Successful Aging

Ruby Hart Neuhaus
Lehman College
The City University of New York

Robert Henry Neuhaus
Sacred Heart University

1807 1982

JOHN WILEY & SONS

New York
Chichester
Brisbane
Toronto
Singapore

9 9 6 6

Library of Congress Cataloging in Publication Data

Neuhaus, Ruby Hart.
  Successful aging.

  Bibliography: p.
  Includes index.
  1. Aging. 2. Aged—United States. I. Neuhaus,
Robert H. II. Title.
HQ1061.N66   305.2'6   81-14807
ISBN 0-471-08448-4   AACR2

Printed in the United States of America

10 9 8 7 6 5 4 3 2 1

Successful Aging

Preface

We are all affected now and will be in the future by the increasing numbers of aged people in America. The group of persons over age 65 has inundated our attempts to care for them, and those of us who are younger must prepare today for growing old and growing old successfully. We have provided information in this book on how we and the aged are coping and how the quality of life and health care can be improved. We consider successful aging a reality; although we have detailed the problems that face older persons, the available resources and the attitudes and behaviors that aid in successful adjustments are also discussed. Myths about the elderly are debunked, and the holistic approach—the concern for the whole individual—is recommended. Team systems that help the elderly and medical, psychological, social, nutritional, spiritual, and health care services are considered. Case histories are included to introduce readers to elderly persons and learn their attitudes, trials, and successes. This book is for those who care about the elderly and about themselves: students, teachers, health care professionals, mothers, sons, uncles, grandfathers, researchers or, simply, society itself.

In preparing this book it was necessary to combine a great deal of information from research studies in different areas of professional expertise, such as psychology, sociology, health, government, and service bulletins and brochures. We acknowledge the help of our students, colleagues, and family who inspired and encouraged us in this endeavor.

Ruby Hart Neuhaus
Robert Henry Neuhaus

Acknowledgments

Our special thanks to Jane Fenjo, Ph.D., who critically reviewed the text and offered thoughtful suggestions and to Mrs. Schlinger, who typed the manuscript. We also acknowledge the encouragement and foresight of the Administration of Lehman College and, in particular, Ruth A. Walker, Ph.D., Associate Dean for the Health Professions, the Faculty of the Health Services Administration Program, the Department of Health Services, and the Health Professions Institute for their support in developing this textbook and their continued commitment to educational programs in the administration of health services.

We are grateful to St. Joseph's College of Brooklyn, New York, for their Grant Award, which assisted in the research for this book, and to Anne Jordheim, Ed.D., Chairperson of the Department of Community Health, for her advice and inspiration in the preparation of the manuscript.

Also, we are appreciative of the interest of our colleagues at Sacred Heart University for their support of scholarly research for this text and their efforts to train health administrators and other professionals.

Ruby Hart Neuhaus
Robert Henry Neuhaus

Contents

CHAPTER 1

Orientation to Aging

All human beings share the common experience of growing older. Some confront the reality of growing old by denial and some by clinging tenaciously to characteristics and behaviors considered youthful; others accept the aging process, with its concomitant changes, as inevitable. Regardless of our feelings, whether we are 19 or 90, we continue to age as time passes. This process begins at the moment of conception and continues until death. It is usually a gradual process, hardly noticed by close associates. However, those who are concerned with the study of aging attempt to answer questions such as "What is aging?", "What causes aging?", and "What happens to people as they grow older?"

This chapter presents definitions of aging, theories about aging and the elderly, and some basic, current concepts about aging. The aging process is examined in terms of its chronological, biological, physiological, and sociological components. Changes that occur as people age are delineated; some reflect decline, while others reveal a potential for growth and development in this period of life. Various psychosocial approaches and theories are described that explore the patterns aged people follow in attempting to cope successfully.

DEFINITION OF GERONTOLOGY AND GERIATRICS

The word *gera* in the original Greek meant to age, to become, to awaken. *Gerontology* is the scientific study of aging and old age. This new science unravels the

1

mysteries of how and why we age. It is also concerned with the antecedents of successful aging and the quality of life of our aging population.

Gerontology is a multidisciplinary study. Growing old and old age involve multifaceted phenomena and changes that are psychological, sociological, and biological. Because there is an interrelationship among our social environment, physical body, and psychological patterns, it is essential that researchers cross academic boundaries to probe areas of knowledge related to the study of old age and aging. For example, significant physiological changes that occur as a function of age are likely to be accompanied by emotional responses. Without information from a variety of fields, it would be impossible to study changes in aging and how people can develop and grow as they become older.

The problems of gerontology fall into four major interdisciplinary classifications: (1) social and economic problems precipitated by the increasing number of elderly people; (2) psychological aspects of aging, which includes intellectual performance, learning, and personal adjustment; (3) physiological bases of aging, including pathological deviations and disease processes; and (4) general biological aspects of aging in all animal species.

Geriatrics is part of the broader field of gerontology and is concerned with health promotion, disease prevention, diagnosis, treatment, and care to be provided knowledgeably and sensitively to older people.

THE MEANING OF AGING

Although there is no consensus of what constitutes aging, several concepts are generally accepted. *Aging* begins with conception, and the pattern is found in the genes. It is a gradual, generally imperceptible process that takes place in all living things; cells, organs, and living organisms change in structure and function with time. All people continue to age, to grow, to develop.

It is a general process that extends over the entire life span. Some of the complex interactions of aging are changes in cells, alterations in chemical activity, and a decrease in *hormone* production. It also involves *behavior, cognition,* and *personality* adjustments. In addition, modifications related to aging pertain to *social roles,* personal interaction, and *status.* Aging, therefore, is the developmental sequence of all these processes as they change with the passage of time.

Aging has many aspects but, as the preceding examples suggest, there are three major categories: biological, psychological, and social. These cover manifested changes and the main factors that influence the changes that occur between maturity and death. They include subjects ranging from heredity to climate to social attitudes.

In human aging the rate of social aging will not necessarily coincide with the rate of physical or psychological aging. Each person is constantly changing, but the individual variability for the types of aging may differ widely. There is obviously an inherited component involved in length of life; it seems that span of life is relatively set by genetic or hereditary characteristics. For example, identical twins have a more similar length of life than fraternal twins, indicating that genetic factors play a role in individual length of life. External or environmental factors such as nutrition, obesity, marital status, smoking, disease, and exercise also influence certain types of aging. In addition, the social environment may enhance or retard aspects of aging. The single most important variable in longevity is to be born of long-living parents.

Old age is the end result of a progressive accumulation of various experiences associated with living over time. Although many changes occur subtly and invisibly, there are gradual reductions in performance capacities. It is therefore apparent that an important aging process is, for example, the gradual reduction of reserve capacity in many important organ systems. Certain measures can be taken to retard the rate of some types of aging, but it cannot be eliminated.

The most common definition of aging is chronological and emphasizes that aging is associated with changes that occur in a living organism over time. *Chronological aging* is a measure of the accumulation of years (or other time units) since a person's birth. At best, chronological aging only provides an index of the passage of time because some developmental processes are time dependent, such as maximum heart rate, which declines with age.

Aging can be represented as a progressive inability to cope with environmental demands and is reflected in an increasing probability of death as individuals age. In this textbook aging is considered an accumulation of pathological processes that eventually kill the individual by interfering with a vital body function. This however, does not take into account that other important developmental processes are not time dependent (such as physical illness or psychological well-being). Therefore, the goal of gerontology is to replace the concept of chronological age with an understanding of processes that cause changes during the life cycle, because chronological age is not an accurate predictor of physical condition or behavior. Instead, it is best seen as an index of many other factors (biological, psychological, and social) that interact and impinge on older people to produce development. This does not mean that age is an unimportant variable in understanding people. It does mean that we should not stop at age but should examine the processes behind age that constitute later mature development.

Biological aging refers to progressive anatomical and physiological changes that take place in cells, organs, and systems of the body over time; the most serious of these is secondary aging, the increased inability to recuperate from various illness. This process is not fully understood, but disease or injury may make biological aging occur more quickly.

Psychological aging refers to age-related changes in behavior that reflect the person's level of maturity and ability to adapt and cope successfully with the stresses of life. Attitudes toward new experiences, flexibility regarding change, curiosity about experiences, and humor perceived in life events all contribute to the impression of a person's psychological age. Psychological age is measured in terms of how a person responds to life. The psychologically young expect to continue to feel and experience life in a vital manner.

Social aging refers to age-related change in an individual or group resulting from defined roles or other social forces. The factor that makes aging most difficult in human society arises from social aging because of the *role* that society imposes on people as they reach a particular chronological point in life. Modern research indicates that a high proportion of the mental and attitudinal changes in "old" people is not the result of biological effects but of role playing. A sociopsychological theory states that aging is a dynamic process enompassing complex bodily changes in addition to psychological adjustment. Another factor is that aging is part of a developmental sequence in the life span. According to this approach, aging is a sequence of events that takes place or is expected to take place during an individual's life.

Some researchers have differentiated between *normal* and pathological aging; they refer to normal aging as the inevitable changes resulting from the passage of time and to pathological aging as changes resulting from illness or disease. Separating normal and abnormal conditions is difficult, since the aged accumulate random trauma and disease effects that may be superimposed on the aging process. Although it is useful throughout this book to look at typical changes that accompany age, the terms normal and pathological do not seem to apply except in specific instances.

Functional aging refers to age-related changes in the ability to perform tasks at the same level of proficiency. Examples of such changes are decreases in immune function, vital lung capacity, maximum heart rate, and reaction time. Functional age distinctions are important and can be used to differentiate changes (both increases and decreases) in capacity that have been noted in the aged.

OPERATIONAL DEFINITION OF OLD AGE

If we accept that *old age* means different things to different people and that no single factor may be employed to define old age, we need a reference point for purposes of research and discussion. As life span increases and mandatory retirement dates become passé, chronological labels will probably also change to reflect increases in human life span. However, at this time, the most commonly used age classification to denote the beginning of old age is 65 years. Therefore, for practicality, we will use 65 years to denote old age. The terms old age and *later maturity* will also be used interchangeably. The term *very old* will be used to describe those 75 years old and over. This is a common distinction, popular in the scientific literature to separate the aged into chronological groups.

THEORETICAL ORIENTATIONS TO AGING

An overview of the human life cycle has developed slowly in the gerontology field. Biological, psychological, and sociological perspectives have not been integrated into an overall theory of human aging, nor have they been combined into a meaningful context against which to view changes over the life cycle as they contribute to an integrated understanding of the aging process. None of the existing theories of aging fit all the facts; therefore it seems that aging is caused by a variety of processes. It is also possible that no one yet knows enough about these processes to construct a workable theory.

Until 1960 most of the medical, psychological, psychiatric, and sociological literature on aging focused on sickness and was based on the institutionalized population, even though this is today only about 7 percent of those over 65 years and represents a much older segment of the elderly population.

Major theories first developed around biological function. The biological effects of aging have been characterized as a decline with time in the production of the necessary free energy for the individual to function and as the increasing inability of the body to maintain itself and perform the operations it once did.

Biological Theories of Aging

Many of the aging trends that have been reported over the years may seem discouraging, such as muscle replaced by fat, decline of physical strength, changes in *nerve* signal transmission, diminished defenses against infection, and decrease in the size of the brain and brain capacity. Some of the recent evidence indicates, however, that the aging process may be slowed down so that the human body might last longer than the present average life span of 65 to 80 years. Recent studies based on hundreds of persons of all ages show a steady decline from 30 years of age in things such as hand-grip strength, breathing capacity, and heart output. Individuals decline in their own way at different rates, but most show some decrement over time. Some older persons seem to have no decline at all for many years; some may even show enhanced function in certain areas. The Baltimore Study has documented kidney function and problem-solving ability as two important measures that do not necessarily decline in all individuals through the passage of time (Anders, 1979). Such findings support and reinforce the truism that functions that are continually exercised are less likely to grow rusty, even with age.

In an attempt to explain these and other changes of aging, a number of biological theories have been proposed. Although each theory may contribute something to our understanding of an aspect of aging, different theories have varying degrees of support. Most theories continue to be scrutinized by the scientific community and are subject to continued modification. Among the most frequently encountered theories of biological aging are: (1) genetic mutation, (2) autoimmunity, (3) cross-linking of molecules, and (4) cellular aging.

Genetic Mutation Theory. The mutation theory of aging is based on the observation that as one grows older, cells exhibiting unusual or different characteristics are noted with increasing frequency. Some theorists now understand the aging process to be related to the accumulation of mutational damage within the genetic mechanism of somatic cells. The *DNA* molecules contain the basic genetic instructions for the orderly behavior of the cell. The processes that DNA undergoes during subdivision and protein synthesis increase the risk of damage to the copying mechanism. If DNA becomes an inaccurate blueprint, problems will arise that lead to a synthesis of defective proteins. Some of these proteins are essential enzymes within the cells whose loss will cause cell death.

Autoimmunity Theory. The *autoimmunity theory* suggests that aging results when various bodily systems begin to reject their own tissues. As a person grows older, there is an increase in *antibody* produced by the body. It appears that defective *proteins* or other changes in the body with age stimulate an immune response. This causes the body to behave in a self-destructive manner, and the immune system operates against its own body cells as if they were foreign bodies. Autoimmune reactions have been observed in connection with various cardiovascular diseases, diabetes, *cancer,* and rheumatoid arthritis. For an unknown reason, with increasing age the body begins to function in ways that operate against the well-being of the organism.

Cross-Linking of Molecules Theory. With increasing age, tendons, skin, and even blood vessels lose elasticity. This led theorists to wonder whether aging of the human body is an instance of a tanning-type process. The aging of protein substances in the body might explain the loss of water and elasticity in aging tissue. With time, the theorists suggest that chemical agents force the molecules of the body to "cross-link," or glue together. Substances capable of cross-linking the body's molecules of protein are found in all living cells. Thus, age-related changes in collagen and elastic fibers are associated with various external signs of growing older, such as wrinkling of the skin, sagging muscles, and slower healing of skin cuts.

Cellular Aging Theory. At the cellular level, studies of aging have been enhanced by the experiments of Leonard Hayflick of Stanford University, who has examined cell survival in cell cultures. Hayflick's studies support the theory that there is a limited doubling potential characteristic of normal human cells, that cells have an intrinsic, finite life span (Hayflick, 1973).

As cell cultures approach their limiting number of divisions, the time interval for cell doubling increases progressively; there is a gradual cessation of activity, few cells will divide, and cellular debris accumulates; finally, there is a total loss of vigor, and death occurs. These degenerative phenomena manifest themselves after about 50 cell population doublings. Hayflick's limit should be considered a limit to what can be, then one must concentrate on the quality of life, or adding life to years instead of years to life.

Even though all theories of biological aging have not been mentioned, it is apparent that physical changes associated with aging can be traced to many sources. We know that cells begin to mutate; autoimmune reactions increase, changes in protein occur, waste products begin to accumulate, and cells stop replacing themselves. Scientists currently believe that aging implicates all these factors. As to how, why, and in what pattern of cause and effect they are implicated, there is little agreement.

Biological theories of aging are particularly valuable for predicting some problems to be faced in later years, but biology and the sciences seek a clear *etiology* in attempting to describe aging phenomena as clinical entities. In recent years, however, it has become clear that aging is an interplay of physical, psychological, and social factors.

Psychological Theories of Aging

A *psychology* of the human life cycle has been slow to develop. Biological and sociological theory have not described a meaningful context for understanding psychological change in the later years. From another perspective, the primary problem seems to be a lack of knowledge about developmental psychology from the viewpoint of adulthood. Adult *development* is the need for a psychology of adulthood in which investigators are concerned with (1) the orderly and sequential changes that occur with the passage of time as adults move from adolescence through adulthood to middle and old age, (2) issues of consistency and change in *personality* over relatively long intervals of time, and (3) issues of antecedent-consequent relationships.

Psychological theories of aging are often the extension of personality and developmental theories into later life. *Personality theories* usually consider the innate human needs and forces that motivate thought and behavior and the modification of these biologically based energies by the experiences of living in a physical and social environment. As people pass through their life experiences, they change more and more. This divergence continues as a response to the large array of possible learning and living experiences.

One problem in the study of aging is that there are still insufficient data on adults. Some data have been reported in which individuals have been studied from childhood into adulthood but, as yet, there have been no major *longitudinal studies* of men and women as they move from youth to middle age or middle age to old age. There have been a few studies at Duke University; in Baltimore under Nathan Shock at the National Institute of Mental Health; at the Philadelphia Geriatric Center; at the Lovelace Foundation in Alberquerque, New Mexico; in Framingham, Massachusetts (the heart study); and in the Veterans Administration Normative Study (Boston Outpatient Clinic). Despite these significant research efforts on aging, no single theory has been formulated that adequately defines aging, accounts for all processes involved in aging, or explains differences in the various types and rates of aging. The enormous complexities of aging and the processes of aging make it unlikely that a comprehensive theory will be forthcoming in the foreseeable future.

In an attempt to explain the psychology of aging, some theories have been proposed. Erik Erikson and Robert Peck have formulated theories of personality development that encompass the life span of the human being. Adaptation and adjustment as related to self-development are emphasized.

Erikson's Life Cycle Theory. Theorists in the psychology of personality have concentrated mostly on the early and not the later stages of human development. However, Erikson's formulation of the stages of *ego development* is the notable exception. Erikson (Table 1) formulated eight stages of ego development, from infancy to old age; each stage represents a choice or a crisis for the expanding ego. The *ego* refers to the aspect of one's developed attitudes and values that objects to or struggles against any behavior that would threaten an individual's existence. The effects of maturation, experience, and social institutions on the developing person are encompassed in the theory, and the resolutions of ego crises are viewed as the determinants of personality success in resolving internal and external demands and one's evaluation of self.

In Erikson's theory a different psychological issue constitutes the basic *conflict* or issue in each stage, but the same issue exists in preceding and later stages. A resolution at any stage of development has its subsequent affect on later development, and an individual who has difficulty at an earlier stage will manifest difficulties in healthy development.

Table 1   Erikson's Eight Stages of Human Life

Opposing Issues for Each Stage	Emerging Value	Period of Life
1. Basic trust versus mistrust	Hope	Infancy
2. Autonomy versus shame and doubt	Will	Early childhood
3. Initiative versus guilt	Purpose	Play age
4. Industry versus inferiority	Competence	School age
5. Identity versus identity (role) confusion	Fidelity	Adolescence
6. Intimacy versus isolation	Love	Young adulthood
7. Intimacy versus stagnation (self-absorption)	Care	Maturity
8. Integrity versus despair (and disgust)	Wisdom	Old age

Source: Based on Erikson (1963, 1976).

Each conflict within the two opposing tendencies at each stage is eventually resolved by a synthesis that represents one of the basic human strengths, such as hope, will, purpose, competence, fidelity, love, care, and wisdom. The struggle is perceived by Erikson as unconscious within the individual. It involves inner psychological processes and effects and is affected by social processes. The resulting psychosocial strengths produce an active adaptation of an individual in the social environment, causing a change in the environment as one makes selective use of its opportunities.

Since our concern is with old age, we will discuss only the last two stages in Erikson's scheme, even though each involves the issues and builds on the strengths of the earlier stages.

The seventh stage of life, which Erikson sees as occurring in later maturity, is probably the longest stage of life. It emerges through the vicissitudes of parenthood or in occupational accomplishment. The struggle is between a sense of *generativity*, or leaving one's mark in the world, and the sense of stagnation, or self-absorption. Although generativity includes the concern for establishing and guiding future generations, it is meant to encompass productivity and creativity in other directions of life. Generativity is an essential stage in psychosexual and psychosocial development. When accomplishment of this stage fails, individuals reflect a need for pseudo-intimacy, often in an atmosphere of stagnation and personal impoverishment. Individuals then seem to others to become self-indulgent and, under certain conditions, physical or emotional invalids. The fact of having or wanting children has little to do with the achievement of generativity. Erikson sees only someone who has adapted to the triumphs or disappointments of the preceding stages and taken care of things and people as experiencing the fruition of the final stages of development. The successful outcome of this stage is the development of care and a widening concern for interests developed in one's lifetime.

The final stage is brought on by a growing awareness of the finitude of life and of one's closeness to death in the later years. The crucial task during this stage is to evaluate one's life and accomplishments and to affirm life as having been and continuing to be meaningful and purposeful. This is known as *ego integrity*. The opposite is a sense of despair often manifested in dissatisfaction with life, a feeling that life has been wasted, and a *fear* of death. The struggle between these two opposing themes is the essence of this period and produces wisdom. Wisdom operates to ameliorate the fear and force of death. In spite of the decline of bodily and mental functions, the person who has accrued an integration of ego can maintain an active concern with life, even in the face of death. A healthy person can integrate these experiences and reflect on a sense of satisfaction with life. In Erikson's view, to become mature, each individual must develop to a sufficient degree all the ego qualities mentioned. Ego integrity thus implies an ability to develop in many areas of life: religion, politics, economics, technology, and arts and sciences, and to accept leadership responsibility. Erikson, like Freud, conceived his ''stages'' of life by examining the psychological problems that require mastery at specific age periods. Erikson's eighth stage, however, ego integrity versus despair, represents all the crises and coping styles developed in the first half of life.

Peck's Developmental Task Theory. The last two of Erikson's stages include most of the middle and late years of the life cycle. In that sense they are more general than earlier stages. Peck therefore defines the crucial issues of middle and old age more precisely (Peck, 1956). He suggests that it is useful to divide the second half of life into different psychological learnings and adjustments. The chief chronological division is between middle age and old age.

In Middle age (after 30) Peck states that decreases in physical powers require an increasing premium on wisdom in a healthy adult. Wisdom is the ability to choose effectively among the alternatives that intellect and imagination offer. Judging from studies of predominantly male business people, he perceives that this occurs from the late thirties to late forties. This issue is called valuing wisdom over physical power.

Allied to general physical decline, but partially separate from it, is the sexual climacteric. This presents itself as an opportunity for the mature adult to redefine male-female relationships based on individual personality. Peck describes this task as a central issue of social versus sexual relationships.

A third phenomenon, the loss of loved ones (death of parents, marriage and relocation of children, changing circle of friends and relatives), requires the capacity to shift emotional investments to other people, pursuits, or settings. The central issue is cathectic flexibility versus impoverishment.

Another challenge faced in the middle years is the ability to achieve a degree of perspective on experience and use it as a promotional guide. Some older people become inflexible in their opinions and actions and are closed to new ideas. Peck defines this issue as mental flexibility versus rigidity.

Peck indicates that old age is usually marked by retirement and occurs for most individuals in their sixties. Peck sees three central issues at this stage. The first requisite for successful adaptation is to establish a varied set of values and self-attributes that can be pursued with a sense of self-worth and satisfaction; thereby retiring persons can redefine their worth beyond their specific work roles. Peck calls this challenge ego differentiation versus work role preoccupation.

Since old age may bring increasing ill health, the second issue of aging requires a successful value system, social and mental resources of pleasure, and self-integrity that transcend physical discomfort. Peck describes this issue as body transcedence versus body preoccupation.

A third crucial issue for successful aging in the later years is to live so that the prospect of death seems less important. Ways may be developed through friendship with one's children, contributions, and culture to achieve enduring significance for life. Peck calls this an ego transcendence versus ego preoccupation task.

These theories of development during adulthood provide a useful outline for understanding the sequential progression of the life cycle. They also sensitize us to some of the main issues of the adult years. In addition, they describe a process of development that is somewhat limited to the ideal of human fulfillment or successful aging as defined in middle-class values of American *society*. However, they do not indicate how cultural differences, sex differences, or social-class differences interact with this general developmental progression.

Sociological Theories of Aging

Several major theories exist that explain social aspects of aging as derived from the particular society in which the individual lives. Expectations about behavior for the aged prescribe an older person's actions and demand that certain standards of behavior be observed. When a person does not conform or comply with the social definitions of acceptable conduct, certain penalties may be imposed or rewards withheld. As a result, most societies expect and demand conformity to certain standards or *norms* of behavior for the aged, and they manage to control the behavior of most of their members. The earliest research in social gerontology was descriptive, but concepts such as "adjustment," "roles," and "changing self-concept" were soon borrowed from the symbolic-interactionist theory in social psychology. This theory suggests that social science looks primarily at the effects of social structure on the experience of aging to understand change and stability in the adult personality. It proposes that situational adjustment is the explanation for many changes noted in aging and that the process of commitment is an explanation for stability.

Two theories have been selected that represent each view and suggest how aging changes can be traced to numerous social sources: the *family* network theory and individual life cycle theories.

Family Networks Theory. There is a growing literature dealing with family networks, relations between parents and adult children, and the position of older people within the family. Research has focused on theories of family structure and the forms the family has taken. Important issues have been raised as to the implication for new patterns of family relationships and experiences of the aging from the perspective of family networks and intergenerational contacts. Descriptions of husband/wife relationships and conflicts during the period of postparental adjustments define the marital roles and adjustments of the aging. These and other investigations elaborate on changes in timing of the family cycles and changes in the life cycle within the family. Finally, survey materials on help patterns and family arrangements among older people and their children describe family patterns and trends in contemporary American society (see Chapter 8).

The facts of social life in the case of aging are too complicated and varied to be encompassed in a theoretical yet functional system. This is particularly true of the social theories as developed to date. Cultural values and meanings are important elements in understanding the social interactions of aging. The neat, integrated system that assumes universals is appealing but is not useful in understanding the phenomenon of aging. Interpreting the facts of aging in a social-historical-cultural context in which the facts and trends of American society are a matrix for the social processes of aging is a better guideline in gerontological research.

Life Cycle Theory. A common view of aging suggested by social scientists is the analogy between seasons of the year and stages of human life. The life cycle is an idealized and age-related progression or sequence of roles and group memberships that individuals are expected to follow as they mature through life. The life course is neither simple nor rigidly prescribed. This approach is helpful in viewing aging because it incorporates various subcultures (whether based on sex, social class, ethnicity, race, or region of the country) that develop unique ideas concerning the timing of the life course. Although later in life options may diminish because of social and physical aging, the older population is considerably more differentiated than the younger one. Yet, even with the increased complexity of life with age, certain generally accepted standards may serve as a timetable for the population. Three major areas are suggested as significant to most individual stages of the life course. The first is related to specific patterns, such as occupational career or family development stage. Second, specific age norms or social roles and expectations accompany various phases of the life course. Finally, people are forced by circumstances, such as the economy or stage of one's health, to make certain choices during the life cycle.

These theories of development provide several useful outlines for sequences in human life. They also alert us to some of the normative crisis points during adult life. However, they do not indicate how cultural or social differences might interact with the general developmental progression. For some older people successful aging and fulfillment must be accomplished under the stress of illness, poverty, and isolation. An awareness of the effects of social class, ethnic background, and male/female differences are important factors in adult development. Even if these theories are useful as guidelines, it is important to look at the effect of historical time on individual development.

Historical Time

The historical time in which a person develops is another age-related dimension that theorists have suggested affects an individual's growth and development. For example, people now in their seventies were born before 1908. These people likely grew up in a household without telephones, televisions, vacuum cleaners, appliances, or automobiles. World War I was important in their childhood years, and they came of age in the flapper era of the 1920s. They grew up when unemployment and economic depression were widespread.

Furthermore, women now in their seventies had the lowest fertility rate of any group of women in the United States. The result is that about 25 percent of those over 70 have no living children. About 29 percent of black women born in the early 1900s never had children. When these women, both black and white, could have had children, the Depression of the 1930s occurred. By the time World War II ended and men returned from war, these women were too old for childbearing. These are crucial elements to consider, not only for understanding, but for research and social policy development.

On the other hand, women now entering their fifties are strikingly different from those entering their seventies. The 50-year-olds are better educated, many have probably spent longer years working, and they had the highest fertility rate ever recorded in this country. When these women reach age 70, some will receive earned pensions. They are, however, even more likely than women presently in their seventies to live without husbands because of the high divorce rate and increasing difference in male/female life expectancy.

Multigenerational studies have indicated that there are many continuities in family life in America, but that there have also been many changes in attitudes, values, and behavior in different generations. However, individual differences, historical events, and changes in social demands and expectations can make developmental categorization problematic.

The central issue raised by this perspective is whether or not all persons experience aging in a similar manner. Studies quoted have stressed the white, middle-class male population. Therefore, in future studies respondents should be selected from a wider variety of social and ethnic backgrounds and life-styles and should include more women.

Some of the diversity in the patterns of development in the process of aging are displayed in the case studies scattered throughout the text. These studies illustrate issues raised in the chapters and bridge the gap between the concepts discussed and real persons confronting the complexity of aging.

Summary

Fewer Americans now die prematurely. The average life span in the United States has increased 26 years in this century, from 47 to 73 years. Since the probability of death increases rapidly with advancing age, changes occur in individuals that make them more vulnerable to disease.

Aging is probably best defined as the developmental sequence of all the biological, social, and psychological processes as they change with the passage of time. Gerontology (the study of aging) is concerned primarily with the changes that occur between the attainment of maturity and death of the individual. The goal of research in gerontology is to identify the factors that influence these changes. The major thrust of gerontology has been to study the process of aging and to discover if and how rates of aging can be altered. The rates of aging in animal research have been changed. The rates of aging in humans have not been changed, but they display so much variation that research has been directed toward this attractive and challenging area instead of toward efforts to examine and improve the quality of old age.

It is not yet known exactly what initiates the decline that occurs with aging. There are four main body system levels in which changes do occur that have been examined. The first is the cellular level. There is evidence that the cells of the aged are different from those of the young, it is possible that these cells may be damaged or mutated in some way. There is also evidence that the body's immune system and metabolic system may trigger the changes we perceive as aging. Other theories stress damage to the organ system such as the brain as the possible source of change responsible for aging. Finally, there are theories that noncellular parts of the body such as bone and blood vessels undergo changes that cause increased vulnerability to disease and death in older people. Other theories have suggested a more general chemical damage process in which a highly active substance (*free radical*) may attack the molecular structure of the body. This has led to the suggestion that antioxidants used to prevent food spoilage may retard aging. There are many facets of gerontological research, but the exact nature of aging in all of the processes involved and why organisms age are unknown. The rate of aging has been slowed; this reflects control over premature causes of death, so that chronic disease such as hardening of the arteries, arthritis, emphysema, and cancer now cause the majority of deaths in the elderly.

The social-psychological literature reveals that there is no significant decrease in activities from 60 to 90 years. Even though many people are unemployed and are prevented from obtaining work, they spend less time watching and listening to the mass media than people in their twenties. Some people disengage from society because of acceptance of old age limitations; this disengagement is not a natural characteristic of aging, but a socially imposed condition. Society begins to withdraw support, positions of status, social roles, available rewards, and opportunities for meaningful social interactions from the older generation.

According to modern gerontology, 75 percent of what we call the phenomenon of old age, which is viewed as an accumulation of deficits and disabilities, is a product of institutional and social attitudes, not of biology.

FURTHER READINGS

Anders, R., "The Normality of Aging: The Baltimore Longitudinal Study," National Institute of Health Publication 79–1410, July 1979.

Busse, E., "Theories of Aging," in C. Busse and E. Pfeiffer (eds.) *Behavior and Adaptation in Late Life,* Little Brown, Boston, 1977, pp. 21–22.

Erikson, E. H., *Childhood and Society,* 2nd rev. ed. W. W. Norton, Hogarth Press, New York, 1963, 1976.

Hayflick, L., "The biology of human aging," *American Journal of Medical Science,* 1973, *265,* 432–445.

Hendricks, T., and C. D. Hendricks, *Aging in Mass Society: Myths & Realities,* Winthrop, Cambridge, Mass., 1977.

Kimmel, D. C., *Adulthood and Aging: An Interdisciplinary, Developmental View,* Wiley, New York, 1974, 1980.

McKenzie, S. C., *Aging and Old Age,* Scott Foresman, Glenview, Ill., 1980.

Peck, R. C., *Psychological Developments in The Second Half of Life.* Psychological Aspects of Aging, Proceedings of a Conference on Planning Research, Bethesda, Md., April 24-27, 1955, John E. Anderson (ed.), American Psychological Association, Washington, D.C., 1956), pp. 44-49.

U. S. Department of Health, Education and Welfare, "Facts About Older Americans," H.D.S. Publication 80-20006, Washington, D.C., 1979.

CHAPTER 2

The Aged in America

If we hope to increase our knowledge of aging and old age, we must dispel personal misconceptions. Various myths and *stereotypes* imposed on the aged by society are presented, and readers are encouraged to distinguish between stereotypic attitudes and valid information concerning old age. The concept of ageism is introduced, and factors that create stereotypes are suggested.

To age successfully, the elderly must confront the social and economic changes that profoundly affect them. Therefore some of the demographic characteristics of this population are examined.

AGEISM

Although most of the population is familiar with various forms of prejudice, when older people are referred to as inflexible, cranky, or senile, the tendency is to accept such phrases with little reflection on the implications. The term *ageism* represents inaccurate prejudgments regarding the elderly. To some extent, the myths and stereotypes discussed here characterize some of the beliefs underlying ageism.

Ageism represents a prejudicial orientation toward the elderly based on misconceptions, half truths, and ignorance. Within the concept of ageism is the assumption that personality, character, behavior, and social traits are determined by chronological age. This is coupled with the notion that the elderly are fundamentally different from and inferior to other age segments.

16

MYTHS OF AGING

In the United States people are changing their views to think of old age as a time of potential health and growth. In western civilization emphasis is placed on life, individuality, and control. These qualities, as well as productivity and power, are becoming more commonly associated with the elderly in America. However, prejudiced views of the aged are fostered and reflected in the mass media and literature. Medicine and the behavioral sciences have reinforced such societal attitudes by presenting old age as negative and emphasizing the concepts of disease and decline. Most medical, psychological, and social science literature on old age has been based on experience with the sick and institutionalized aged, thereby creating distortions, myths, and stereotypic thinking.

Many stereotypes and myths surround aging and old age. A stereotype is a standardized picture or rigid perception of persons or things. A myth is a collective belief about people, in this case, the aged, with little factual foundation; specifically, it is the imposing on an entire group some characteristic seen in a limited but highly noticeable few.

Myth   *After age 65, everyone goes steadily downhill.*

The dominance of chronological aging is a myth because it is well established that large disparities exist among physiological, chronological, and social ages. People age at different rates; physiological indicators show a greater range from the mean in old age than in any other group. Some old people do not show decrements over time for specific functions such as kidney and problem-solving activities; they perform as well or better in these areas than they did at a younger age or when compared with younger people with similar backgrounds. In the Duke University Longitudinal Study more than 50 percent of the people over 65 had no detectable deterioration in physical condition. More than 50 percent rated their health as "good," 33 percent as "fair," and 16 percent as "poor." More than 50 percent of the decline noted by observers was related to boredom inactivity and the anticipation that poor health or infirmity was expected.

Myth   *Old people are all pretty much alike.*

The idea that individuals are a group who all have the same needs is perhaps the most widespread stereotype imposed on older citizens. Contrary to popular belief, increased heterogeneity appears more characteristic of aging. In essence, as a person grows older, there is a constant and gradual accentuation of uniqueness as a result of varied experiences that exert a diversifying influence. Although people willingly perceive the uniqueness of each child, they do not often extend such perception to older persons.

Myth   *Old age is a disease.*

Senile behavior is frequently considered synonymous with the behavior exhibited by people in old age. *Senility* is a term loosely used to describe certain pathological brain dysfunctions characterized by confusion and forgetfulness, yet such conditions are not inherent in normal aging. All age groups are susceptible to such a condition, which can be caused by a variety of trauma. The statistical probability of a person becoming senile as a result of old age is extremely small (see Chapter 7).

Myth   *Old people have it easy.*

This preconception envisions old age as a time of serenity when older people, unburdened by the responsibilities of earlier stages of life, can relax and enjoy the benefits of old age and retirement. The reality, however, often includes poverty, fear of crime, lack of transportation, bodily decline, loss of prestige, and death of loved ones. No other age group faces more potential external and internal stress than the aged.

Myth   *People should retire at 65 or before; older people cannot do a good day's work.*

The myth of unproductivity and lack of creativity with age stems from society's view of retirement as a time when old people withdraw from society, lose interest in work or things they have always done, and pursue their retirement hobbies or interests.

Although the majority of older people voluntarily or mandatorily retire at 65, about 3 million (or 13 percent of older people) continue in the work force. These people are slightly more productive, have a 20 percent better absentee record, and have fewer accidents than younger employees. Dependability and persisting usefulness is the rule, not the exception, for people over 65. However, at this point, convention decrees that we stop employing them.

Myth   *The older you get, the more rigid you become.*

Inflexibility or rigidity refers to a psychological orientation characterized by rigid resistance to change and inability to adapt to new circumstances. Some older people are rigid, but *inflexibility* is a personality trait that may be manifested by individuals at any stage of development and is not inherent in old age. Not only do older individuals change, but the majority must, by necessity, adapt to major events of later life such as retirement, changes in income and life-style, loss of loved ones, and discomforts of illness and disease.

Myth   *Old people have trouble learning new skills.*

It would be incorrect to say that differences in learning rates as reflected in performance are not noted in some skills with different age groups. For example, eye-hand coordination is generally greatest in younger age groups and declines with age. Learning, however, is a relatively permanent change in behavior resulting from experience. To assume that decreases in performance rate represent a decrease in ability to acquire new information is untrue. According to research findings (Chapter 4), even though there is a slowdown in reaction time with normal aging, general mental abilities, or the capacity to learn, were not found to decrease with age.

Myth   *Everyone knows old people are through having sex.*

Within our society there is an unfortunate belief that sexuality is a function of youth. When engaged in by older adults, it is perceived somehow as inappropriate. Such beliefs, which seem to be widely accepted by both young and old, can be psychologically harmful. If older people believe sexual activities are abnormal or impossible, they may deprive themselves of a healthy sexual outlet and mode of communication. In addition, if they feel it is wrong, they may experience fear, guilt, depression, and loss of self-esteem.

Research has found that individuals possess the capacity for sexual intercourse and orgasm up to and beyond the 80-year level. Among variables cited as contributing to successful sexual functioning in later life are physical health, a sense of well-being, the availability of a willing partner, and a history of interest and enjoyment in sexual activities (Busse, 1977).

Myth   *Most of the elderly are bedridden and dependent.*

Few of the elderly over 65 are bedridden; only about 5 percent of all old people are confined to their own home (homebound). Only 4 percent of older Americans live in institutions at any point in their lives. This leaves the vast majority, or 89 percent, of those over 65 who are self-sufficient. Chronic conditions, however, are more prevalent among older people over 65 and may restrict activity. According to the Census Bureau (1980), about 37 percent of older people are limited in their major activity. About 18 percent of those over 65 have mobility interference because of chronic conditions; of these, 6 percent have trouble getting around alone, 7 percent need a mechanical aid to get around, and only 5 percent are homebound. Even among those 85 years old and over, only 20 percent live in institutions; the other 80 percent are living independently.

Efforts to dispel ageism, myths, and distortions concerning the aged are supported by valid information in the field of gerontology. In an effort to meet the need for such information, recent knowledge about U.S. citizens in the 65-and-over population is presented next. A brief statistical sketch of the individuals in this age category provides a more realistic understanding of: Who are the elderly? How many older Americans are there? Where do they live? Has life expectancy changed? What are the living arrangements of older persons? What is the marital status of older persons? How many older persons work? What is the economic and health status of elderly persons?

WHO THE AGED ARE

Number of Elderly in the United States

Vital statistics that characterize the elderly in the United States recognize that this population may be very different from elderly populations in other cultures.

According to the recent census, there are over 24 million people in the United

States, of which 1 out of every 9 was over the age of 65. This population is not homogenous in age structure, and each age group warrants separate consideration. Concretely, there are about 1 million Americans over the age of 75, most of them women. Also, there are 1 million women over 85, and more than 106,000 reportedly over 100 years old.

In the perspective of time, the percentage of the elderly has risen markedly; in 1776 about 50,000 of the 2.5 million people in the United States, or 2 percent of the total population, were 65 and over. In 1900 there were 4.9 million older people, or 4 percent of the total population. It is estimated that in 2030 there will be approximately 33 million older people, constituting 17 to 23 percent of the total population.

The forces that shaped the increasing number and proportion are well known. Except for the baby boom after World War II, fertility rates have been steadily declining. At the same time, medical advances, especially those reducing infant and maternal deaths, have added about 26 years to the average life span since 1900. Although the average life expectancy for persons at age 60 has not increased dramatically, many more people are now surviving to that age. Immigration from abroad brought 17 million (primarily young) persons to this country in the first quarter of this century. The survivors of the turn-of-the-century waves of immigration are now elderly, as are many of their children.

The elderly have become increasingly older. The size of the population 60 years and over has increased nearly 7 times since 1900; the population 75 and over has increased 10 times; and the 85-and-over group has increased 17 times. Currently, 40 percent of the elderly are 75 and over, and this proportion is projected to increase to 44 percent by 2000. It has been projected that by 2035 10 percent of the elderly will be 85 and over (Census Bureau, 1980).

The growth of the older population will have a profound impact on industry, consumption sales patterns, and family life and will significantly affect the demand for and delivery of services.

Life Expectancy

Life expectancy is the number of years one can expect to live based on statistical probability. According to the most recent evidence, a child born in the 1980s can be expected to live about 73 years (69 for males, 77 for females), about 26 years longer than a child born in 1900. The major part of the increase occurred because of reduced death rates for children and young adults. The life expectancy for people who are 65 is 14 years for a male and 18 for a female.

Marital Status of Older Persons

One experience that most elderly women eventually have in common is the loss of a spouse. The vast majority of women in their younger adult years are married, but fewer than 50 percent of all women 60 years old and over are currently living with a spouse. According to the Census Bureau, there are 8 million widows, and the rate of widowhood rises from one in four for women 60 to 64 years old to 70 percent for those 75 years old and older. Future growth in the number of elderly women will increase the number of elderly requiring a variety of supportive services in order to cope with living alone, declining health, and poverty-level income.

WHERE THE ELDERLY LIVE

Geographical Distribution

Most elderly people live in the Middle Atlantic States, followed closely by the East-North-Central area, the South Atlantic States, and the West. Elderly people, both black and white, frequently live in the inner city or rural areas. The Midwest and New England have concentrations of older people because they remain on the farms. About 67 percent of older people in America live in urban areas, with 33 percent in center cities. Less than 50 percent of the elderly live in nonmetropolitan areas; only 5 percent live on farms, and the other 35 percent live in towns.

The geographic concentrations of elderly blacks and whites differ. White persons aged 65 and over are evenly distributed among the four major regions, except the West where less than 17 percent live. Older blacks are more prevalent in the South, but New York, Texas, Georgia, Louisiana, Alabama, and Illinois also have large numbers of older blacks (U.S. Department of Health, Education and Welfare, 1980).

Living Arrangements

Most older persons in the noninstitutional population live in a family setting. The numbers of older men and older women living in families are about the same (7.5 million men, 7.6 million women).

One of the most striking phenomena that has occurred in recent decades has been the rapid growth in the number of elderly living alone, from 3.8 million in the 1960s to over 7 million in 1980. The trend toward living alone is particularly noticeable among the oldest subgroups of the elderly population. The number of elderly men living alone grew by 600,000 between 1960 and 1980. However, the number of elderly women maintaining households by themselves grew by 3 million (or 132 percent) in the 20-year period since 1960 (Fowles, 1980).

There are many contributing factors to this trend. A principal factor is the longer life span of women, coupled with the fact that women are often younger than the men they marry. Other factors include greater numbers dependent on federal or other private pension plans that require the elderly to remain single or lose the spouse's benefits; the increasing geographic dispersal of the family; and smaller families (most of today's elderly have fewer children than earlier generations).

The majority of elderly people live within, and continue to maintain independently, their own homes during their older life. A small portion of the 65-and-over group may expect to spend some time in a nursing home or institution, but these periods of confinement are temporary and short.

Crime

Because the elderly are more likely than young persons to be perceived as easy prey, specific precautions become more important to prevent such attacks. Households with heads over age 65 experienced over 2.5 million household crimes and more than 2 million personal crimes. The household crime rate for blacks aged 65 and over was higher by 25 percent and the personal crime rate was higher by 33 percent than for their *white* counterparts (Williams, 1980).

The elderly are more likely to be the targets of thefts, muggings, and burglaries. Crimes of violence are relatively low compared to crimes of theft, which include purse snatching and pocket picking. In addition, the impact of crime is disproportionately more severe for older victims, particularly in terms of economic loss, physical harm, and the resultant fear for personal safety. Many crimes directed toward the elderly may be avoided by the adoption of precautionary behavior. Local police departments can provide the elderly with specific measures designed to protect them from becoming easy prey.

WORK, EDUCATION, INCOME, AND HEALTH OF THE AGED

Employment

Presently 3 million, or 13 percent of, older people are in the labor force—either working or actively seeking work. Of the 65 or over employed males, more than 50 percent are working full time (nonagricultural), and more than 33 percent of employed females over 65 are working full time. This group of working elderly makes up about 25 percent of the total U.S. labor force. Twenty percent of the 65-and-over men (1.9 million) and 8 percent of the older women (1.1 million) are in the labor force. Thus the occupational history of tomorrow's elderly retired population will be considerably different from today's.

One of the effects of these changes has been to increase the average income of older persons and decrease the number whose incomes fall below the poverty level. Other factors that have contributed to the somewhat improved picture in the economic situation of the elderly have been the increasing concern about coverage of the elderly under a variety of public and private pension plans, the implementation of new income support programs, and increased benefit levels and cost of living clauses for the Social Security program. It may be, however, that the continued rapid growth of minority, racial, and ethnic groups, together with a declining economy, will keep a substantial number of elderly persons at incomes near or below the poverty level.

Educational Values

Many of the changes that have occurred in the social and economic structure of the United States are reflected in the characteristics of the elderly population only after a delay of years or even decades. For elderly persons who received their education during or before the Depression of the 1930s, the median number of school years was 8 years and remained at 8 years between 1940 and 1960. The Census Bureau (1980) reported that by the 1980s older persons had completed an average of 9.7 years of school. In the 1980s census, 33 percent of the population over 65 had finished high school, but only about 50 percent of those 65 and over had not completed 1 year of high school. About 9 percent of older Americans (2.5 million) were functionally illiterate, which meant they had no schooling to less than 5 years of schooling. At this time, the average urban person over 65 has had 9 years of education; the rural elderly usually have had less. This educational deficit among the elderly contributes to job difficulties and may hamper full use of leisure opportunities. At the same time, a rising number of elderly are college graduates (8 percent). By 1990, it is projected that 50 percent of the population over 65 will be high school graduates. Note that high school "then," "now," and "in the future" cannot be taken as a constant measurement on which to use comparisons.

According to the current population survey, the median number of years of school completed by older blacks was only 70 percent that of elderly whites in both 1970 and 1980. The median number of years of school completed by black elderly was 2.4 years in 1970 and 3.2 years in 1980. About 20 percent of this older group had received high school diplomas; however, 764,000, or over 25 percent, of older blacks had 0 to 5 years of schooling. Older blacks in the future will have more formal education. By 1980, over 33 percent of blacks 45 to 59 years old and a majority (66 percent) of blacks 25 to 44 years old had completed 12 years or more of school.

Income

Even though there are some wealthy aged people, the older population is identified with low income. People who were poor all their lives can expect to become poorer in old age. They are joined by people who become poor after becoming older.

Because of the way incomes are reported by the Census Bureau (1980), money income data should be interpreted cautiously, since the designation of a person as head of a household may be arbitrary. Money income of a family headed by a person aged 65 and over may include substantial amounts of income received by adult children and other family members. Furthermore, elderly family members who are not classified as family heads are lost in an analysis using family data based on age of family head.

Ten percent of couples with a husband 65 and over received incomes less than $4000 in the late 1970s. The income of elderly persons living alone or with nonrelatives was more skewed to the lower end of the income distribution. Nearly 30 percent received incomes under $3000, while only 25 percent received $6000 or more. The *median income* for these individuals was $3829. At the other end of the income scale, one of every five elderly couples had incomes of $15,000 or more. The median income for these couples was about $8000.

Elderly families and individuals spend relatively large amounts of money from their incomes on housing, food, and medical care. The most expensive item is housing, followed by food, transportation, and medical care.

Approximately 14 percent of the income of the elderly derives from accumulated assets. Rent and certain forms of dividends are not penalized by reductions in *Social Security* payments. However, only about 9 percent of families with heads of households over age 65 have incomes of $25,000. Today, of the 24 million older people, over 80 percent receive Social Security checks. For most people, Social Security payments have become the largest single share of their income. It is the source of 50 percent of the income of nearly 4.3 million elderly families, only 15 percent of whom are poor. It is essentially the sole source of income for about 30 percent of retired workers and over 14 percent of elderly couples (Census Bureau, 1980).

It is a common belief that Social Security and *Medicare* adequately supplement the needs of the elderly. However, while increasing numbers of elderly are dependent on governmental programs for support, there are major problems with the concepts and benefit levels of income maintenance for the elderly. By April 1979, the average monthly Social Security benefits amounted to $283 for individuals and $482 for an elderly couple.

The maximum monthly benefit is $752. In 1981 retired persons eligible for Social Security benefits could earn up to $4,080 if they were under 65 and $5,500 if they were between 65 and 72 without losing benefits; benefits were reduced 50¢ for each dollar earned over these amounts. Persons over age 72 could earn any amount without losing benefits. The average Social Security income for a couple was $5684.

Older persons with low Social Security benefits may also be eligible for *supplemental security income* (SSI) if they have less than $1500 in resources and earn not more than $65 per month. As with Social Security, federal SSI benefits are adjusted in July to reflect changes in the *consumer price index*. In the beginning of 1980 the maximum federal SSI benefits were $264.70 for an individual and $397 for a couple. Each state may supplement these benefits. Thus, as of August 1981 in New York State (which has one of the highest SSI supplements), an individual living alone with no other income would receive $327.91 each month, about $28 in food stamps, and would be eligible for Medicaid (which covers all medical care without charge for those 65 and over).

During the past several years, the high rate of inflation experienced in the United States has posed great problems for older individuals who frequently must live on fixed incomes. Pensions and Social Security payments are often inadequate and have failed to keep pace with inflation. The effects of fixed incomes, limited employment opportunities, and inflation have imposed financial hardships on many older persons.

Poverty and the Elderly

One of the most prevalent measures of economic status is the *poverty index,* the federal government's official statistical measure of poverty or low income. Many analysts believe that the dollar amounts of the poverty thresholds are unrealistically low. For example, the average poverty threshold for a nonfarm family of four was $5500, and the comparable mean poverty threshold was $6875 (Goules, 1980).

Of the 8.2 million families with a 65-and-over head, 710,000 (about 10 percent) were below the poverty level, but over 33 percent of elderly blacks and over 20 percent of elderly Spanish persons were below poverty. Most (88 percent) of the income received by poor families was derived from public sources such as Social Security, supplemental security, and public assistance. For nonpoor families with a head 65 and over, only one-third (36 percent) of the income for nonpoor families was in the form of wages, salaries, and self-employment income. Sixty-six percent of black families with heads over 65 received earnings from employment compared to about 50 percent of white families with heads over 65. The reason seems to be that elderly black workers were much less likely to be covered by pension. Elderly black workers were less likely to have been employed in manufacturing industries and, more likely, were found in lower-paying nontechnical or nonprofessional jobs and had worked fewer years in pension-covered occupations than whites. Analysis of the recent income data by family status shows that about three times as many black families with heads of 65-and-over were below poverty as white families.

The proportion below the poverty level was much higher for elderly persons living alone or with nonrelatives (27 percent) than for those living in families (8 percent). About 67 percent, or 2 million, of those 65 or over are poor who live alone or with nonrelatives, and 51 percent of the nearly 900,000 65-and-over black elderly who live alone were defined as poor. As with elderly families, almost all (93 percent) of the income received by poor individuals 65 and over was from public sources.

Health Status

Acute and chronic health problems do not keep the majority of the elderly from independent living. Less than 5 percent of older Americans after 65 live in institutions (over 85, 20 percent do). Eighty-one percent of the elderly are able to function without assistance and remain in reasonably good health. The majority of the elderly can expect to feel physically well in old age.

Physical and psychological problems should not be ignored and attributed to aging. Unless identified and confronted, such problems are not likely to go away.

The increase in the elderly population will have an obvious impact on the need for health and supportive services in this country. The bulk of the physical health problems of the elderly are chronic conditions such as high blood pressure, arthritis, diabetes, heart disease, arteriosclerosis, and emphysema. These conditions require more medical care and result in more physical and emotional disability. Recent facts about older Americans (Census Bureau, 1980) show that about 18 percent of the 65-and-over group had an interference with their mobility caused by chronic conditions, 6 percent have some trouble ambulating, 7 percent need mechanical assistance to move about, and 5 percent are homebound, compared to 7 percent of younger persons.

Persons over 65 have a greater chance of being hospitalized during the year than those aged 60 to 64. Persons 75 years and older spend an average of 4.5 times as many days in short-stay hospitals as the national average and 70 percent more than persons 65 to 74 years of age. In addition, 75 percent of all nursing home residents are 75 and over, and more than 33 percent are 85 and over.

Recent reports show that the United States spend over $140 billion for personal health care. About $41 billion, or about 33 percent of this amount, was spent for persons 65 and over. The per capita health care cost for a person over 65 years old was $1745, more than two and one-half times as much as the $661 spent for a young adult. Benefits from government programs, including Medicare ($18.3 billion) and Medicaid ($6.9 billion), accounted for about 67 percent of the health expenditures of persons 65 and over, compared with only about 30 percent for adults under 65.

The extent of mental disorders in the elderly is difficult to judge. About 1 million persons over 65 are in institutions, primarily nursing homes, and well over 50 percent of them have some evidence of psychiatric symptoms.

Suicides tend to increase with age among severely depressed individuals. All indications of potential suicide and mental disorder should be perceived as an opportunity for others to help and should be treated accordingly. The importance of accurately identifying and effectively dealing with emotional reactions that occur in the aged will be discussed in Chapter 6.

Significant hearing loss is found in only about 29 percent of the elderly, but it is more common than visual loss. Only about 10 percent of the elderly have vision impairment, usually caused by cataracts, glaucoma, diabetes, and degeneration of the retina.

Diminished sensory acuity should not be ignored or tolerated, especially since aids designed to compensate for some sensory decline are readily available and can be obtained when needed. Health and effective sensory functioning should not be relinquished under the guise of old age.

MINORITY GROUP AGED

Minority group elderly live in multiple jeopardy because of the effects of both racism and aging. Blacks, Hispanics, American Indians, Asians, and Pacific Island Americans are among the minorities whose old age is usually marked with poverty; their likelihood of being poor is twice that of the total population of all ages.

These minorities must live in the United States through six decades of poverty, discrimination, poor education, ghetto conditions, unemployment, and inadequate medical care. In addition to generally poor living conditions, Hispanics and Asian Americans particularly suffer from cultural and language barriers.

Black Americans

There have been significant increases in the life expectancy for all racial groups, and the size of the black and other populations grew greatly between the 1960s and the present (an increase of over 30 percent). The segment 60 years and older more than doubled. The Census Bureau estimated there were 2.8 million black and other racial Americans age 60 and older. These 60+ persons are identified with characteristics such as lower incomes, greater health problems, higher incidence of widowhood, and faster growth rate than comparable whites or younger blacks.

More than 50 percent of both the 60 to 64 and 65-and-over black age groups are women, and the female proportion continues to grow—56 percent of the 60-and-over group in 1970, more than 57 percent in 1978—with growth of similar proportions for those 65 and over during the same periods. The Census Bureau has projected that by 2000 there will be over 4 million black persons 60 and over years old and over 3 million 65 and over. If these increases are realized, they will exceed the rates of growth of the 65-and-over white population by over 25 percent. The ratio of older black women to older black men is also expected to continue to increase. These changes occur because of socioeconomic improvements and increasing efforts to provide better medical services for minorities (Williams, 1980).

Spanish Americans

Recent census figures suggest that the Spanish American population of 11.2 million is the second largest racial minority in America. Persons of Hispanic origin include Cubans, Central and South Americans, Mexicans, Puerto Ricans, and other Spanish. These figures do not include the 2.8 million Spanish-speaking people of Puerto Rico or the estimated 8 million illegal (there are many more) alien Spanish population living in America. Approximately 7 million of the 11.2 million Spanish-speaking Americans are of Mexican background, and approximately 80 percent live in urban areas of the Southwest in five states (Arizona, California, Colorado, New Mexico, and Texas). In the Spanish-speaking population, it is estimated that 4 percent, or about 440,000, are elderly.

The National Council on Aging (1980) reports that Spanish-speaking Americans suffer from a much lower life expectancy than blacks or whites; for example, in Colorado their life expectancy is 56.7 years, compared to 67.5 years for other Colorado residents.

American Indians

The Census Bureau recently estimated the total American Indian population at about 792,730. The criteria for numbering in this group were at least 25 percent Indian blood and registration on an approved tribal roll, but the aged in this population have not been reliably estimated. The American Indian life expectancy of about 47 years is extraordinarily low and 33 percent shorter than the national average.

Services to the Indians are provided by the U.S. Public Health Service, which has no outreach or prevention programs. The Indian Health Service of the Bureau of Indian Affairs is offered only to Indians on the reservations. Those off the reservations do not qualify for service (Williams, 1980).

The Indian population are the poorest people in America. The most recent census (1980) indicates that 50 percent of the families have incomes of less than $4000 per year. Unemployment, abject poverty, hunger, and malnutrition are constant problems. The population of 63,000 Indians over 60 represented only 8 percent of the population, compared to 14 percent of the U.S. total. If such conditions are the rule, we can be certain the Indians are in desperate condition. Traditional family support is unfeasible in families with no resources, and many of the elderly are left impoverished, especially if the children leave the reservation. The sole source of income for many Indian elderly is welfare, with only the minimal level of Social Security. The federal government, through the Bureau of Indian Affairs, did not set up funding programs so that Indians could participate in company retirement, insurance plans, or in many cases, Social Security. Because of jurisdictional disputes, for example, some states have refused to license nursing homes on reservations with the result that federal funds for use with this group are not authorized.

Asian Americans

As a combined minority group, the Asian-American elderly (Chinese, Filipino, Japanese, Korean, Samoan, Malaysian, Vietnamese, Cambodians, and a few others) constitute about 1 percent of the U.S. population. Although these groups have different languages and cultures, they are identified as "Orientals."

More than 90 percent of Asian Americans live in metropolitan areas. The majority live in California and Hawaii as a result of direct immigration to these areas. Sixty-seven percent of the Asian-American population have settled in San Francisco. Immigration practices have affected this group profoundly, particularly with regard to family life and male/female ratios. About 67 percent of the Asian elderly are males who have no female to call on in times of need.

In most areas of Chinese-American populations, there are large groups of single men, a partial reflection of pre-World War II imigration laws, not liberalized until 1975 that forbid Chinese men from intermarriage or bringing their families over. Another group, the "young-old" Chinese, is beginning to appear as a result of the reunion of long-separated families and seems to have more elderly women than men. Added to these are the aged Chinese born in the United States, again a higher proportion of women.

Recent Census figures reveal that there are 26,856 elderly Chinese over 65 years old, about 6 percent of the total Chinese-American population. However, these figures do not reflect the high number of illegal immigrants living in the ethnic community. Older males numbered 15,244 and females numbered 11,612. Only about 27 percent of the elderly live with a spouse, compared with 43 percent of the general elderly population. Nationally, the Census showed 28 percent of all elderly Chinese in America are below the official poverty index. In San Francisco's Chinatown, about 50 percent of the elderly subsist below the poverty level (Carp, 1976). About 80 percent of the households have annual incomes below $4000, and about 33 percent have incomes below $2000. In New York City, about 33 percent of Chinese elderly are below the poverty level. Note that Asian and Pacific Island elderly account for 70 percent of the city's elderly "other *nonwhites*" (Daum, 1980). It is of interest that the rate of poverty among elderly "other nonwhites" is comparable to that of blacks and Puerto Ricans. The disruption of traditional patterns of alien cultures is exacerbated because many of the elderly do not speak English. Almost 80 percent of Asian and Pacific elderly are foreign born.

Japanese elderly receive more family support and economic security because they were allowed to emigrate as families. Recent census figures (1980) show the elderly numbered 47,159, or about 8 percent of the total Japanese-American population. Twenty percent of these elderly are poor and live in California and Hawaii. Fifty-eight percent live alone, and 67 percent of these are widowed females. The elderly male Japanese tends to speak some English, although older women tend to speak only Japanese. Health surveys have found this elderly group to be among the physically most healthy and long lived.

The Filipino-American elderly are a smaller group; 21,249 persons over 65 represent about 7 percent of the Filipino population here. About 81 percent of Filipino Americans are male; 30 percent of them still living with a spouse in an interracial marriage. The majority of Filipino Americans live in urban areas in poverty-stricken circumstances. Some Filipinos came to the United States as laborers, and many were awarded citizenship as veterans of the American army after World War II. Perhaps because of living isolated lives, the Filipino population has an unusually large proportion of men in psychiatric hospitals. Poverty, discrimination, poor housing, and health problems are widespread among minority groups and, even in Asian-American families usually thought of as much better off financially, the needs of the elderly are beyond the families' ability to help them.

Rural Elderly

There were 6 million farms in the United States in 1940 and only 3 million in the 1970s. According to the Census Bureau (1980), only about 5 percent of the elderly now live on farms. About 33 percent of them lived outside the nation's metropolitan areas compared to 26 percent of all other age groups. Migration from the farms has followed the decrease of smaller marginal farms. Agricultural business has taken over in the upper central Midwest (Minnesota and North and South Dakota) and upper New England (Maine, New Hampshire, and Vermont).

Older people become part of the problem of *rural* poverty, where 67 percent of the nation's substandard housing is to be found in small towns and villages. Other unfavorable features that affect the elderly include inadequate transportation (and dependence on private transportation), inadequate medical facilities, and low income levels. Agricultural workers have lower Social Security payments, and the self-employed farmers have only recently come under coverage. There is also a shrinking tax base and loss of services because of the migration of younger people to the cities, so that the rural elderly are left with rising property and sales taxes to maintain community services. The shortage of paid jobs has also hampered older rural elderly. Present job programs have done little to help, since 33 percent of the country's poverty is found in rural areas, but limited federal manpower funds are allotted these areas.

Summary

The elderly population has been growing much faster than the nation's population as a whole during the twentieth century and can be expected to continue growing rapidly in the first third of the next century. The demographic and socioeconomic characteristics of this population have also undergone considerable changes in the past that will continue into the future.

However, the segments of the elderly population that will be growing most rapidly (the oldest of the old, women, and persons of races other than white) will be the same groups that have suffered more from common problems such as social isolation, poverty, and poor health. A striking phenomenon that has occurred in recent decades has been the rapid growth in number of elderly who live alone and rent instead of owning their homes. In addition, the elderly are concentrated in the larger states and are living more and more in the nation's metropolitan areas.

Although the 1960s were a period of economic progress for the population as a whole, the same subgroups that experienced little or no decline in poverty were females, minorities, and those who live alone. These subgroups, particularly women and minorities, tend to have worked less than in the past and to have worked in lower-paying occupations and, therefore, tend to have fewer financial assets after retirement. Clearly, the increasing size of these subgroups will enlarge the number of elderly poor in the future. More and more elderly are dependent on income support programs, including Social Security, supplemental security income, Medicare, food stamps, and housing subsidies.

Many of the changes that have occurred in the social and economic structure of the United States are reflected in the elderly after a delay of years or even decades. For example, the advent of universal education and emphasis on the benefits of education have been reflected in the constant rise in the median number of years of school completed by the elderly. In addition, the occupational history of the elderly, indicating more professional training and higher earnings, is evident. It is likely that tomorrow's elderly will be more highly educated and involved in higher-paying occupations. Besides Social Security, many will receive increased pension benefits, and a higher proportion of elderly women will be eligible for retirement benefits of their own. The most difficult problem will continue to be economic inequities between white male elderly and female and nonwhite elderly. Regardless of the national economic situation, these data indicate that the elderly population will be rapidly growing and changing, and the trend toward early retirement, coupled with longer life expectancy, will mean many more years of retirement. The increasing proportion of the elderly who will fall in the 75-and-over and 85-and-over groups will require additional resources to handle their more frequent physical and emotional problems. The growing proportion of women, many of whom will be widowed and living alone, will also require additional resources to meet their needs. The rising number of elderly living alone will require housing alternatives to institutionalization in order for them to continue to live independently while coping with the problems of age. The nation as a whole, as it becomes older in age composition, must learn to deal with the changing needs of its members.

FURTHER READINGS

Brophy, A. M., *Facts for Action: The Elderly in the Inner City,* New York City Office of the Aging, 1980.

Butler, R. N., *Why Survive? Being Old in America,* Harper & Row, New York, 1975.

Busse, E., "Theories of Aging," in C. Busse, and E. Pfeiffer, (eds.), *Behavior and Adaptation in Late Life,* Little Brown, Boston, 1977.

Carp, F. M., and E. Kataoka, "Health Care Problems of The Elderly in San Francisco's Chinatown," *The Gerontologist,* 1976, *16,* 30–38.

Current Population Reports, "Marital Status and Living Arrangements: March, 1975" Series P-20, No. 287, U. S. Department of Commerce, Bureau of the Census, Washington, D.C., 1975, 1980.

Current Population Reports, "Money Income and Poverty Status of Families and Persons in the United States," Series P-60, No. 103, U. S. Department of Commerce, Bureau of the Census, Washington, D. C., 1975, 1980.

Current Population Reports, Special Studies, "Demographic Aspects of Aging and The Older Population in the United States," Series P-23, No. 59, U. S. Department of Commerce, *Bureau of the Census,* Washington, D. C., May 1976, 1980.

Current Population Reports, "Projections of The Population of The United States," P-25, No. 75, 1977, 2050, U. S. Department of Commerce, *Bureau of The Census,* July, 1977, Washington, D. C., 1978, 1980.

Developments in Aging 1976–1977, Part 1, *A Report of The Special Committee on Aging,* U. S. Senate, U. S. Government Printing Office, No. 95, 771, Washington, D. C., 1978, 1980.

Facts about Older Americans, U. S. Department of Health, Education & Welfare, Washington, D. C., 1975, 1980.

Fowles, D. G., "Some Prospects for the Future Elderly Population," *Statistical Reports on Older Americans, January 1978,* U. S. Department of Health, Education and Welfare, Office of Human Development Administration on Aging, National Clearinghouse on Aging, No. 3, Washington, D. C., 1978, 1980.

Daum, M. "Selected Demographic Characteristics of Elderly Asian and Pacific Island Americans in New York City," *Facts For Action,* New York City Office For The Aging, Vol. 9, No. 1, January 1977, 1980.

New York City Department for the Aging, *Recent Developments in the Economics of Aging,* June 1975, 1980.

Goules, D. G., "Income and Poverty Among the Elderly: 1975," *Statistical Reports on Older Americans, April 1977,* U. S. Department of Health, Education, and Welfare Publication No. OHD, 77-20286, Washington, D. C., 1977, 1980.

Fowles, D. J., *Statistical Memo No. 33,* "Elderly Widows," July 1976, "Administration on Aging," Washington, D. C., 1976, 1980.

Facts and Figures on Older Americans, No. 5, U. S. Department of Health, Education and Welfare, January 1978.

Thompson, G. B., "Black-White Differences in Private Pension; "Findings from the Retirement History Study," *Social Security Bulletin,* February 1979, *42* (2).

U. S. Department of Commerce, Persons of Spanish Origin in The United States, March 1975. Population Characteristics, Advance Report, Bureau of The Census, Series P-20, No. 283, Washington, D. C., 1975, 1980.

Williams, B. S., "Characteristics of the Black Elderly-and Older American Indians 1980," Statistical Reports on Older Americans, No. 5, April 1980. U. S. Department of Health and Human Services, Office of Human Development Services, Administration on Aging, National Clearinghouse on Aging, DHEW Publication, No. OHDS 80-20057, 78-20289 Washington, D. C., 1980.

CHAPTER 3

Changes in the Body with Age

This chapter examines age-related changes in the body systems and describes the prevalence and effects of disease among the aged. In general, it is difficult to separate physiological, social, and psychological effects of disease because aging and disease seem highly correlated. For example, aged persons experience growing effects of disease, gradual reduction of sensation, more social losses, and more situations of increased emotional stress.

Age-related changes in hearing, vision, taste, smell, and touch are considered; since behavior is directly related to the individual's ability to perceive the environment through the sensory organs, it is important for the aged (and for those working with them) to know the consequences of sensory deprivation. Some measures are suggested that may alleviate the negative effects of sensory decline in old age.

HEALTHY OLD AGE

The study of natural development has seldom gone far beyond early adult years. The healthy aged tend to be invisible, yet old age can be an emotionally healthy and satisfying time of life, as the following case demonstrates.

GOOD AS EVER

Mr. E. is a 78-year-old man who recently suffered the loss of his second wife of 3 years. He is well dressed and appears in excellent health, looking much younger than his stated age. He is living with a 76-year-old widowed sister in three rented rooms. He was first married for 50 years to a woman who died shortly after a heart attack 7 years ago. He has only limited contact with his children, who live close by. He had been employed all his life as a meat packer but was forced to retire at 65. After the death of his second wife, he returned to work part-time to supplement his Social Security and union pension but mainly, "to be with people." He had always lived in a central part of the city, but he and his second wife moved to Florida because of crime problems in the housing project in which they lived. When interviewed, he was spontaneous and talkative; he showed a keen interest in and awareness of events and had no memory impairments.

He was born in a large metropolitan city, the second of six children. He was employed at age 9 and worked as a butcher with his brother-in-law when he was a teenager. He married at 21 and moved to the apartment where he lived with his first wife for 50 years and raised two children. His marriage was viewed by him as an excellent one, and his wife was in good health until a week before she died. Mr. E. described trouble with his prostate in recent years, but he was able to have normal sexual relations on a less frequent basis. His relationship with his second wife "was like starting life all over," but her children opposed their marriage because he was of a different religion.

His relationship with his children and grandchildren was described as satisfying, but he has almost no contact with them.

Mr. E. made plans for his retirement and continues to plan for the future. He describes little concern for death and only hopes he will die without pain or "like my second wife, in her sleep." He describes himself as always being "very religious" and an active member of his church.

In viewing his aging condition he relates that "my legs are not as steady and I can't work as long but I'm just as good as ever." He did recognize that for any physical problems "there was no one to care for him," and he knew he had "a bladder problem that should be fixed." He made application for a retirement home associated with a fraternal order and was "on the waiting list." He seems to have accepted his physical changes and is extremely active, still walking about the house and participating in daily activities. There is no history or evidence of physical, social, or psychological difficulty, and there is no indication that he will in the near future experience functional breakdown.

When Mr. E. was contacted again recently, he had to have a prostatectomy. Because of his concern that he might need further medical care in the future, he was able to enter the retirement home sooner than expected. In this new location (upstate), he has already made many new friends, is in charge of contacting and visiting some of the older residents as part of a peer counseling service, and is given some renumeration. He shows a reasonable recognition of his limitations and capacities. His only wish is that he could visit his old friends, and he is making plans to do so in the summer.

In considering health one realizes that, in addition to the general lack of interest in the elderly, science and medicine have been more concerned with treating the sick than clarifying the complex interwoven elements necessary to support health and prevent illness. The less dramatic process of prevention requires an understanding of what supports and what interferes with healthy development in the life cycle.

The World Health Organization has defined health as "a state of physical, mental, and social well-being and not merely the absence of disease or infirmity." If one conceives aging to be a process of change involving many physical, psychological, and social elements, these elements are the framework for analyzing the changes that occur with advancing age.

The aging person has a unique set of developmental tasks to accomplish, primarily to clarify, deepen, and find use for what one has experienced in a lifetime. Ability to adapt is related to physical health, personality, earlier life experiences, and social supports such as finances, shelter, medical care, social roles, family interests, and recreation.

Becoming "Old"

The term "aging" is used to denote characteristic patterns of late life changes; however, models of aging differ, and various biological, environmental, social, or random antecedents have been suggested. However, we wish to examine the more general physical and physiological characteristics and changes of aging that are fairly common in America.

Types of Change

To understand common aging changes, one may distinguish between those that are (1) intrinsic, age-specific, and perhaps immodifiable, and (2) extrinsic, variable, and imposed by exposure to active forces such as disease, social loss, and preexisting personality. Age changes, however, are often due to a complex of interacting forces, and it is sometimes difficult to be sure which are inevitable intrinsic changes and which are extrinsic. In this chapter we will discuss these changes without considering theoretical controllability.

Some of the physical changes may have major effects on the concept of self; others, especially decreased perceptual acuity and central nervous system slowing, may have more effect on psychological and social adjustment. There are, however, individual variations in changes in this area, since they reflect the combined effects of heredity, environment, and aging. Age-related changes in the structure and function of body systems are poorly understood, as are the relationships between such changes and the psychological and social behavior of an aging person.

SKIN CHANGES IN AGING

One of the most apparent changes in old age occurs in the skin in the form of increased paleness, change in texture, loss of elasticity, dryness, and appearance of spots of pigmentation; much of this is attributed to changes in fibrous protein (collagen), as noted in Chapter 2. Collagen also affects stature and joint diseases and causes wounds to heal more slowly.

Compounding the loss of elasticity of the skin, there is a thinning of the epithelium, the outermost layer of the tissue covering the body's free surfaces, and of *subcutaneous* fatty layers. Multiple factors including age, sex, race, and state of nutrition determine the amount of fat in the subcutaneous layers of the skin. However, the loss of fatty tissues is particularly observable on the legs and forearms of older individuals. Skinfold measurements indicate this diminution begins with regularity at age 45. With the disappearance of fat, one observes deepening of hollows, increase of boniness, and increased prominence of muscular markings.

Other constituents of the skin undergo regression, including the elastic fibers in the subcutaneous layer and sweat glands, which also diminish in number. The net effect leaves the skin in a dry, thin, inelastic state. The loss of sweat glands means an important change in body temperature regulation. Since older people cannot perspire as freely, they are more likely to complain of the heat and are more subject to heat exhaustion. Sensitivity to the cold is also common and is due to the loss of insulating fat and diminished circulation. Among the cellular changes of aging are the loss of the epidermic cells (melanocytes) that produce *melanin* (the brown pigment that colors the skin and protects it from ultraviolet rays). The skin of Caucasians tends to become more pallid; this is sometimes further accentuated by the loss of ruddiness because of decreased peripheral circulation in the small blood vessels. Deposits of pigmentation are also seen (melanotic freckles), although the skin overall seems paler. In additin, brown plaquelike growths (seborrheic hyperkatoses) the size of a small coin appear more and more after age 50.

Graying of hair, also a failure of pigment cells, is a familiar sign of aging. In general, there is a marked thinning of scalp hair and of hair on the extremities. Oddly, in older women particularly, changes in the androgen/estrogen ratio may produce bristly facial hairs that require depilation.

Wrinkling or permanent infoldings of the skin, a result of skin sagging and loss of elasticity, are most often noted on the face because of repeated stress on facial skin produced by the muscles of expression. Wrinkling is more severe in those exposed to the sun. The neck is perhaps the most reliable area in which to observe aging change, usually quite obvious by age 50. Other common sites are above the eyebrows and at the outer edges of the lips and mouth. By age 50, the lobes of the ear become fuller, and the ear seems more elongated.

Changes in the hair and skin certainly affect one's self-concept, confidence, and sense of value and mark one as "old." No medication or creams remove wrinkles, although some people do use mild hypoallergenic creams or simple wax moisture creams, estrogen supplements (if prescribed by a doctor), or cosmetic surgery (if it is within the means and is important to self-esteem). However, the best preventive measure for most people is to begin at an early age to protect skin and hair from overexposure to the sun, chemicals and from other factors (such as inadequate diet) known to contribute to such changes. Some of the practices of modern hairdressing, such as the use of dyes, can be used if one's body can tolerate them. Fortunately, loss of hair in women is uncommon. In men, baldness is genetic and cannot be prevented or even slowed by any of the routines promoted to delay it. If loss of hair is upsetting, it is possible, although still expensive, to buy natural-looking hairpieces or to undergo transplant procedures.

DENTAL CHANGES IN AGING

Although one does see older persons with a full set of natural teeth, loss of teeth is a frequent difficulty for older people. The adjustment to dentures has implications for the ability to chew food properly and for readjustment of self-image. Unlike the tooth loss of earlier years (because of cavities or tooth decay), most tooth loss in the middle and later years results from the effects of *periodontal disease* (often called pyorrhea) and the inflamation of the tissues surrounding and supporting the teeth, and it involves bone factors, essentially a degree of osteoporosis. Removal of teeth aggravates the process of osteoporosis, so it is desirable to use dental procedures that maintain the teeth and jaw.

MUSCULOSKELETAL CHANGES IN AGING

In this section a few common muscle changes, prevalent joint diseases, skeletal disorders, and the disability they cause are discussed.

Muscle Changes

Muscle changes and disorders brought on by natural processes are examined here. In general, skeletal muscles waste, and there is a decrease in strength, endurance, and agility, but the extent and rate of such loss vary among aging individuals. Considerable retention of muscular ability may be seen in some. Decrease in bulk is part of the general atrophy of organs and tissues; atrophy of the small muscles makes the arms and legs seem thin and bony. There is a general picture of flexion in the posture of the aged caused by changes in the vertebral system, shrinking of tendons and muscles, and degenerative changes in the *central nervous system.*

Prevalent Musculoskeletal Disorders In The Elderly

Osteoarthritis. The most common human arthritic affliction is osteoarthritis. Symptoms are usually mild or absent until degeneration of the inner vertibal disk begins. When nerve compression develops, there may be pain.

Rheumatoid Arthritis. Joint inflamation is the predominant sign of this disease of connective tissue. It usually begins between 20 and 60 years of age and is three times more prevalent in women. Its relatively early onset, usually gradual, marks it as a condition not limited only to the aged. Joints become stiff after inactivity, and motion is limited by pain and stiffness. Signs differentiating rheumatiod arthritis are gradual swelling, warmth, redness, and tenderness, with periods of exacerbation and remission.

Studies indicate that distinct losses in height occur during later life. By age 50 to 55, a decrease of 0.25 to 0.75 inch occurs because of shrinkage of the disks between the vertebrae. Subsequently, major losses of height occur because of osteoporosis.

Osteoporosis. This most prevalent metabolic disorder of the bone develops slowly and is characterized by decreased skeletal mass and density. It is not certain, however, that age-related bone changes and clinical osteoporosis are the same. There is no alteration in the composition of the bone, but the body cannot sustain the mechanical stresses of daily life. The result is susceptibility to fracture, particularly fracture of the hip, vertebrae (spinal column), and wrist. Approximately 6.3 million older people in the United States suffer from acute problems related to this disorder. Thirty percent of postmenopausal women have major orthopedic problems related to osteoporosis, since women tend to have bone changes earlier and are more likely to develop it. Causes of the disease have been related to immobilization, decreased estrogen levels, high steroid levels, and environmental factors. The major presenting symptom is back pain and increasing spinal curvature (particularly dowager's hump). Although it is prevalent, it is not listed among the most common ailments of the elderly. Osteoporosis is believed to precipitate about 195,000 hip fractures annually, primarily among elderly women, with such fractures a major cause of physical disability in old age.

Disability Related to Chronic Muscloskeletal Disorders

Disability caused by chronic muscloskeletal diseases (discussed in the preceding section) is, as expected, more severe in the elderly. In a survey by the National Institute on Aging (1980) about 30 percent of those over 65 consider themselves limited in one or more daily activity (such as moving about, feeding themselves, and climbing stairs) by their chronic condition. The limitation was usually at the level of inconvenience or discomfort; fewer persons require assistance from others. Less than 1 percent of persons surveyed were limited in their ability to feed, dress, bathe, or perform self-care toilet functions but, if so limited, help was often required. Sixty-seven percent of those reporting limitation of ability to move about still functioned without outside help. Sixty percent of those reporting difficulty climbing stairs still were able to function alone. Of particular importance is that travel on public transit was an exception to the limitations; seventy-five percent of those who reported such limitations required help to travel or were unable to travel at all. This fact has obvious implications in planning for the delivery of proper health care.

Ideally, from the age of 50 onward, people should see a physician if they have persistent pain or stiffness in joints, especially on waking up or when resuming an activity. Early medical attention can halt muscular skeletal damage before it becomes disabling; however, if a disabling condition is already present, active medical treatment is still important. If medication or other treatment is not effective, painful joints can be fused or replaced artifically. Early prevention, however, is still the best course.

CENTRAL NERVOUS SYSTEM CHANGES IN AGING

Several neurophysiological changes occur with age. Independent of disease, neuronal depopulation (gradual reduction of the number of neuron cells) of the central nervous system and progressive loss of function invariably occur with time and are, therefore, an aspect of aging, occuring at a varying rate individually.

The slowing of the central nervous system with age is most apparent in tests of reaction time, that is, the time between a signal and the subject's response is consistently found to increase with age. Reaction time involves several facets: perception, attention, short-term memory, and transmission of neural impulse; it is not clear whether all these processes slow with age or whether slowing occurs in only some of them. It has been posited that at least some of this slowing may occur in the transmission of neural impulse. Perhaps the most important single feature of the nervous system and nerve conduction is the establishment of a complex network of synapses (the junction of two *neurons)*. By these anatomical connections, the central nervous system becomes a confederation of functional units. It is likely that physical-chemical changes at the synapse may slow the transmission of impulses in the nervous system.

There are several additional factors that may affect the functioning of the central nervous system with age; however, they are too complex to discuss in detail here. For example, changes in hormone levels that affect the level of brain function or changes with age in vital cell components such as nucleic acid (*RNA* and DNA), ammino acids, proteins, and enzymes have been suggested as possible factors affecting the efficiency of the central nervous system in the aged. Another important factor is that many metabolites need to reach the central nervous system, which establishes its critical dependency on the integrity of the circulatory system. It was found that when such changes do occur, as in vascular accidents, physiological and intellectual functions are impaired. Irreversible vascular problems are frequent, and cerebral arteriosclerosis is common in the aged.

Changes have been found in sleep patterns with age. Spontaneous interruption of sleep and the amount of time spent awake before sleep occurs more frequently. Alterations of the sleep/wakefulness ratio and the ability to regulate body temperature suggest aging modification in hypothalomic function. The *hypothalamus,* in addition to its role in sleep and temperature regulation, is important to appetite and thirst, control of body fluids, expression of emotions (rage and fear), sexual activity, growth control of the thyroid and adrenal systems, and control of the autonomic nervous system.

The control of the autonomic nervous system over various organic functions in aging seems unstable and unpredictable, probably contributing to intestinal movement and resulting in irregularity and constipation. By contrast, loss of cortical inhibition in the elderly may contribute to diarrhea or urinary incontinence. These losses do not necessarily begin early and often appear only in later years or even not at all until close to death.

Reduction of sensitivity to bodily discomfort is also evidenced by the fact that the aged tolerate space-occupying growths with little discomfort. Aging of the nervous systems could contribute to inadequate mobility; delay in feedback for enzyme and hormone release; diminished response to pain; and decreased vasomotor response during exercising, eating, or displaying strong emotion.

The brain and central nervous system do deteriorate with age but, with most people, it functions effectively and well through nine decades. Brain damage is no longer considered a general or common part of normal aging (see Chapter 1). The main way in which the brain can be damaged is by interference with its blood supply.

ENDOCRINE SYSTEM CHANGES IN AGING

The endocrine system is the group of ductless glands or tissues that secrete highly specific substances into the bloodstream for use by other tissues. In the aged the thyroid gland, adrenal glands, pituitary gland, ovaries, testes, and uterus are the major organs most frequently subject to change. Of course, all the endocrine systems will become subject to the usual phenomena of disorder in terms of circulatory dysfunction, degenerative changes, and disease processes.

Alteration in responsiveness to hormones may be a major part of the deterioration of biochemical activity during aging. It is known that under certain conditions the ability to secrete insulin and glucocorticoids is impaired with age. In addition to deficiencies in thyroid and pituitary hormones, changes in hormone transport, action, and feedback systems seem to occur. There have been some reports of changes in the ability of hormones such as estrogen, androgen, progesterone, and glucocorticoids to bind to target cells and tissue receptors in the brain, liver, prostate, white blood cells, fatty tissues, muscles, and uterus.

BLOOD SYSTEM CHANGES IN AGING

The blood normally consists of a circulating liquid *plasma* that maintains a slightly less than equal volume of three solid constituents: white cells, blood cells, and *platelets,* the elements that cause clotting. The red cells are made in the bone marrow and carry oxygen to the tissue. *Red cells* constitute the main solid portion of the blood. Two types of white cells—*lymphocytes* and *phagocytes*—constitute 1 out of every 500 blood cells. Lymphocytes are made in the marrow and lymph system and are important in fighting infection; phagocytes ingest undesirable cells.

There is no evidence in the aged of a systemic change in the resting levels of blood sugar, blood acidity, osmotic blood pressure, or total volume and, even though the rate of red cell formation is unchanged in older persons, there is an unexplained increase in cell fragility that possibly is the cause of increased anemia.

Blood Disorders

Disorders of the blood in the elderly such as anemia most commonly affect the ratio of the red and white cells, but platelet levels are not significantly altered in later life.

Anemias. These may be present when the concentration of hemoglobin in the blood falls below the normal range.

Iron deficiency is the most common form of anemia in the elderly, and evidence suggests that the response of older people to iron is delayed.

Pernicious anemia resulting from a vitamin B-12 deficiency is most prevalent in later life. The presence of antibodies in the cells lining the stomach found in persons with this condition suggest some abnormality of immune surveillance in later life. Similarly, a decrease in acid and other secretions accompanying normal aging is accentuated in this condition.

Nutritional disturbances are common in anemic older people. Nutritional studies of older people reveal that diets are not as balanced as they look or as they are reported. Anyone living on a full, well-balanced American diet should not need added vitamins. It would do no harm for older people to add the approved standard daily dose of a full (brand) multivitamin preparation and, if in doubt, to ask a physician if a pharmacy preparation is recommended.

High Blood Pressure

Studies have demonstrated that the blood pressure, especially the systolic pressure, is higher in older subjects than in younger ones (Comroe, 1980). The role of factors such as stress, salt intake, and age changes on arterial stiffness, elasticity, or distensibility remains unclear. It is also uncertain just what levels of blood pressure should be considered normal for the aged. Nevertheless, it has been demonstrated that identifying the hypertensive-prone individual early in life and lowering the blood pressure is highly beneficial in delaying the onset of vascular disease and prolonging life. (See hypertensive kidney disorder, discussed in this section.)

IMMUNE SYSTEM CHANGES IN AGING

The immune system includes the bone marrow, spleen, lymph nodes, and white cells. It is intimately involved with the body's ability to adapt to environmental *stress* and change. Its main function is to defend the body against infection. The immune mechanisms are generally classified as specific or nonspecific. The words *immunity* and *immune system* are frequently used only to refer to specific mechanisms.

Nonspecific Mechanisms

Nonspecific mechanisms include the skin, mucous membranes, secretions (such as tears and mucous), actions of *enzymes,* and some organisms, fluids, and biochemical processes of the gastrointestinal tract. Emphasis in the changes of age on the immune system, however, has focused on specific mechanisms.

Specific Mechanisms

Adaptive immunity is the result of contact with specific organisms or substances and is a function of the white blood cells (lymphocytes). There are two types of white cells involved in immunity: B cells and T cells.

B cells. These carry on their surface a kind of molecule known as an antibody that is highly specific and able to locate and react to a portion of another molecular pattern in some molecular substance entering the body.

The molecular patterns that antibodies can identify are called antigenic determinants. The particle or foreign organism carrying the antigenic determinants is called the antigen. This combination of antibody with foreign *antigen* leads to the inactivation and removal of substances that invade the body. Any organism or particle presents many *antigenic determinants,* and one (or more) of these is certain to come in to contact with B cells carrying the antibody that will combine with it.

T cells. Like B cells, T cells react to antigens and divide and proliferate in contact with them. They release a number of materials that accelerate the removal of antigen. They also release other substances that stimulate B cells to divide and produce antibody, but T cells themselves produce little or no antibody. T cells are able to identify changes in cell surface and can bind to these modified areas and destroy or neutralize the altered cell before it can begin to replicate.

Recent studies have established that certain normal functions decline with increasing age, among them the immune function, with a consequent rise in autoimmune diseases and susceptibility to infection.

Disorders of the Immune System

Response to Infection. Older persons respond differently to infection than younger people. Often, no fever and no increase of circulating white cells is evident. Older persons are more likely to suffer adverse reaction to antibiotics because their immune responsiveness is reduced, with a significant decrease in T cell reaction. They are also less responsive to vaccination.

Cancer. Chronic lymphatic cancer is closely age related and occurs with high frequency in the elderly. This is the most common leukemia of older people, usually being diagnosed at age 60 or above. Men are affected twice as often as women. This disorder of the lymphocytes is accompanied by a decline in the percentage of T cells essential for immunological protection.

Autoimmune Disease. The body's self-recognition mechanisms break down fairly often. When such failures occur, the immune system may attack one of the organs of the body. Autoimmune responses are suspected in many diseases of the aged, including rheumatoid arthritis and cancer.

CIRCULATORY SYSTEM CHANGES IN AGING

Strehler (1977) points out that disorders of the heart and circulatory interference with blood supply to the brain are the leading causes of death in the aged.

The pulse of an older person gives some insight as to general circulatory changes in aging. The artery is more prominent because of the loss of supporting tissue and increased stiffness of the arterial wall; these changes are referred to as *arteriosclerosis* but, more accurately, are a combination of *atherosclerosis,* deposit of fatty materials in the artery, and calcification of the middle lining of the vessels.

Even though heart disease is the leading cause of death in people over 65, it can lead to secondary *pulmonary* abnormalities, which in turn cause cardiac involvement. The cardiovascular and pulmonary systems are closely related, and each has its own normal aging features.

Cardiac Features of Aging

There are three major features of cardiac aging: (1) structural changes in the heart and valves, (2) physiological characteristics, and (3) electrocardiograms.

The heart may shrink with age and, in addition, fatty tissue appears in the veins and arterial walls. Endocardial thickening and sclerosis also occurs; the walls of the left side (ventricle) show a 25 percent increase in thickness from age 30 to age 80.

The change in the heart's structure is also manifested in the valves, which become more rigid, thickened, and distorted because of sclerosis and fibrosis, rendering the valve closing less accurate and producing heart murmur.

The most significant physiological changes to the heart as a result of aging are that: (1) cardiac reserve diminishes and the heart reacts poorly to stress; (2) the aged heart has a decreased ability to use oxygen; (3) the heart's rate of recovery is slower and reacts poorly to fast beating; (4) the maximum blood flow through the coronary artery at age 60 is about 35 percent lower than in younger people.

With loss of elasticity in the walls of the arteries and increased instability of control in extreme old age, blood pressure may vary between 100 to 140 systolic and 70 to 90 diastolic. There is generally a significant increase in the relaxation phase (diastolic) in older men of 10 to 15 percent (compared to men 30 years old).

Electrocardiogram changes generally reveal that heart voltages diminish and slowing of impulse conduction occurs as people age.

Major Cardiovascular Disorders

Several disorders increase in frequency and severity with old age and may become a determining factor in life span.

The leading cause of death at all ages is heart disease; cerebral *vascular* accident (stroke) ranks second. Hypertensive heart disease is the third most common cause of death from 65 to 84, and it is an important cause of death of people past 85, together with arteriosclerosis and cerebral vascular accidents.

Most of the 20 listed causes of death, except for lung cancer, show an increasing rate in the older age ranges. The death rate from emphysema is also relatively constant in older persons.

Heart Abnormalities. Regardless of causes, the two most important diseases that increase with age are hypertension and heart involvement and arteriosclerotic heart disease. However, various factors in addition to aging contribute to heart disease, such as heredity, infection or disease, and stress.

Hypertension. Hypertension or high blood pressure affects an estimated 23 million Americans. Only 50 percent are aware of it, and only 50 percent of these are being treated. Hypertension plays a direct role in the death of at least 60,000 persons yearly, the majority in their fifties. Government figures show that one in seven black people have high blood pressure and that hypertension kills 13,000 black people compared to sickle-cell anemia's toll of 340 per year. The nonwhite death rate for hypertension is 58.4 per 100,000, more than twice the 27.1 per 100,000 rate for whites. There are data showing that blacks living in urban areas have the highest blood pressures of all.

Hypertension Characteristics. According to authorities, many factors regulate blood pressure: blood thickness and volume, heart output and elasticity of arterial walls, resistance due to peripheral changes, kidney dysfunction, and malfunction of the endocrine system. In the aged arteriosclerosis is one of the principal causes of hypertension.

Hypertensive arterial disease is a severe problem for the aged because it impairs circulation to the vital organs of the body (brain, heart, and kidneys), increases the work of the heart, aggravates arteriosclerosis, and precipitates congestive heart failure. Hypertension is not an isolated problem; it can lead to neurological, cardiac, and kidney involvement. Neurological symptoms of hypertension include dull morning headache, memory impairment, and body tremor. Prolonged hypertension in the aged can lead to cerebral problems and injury to the eyes. These symptoms may be compounded by normal visual changes. In either case, people will experience blurred vision.

The second major consequence of hypertension in the elderly involves the risk of heart damage. Hypertension eventually leads to acceleration of heart damage. Such damage is in the form of impaired heart nutrition and oxygenation, which leads to severe chest pain (angina pectoris), and coronary occlusion. The last consequence of hypertension is damage to kidney arteries.

Recent studies have demonstrated that lowering elevated blood pressures is highly beneficial in delaying the onset of blood vessel disorders and prolonging life. The role of factors such as stress, salt intake, and age-related arterial changes is still unclear. Nevertheless, hypertension is treatable using simple diuretics that reduce salt levels or stronger, specific drugs for more severe cases. Regular checking of blood pressure and medical supervision for control at an early age can aid in avoiding illness later in life.

Incidence of Heart and Cerebrovascular Disorders. Of the 10 leading causes of death, diseases of the heart, malignancies, and cerebrovascular disease account for about 70 percent of annual deaths for older people. A recent governmental task force on arteriosclerosis called for a national effort against the epidemic of heart disease, mainly caused by arteriosclerosis. More than 1 million people die annually from arteriosclerosis and its effects, and heart disease is the most common affliction of persons under 65 receiving Social Security disability benefits.

About 33 percent of all cases of acute coronary infarction terminate fatally before they receive medical attention. However, about 70 to 80 percent survive the high-risk period of the first 24 hours. Acute arrythmia, congestive failure, or cardiac shock account for the deaths.

Valve Disorders. The National Institute on Aging (1980) says that valvular damage and deformities are usually caused by previous rheumatic infections and arteriosclerosis. It has been suggested that valvular heart disease is rare in a person of 65 or even 70 when it is not related to some precondition. In normal aging the speed with which the mitral valve that controls blood flow in and out of the heart decreases by 5 percent.

Conduction Disturbances (Arrythmias). Rate and rhythm of the heartbeat are determined by a highly specialized conducting system in the heart. The aged are especially susceptible to alterations in normal rhythm. The normal pulse rate is between 60 to 100 beats per minute; there are, however, times when rates as low as 30 beats per minute occur in the aged and, conversely, a rate of 90 beats per minute in an aged person who normally maintains a rate of 50 beats per minute may constitute a rapid beat (tachycardia). Conduction irregularities such as premature contraction, rapid heart fibrillation, and heart block increase with age. While these disturbances are more common in aging, they are also far more serious. The initial symptom of this age change is usually a sudden slowing of the heartbeat (called atrial fibrillation) with various other signs, including loss of consciousness. The aged may not realize that they are experiencing fibrillation because the heart rate becomes slower with aging. When fast heartbeat occurs, it is often a compensatory mechanism in older people; when heart congestion is relieved, the heart rate will return to normal.

Another conduction irregularity is heart block. The causes of conduction interruption are usually related to one of two processes: atherosclerosis, the less common cause; and true changes in specialized tissue. Heart block was generally attributed to arteriosclerosis, but more recent observations have shown that it is usually the result of fiber changes extending into and interrupting conduction.

Drug therapy is relatively ineffective, but the problem can be alleviated by the use of surgically implanted electronic pacemakers, which have saved many lives. Over 120,000 pacemakers have been implanted in American patients, the majority of them old.

Cerebrovascular Disorders. There is a marked, steady increase in vascular disorders with increasing age after the age of 50 (National Advisory Council of Aging, 1980). Unlike in heart disease, women seem as vulnerable as men. Approximately 1 out of every 20 persons over age 65 is affected by stroke. *Stroke* is a lay term for destruction of parts of the brain. It is a result of arterial rupture. Before age 50, the majority of strokes are based on a congenital weakness of the arterial wall (*aneurism*). After age 50, the most common cause (80 to 85 percent) is arteriosclerosis and the resulting clot formation in narrowed blood vessels. Generally, the most important contributing factor in strokes is hypertension, including the asymptomatic kind. Stroke may be caused by the rupture of small blockages found in certain sites of the brain; it is closely related to advancing age and hypertension. These *ischemic attacks* in older people may be the explanation for blackouts and temporary loss of memory. What seems to happen is a cutoff of blood to part of the brain; this may occur suddenly and, if it is not fatal, can be damaging. Such a sudden event does not impair intellect as much as function; it may impair speech, cause paralysis, or result in perceptual or emotional changes and other disabilities.

As many as 85 percent of elderly stroke victims can learn to move about, either with complete control or with an aid such as a walker or cane. Methods of care during the active phase of stroke and vigorous rehabilitation programs during the recovery stage of stroke have been developed but are not yet widespread.

RESPIRATORY SYSTEM CHANGES IN AGING

The *respiratory system* pertains to the process whereby oxygen is carried into the body system and gaseous by-products of oxidation are carried out of the body. Respiratory conditions have a profound but poorly understood effect on the general health of the aged for several reasons: (1) normal performance on breathing tests is scanty; (2) the aged commonly have heart disorders, which can cause shortness of breath; and (3) muscle weakness caused by aging disease can contribute to breathing difficulties.

Pulmonary Lung Changes in Aging

Three major areas of pulmonary lung changes are associated with aging: living structure and functioning, gaseous exchange and circulation, and ventilation control.

Lung structure significantly changes in the aged and affects control of ventilation and capacity of exercise. The aged lungs lose elasticity. There is a decline of water absorption into the lungs, a 50 percent loss of blood vessel elasticity, a resultant decrease in lung elasticity, and a change in the volume pressure behavior of the lungs. The aged thus require increased energy to maintain an adequate level of ventilation.

A second major factor in pulmonary aging is changes in gaseous exchange and pulmonary circulation. The ability of the lungs to exchange air with the pulmonary blood system depends on the surface area of capillaries exposed to ventilated oxygen. There is, by age 65, about a 48 percent decrease in diffusing capacity.

The last major respiratory change deals with ventilation control. Although volume and plasma levels do not change with age, the bellows function of the lung decreases, ventilation capacity declines, the lungs lose their retroactive force, and the chest wall becomes less compliant. Both the heart and respiratory systems are altered significantly by aging. Stress or major illness superimposed on these reduced functions may seriously limit the elderly.

Major Respiratory (Pulmonary) Disorders

The primary respiratory abnormalities that will be discussed are bronchitis, emphysema, and lung cancer. Keep in mind the word "abnormalities" and remember that individuals differ in susceptibility over the long span from 65 to 90 and that such disorders do not necessarily occur to all aged. It is difficult to know whether aging is primarily a genetic or environmental problem.

Bronchitis. Chronic bronchitis is the most common respiratory problem of the aged. It is not believed to be due to bacteria but to a disturbance of the respiratory autonomic nervous system. Changes in bronchitis include shrinking or swelling of the mucous membrane, fibrostic change in the bronchial wall, destruction of the muscle elements, and impairment of all factors involved in raising sputum. Signs include a persistent cough and spitting. This respiratory problem is often difficult to distinguish from emphysema.

Emphysema. Emphysema increases with age and reaches severity in the seventies. Increased volumes of air not evacuated from the lungs and decreased vital capacity are found in all aged. The chief dysfunctional lung change in emphysema consists of a greater degree of flow resistance, more uneven lung ventilation, and more impairment in diffusion. There are two principal elements in chronic emphysema: inelasticity of the lungs and obstruction to the free flow of air in and out of the air sacs (alveoli) in the lung. Spasm of the muscle because of inherited hypersensitivity or allergy causes narrowing of the air passages. The disparity between the phases of respiration causes air to be trapped within the lung and not be completely evacuated. In addition, smoking or other factors may have impaired the elasticity of the lungs and further impeded respiration.

Lung Cancer. The incidence of lung cancer is continuing to increase in the general population. Since most pulmonary cancers are related etiologically to the carcinogens in tobacco smoke, it is likely that the duration of regular exposure is more important than age alone.

Factors that lead to respiratory cancer are chronic damage to lung tissue resulting from scar formation, smoking, and environmental pollution. Chronic scarring of lung tissue by pneumonia, fibrosis, and the like has been recognized as an important predisposing cancer factor. Twenty-five percent of lung cancer cases seem to be related to lung scarring and is the most serious consequence of occupational and environmental pollution.

Ninety percent of individuals with lung cancer are smokers. Many older persons have been exposed to occupational carcinogens in combination with other noxious environmental agents. For example, the incidence of lung cancer among older asbestos workers was eight times what it was for smokers in other industries and 92 times the incidence in nonsmokers. A vast majority of both young and old with lung cancer will die of it (Seligman, 1979). It is not operable in most cases and, even if it is, survival to 4 or 5 years is limited.

Smoking Effects

Smoking is one of the major life shorteners, not only because of cancer and heart disorders but because it damages lung elasticity and promotes pulmonary disorders. Cigarette smokers are up to 18 times more likely to die from pulmonary emphysema and chronic bronchitis than nonsmokers. Smokers with chronic bronchitis face a greater risk of lung cancer, no matter how old they are or how many (or few) cigarettes they smoke. Chronic bronchitis seems to be directly related to lung cancer. Smokers with emphysema or chronic bronchitis are also more likely to suffer from chronic cough, excess phlegm, and breathlessness (Seidman, 1978). It is well worth giving up smoking at any age, but is vital for life and breath in older people.

DIGESTIVE SYSTEM CHANGES IN AGING

The digestive system is the system least likely to be affected by aging. However, coordinated motor function of the gastrointestinal tract deteriorates with age. In elderly individuals constipation, difficulties in swallowing, and the indications of formations of blind sacs in the digestive tract may reasonably be considered manifestations of aging in the nerve supply to the tract. In addition, digestive function changes involve modifications of secretions, digestion, reduction, absorption, or motility. Any one or all of these processes can be affected by aging.

Esophagus

After years of functioning as a conduit for food, the esophagus can become an important concern for the elderly. When the intestinal tract is distended, it normally causes rhythmic waves called peristalsis in the entire length of the gut. The dependence of this tract on nervous regulation makes it vulnerable in aging. Studies have shown a decrease in the amount of peristalsis, lack of synchrony in the waves, defects in sphincter relaxation and, therefore, dilation of the esophagus. Dilation and delay in emptying the esophagus allow food to putrify, usually causing spasms and pain. The most common symptom is chest pain, which in the aging is difficult to distinguish from cardiac pain. Some authorities feel that this is one of the most common causes of heartburn in the aged (NIH, 1980).

Stomach

Whereas the esophagus acts as a tube to convey food, the stomach is active in the process of digestion. The stomach secretes gastric juices, which are a combination of hydrochloric acid, pepsin, lipase, and mucous. Absorption in the stomach is minimal (although greater than in the esophagus). Water, protein, and carbohydrate are hardly absorbed at all; some fats and fat-soluble materials, however, are absorbed.

There are three major alterations of gastric secretion in aging. Although excess acidity is seldom found in the aged, a decrease in gastric juices is prevalent. Whatever the approximate year of onset, secretions are lessened by 50 percent by age 70. In gastric atrophy there is first a failure of acid secretion, then pepsinogen and, finally, the intrinsic factor necessary for sustaining vitamin B-12 absorption.

Small Bowel

Studies on the small bowel function of the aged are difficult because of changes in other systems and physical and psychological disabilities of the population. Absorption is the major function of the gastrointestinal system; however, digestion must be complete before absorption takes place.

There are also some changes in aging related to the essential digestive enzymes. Carbohydrates are absorbed in the form of monosaccharides, a process that begins with salivation in the mouth. The secretion of the salivary glands remains relatively stable until age 60, when there is a rapid decline. The pancreas, which is important in enzyme production, also undergoes atrophy and reduces its secretions but, since the pancreatic secretions are very active, they are apparently sufficient into old age.

Lipids or fats are split by the action of bile into glycerol, fatty acids, and sterols by the lipases of the stomach intestine and pancreatic secretions. Absorption of lipids slows with aging. The peak of lipid serum concentration occurs 7 hours after eating a high-fat meal in the aged, compared to 3 hours later in young adults.

The first stage of protein absorption is limited with aging and, when coupled with other decrements in pancreatic or intestinal secretions, can lead to marked digestive and absorption impairment.

Reduction of pancreatic enzyme activity begins at about age 40 and decreases with age. Of these, trypsin is probably most important because of its specific action of initially breaking whole complex proteins into less complex molecules.

In addition to foodstuffs and vitamins, the intestines absorb electrolytes and water, the bowel must absorb about 7 or 8 quarts of these each day to maintain bodily volume necessary for temperature and circulation control. The elderly can be jeopardized by too little water intake, improper use of high concentrations of salt and sugar, and other gastrointestinal disturbances.

Bacteria in the intestine also change with aging. Organisms such as strep-
tococci, which are normally inhibited by the gastric juices of the young, begin to
flourish in the aged.

Pancreas

The pancreas empties its chemically basic solutions into the duodenum, the first
portion of the small intestine but with aging, degeneration of the cavities of the
pancreatic ducts is marked. Since the pancreas is under hormonal as well as neurological control, this presents serious difficulties. When blockage occurs, as often
happens in aging, the release of secretion continues in response to hormonal formation, and pressure can begin to build up. Activation of secretions can occur, and the
ducts begin digestive action on the pancreas itself, causing pancreatitis.

Other than in acute pancreatitis, symptoms of pancreatic disease are vague and
varied; pain accompanied by rigidity and tenderness is often experienced in the
upper and middle part abdomen.

Pancreas and Diabetes. A highly age-related disease, diabetes mellitus, has only
recently been recognized as a major scourge of our time. Its role as a cause of
disability (blindness, kidney failure, neurological problems, and arteriosclerosis of
the coronary and leg vessels) and early death has been underestimated in the past.
The difficulty in differentiating normal aging processes from disease states makes
diabetes a classic example of the aging-versus-disease problem.

Nevertheless, there are probably more than 2 million diabetics in the aged
population. Although the exact cause of the disease is unknown, at least 33 percent
of all diabetics report the occurrence among relatives. Excess weight also is predisposing factor in older adults. In the older population, diabetes is more common in
women than men by a three to two ratio. The older black population has a higher
incidence than the white elderly by a two to one ratio.

The sugar seen in the excess urine of diabetes mellitus victims results from a
lack of insulin to control the blood sugar level normally in the body. This lack may
be in the production of the pancreas or at the level of availability in the blood. This
is an area where older people must be examined regularly because even mild diabetes
predisposes to vessel and vital organ damage. Diabetes is, moreover, often asymptomatic. There is a marked change in rate of sugar removal for the elderly that may be
mistaken for the disease.

Gall Bladder

The gall bladder is a small sac attached to the liver; it receives bile from the liver
(hepatic) ducts, concentrating it and discharging it after meals. Bile is a liquid that
aids in digestion, principally by emulsifying fats. Gall bladder changes in aging are

functional and relate to discharging bile. In the aged bile is thicker, higher in cholesterol, and of smaller volume, and bile tract disease and the presence of gallstones increase with aging. Pain below the rib cage is the most important symptom of gall bladder disease and is usually accompanied by nausea, vomiting, and fat intolerance.

Intestinal Disturbances

The small intestine is comprised of the duodenum, jejunum, and ileum; the large intestine is constituted of the caecum, *colon,* and intestine. Both the large and small bowels are susceptible to four main difficulties: obstruction, vascular or hemorrhagic problems, malabsorption, and *diverticulosis* (or branching into a blind sac). As with other portions of the digestive tract, malignancy occurs more frequently in the elderly. Cancer of the colon and rectum are reported as the leading form of malignant disease in old age.

Internal obstruction from whatever cause in the older person is a critical condition. Distension, constipation, nausea, and severe pain suggest mechanical obstruction, but lack of pain may herald paralysis. Both causes lead to loss of color, dehydration, shock, abdominal tenderness, and possible fever. Feces from digestive processes continue to form, even in obstruction, but cannot be absorbed because of the related pressures and inflammation.

Aging of the vessels affects the digestive tract in several ways. Arterisclerosis can narrow the cavity and form blockages. A decrease of cardiac output decreases blood flow to the intestines, and this can lead to tissue damage.

Two problems of concern to the elderly involve incontinence and constipation. A defecation center in the brain (medulla) controls this activity, and mass distension of the rectum arouses the reflex. Aging of the large bowel brings atrophy of the mucosa and muscle layers, abnormality of the intestinal glands, arteriosclerosis, and delay in nerve transmissions.

Although old people are concerned about constipation, there is no evidence to support the contention that constipation is a function of aging. Constipation can mean either insufficient feces (amount decreases with age) or hard, dry stools that are difficult to pass. There is a possibility that elderly people develop an enlarged colon, but constipation with impaction seems to be due more frequently to inactivity, inadequate water intake, lack of bulk or fruit in the diet, and weakened abdominal muscles.

Fecal incontinence is a real problem with the aged and can be caused by fecal impaction with overflow because of irritation, neurological damage with resultant loss of sphincter control, or as a side effect of an underlying disease condition.

The incidence of diverticulosis markedly increases with age, is more common in men, and tends to recur. It is usually due to the formation of blind pockets;

atrophy of the stomach wall is a factor in its development. The onset is sudden, with spasms, tenderness in the affected area, and signs of inflammation in the membrane wall of the abdominal cavity.

Gastrointestinal Cancer. The incidence of cancer rises sharply as the population ages. Gastrointestinal cancers comprise 25 to 44 percent of all cancers occurring after 75 years of age, but it is treatable, if operable, and not more painful by nature than any other disease. The initial approach to gastric or colorectal cancer in older people is surgical. However, if such cancer is diagnosed and found operable, age does not affect the median survival rate in patients under 80 years of age because its course, like that of most cancers, generally is nearly always less acute than at younger ages. The steady increase in the proportion of long-term survivors suggests that many elder patients with gastrointestinal cancer have more slowly growing tumors.

THE EXCRETORY SYSTEM CHANGES IN AGING

Renal Excretory Function

The aged may move through life without the threat of renal disease, experiencing only the normal physiological changes caused by kidney alterations that are associated with aging. The kidneys in the elderly are primarily affected by atrophy and other involutional processes, secondarily arteriosclerosis, and other diseases and conditions imposed on these.

Normal Kidney Responses

Approximately 33 percent of people over 65 have normal tubular function, and more than 67 percent have a normal kidney capillary function.

The kidneys are a pair of bean-shaped glandular organs about 4 inches long located in the back of the abdominal cavity. The functional activities of the kidneys include filtering blood plasma, resorption of various selective substances from the blood, and formation of new compounds for excretion as urine. To accomplish these tasks, the kidneys are supplied with over 1 quart of blood per minute, which represents 20 percent of the total cardiac output.

With increased age there is a gradual decrease in kidney function, as indicated by the reduced rate of capillary filtration, which is primarily based on changes in the blood vessel system. There is narrowing and loss of vessels; this reduces the flow of blood through the organ, apparently caused more by circulatory dysfunction than renal structural change (Shock, 1978). Examination of the aged kidney has shown that by age 70 the number of capillaries (glomeruli) equals only 50 to 67 percent that of the young adult. Arteriosclerosis brings about a reduction in the bulk of the kidney's tubes (*nephrons*). The connective tissue framework between the cells (interstitial) are condensed, and the renal arteries become narrower.

Besides structural changes, the aged kidneys also undergo functional changes associated with sclerosis, and some blood that formerly passed through the kidney is directed without modification directly to the tubules.

Bladder and Urinary Tract

The process of voiding is taken for granted until altered through problems such as incontinence or retention, as is the bladder, an organ comparable in importance to the heart. The bladder is a distensible pelvic sac with membranous and muscular walls for storage and expulsion of urine secreted by the kidney.

The voiding mechanism is a complex interaction of voluntary and involuntary processes. A delicate balance exists between the bladder muscle and the outlet. Changes that diminish the efficiency of the muscle or increase outflow resistance result in incomplete emptying of the bladder. The bladder, like the heart muscle, responds to gradual distention by producing a spasmodic contraction when a certain point is reached. Overdistention may stretch muscle fibers and decrease efficient coordination of contraction.

The lower urinary tract has particular significance for the elderly. Urinary incontinence in the female can lead to genito-urinary infection. In the aged male problems associated with urination are often caused by enlargement of the prostate gland. This is a composite gland that surrounds the urethra (urinary canal) of males at the base of the bladder. Some degree of prostation (outlet symptoms) are present in 75 percent of males over 65.

Incidence of Kidney Vascular Change

As indicated in previous sections, an estimated 23 million Americans suffer from hypertension. Hypertension also exacerbates the problem of aging kidney function. It has been said that eliminating cardiovascular diseases would add about 11 years to life expectancy at birth in the United States (Comroe, 1980).

Renal Abnormalities in the Aged

Renal abnormalities can be ordered according to their cause in the aged. The following categories will be used: prerenal, intrarenal, and extrarenal (postrenal).

Prerenal. A prerenal problem describes a dysfunction in the system before actually reaching the kidneys. The overall problem usually begins as a result of deficits in blood flow to the kidneys. Other problems include inadequate fluid intake, fluid loss due to vomiting or diarrhea, hemorrhage, or shock, coronary failure, infection, and improper use of medical substances to increase urine.

When reduced renal blood flow occurs, a chain of events occurs in an attempt to stabilize kidney function. The body, to maintain circulation, secretes large amounts of steroid hormone (aldosterone), an antidiuretic hormone. Aldosterone causes salt retention and, therefore, water retention by increasing its reabsorption in the tubules. The overall effect is increased circulating volume until stability in the system is restored, but the process is ineffective if the use of diuretics is continued. Prerenal problems, however, tend to be transient. Once the cause is identified, it can usually be corrected before contributing to the more serious problems associated with damage to the kidney organ itself (intrarenal).

Intrarenal. Intrarenal problems affecting the aged primarily involve the kidneys themselves. The condition can be acute or, with repeated infection or disease can become more chronic. The ultimate chronic kidney dysfunction is uremia. The major organ tissue problems confronting the aged are pelvic infections that spread to the kidney, inflamations because of allergic reaction, renal stones, and kidney failure.

Pyelonephritis. This bacterial infection process originates in the pelvis and spreads to the kidney. It usually affects the soft, marrowlike center of the kidney called the medulla, which is responsible for the mechanisms that concentrate the urine; therefore, with such infection, kidney function is impaired. This is probably the most common renal disease in the aged male. The underlying cause is usually obstruction caused by bladder neck infection but, even after infection, autoimmune mechanisms may be involved in the continued progress of the disease. The elderly often manifest symptoms of pain over the kidneys and may have fever, chills, and gastrointestinal upset.

Glomerulonephritis. This inflammation because of allergic reaction causes total or partial blockage of many cell capillaries and allows protein to leak into the urine. Symptoms vary, but they may include headache, fever, and vomiting, accompanied by severe abdominal pain. More specific signs include puffiness and swelling (edema) of the extremities, hypertension, and protein in the urine.

Kidney Stones. Kidney stones in the elderly are particularly important because blockage may result in acute or chronic symptoms and, if unrecognized, may lead to the loss of one or both kidneys. The stones are caused by increased excretion of calcium phosphates, uric acid, and *systine* or by renal infection. One other common factor that contributes is immobility for periods beyond 2 weeks.

Renal Failure. Renal failure signifies that the kidneys are unable to excrete the normal load of bodily metabolites. First, the body begins to catabolize its own body cells, perhaps for several days to several weeks. Then, as the kidney begins to stabilize, urine output may diminish or cease. Finally, if not seriously damaged, the kidneys will begin to heal but, if not, the person may experience uremia, the ultimate kidney abnormality.

Uremia. Uremia is the term applied to the clinical syndrome resulting from severe reduction in excretory kidney function. Its chief biochemical sign is an extreme degree of azotemia, which involves malnutrition, anemia, poisoning by acids forming in the body, fluid imbalances, hypertension, cardiovascular disease, and circulatory difficulties. Chronic uremia is most frequently the result of the destruction of kidney organ tissue by various renal diseases.

Postrenal. The major postrenal or extrarenal problems confronting the aged are increased potential of obstruction in the lower urinary tract, susceptibility to urogenital infection, urinary incontinence, retention, prostatism, and impotence.

Lower Urinary Tract Infection. One of the most common problems of the aged is lower urinary tract infection, which affects approximately 20 percent of those over age 75. Females usually suffer from the falling down of the mucous lining of the urethra (prolapse), urethral closure, formation of cysts, and contracted bladder. Males more often suffer from inflamation of the urethra, prostate enlargement and irritation, and weakened bladder muscles.

Urinary Incontinence. Urinary incontinence is a common problem that may increase with age and can consist of any combination of elements of neurogenic disease, urgency stress, and overflow incontinence. Diabetes, Parkinson's disease, and brain lesions often lead to neurogenic incontinence. Urgency incontinence depends on local mechanisms, but it may not be noticed until irritation develops. Common contributory factors include vaginitis, urinary tract infection, or prostatic enlargement. Stress incontinence seems to be dependent on psychosocial factors as well as bladder pressure. Persons with this problem complain of loss of control when they cough, laugh, or sneeze. In the female this condition may be caused by the dropping of the uterus organ from its original position (uterine prolapse). Finally, overflow incontinence may be caused by lesions or drug effects.

Acute Urinary Retention. Acute urinary retention can be a serious or even life-threatening problem to the aged. Extreme bladder distension can occur within 24 hours; urinary retention can progress to renal failure if it is not corrected.

Prostatism. A problem confronting a vast majority of males is prostatic enlargement. Early symptoms are hesitancy in voiding, decrease in force of urine, and increased frequency, including night-time urination. As the condition becomes more severe, obstructive symptoms usually appear, including dribbling after urination, poor control, overflow incontinence, irritation at the outlets, and local infection. There is little correlation between urine volume and the degree of obstruction.

With total removal of the prostate, sterility does occur. If, however, even a small portion of the prostate remains, it is possible to have viable sperm. Even though surgery itself does not cause impotence, lack of knowledge and incorrect conceptions regarding impairment of sexual function makes it a problem among aged males.

Postrenal problems are generally not as physiologically serious as intrarenal ones; however, both types have the potential of leading to renal insufficiency or failure.

CHANGES IN THE SENSES WITH AGING

Vision

About 10 percent (2.3 million) of the elderly have some vision impairment. However, in studies of people over 100 years old, only 5 percent were totally blind. Although most older people need glasses, poor vision is not as widespread as is usually thought. About 80 percent have fair to adequate visual sharpness to age 90 and even beyond. Often one eye continues to function even if the other does not (NIH, 1980).

As we get older, the acuity of our senses begins to decline. Visual acuity (the ability to see clearly at a distance) remains fairly constant until age 45 to 50; it declines gradually so that in people over 65, 40 percent of men and 60 percent of women have vision poorer than 20/70. Another common normal age change is that the eye loses its ability to keep images sharp at close range (accommodation). A decrease in this control is a result of changes in eye structure and muscles. Most of the more serious problems relate to the lens and retina. In general, with aging, the lens of the eye usually allows less light to pass through the retina; however, more light is required by the aging retina than in younger years, and the ability to see clearly in low illumination decreases (as in night driving). More time is needed for both light and dark adaptation. Additional changes may occur in the pupil of the eye (the expanding and contracting opening in the iris through which light passes to the retina). A common change is the diminution in pupil size and regularity. A dropping of the lids is often seen, and changes associated with chronic infections and scarring sometimes occur. The tear glands, which secrete the fluid necessary for continual cleansing and lubrication, lose function with aging, contributing to dryness and eye irritation. Three serious eye conditions are common with aging. One is glaucoma, in which pressure in the eye fluid increases because of fluid drainage obstruction. Glaucoma starts imperceptibly, and one of the first signs is a halo effect perceived around sources of light. Although an easy test is available for detection, it is a common cause of blindness if neglected and accounts for about 20 percent of blindness in people over age 65.

Practically nothing is known about the treatment of the second condition, retinal blindness, even though a decline in retinal function accounts for a high percentage (about 20 percent) of the visual problems that develop during aging. Such decreased function is usually caused by slow degeneration of the central region of the retina (the *macula*). This disease process is called macula degeneration and is caused by hardening and obstruction of the retinal artery. Although the victim will have perimeter retinal vision, the ability to read will be lost. This disorder can be detected by an opthamalogist.

Diabetic retinopathy accounts for about 12 percent of blindness in people over age 65; it is caused by chronic diabetes.

Cataract is the major cause of visual disability and blindness throughout the world. In the United States, it causes 17 percent of the blindness in the elderly. In this case the aging process transforms the normally transparent organ called the lens into an opaque (cataractal) one.

According to the National Society for the Prevention of Blindness (1980), the prevalence rate for legal blindness in the United States is estimated to be 225 per 100,000 population. New cases occur each year at the rate of 21 per 100,000 population. In the late 1970s the number of legally blind persons was 479,000, of which 47 percent were 65 or over: the number of new cases was estimated at 44,750, of which 50 percent were 65 years of age or older. Few older people go blind, but 60 percent of blind people are older than 70, yet most of this blindness is preventable with early detection and treatment.

Hearing

The loss of hearing is more usual in older people than the loss of sight; hearing is an area in which more disabilities are related to aging than to any other factor. This decline is especially noted in the ability to hear high-pitched notes (e.g., doorbells and bells), which is first noted after 50 but varies with each individual. The changes are so gradual that many older people fail to recognize them until the disability is extreme.

One of the major sources of such hearing impariment involves the cochlea, a spiral tube of the inner ear that resembles a conch shell. At birth, the cochlea contains about 20,000 hairlike nerve cells that gradually die off and are not replaced. Loss of these cells is called presbycusis, and it impairs the transmission of high-frequency sounds.

These and other changes seldom occur where there is little noise; hearing is aggravated by acoustic trauma, and noise pollution is more and more a factor in hearing loss. The decibel level of one's environment can become great enough to damage the hairlike nerve cells of the inner ear permanently. The decibel is the smallest difference in loudness the human ear can detect. The decibel scale is logarithmic, so a tenfold decibel increase in sound strength is a 10-decibel increase, but a hundredfold increase in sound strength is a 20-decibel increase. Noise levels at

50 to 55 decibels may interfere with sleep and cause excess fatigue. Evidence suggests that noise above 90 decibels can cause irreversible damage.

About 5 percent of the population have hearing difficulties at age 50. After age 65, 30 percent of the population have hearing difficulties. In the older age group (+74) 27 percent have hearing difficulties, and 450,000 were profoundly deaf and totally cut off from sound. Men show more significant hearing loss than women (probably because of noise in the working place). Hearing loss is a severe impediment because it isolates the aged from the verbal communication vital to interaction with others.

Most hearing difficulties can be partially reversed by surgery, use of a hearing aid, or both. However, this is an area in which action must be taken; in a U. S. study 34 percent of deaf older people had never had a hearing test, and only 18 percent had had one in the previous 2 years (NIH, 1980).

Taste and Smell

Smell also declines with age, and up to 30 percent of people over age 80 have difficulty identifying common substances by smell. Taste, too, is affected, since 67 percent of taste sensations are dependent on the ability to smell; in addition, taste buds decrease sharply with age. Originally there are 250 taste buds in each capsule (on the tongue) but, by old age, the number may drop to 100. Thus higher levels of stimulation of taste and smell are required for older persons than for younger persons; this need may be partly responsible in some older people for the complaints about and lack of interest in food that result in poor nutrition.

Touch

Special receivers for the sense of touch are located in the skin. These receivers are sensitive to five types of stimulation: cold, heat, touch, pain, and pressure. The use of the term touch in the present context indicates the generic concept that encompasses these tactile and temperature sensitivities. Of the five senses, the least is known about touch, and most available information regarding age-related changes are derived from subjective reports of elderly individuals.

Sensitivity to Cold and Heat. On the basis of present knowledge, it is believed that there are two significant changes in cold/heat sensitivity with aging. Although it is not certain why, with advancing age most older people experience a general reduction of resistance to and ability to recover from temperature stress and change (Butler, 1977).

This sensitivity can lead to hypothermia, an abnormally low body temperature (under 95°F) in the presence of relatively mild cold. Excessive heat can also create problems. *Hyperthermia* (or heat stroke) occurs following exposure to high temperatures; it is characterized by a failure of the body to control its temperature. In this condition perspiring, a major regulatory mechamism, ceases and temperature rises above 104°F.

It is thus clear that all aged, and especially those over 75 years old, should avoid prolonged exposure to even mild cold temperatures or sustained/extreme high temperatures (e. g., heat waves).

The number of deaths from accidental temperature sensitivity among the elderly is not known, but at least 2.3 million elderly in the United States could be vulnerable. This risk is due to the many geographical areas with harsh or quickly changing weather. In addition, many of the older population are taking drugs that increase the body's susceptibility to temperature change.

Sensitivity to Pain and Pressure. Sensitivity to pain and pressure as a danger signal is extremely important. Its loss in older persons seems to be related to a loss of tactile response as both perception and motor abilities decline in reaction to stimuli. However, the slowing of reaction times that at first was found to characterize aging is apparently also related to environmental deprivation and depression.

Pain is a more frequent concern for the aged. The periodic daily aches of rheumatism, the unrelenting pain of arthritis, and the sharp distress of angina are examples. The elderly learn to deal with these according to their personality, background, and the nature and extent of the pain. As sensitivity to pain decreases, elderly individuals may fail to attend to minor injuries when they occur, may not be alert to potential sources of harm, and may repeatedly incur injury or damage.

Summary

The data indicates that with advanced age certain changes are characteristic of individuals in the population. Examination of test data now available on normal human subjects leads to the conclusion that there presently is no evidence for the existence of a general aging process other than of chronological time.

Numerous studies have linked performance of specific organ systems to chronological age, and many exhibit linear decrements in function with advancing age.

Not all physiological characteristics show progressive changes with age. Most of the characteristics of blood plasma that require close regulation for body cells to function effectively are adequately maintained into advanced age. Thus, for example, there is no evidence for systemic changes in fasting sugar levels of blood acidity (ph), its osmotic pressure, or its total volume.

There are, however, significant changes in other functions, even in the resting state. These are primarily characteristic of more than one organ system. For example, the amount of blood pumped by the heart decreases on the average of about 30 percent between 30 and 75 years. Blood plasma flow through the kidney is reduced by almost 50 percent for the same age span. On the other hand, the age decrement in the speed of nerve impulses falls only about 10 percent and the basal metabolism rate only by about 16 percent.

Although all of these characteristics diminish gradually in a linear fashion throughout the life span, other functions show different rates of change. For example, the changes in the ability of the eye to see shows a rapid decline between the ages of 20 and 50 but is fairly constant for the remainder of life in most people. There may also be sex differences in the pattern of age change. For example, osteoporosis appears in women more frequently at an earlier age than in men.

There are also wide individual differences in the effect of age on any physiological system. Observations have been made of various individuals at the age of 90 who showed kidney function as good as the average 50-year-old. In one test of kidney function ability increased after age 60.

It is not clear to what degree change in body function is related to aging or to the presence of disease processes. Many capacities decline so gradually that compensation for any loss is automatic, except when disease or injury brings a sudden and drastic change.

It is important to examine physiological changes in terms of the kind of physical, social, and psychological environment suited to maximum healthy adjustment in older people.

We must also conclude that preparation for a healthy, old age may begin with changes in habits or life-style in the young. Many of the functional deficits of the elderly population are not the inevitable results of aging but the lack of prevention, early detection, or proper treatment.

FURTHER READINGS

Asimov, I., *The Human Brain: Its Capacities & Functions,* The New American Library, New York, 1974, pp. 112-188.

Brocklehurst, J. C., "The Large Bowel," in J. C. Brocklehurst (ed.), *Textbook of Geriatric Medicine & Gerontology,* Churchill Livingstone, London, 1973, pp. 346-363.

Butler, R. N., and M. I. Lewis, *Aging & Mental Health, Positive Psychosocial Approaches,* Chapter 6, "Special Concerns," C. V. Mosby, St. Louis, 1977.

Butler, R. N., *Energy and Aging,* U. S. Senate Special Committee on Aging, Washington, D. C., April 5, 1977.

Corso, F., "Auditory Perception and Communication," in J. E. Birren and K. W. Schaie (eds.), *Handbook of the Psychology of Aging,* Van Nostrand Rheinhold, New York, 1977.

Comroe, J. H., and R. D. Dripps, "The Ten Top Clinical Advances in Cardiovascular-Pulmonary Medicine and Surgery. Between 1945 and 1975, How They Came About," Final Report National Heart Lung and Blood Institute, U. S. Government Printing Office, Washington, D. C., January 31, 1977, 1980.

Engel, B. T., "Using Biofeedback With the Elderly," National Institute on Aging, M. & H. Publication No. 79-1404, Washington, D. C., July 1979.

Groh, I., "Common Disorders of Muscles in The Aged," in A. B. Chinn (ed.), *Working with Older People: A Guide to Practice,* Vol. 4, *Clinical Aspects of Aging,* U. S. Public Health Service Publication No. 1459, Washington, D. C., pp. 156-162, 1980.

Hall, I. A., "Metabolic and Structural Aspects of Aging," in J. C. Brocklehurst (ed.), *Textbook of Geriatric Medicine and Gerontology,* London, 1973, pp. 426-435.

Jaffe, J., "Common Lower Urinary Tract Problems in Older People," *Working with Older People,* Vol. IV, U. S. Department of Health, Education and Welfare, pp. 141, 143–145, 1971, 1980.

Kahn, A., and I. Snapper, "Medical Renal Disease in The Aged," in *Working with Older People,* Vol. IV, U. S. Department of Health, Education and Welfare, pp. 131, 133–139, 1971, 1980.

Kammel, W. B., "Framingham Study and Chronic Disease Prevention," *Hospital Practice,* 1970, *5,* 78.

National Advisory Council on Aging, "Our Future Selves: A Research Plan Toward Understanding Aging," N.I.H. Publication No. 80-1444, and 45. U. S. Government Printing Office, Washington D. C., January 1980.

National Institute on Aging, "Special Report on Aging: 1979"; U. S. Department of Health Education and Welfare, N.I.H. Publication No. 80-1907, Washington, D. C., February 1980.

National Society for the Prevention of Blindness, *National Society for Prevention of Blindness Factbook,* New York, 1974, 1980.

Peterson, B. A., and B. J. Kennedy, "Aging and Cancer Management Part I: Clinical Observations," *Cancer Journal for Clinicians,* November/December 1979, *29,* (6).

Seidman, H., E. Silverberg, and A. Bodden, "Probabilities of Eventually Developing and Dying of A Cancer (Risk Among Persons Previously Undiagnosed with the Cancer)," *Cancer,* 1978, *28,* 33–46.

Seligman, I., "What Causes Cancer," *Newsweek,* January 26, 1976, in Helene Sloan (ed.), *Readings in Health, 1978–79,* Dushkin Publishing, Guilford, Conn., 1978.

Shock, N., *Biomedical Science: Prospects in Aging,* Presentation to Convocation Andrus Gerontology Center, University of Southern California, February 1973.

Shock, N. "Systems Physiology and Aging," Symposium of the Gerontological Society, Biological Sciences Section and The American Physiological Society at the 62nd Annual Meeting of the Federation of American Societies for Experimental Biology, Atlantic City, N. J., April 13, 1978.

Strehler, B. L., *Fine Cells and Aging* (2nd ed.), Academic Press, New York, 1977.

Timiras, P. S., "Diseases of Aging," in P. S. Wimiar (ed.), *Development Physiology and Aging,* Macmillan, New York, 1972, 1980, p. 474.

Vogel, F., "The Brain and Time," in W. Busse and E. Pfeiffer (eds.), *Behavior and Adaptation in Late Life,* Little Brown, Boston, 1977.

CHAPTER 4

Changes in Intelligence and Cognition in Aging

This chapter discusses findings bearing on cognition and learning in healthy older people; an analysis of some of the characteristics of the elderly in regard to style of learning and memory; and some of the implications for learning and the aged.

COGNITIVE PROCESSES

The term "cognitive processes" refers to a series of orderly steps that seem to underlie how people handle information. Intelligence is an important factor, but research indicates that many other processes are involved, including how information is perceived, how it is evaluated, how thinking is generated, and how new material and experiences are handled. Although popular opinion before 1960 presumed a steady decline in cognitive processes with age, recent research findings indicate this is not true.

DEFINITION AND CONCEPT OF INTELLIGENCE

Intelligence has been the central focus of study for research psychologists and a variety of other disciplines. For the practitioner, intelligence is a descriptive concept with a variety of meanings, the most important of which are the ability to communicate and the ability to care for oneself. Educators define it as a person's capacity to acquire new knowledge and to utilize information for the purpose of attaining some meaningful goal. This definition and approach, stressing particular goals with certain judgments of what is healthy/reasonable in contrast to what is unhealthy/ineffectual, has a high cultural loading.

Accordingly, poor judgment in interpersonal relationships or in managing personal resources (even though the reason for such responses may be faulty health bearing on any number of factors in the aged) may be seen as implying loss of intelligence and inability to continue to function responsibly in the larger community.

Intelligence is not directly measurable; it must be inferred. The criteria for intelligence are therefore variable, and different measures have been used in attempting to make meaningful statements concerning the intellectual capacity of a person or group of people. Thus inferences concerning intelligence are based on the supposition that the portion of behavior seen at the time of testing was representative of the individual behavior and function. Many factors, such as maturation, conditions at the time of testing, and previous experience, all affect test performance. The problem of accurate sampling is particularly important with the aged.

Definition of Intelligence

Until recently, attempts to understand intelligence were guided by the idea that development of intellect involved fixed intelligence and predetermined development. These beliefs lead to the assumption that intelligence is a genetically programmed dimension of human personality. From this viewpoint, a person's capacity is fixed in relation to others; development occurs in the life span in a predetermined, orderly pattern of increment and follows a course of decline in aging.

Type of Intelligence

Most recently, a concept of intelligence as a multidimensional, multivariable ability has emerged. According to this concept, there is no such thing as general intelligence; a set of cognitive abilities exists whose pattern and level vary individually.

One way of looking at the dimensions of intelligence has been to distinguish between "fluid" and "crystallized" intelligence. Fluid intelligence is the ability to reorganize one's perceptions. It depends on biologically mediated functions that are reported to peak in adolescence and then decline. Crystallized ability is the capacity to organize and utilize ordered information; it is assumed to be a function of experience. As such, it is reflective of individual experiential processes in acculturation. Crystallized intelligence seems to increase through adulthood and shows little or no decline with age, thus not supporting the common assumption that intelligence declines with age. Although such approaches are controversial, they reflect a more sophisticated approach to intellectual functioning and development than has been suggested before.

RESEARCH DATA ON LEARNING COGNITION IN THE AGED

As recently as the 1960s, most research in adult learning reinforced the idea that general ability to learn declined as a function of age. Eisdorfer (1963) in a 3 to 4-year follow-up study of the Duke longitudinal sample found no demonstrable decline in a group of subjects aged 60 to 94. In addition, Eisdorfer and Wilkie (1973) in a 10-year follow-up study of the survivors of the original Duke University group found that a group of relatively normal persons aged 60 to 69 did not show any systematic intellectual decline over the 10-year period; by age 70 to 79, they showed a few minor changes, but these were not striking.

Schaie and Stroher (1968) studied a stratified random sample of 500 subjects ranging in age from 20 to 70 years old and found that while there were significant age group differences cross-sectionally, only performance on tasks emphasizing speed declined appreciably over time. They concluded that, generally, if older people were given enough time on tests they functioned as accurately as those who were younger.

Eichorn (1973), reported on one of the Berkeley longitudinal studies, noted that mental ability is incremental during adulthood with an overall increase for both sexes between the ages of 16 and 36, beyond which there is some deceleration. These findings reveal the need for reappraisal of the concept of a normal, age-related loss of intellectual function.

A suggestion that emerges from such findings is that age differences in intelligence reported in cross-sectional studies may be a function of various factors that have affected the intelligence of the subject in earlier stages but may not be consistent from one age group to the next. The American Psychological Association Task Force on Aging (1973) proposed that a major portion of the variance attributed to age differences in past cross-sectional studies should be assigned to differences in ability between successive generations.

CHARACTERISTICS OF LEARNING IN THE AGED

Learning is the ability to gain knowledge or understanding of a skill by study, practice, training, or repeated experience.

Recent data note little decrease with advancing age in capacity to learn (Eisdorfer, 1973; Schaie and Strohen, 1968). Differences that appear are attributed to perception, habits, motivation, attention, and physical states. What we really measure is evidently performance, and learning ability can only be inferred. The ability to identify factors that affect learning in the aged are important in order to suggest approaches to minimize observed deficits and facilitate learning of new skills.

In recent years age-related studies have shown that noncognitive factors such as pacing, anxiety, inhibition, meaningfulness of the learning material, differences in learning procedures, and other factors within the learning situation profoundly influence task performance in the elderly.

Pacing

One factor found to be important in learning by older people is pacing, or the speed of presentation of the material to be learned. It has been demonstrated, using different learning models, that older people with average intelligence do better at slower paced or self-paced tasks. This is reminiscent of observations that older workers generally are less efficient in assembly-line situations than in untimed tasks.

It was also demonstrated that improved learning resulted when older people were given more time to respond. An increase in the total number of responses may also be due to their greater willingness to respond to slower-paced material. Investigators have demonstrated that the time taken by older subjects for making a response was short enough so that the response could have been made under the rapidly paced conditions (Eisdorfer, 1973).

Motivation and Fear of Failure

This inhibition of responses, with consequent apparent failure, may be related to a characteristic on the part of older people that might best be termed fear of failure. In a number of investigations indications are that older subjects experienced greater stress in the learning situations and took longer to recover than younger people did and that older people responded more and learned faster when stress was chemically blocked. Familiarizing the older person with the examination situation prior to the time of testing also helped to alleviate arousal levels.

Risk Taking

Research demonstrated that older people are less prone to risk-taking behavior. This may also be a possible explanation for the failure of older people to respond in a learning or cognitive task situation. Thus their inhibition in learning may be seen as either a fear of failure of a lack of desire to achieve.

Relevance of Task and Information

Meaningfulness of test tasks and relevance of information to be learned may also be factors related to age differences in learning. Most testing materials are geared to the young and measure knowledge and abilities related to their closeness to school years. The aged, therefore, may see many of the tasks on typical intelligence tests as uninteresting, silly, or dull. Studies have shown that as the amount of irrelevant information increases, the performance of older people declines and, conversely, that their performance is better on tasks that are more meaningful to them (Rabbitt, 1971; Botwinick, 1978; Arenberg, 1973). One problem in interpreting data is that some researchers, in making tasks more meaningful, may make them easier. Older people do perform proportionally more poorly on tasks as they increase in difficulty. Nevertheless, findings suggest that simplifying tests and making them more meaningful seem to be factors in facilitating learning in older people.

Other Relevant Factors

A number of other factors have been suggested that may be relevant in learning for older people. Several studies reported that older women perform differently than older men and do not show the same performance deficits during learning (Eisdorfer, 1977; Cohen, 1975). These findings evidently are related to factors such as the value of lifelong learning strategies of men and women and differential rates of responsiveness.

Another factor that seems to put older people at a disadvantage in learning is the organization of information. A task becomes easier when the information is organized into larger units; many older people are not able to take advantage of this. When suggestions are given on how to organize material, improvements are often seen, especially in those with low verbal ability.

Aids to learning and memory suggested to the elderly result in variable responses. When mediators such as mental pictures and word association are suggested, performance is enhanced, but note taking, when suggested, does not seem to help. Research suggests that older people apparently understand the purpose of note taking but do not make use of it. Note taking is a skill of summarizing and categorizing as well as listing data. This skill has to be learned in school. Although older people grasp the reason for note taking, they apparently do not possess the skill to make use of it.

LEARNING AND MEMORY

Although conceived differently, learning and memory are closely related. Most distinctions between memory and learning are arbitrary and are distinguished by various time bases. In the literature of cognition, learning refers to changes measured from one trial to another; memory refers to the temporal interval between the trials.

Since older people are generally exposed to fewer learning settings than young people, one might expect that older people do not remember as well as the young. However, to establish that older people have decrements in memory compared to younger people, it must be established that they have learned the task just as well. Clearly, confusion exists about the interaction between learning and memory. When age changes are noted, research often does not indicate what differences mean. They may result from variation short-term or long-term memory or from differences in the three stages of registration, retention, recall involved in each. Registration is the stimulus entering the memory system; retention or storage is the ability to maintain the stimulus trace in the memory system over time; recall is the ability to retrieve the material that is registered and retained.

Very Short-Term Memory

Very short-term memory is defined as information that is retained, with exposures to stimulus, for under 1 second. This involves stimulus traces whose effects are so transient that recall normally fades quickly. Age differences in this phase of memory show great individual variation.

Short-Term Memory

Short-term memory refers to measures of recall of information that has been presented for more than 1 second and up to several minutes. Capacity of short-term memory storage normally is limited, and the underlying neural activity is transitory. This type of recall shows some decline with age.

Long-Term Memory

Long-term memory refers to information retained over a 10- to 20-minute period. Long-term memory storage evidently is an unlimited capacity in the healthy, normal adult. Declines in long-term memory are observed even when short-term memory is comparable to the young.

Old Memory

Old memory involves storage and also recall or retrieval abilities; it is measured by recall of past events. It is difficult to establish the needed experimental controls for studying this area. Nevertheless, evidence that is available indicates little impairment of old memory in the aged compared to the young.

Factors Influencing Age Differences in Memory

It is important to ascertain where differences exist in short-term and long-term memory in the aged. It is also necessary to identify factors that may be involved in the etiology of decrements where they have been identified in the aged. Just as with learning, memory deficits are often found in tasks that are paced and identified as not meaningful to the elderly; they are also reported in tasks requiring a constant switching of attention, or change of set. The elderly are also found more impaired on visual as opposed to auditory memory tasks. Age differences in memory appear in tasks that require free recall but are minimal on recognition tasks that involve choosing a right answer from those supplied versus supplying one's own response in free-recall tasks. These findings suggest that older people may have more difficulty in retrieval memory even if they may have stored the information. Also, age differences in recognition studies show that material presented graphically to the elderly is better recalled than that presented verbally. The most positive memory results seem to come in test situations that measure what the aged really notice and want to remember.

The concept of interference is frequently used to explain differences in learning and memory. Interference refers to the idea that people do not remember or retain what they have learned because of the competition of previously learned material. Interference is minimized in older people when a task is well learned with slow or self-pacing.

Summary

An understanding of intellectual and cognitive function in aging evidently involves social, psychological, behavioral, and physiological (including genetic) factors. Physiological changes seem to make responses to new situations more difficult (particularly of the type involved in typical learning and memory laboratory tests).

This chapter has described cognitive and noncognitive factors that affect the learning process in normal, healthy, aged people. The latest studies indicate that broad generalizations are not useful, especially when applied to the elderly. It has long been assumed that cognitive function would show individual but steady downhill slope from about the age of 30, but recent longitudinal findings have shown that some persons simply do not decline in cognitive function, particularly in the simple straight-line fashion suggested by earlier studies (Shock, 1979).

Perhaps one of the most important findings in this chapter's review of the literature on cognitive function is that old age is not necessarily a process of cognitive decline. There were some subjects, aged 65 to 80, who were not showing decrements. This was particularly true in maintenance or stability of intellectual problem-solving abilities; some members of the study groups seem to be at least holding their own against aging. These tend to be persons for whom problem solving has been a way of life for years. These new behavioral evidences reinforce the truism that functions that are continuously exercised are less likely to suffer decrements even with age.

Some common notions also do not hold true. Lack of flexibility generally is not common to the aged; if one does encounter such traits, it is probably a function of personality or other factors. Such perceptions of the aged lead to stereotyping and make it difficult for those working with older people to see them as individuals.

Probably the most useful findings are those on learning and memory. Understanding the factors that are most conducive to an effective learning situation is important to those teaching older people or working with them in health service settings. Older people, more so than the young, operate poorly when threatened, placed under stress, faced with meaningless tasks, and the like. On the other hand, research suggests that dealing patiently with them in a nonthreatening manner, allowing them to pace themselves, making tasks meaningful, avoiding irrelevant information, keeping tasks simple, and providing cues are important factors in the learning and memory performance of the elderly.

FURTHER READINGS

Arenberg, D., "Cognition and Learning: Verbal Learning, Memory and Problem Solving," in C. Eisdorfer and M. P. Lawton (eds.), *The Psychology of Adult Development and Aging*, American Psychological Association, Washington, D. C., 1973, pp. 157-219.

Botwinick, J., "Intellectual Abilities," in J. E. Birren and K. W. Schaie (eds.), *Handbook of the Psychology of Aging*, Van Nostrand Reinhold, New York, 1978.

Cohen, D., *Sex Differences in the Organization of Spatial Abilities* in *Older Men and Women*. Unpublished doctoral dissertation, University of Southern California, Los Angeles, 1975.

Eichorn, D. H., The Institute of Human Development Studies, Berkeley and Oakland. In L. F. Jarvik, C. Eisdorfer, and J. E. Blum (eds.), *Intellectual Functioning in Adults*, Springer, New York, 1973, pp. 1-6.

Eisdorfer, C., "Intelligence and Cognition in the Aged" in E. W. Busse and E. Pfeiffer (eds.), *Behavior and Adaptation in Later Life*, Little Brown, Boston, 1977, p. 213 ff.

Rabbitt, P. M. A., "An Age Decrement in The Ability to Ignore Irrelevent Information," *Journal of Gerontology*, 1971, *26*, 133-136.

Schaie, K. W., and K. Gribbin, "Adult Development and Aging," *The Annual Review of Psychology*, Annual Reviews, Palo Alto, Calif., 1975.

Shock, N., National Institute of Aging, Baltimore, Md., "Reported Surprising Findings in The Process of Aging," Science Times Section, *The New York Times*, June 19, 1979.

5

Sexuality and Aging

In this chapter we dispel some of the myths about sex and aging. We distinguish between sexuality and sexual activity and describe the importance of differentiating between the two concepts. The importance of sexuality to the older person is reviewed, and the role of sex in later life presented. Facts concerning sexual activities in old age are given, and factors influencing such activities are detailed. Physiological and functional sexual changes in older males and females are surveyed; finally, sexual dysfunction and healthy adjustment in the aged are discussed.

SEXUALITY (DEFINITION)

Sexuality has several separate but related aspects. In the broad sense, sexuality refers to the aspects of personality structure related to our ideas of who we are as sexual beings that form the basis for self-identity. Sexuality is also often defined in the literature as the capacity to experience pleasure through intimate physical contact. Sexual activities are more connected with what we do, but they are influenced by individual sexuality.

Sexuality and the Person

The sex hormones involved in the development of reproductive function and structure through old age stimulate sexual interest and activity. The total personality participates in sexuality and is not separable from the physiology involved. Acts of intimacy associated with sexuality have significance beyond release of sexual tension.

Sexuality and Society

A series of fictions or cultural stereotypes exist with regard to sexual behavior in old age. Some of these erroneous ideas include the following: sexual desire disappears with age; older people are too weak and fragile to engage in sexual activity; it is indiscreet for the elderly to show evidence of continued sexual interest and concern; and older people who say they are sexually active are immoral or deceiving themselves.

ROLE OF SEX IN LATER LIFE

There is increased agreement among those who study sexual responses among the aged that sexuality can provide important psychological and physiological outlets in advancing years.

Studies began with Kinsey's classic works on sexual behavior in humans. Kinsey found that the rate at which males declined in sexual activity in later years does not exceed the rate at which they declined in previous age groups. This should be contrasted, however, with data stating that the proportion of impotency reported rises from 20 percent at age 60 to 75 percent at 80. In women over 65 Kinsey et al. (1948, 1953) noted a gradual decline in frequency of intercourse but found little evidence of decrease in sexual capacities; they further observed that in contrast to men, single and postmarital females had lower rates of sexual activity than their married counterparts.

Masters and Johnson (1966, 1970) report in their sample that human sexual response seems to be related to declining physical capacity.

Pfeiffer (1974), reporting on the Duke longitudinal studies, briefly summarized the finding on sexual activity in two major statements: sexual interest and coital activity were common in persons over age 60, and patterns of interest and activity differ for men and women of the same age. About 80 percent of men whose health was not impaired at the start of the study reported continuing sexual interest and, 10 years later at age 70, interest had not declined significantly. In contrast, although 70 percent were still sexually active at age 60, by age 70 the sexually active proportion was only 20 percent.

In the sample of women from the same study whose health was good, only about 33 percent reported sexual interest. Ten years later this had not changed significantly. Only about 20 percent of those same healthy women reported they were sexually active at the start of the study. Again, this proportion did not decline over the next 10 years. Obviously, however, far fewer older women than older men were sexually interested or active. Another important finding from the Duke studies has been the observation that sexual expression in later years is greater for persons who were highly interested and active sexually when they were younger.

There are several tentative explanations for the disparity of the sex urge in the young and the elderly. Women today had their attitudes formed in a period of time that dictated women's primary sex role as procreative and interest in sexual activity as improper. In terms of appearance and sexuality, there exists what Sontag (1972) has termed a "double standard of aging." Middle-aged men are perceived as virile in later life, and it is only on reaching 65 years of age that they are viewed as declining in both sexual interest and activity. Women, however, are conceived as asexual on reaching menopause, and any indication of either sexual interest or activity during the remaining 30 years of life is decried.

PHYSICAL CHARACTERISTICS AND THE EFFECTS ON SEXUAL ACTIVITY IN OLDER PEOPLE

Loss of sexual vigor should be no greater than loss of other capabilities, and impotency before 80 to 90 years of age often seems to be a function of psychological problems. For many, however, sexual interest and capacity extend into old age.

The Duke studies found that more variables affected men's sexual behavior than women's. Increased age, declining health, anxiety over performance, and drugs all had a negative effect for men. Past enjoyment, interest, and frequency correlated highly with present interest and sexual activity among both men and women. For women, however, current interest and activity were more dependent on marital status. People are generally aware that sexual opportunities for aged women are less available in the older population and more disapproved of by society if the man is appreciably younger. The Duke studies also emphasized that patterns of coitus are typically controlled by the husband's interest and activity and not the wife's.

Sexual Activity of Older Men

Rubin (1976) found that 50 percent of men aged 75 to 92 reported continued sexual coitus. Tarail found that the average frequency of coitus for 67 percent of males over 65 is four times per month. Masturbation is less prevalent among married men, but it is a sexual outlet in almost 25 percent of those studied.

Physical Sexual Changes in Older Men

Although testosterone in older men is available at a high rate compared to estrogen levels in women, concentrations decrease markedly after age 50 and affect the genital tissue. The testes become smaller and less firm with age. Interstitial cells where sperm is produced thicken and begin to degenerate and inhibit the production of sperm. A gradual decline in sexual energy, erectile strength, and viable sperm results from the hormonal declines of aging. As the prostate becomes enlarged with age, contractions become weaker. There is also a marked decline in volume and viscosity of sperm, so that ejaculatory force becomes weaker.

Sexual Responses of Older Men

Masters and Johnson (1966) have documented aging changes in the physiology of sexual response in the aged.

In the excitement phase, excitation builds more slowly. Erection, which takes longer to attain and may require more direct stimulation, elicits less testicular elevation or scrotal sac vasocongestion. Intensity and duration of sex flush and involuntary spasms on ejaculation diminish. The plateau phase lasts longer than with the young, with minimal testicular engorgement. Older men experience a reduction in volume of sperm, which reduces pressure on the testes. Increase in penile circumference is marked by the absence of preejaculatory fluid, which also decreases with age. The orgasmic phase in older men is experienced in a shorter one-stage phase compared to two stages in earlier life. The loss of the first ejaculatory stage, which is marked by a sensation of inevitability and loss of control in the young, is explained by the decrease of the pressure to ejaculate (because of decreased semen volume) in older males. The second stage, expulsion of seminal fluid through the penis, may be complete within one or two contractions compared to three or four at a younger age. Orgasm itself may become less frequent and may not occur in every act of intercourse. In the resolution phase there is, after age 50, a physiologically extended refractory period. This means that the capacity for erection following ejaculation cannot be regained for 12 to 24 hours compared to the 2 minute to 1 hour refractory time of the young male. In the older man the loss of erection also takes place more quickly than in the young.

One of the advantages of aging is that the older male (50 to 75 years) can remain erect and engage in coitus longer before orgasm. This reduction in ejaculatory demand is appropriate to slower response in the woman and may enhance satisfaction for both. Rubin (1976) has found that most men over age 60 had erections with sexual dreaming. Most men over age 60 also were satisfied with one or two ejaculations per week but could enjoy sex more frequently.

A consistent pattern of sexual expression helps to maintain sexuality. Older men are thus able to continue an active sex life until their seventies and eighties and probably beyond.

Sexual Activity of Older Women

Physiologically, the older woman with moderate good health can expect to have few physiological difficulties that would affect sexuality. Nevertheless, there is reason to believe that the clearly demarcated menopause in women, signaling the end of reproductive capacity, may have a negative influence on sexual interest and activity in some women. There is no time limit drawn by advancing years to female sexuality. Masters and Johnson (1966) found significant sexual capacity and effective sexual performance among menopausal and postmenopausal women age 48 to 78. There is no inevitability about major physical or psychological crises, pre-menopausal, menopausal, or postmenopausal.

Physical Sexual Changes in Older Women

At the menopause, two things happen. Women stop ovulating and producing hormonal cycles, usually between the ages of 48 to 52, and they can no longer become pregnant; women do *not* become "neuter," and their sex life does not end. Whether or not menopause is upsetting seems to relate mainly to previous adjustment in life, although misleading notions of loss of function, overemphasis on youth, and perceptions of no longer being loved may also influence response to menopause. Secondary sex characteristics are maintained until the late sixties. The absurd ideas relative to the cessation of menstruation, propagated through the years, are annoying to sensible people. There is nothing, however, in the menopause itself, once hormone changes subside, to make a person ill.

The onset of menopause often begins with a 2- or 3-year period of irregular or absent menses prior to total cessation of menstruation. Statistics indicate that 70 to 75 percent of the heavy menses in women in this period will cease without medical attention. In addition to heavy and irregular menstrual bleeding, other common complaints include headache, depression, loss of appetite, insomnia, irritability, anxiety, and heart palpitations, but only about 25 percent of all women experience any sort of distressing symptoms. On the whole, the better the emotional health of the woman before the climacteric, the fewer symptoms they report (Ryan, 1979).

For some menopausal women a common transitory discomfort is the "hot flashes" that occur because of a periodic fluctuation in the diameter of the blood vessels. The flush involves heat, perspiration, and red blotching, starting on the neck and spreading to the neck and face. The flushing may be due to a glandular imbalance that accompanies the climacteric, causing more blood to flow at one time than at another. It is when the greater amount of blood flows that the flashes, lasting from a second to several minutes, occur. The vascular instability may be due to the increased secretion of pituitary hormones without the moderating effect of the estrogen/progesterone ratio in the young female.

Finally, between the ages of 60 and 70, the effects of gradual hormonal insufficiency cause thinning of the walls of the uterus and vagina and shrinking of related genital tissue. Skin elasticity also decreases, and glandular tissue and tone diminish, causing loss of firmness and changes in breast and body contour. Vaginal mucous linings thin in menopause, and there may be vaginal itching and burning (called senile vaginitis). The cervix, ovaries, and portions of the urinary tract (including the urethra and bladder) also shrink. The loss of sex steroids also decreases the size of the vagina, vulva, labia, and clitoris but, for the clitoris, there is no objective evidence to suggest any appreciable loss in sensate focus.

Sexual Responses of Older Women

The effects of neuronal decrease in rate of responsivity and steroid insufficiency combine to produce changes in physiology and function of older women's sexual activities. Although physiologic and functional changes are common in older women in relation to sexual activity, not all women report significant discomfort, despite some thinning of the vaginal walls and decreased lubrication. For others, cracking, bleeding, and pain can result during sexual intercourse. Uterine contractions in orgasm may also cause pain. The urethra and bladder are more subject to irritation with the decreased cushioning of thinning vaginal walls, and there can be burning and frequency of urination for several days after sex.

All four phases of sexual response to stimulation are generally diminished in the aged woman. In the excitement phase lubrication of the vagina increases from 15 to 30 seconds in the young to as long as 5 minutes for older women. Expansion of the vagina is reduced in extent. Vasocongestion is reduced, and purple coloration changes in younger women become pink in menopausal females. At plateau phase, the deep skin coloration in younger women, predictive of impending orgasm, is absent in older woman. The labia majora no longer elevate and flatten out. Involuntary uterine elevation is diminished, although clitoral response, including elevation and flattening, is similar to that in younger women. Duration of orgasm is reduced considerably between 50 and 70 years of age. Uterine contractability is similar to that of younger women but is spastic rather than rhythmic, and contractions are reduced from three to five to one or two. Muscle tone reduces the tightening of the vagina on the penis. Vaginal orgasmic platform is still initiated in 8-second intervals, but contractions are reduced from 8 to 12 for younger women to 4 or 5 in older women. Resolution is much more rapid in uterine declevation and vaginal, uterine, and clitoral detumescence. Labia minora color changes are faint or absent and disappear even before orgasm occurs.

Menopausal and postmenopausal women, however, maintain the multiple orgasmic capacity of their younger years.

SEXUAL DYSFUNCTION

The factors that lead to sexual dysfunction of the aged tend to be the same for any age: disease or trauma to the urogenital system, systemic disease, social attitudes, and emotional disturbances. Some decline in sexual functioning in the aged is known to have physiologic bases. In some cases, it is secondary to diseases, such as diabetes; in others, it is caused by the side effects of medication. The role of sociopsychological factors in the sexual functioning of the elderly is less clear. The cultural myths and loss of self-esteem that accompany aging in our society may combine to make the aged more vulnerable to psychological stress. Part of the problem lies with health professionals who may refrain from discussing sex in their contacts with older people. Thus concern with erection or painful intercourse, for example, may be overlooked or avoided.

The most common sexual dysfunctions in aging are (1) impotence, (2) painful coitus, and (3) female orgasmic dysfunction. Sexual dysfunction in the male can severely limit the pleasurable aspects of intercourse for both partners. Function in males means erection for a reasonable length of time under voluntary control. Dysfunction is defined as (1) impotence, the inability to have an erection or to maintain an erection to ejaculation, or (2) premature ejaculation, the inability to exert some voluntary control over ejaculation. Problems of failure of ejaculation are rare in the general population and usually relate to inability to ejaculate intravaginally, not to absence of ejaculation in the presence of erection and adequate stimulation. Putting aside for the moment disease, trauma, or physical problems, the orign of these problems is usually psychosocial. Three types of impotence are recognized: organic, functional, and psychogenic.

Organic impotence is relatively rare and is caused by some defect in the reproductive or central nervous system. Functional impotence is much more common in the elderly and may be caused by a nervous condition, excessive use of drugs or alcohol, deficient hormonal functioning, circulatory or other physical problems, the aging process itself, or physical exhaustion—any of which can interfere with sexual function. With advancing age, there is the increased possibility of one or more chronic diseases that, alone or in combination, may have physiological effects on the reproductive system. Diabetes is common in old age and causes impotence two to five times as often as in the general population, although sexual interest may persist. Impotence can occur from poorly controlled diabetes. Adequate control of diabetes usually restores function, but the adequately controlled diabetic who develops impotence usually has a more permanent problem. The effects of diabetes on sexuality in women is unknown. The high incidence of heart disease and cardiovascular accident may also contribute to impotency in older people. During sexual intercourse, heart rate, blood pressure, and oxygen consumption increase in the elderly to levels comparable to light to moderate physical excercise. The heart rate ranges from 90 to 150 beats per minute, with an average of 120 beats. A conservative estimate is that only about 1 percent of sudden death occurs around the time of intercourse. There is not yet a mass of conclusive data regarding death at the time of intercourse, but it does not seem to be a factor that should be of any great concern to the aged. Only extreme coronary disease calls for abstinence.

Perhaps the most common reasons for an effective loss of desire for or end to sexual activity for many is difficulty with urogenital function or surgery of the urogenital system. Pelvic surgery must be carefully planned to avoid unnecessary sexual impairment.

With the passage of time, the prostrate gland enlarges in males. It is almost universally present in men and systematically troublesome in at least 25 percent of men over age 60. Surgical treatment is generally effective, but it does have some physical side effects that can be distressing. A prostatectomy need not affect sexual potency, although it sometimes alters the sensation of ejaculation or even abolishes ejaculation. The loss of capacity for erection is a major unnecessary worry in prostate surgery. It can become impaired by performance anxiety, medication, or merely by thinking that it was impaired. It is not unusual after prostate surgery to experience temporary loss of erection; however, the capacity is seldom destroyed by age or simple prostate operations. Radical operations that cut the nerves controlling penile erection can produce impotency. Cancer of the prostate requires radical surgery, but this is one of the easiest cancers to treat. It does result in loss of sexual capacity; this must be balanced against the possibilities of painful disability or death if there is no treatment. Seventy percent of the men who have had prostate operations remain potent. Potency is rarely effected when gland tissue is removed by surgical procedures through the urethral transurethral resection canal or when an incision is made in the abdomen (suprapubic), although impotence may occur for psychological reasons. Nonpsychological physical impotence is most often associated with prostate removal when an incision is made between the scrotum and rectum (perineal).

There is no evidence that a hysterectomy with or without ovariectomy produces any change in sexual desire or performance in women. More than 70 percent of women who have had hysterectomies retain potency and coital enjoyment. If change does occur, it is usually psychological. Fear of sexual impairment, loss of desire, and loss of attractiveness are the most frequent occurrences. People tend to become more upset after major subtractive surgeries such as mastectomies, ileostomies, and colostomies. Fears and anxieties associated with surgery lead to sexual concern and problems.

Declining levels of health and current medical practice often lead to drug abuse in the elderly. Alcohol and tranquilizers can weaken erection and delay ejaculation in older men. Anemia, fatigue, poor nutrition, and a variety of metabolic abnormalities may inhibit desire and abort arousal or sexual climax at any age, but the aging are more susceptible. Obesity is a common problem of older people that negatively affects health and sexual functioning in both sexes.

Older people who have chronic illnesses may want to live as normal a life as possible, including sexual activity, with the help of medical treatment. Sexual activity, moreover, may actually help older people to stay in good physical condition, since it helps to reduce tension that can have physical and psychological components. Of course, at any age, cerebrovascular accidents, coronary attacks, diabetes mellitus, prostatectomy, hysterectomy, and other surgical procedures may lead to sexual concern and possible problems. (See the Case of Sexual Therapy.)

One group of dysfunctions of sexuality more common to the aged than the young arises from varying degrees of discomfort with intercourse. The most common cause in older women is probably insufficient vaginal lubrication, which does not occur in women who have weekly intercourse.

In older men painful intercourse is usually a sign of infection or disease. Infections of any reproductive structure or even general bodily dysfunction can result in sexual dysfunction.

Another female sexual dysfunction is entirely identified by the lack of desire or total or partial loss of interest in sex. In recent years the term has been discarded in favor of the more descriptive term for this common female sexual dysfunction—female orgasmic dysfunction.

The major manifestation of female sexual orgasmic dysfunction is as the inability to go beyond the plateau stage in sexual response. Nonorgasmic women are placed in one or two classes, those with primary orgasmic dysfunction and those with situational orgasmic dysfunction. The women in the first category have never achieved orgasm. The women in the situational category, have achieved orgasm in the past, but no longer do so.

Three major areas are worth examining when orgasmic experiences are infrequent or lacking: (1) the time involved; (2) the actual physical technique; and (3) the wide range of attitudes about sexual activity. Decreased interest, from a previous moderate or normal level of interest, is often associated with a situational disturbance and is usually amenable to treatment.

Nonorgasmic women are often more severely disabled and more difficult to treat. They are more apt to show evidence of personality disorder or difficulties in other areas of their lives that predate this type of sexual dysfunction. Treatment focus in orgasmic dysfunction must be directed at the relationships in which the older woman is involved. In orgasmic dysfunction at any age, problems usually extend beyond the sexual area by the time help is sought.

Many elderly have personal feelings, fears, and misunderstandings about sex in old age. Professional help can be beneficial in evaluating and treating sexual dysfunction. Sexual education for older people is important to enable them to understand normal, age-related changes and to explore techniques of sexual activity that may be especially pertinent in order to enjoy sexual activity until late in life.

Sexuality is only one of the many areas of human functioning. For many older patients it is not a central concern. For couples who do enjoy sexual activity in their later years, it is important to remove the cultural barriers, embarrassment, shame, guilt, or ridicule from sexual expression and to accept sexuality as a potentially life-long experience not bound to age or body appearance. Even if and when actual intercourse is impaired by infirmity or disease, other sexual needs persist, including closeness, sensuality, and being valued as a man or woman.

SEXUAL THERAPY

Mr. P., 68, a retired postal worker, and his wife, 66, a retired employee for a public utility, sought help on a daughter's recommendation. The daughter wrote of their relationship, "My mother keeps accusing my father of meeting people at the store, talking to strange women, and not paying attention to her. He bitterly resents her nagging and suspicions. His answer to her frequent concerns about other women and lack of attention to her is, ''You're driving me crazy, it's ridiculous?' He is extremely frustrated by these conditions. She is crushed by his anger but only seems to be more agitated and persistent in her nagging.''

Mrs. P. was a pleasant woman who appeared anxious and tense. She denied any trouble with her husband but said he was not at all affectionate since his prostatectomy in the early part of the year. She described herself as always active and fidgety but admitted that this trait had increased since her voluntary retirement the past year. She said she retired without any plan; she was ''tired of going to work every day and wanted to retire like everone else.'' She said that time dragged heavily, and she missed feeling useful. She had considered local, part-time work but had never pursued it.

When Mr. P. was interviewed, he was friendly and cooperative. His facial expression was animated, and he talked very openly. He said he felt well, particularly after his prostate operation; it had relieved his constant urination, which had been accompanied by itching and burning. He then confided that he wondered if something could be done for his wife, who was ''driving me crazy.'' The conflict at home apparently was a situational reaction to the stress of the husband's organic impediment to sexual expression and the wife's fears that she was no longer attractive to her partner.

Therapy was undertaken, first with each one individually, to provide information about the effects of prostate surgery, psychological counseling to understand how each was affected, and the opportunity to express some form of affection until the expected return of normal function in the male.

It was discovered that the couple had both reacted with some anxiety to threats to sexual fulfillment. As often happens, the consequences of surgery— changes in sensation of ejaculation and temporary loss of erection—had not been fully discussed. In addition, one of the common fears that presented itself in the husband's case was fear of damage to the genital system. Factual information was presented to aid both spouses in joint sessions to understand prostate-related function better. Individual counseling focused on helping the individuals to talk about and confront their fear and anxiety about limitations in sexual performance. The couple was encouraged to relax and enjoy other aspects of sex, such as touching, feeling, and holding one another, until the return of full sexual capacity.

After several months, the husband began to experience erection on waking. He found it reassuring that the capacity for erection had not been lost, potency was not effected, and only the sensation of ejaculation had changed. As soon as the stress of loss of function was removed, the couple showed a return to normalcy.

Summary

Sexuality is intimately involved with their personhood for most people. The research shows that in the absence of true disabilities, actual disease, and the belief that the aged should no longer be active sexually, sexual needs and capacities are lifelong.

As with all other body systems, normal aging of the reproductive system brings decrements in efficiency, increased time for responsivity, and tissue changes in the sexual area.

The following generalizations concerning sexual activity in old age are now widely accepted by researchers. Although sexual activities decrease in frequency, this is more common among women than men. In patterns of sexual response, the sequential patterns do not change, and enjoyment of sex seems heightened in many older couples. There are indications of wide individual variety in sexual activity, but earlier established sexual patterns (particularly between spouses) tend to continue. Those who are sexually active at an early age continue to be active in later life. It is found that menopause, far from marking the end of sexual response in women, often results in an upsurge of interest in and enjoyment of sexual contacts.

In later life adjustment difficulties in the sexual area are more related to emotional threats to sexuality than physiological incapacity or change. Sexual dysfunction in both sexes rarely has anthing to do with age; it is most often caused by anxieties related to performance or how one views oneself or one's partner. When sexual decline or dysfunction is emotional, sex therapy involving education and counseling are available. Both have been successful in eliminating sexual dysfunction arising from psychological causes in older couples.

The sexual function is a major means of interpersonal contact and communication, particularly in older people. Healthy sexuality may be therapeutic in reducing tensions, which are physical and psychological, and imparting feelings of well-being and self-esteem among older people, whose basic needs for intimacy, love, and self-concept are at greater risk at this time of life. Even when actual intercourse is impaired or no longer possible, other sexual needs persist and can and should be expressed and satisfied in a healthy way.

FURTHER READINGS

Bastani, J. B., "Sexuality in Later Life," *Nebraska Medical Journal,* 1977, 62(3), 62–64.

Butler, C. A., "New Data About Female Sexual Response," *Journal of Sex and Marital Therapy,* 1976, 2(1), 40–46.

Calderone, M. S., "Sexuality and the Later Years," in *Learning for Aging,* U.S. Educational Resources Information Center, Washington, D.C. 1974.

Cherry, S. H., *The Menopausal Myth,* Ballantine, New York, 1976.

Jones, T. (ed.), "Going Strong in your Eighties," *Quest,* 1978, 2(2).

Kinsey, A. C., W. B. Pomeroy, and C. R. Martin, *Sexual Behavior in The Human Male,* Philadelphia, Saunders, 1948, 1953.

Masters, W. H., and V. E. Johnson, *Human Sexual Inadequacy,* Little Brown, Boston, 1970, pp. 337–339.

Masters, W. H., and V. E. Johnson, *Human Sexual Response,* Little Brown, Boston, 1966.

McClay, J. L. *Human Sexuality* (2nd ed.), Van Nostrand, New York, 1973.

National Advisory Council on Aging, "Our Future Selves," Report of the Panel on Biomedical Research, N.I.H. Publication No. 80-1445 U.S. Government Printing Office, Washington, D.C., January 1980.

Nudel, A. *For the Woman Over 50,* Taplinger, New York, 1978.

Peterson, J. A., and B. Payne, *Love in the Later Years: The Emotional, Physical, Sexual and Social Potential of the Elderly,* Association Press, New York, 1975.

Pfeiffer, E., *Successful Aging,* Duke University Center for the Study of Aging and Human Development, Durham, N.C. 1974.

Pfeiffer, E., "Sexual Behavior in Old Age," in E. W. Busse and E. Pfeiffer, *Behavior and Adaptation in Late Life,* Little Brown, Boston, 1977, pp. 130-140.

Rubin, I., *Sexual Life after Sixty,* Basic Books, New York, 1976.

Ryan, K. J., and D. C. Gibson, *Menopause and Aging,* U.S. Department of Health Education and Welfare, N.I.H. No. (NIH) 73-319, Bethesda, Maryland, 1979.

Shearer, M. R., and M. L. Shearer, "Sexuality and Sexual Counseling in the Elderly," *Clinical Obstetrics and Gynecology,* 1977, *20*(1), 197-208.

6

Psychological and Social Aspects of Aging

Individuals go through a life cycle during which developmental stages are marked by critical events: marriage, birth of children, the "empty nest" experience when children leave home, retirement, and widowhood. These events suggest that, at each stage in one's life, there are differing demands, challenges, and periods of stress. They also reflect to some extent the expectations, attitudes, personality, and social and cultural experiences of the individual. Moreover, these events call attention to their psychological and social effects on the individual. For example, widowhood brings a shift in role, with consequent shifts in expectations, but it also may bring concomitant feelings of loneliness, depression, anger, *anxiety,* and a possible reawakening of unresolved conflicts and needs.

This chapter examines some of the psychological and social aspects of aging associated with these critical events in the developmental life cycle; it also discusses different social expectations of aging that characterize social *roles* and behavior. The impact of individual attitudes on the aging process and how these attitudes affect adaptation and satisfaction are considered.

Special problems of the elderly, such as emotional and social losses and loneliness, affect *adaptation.* These problems are discussed in conjuction with the emotional reactions and behavioral manifestations of old age—manipulation, anger, and anxiety.

The defense mechanisms of the aged, which represent attempts by the individual to avoid, reduce, or defend themselves from the disabling effects of anxiety and stress, are studied.

Finally, constructive ways of coping with anxiety, frustration, and stress to facilitate success and satisfactory adjustment to aging are discussed.

Many individuals accept aging gracefully. In America the prospect of aging is not always regarded favorably. It is dreaded by some people who feel that growing old is shameful. It is usually perceived as a time of deterioration in health, appearance, loss of friends and family, and *ability*.

The fact that the process of aging is not limited to the elderly is often overlooked. It begins at conception and continues to death. Aging is the changing of structure and function over time. Every human being "ages" with the passage of time. There is much confusion about what aging is all about. There is little understanding that individuals can have some control over the length and the quality of their lives. This chapter looks at some of the psychological and social implications of aging.

Aging is the gradual loss of adaptive ability with age. It embraces a loss of physiological adaptability but encompasses mental *adjustment*. The goal of gerontologists is to keep as many people as possible vibrantly alive, growing, and involved in later life. This process does not happen by accident. It depends on circumstances in the environment, some of which can be controlled and positively effected.

Aging is an important consideration for adolescents, adults, the middle age, and older people. What we are and do in later life is greatly affected by and dependent on what we are and do throughout our lives.

Some older people find their lives and dreams faded. Forced retirement, greatly reduced incomes on which individuals can barely exist, and loss of loved ones can place exceedingly great stress on the adjustment of older persons. The changes in appearance brought about by age may be seen as totally negative and worsen the effects of attitudes of the elderly toward themselves and those directed toward the elderly by others.

Some individuals view aging synonymously with isolation, loneliness, rejection, dread of institutions, and physical devastation. These feelings are enhanced by the negative ways of dealing with age often actively promulgated by society and affect the self-esteem of many elderly persons.

Illness often makes an elderly person's daily life a miserable, prolonged wait for death. Social welfare programs, Medicare, and other health insurance plans do not change this basic circumstance; however, for some, quality care makes the wait easier and more tolerable. Although there seems to be a great deal of expressed concern, little significant change has occurred in our society to improve the lot of the elderly. The needs of older persons are similar to those of all age groups—to have their basic need requirements satisfied and to have a chance to lead a meaningful, useful existence.

WHAT SOCIETY EXPECTS OF THE ELDERLY

Society has expectations about what is desirable behavior for a person at a certain age. These norms differ somewhat, depending on the culture, sex, and social class of the group, but they place social controls on behavior that, to some extent, shapes the expectations of others in society toward the elderly.

These ascribed characteristics are important considerations for aging because they include social role expectations of behavior, privileges, and responsibilities. Elderly persons have grown up learning how to enact a variety of roles: student, wife, husband, mother, father, friend, and group participant; each role has its rewards and satisfactions and gives purpose, content, and meaning to everyday living. When roles change, however, dire repercussions may result for the elderly.

In this complex modern society age is a universal criterion for assigning social roles, expectations, and behavior. There is a prescriptive expectation of age-appropriate and age-linked behavior pertaining to various stages of the life cycle, such as marriage, being settled in an established career, and retirement. These normative systems of social controls place constraints on behavior that are particularly felt by the elderly.

The social expectations for the period of old age in the progression of the family cycle are often characterized as changes in health, retirement, social responsibilities, and role, the implications being that if individuals are off-schedule with regard to major life events, negative consequences may result. Middle-aged and older people for the most part regard age and age appropriateness as reasonable criteria for evaluating behavior. Individuals who are not fulfilling social expectations at an age-appropriate time may be vulnerable psychologically and socially, thus affecting self-esteem, mobility, aspirations, anticipated and real adjustment to changing roles, perception of status, and degree of social integration in the community. There are frequently different expectations of aging of men and women.

Many prejudices toward aging are perpetuated by mass media. Vigor, power, sexual prowess, attractiveness, and femininity are usually valued and attributed to young and middle-aged persons, while frailty, senility, rigidity in thought and manner, helplessness, and feebleness are stereotypes associated with aging. These attitudes of ageism influence the perceptions of self and the concomitant behavior of its victims. The elderly tend to adopt negative attitudes toward themselves and to develop the very prejudicial stereotypes directed against them, thereby reinforcing society's view of them.

Common conversations among the elderly concern the plight of life they are enduring, frustration, anger, passive resignation, and a quality of depressive defeatism. It need not be this way. For many elderly persons, this stage of life is a pinnacle, a time of potential knowledge gain, creativity, with time to pursue interests, hobbies, and richer and deeper experiences in faith and family relationships.

The lack of empathy on the part of *family, society,* and significant others also reinforces the elderly's negative attitudes and ambivalent feelings. These feelings can be manifested into negative behavior. Older people are not always the victims of rejection, isolation, and prejudice reflected in circumstance and relationship; they may also exploit their age and attempt to manipulate others to demand and gain something they want or need. They can initiate action and stimulate angry, hostile, frustrated defenses from well-meaning relatives and friends who feel exploited by excessive requests and demands. Younger relatives and persons working in various roles with the elderly may find themselves feeling repeated cycles of pity, over-protectiveness, anger, rage, and guilt. Very often the middle-aged children or relatives of the elderly bear the heaviest personal, physical, emotional, social, and financial responsibilities, since they are called on and expected to help provide care and support. These responsibilities are often superimposed on the family at times when career responsibilities are demanding and onerous. Furthermore, as the average life span increases, parents and grandparents live longer, and responsibilities grow and produce added strains on the family.

ATTITUDES OF THE ELDERLY TOWARD AGING

The flow of human life from birth to death is called aging, but aging also refers to patterns of late-life changes that vary only in rate and degree that can be seen in all persons. The aging process and the period of old age can be an emotionally healthy, fulfilling, and satisfying time of life, with a minimum of physical and mental impairment. The World Health Organization describes health "as a state of complete physical, mental and social well-being and not merely the absence of disease or infirmity."

Each stage of life has a period of unique developmental tasks. The tasks of old age are to clarify, enrich, and discover what one has attained in a lifetime of learning and to adapt to the changes and losses in strength, relationships, and resources that occur as part of the aging experience.

The ability of the elderly to adapt is contingent on the individual's attitude toward the aging process; on physical health, personality, earlier life experiences, and adaptation; and on societal and familial supports such as adequate finances, housing, health care, *social roles,* and recreation. In order for the elderly to live a satisfying, meaningful life and for total health to be promoted and maintained, their needs must be met and they must continue to grow, develop, and adapt flexibly to change. Failure to adapt at any stage of development or under any circumstance can result in physical or emotional illness.

At every stage of life, including old age, individuals require confirmation of their worth. This confirmation can be enhanced by participating in activities that have meaning and value, by maintaining personal qualities of affection, and by showing caring through a living, vital spirit. Satisfying activities enable a person to sustain self-respect and involvement and to elicit respect from others. Satisfaction in interpersonal relationships encourages people to share themselves in various ways and thus maintain a sense of efficacy, purposefulness, and hope. One of the greatest handicaps older people face is not necessarily the aging process itself but their attitudes toward it. Many elderly persons feel overwhelmed by feelings of doubt and inferiority. They fear what may happen if their capacities begin to wane. The thought of physical aging and intellectual deterioration can be terrifying for some people, who conjure up painful ruminations of a life without dignity or purpose, such as total dependence on others or confinement to a wheelchair. Other fears include being a burden to oneself and others, suffering pain or wasted flesh and illness, being forced by others into a nursing home or an unfamiliar home for the aged, and being unwanted, useless, lonely, and rejected. Living in unfamiliar surroundings, however, or being put away from family and friends in isolation is tantamount to death for many persons; at a time in life when one needs most to be close to those one loves, the older person is too often terribly, dreadfully alone.

It is important for society to present a new perspective about later years. Age itself is not the cause of all ills. Much of the misery of the aged represents conflict and unsolved problems that have also existed in earlier stages of the life cycle. Failures, regrets, depression, feelings of inferiority, and inability to adjust to change are common problems but, as these problems are manifested throughout childhood, adolescence, young adulthood, and middle life, they will also be apparent in old age. The lack or loss of ego integration and of the ability to adjust to changes precipitated by the aging process may nevertheless result in despair, fear of death, disgust and displeasure with life, institutions, and particular people, and even contempt for oneself.

Maslow's (1970) concept of a hierarchy of needs is valuable in understanding the behavior of the elderly. According to his theory, human behavior is motivated by needs at various levels. The most basic needs are for physiological satisfactions (food, rest, warmth) and safety (security, freedom from fear). The needs for belonging and love emerge only when and if these basic needs are fulfilled. Self-esteem needs include the desire for competence and prestige but, when these needs have been met, a new restlessness may appear that propels the individual toward "self-actualization," a higher level of needs that, if met, produce more profound feelings of satisfaction. The human needs for survival and safety, adequate suitable housing, nutritious food, medical care, and protection from physical harm must also be met. Only then will the aged be able to focus on a full range of higher needs, attainments, and abilities and to acknowledge, appreciate, and use their attributes in order to become creative, competent, purposeful, fulfilled individuals.

The self-concept—how we see and feel about ourselves in relation to the world—will have an important affect on how we grow older. Negative feelings about oneself, physical appearance, sexual attractiveness, and job may become more intense in later years, when significant changes take place in these areas. Individuals may feel less positive about themselves, their adequacy, and their potential. However, people who are inquisitive and want to learn continue to become more self-actualizing, grow in self-awareness and in spirit, maintain friendships and interests, accept themselves, develop, and change. The sense of identity includes an inner assurance of continuity with the past but an awareness and acceptance of the change in the present. The attitude toward oneself and identity in childhood and the stages of life will greatly influence the elderly person's self-view as competent, capable of taking responsibility for daily living, worthy of respect, and acceptable. If people view themselves throughout life as basically incompetent and dependent on others to decide, think, and feel, in later life these attitudes will be reflected in their adjustment.

INDEPENDENCE VERSUS DEPENDENCE

Individuals who are realizing their potential and who have a positive self-concept usually feel in old age that they have some control over the decisions affecting life; individuals who have been hesitant to explore alternatives in the process of decision making of life's choices usually feel in old age that they are unduly controlled by fate, circumstance, or decisions made by others.

Dependence on others can occur at any age. Children depend on their parents. Parents in the later years depend on their children and other relatives and friends for emotional satisfaction. At what point does the attempt to meet dependency needs in inordinate ways mask psychological problems?

Some adults never resolve the personality problems of childhood, adulthood, and middle age. If an individual has been passive and dependent throughout life, that person will likely manifest these personality characteristics in later life.

Research done by Newgarten, Havinghurst, and Tobin (1964) on personality and aging studied patterns of personality type, role activity, and life satisfaction in people aged 70 to 79; the research seems to support the concept that aged individuals continue to make choices in life and to select activities and relationships from the environment according to their own established needs and patterns of adaption to the end of life.

SPECIAL PROBLEMS OF THE AGING

Certain life crises in old age, regardless of socioeconomic and cultural circumstances, can have serious effects.

The experiences most often cited by the elderly as being most stressful include: death of a spouse, close family member, or friend, marital separation or divorce, personal injury or illness, retirement, change in health of a family member, sexual difficulties, change in financial state, separation from family members, trouble with family or in-laws, change in living conditions, revision of personal habits, change in residence, and change in activities.

Emotional and social losses place the elderly in an especially vulnerable position in coping with life.

Emotional and Physical Losses

Loss is a major characteristic of the emotional experience of the elderly. Loss and change in every aspect of life have adverse affects, but the elderly expend a good deal of energy grieving and adapting to changes resulting from loss. The loss of family, friends, social position, residence, or occupation all have negative components; if several losses occur simultaneously, they place added emotional strain on the elderly.

The death of a marital partner, other significant relative, or friend may occur just when an older person is trying to adjust to loss of income, status, prestige, and role. Separation from adult children who change employment and move to other regions can seriously affect the elderly when compounded by frequent feelings of rejection, neglect, and the loss of emotional support and usefulness, as illustrated by the experience of Alvin P.

HIS ONLY SON

Alvin P. was an 81-year-old man who lived with his 76-year-old wife. He had lived in a semirural small town in Kansas for most of his life. Mr. and Mrs. P. had owned a wheat farm and successfully worked the farm for many years. They also had some cattle and hogs from which they got their own supply of meat.

Although his only son, 55 years old, helped to run the farm, in recent years he had become ill and moved with his family to a large city out of state to take another job. Visits became less frequent with time. Mr. P. and his wife felt alone, abandoned, and resentful toward their son. Since they were no longer able to run the farm by themselves, they let it "go to seed" and lived on Social Security benefits. Mr. P. was finding "getting around" more difficult. There was no public transportation to the village, and driving was becoming more hazardous because of his failing eyesight and other physical problems. In the village there were no social services, and medical care was inaccessible.

Many of his close friends had died, and he did not feel he wanted to burden others with his problems. "We will just try to make the best of it."

The loss of energy and strength, often accompanied, caused, or increased by types of illness prevalent during aging, can generate feelings of helplessness and anxiety and threaten an elderly person's sense of identity. The loss of physical capacities and illness elicits appropriate, but distorted, emotional reactions. Fear and anxiety about the appearance of an illness or a debilitating disease may cause further behavioral changes. Individuals who have been self-sufficient, mature, and have functioned well in their jobs and with their families for most of their lives find the thought of implacable illness in the aging process inherently frightening, and they may be disturbed more than their accustomed personality would suggest.

As physical bodies change in size, appearance, and shape, some elderly persons report shock and disbelief at the loss of youthfulness. Common preoccupations of the elderly include concern about bodily processes, the need for special diets, the effects of drugs, and bowel and urinary monitoring. Some elderly persons absorb themselves in their ruminations about their own bodies, ill health, and physical decline.

Elderly individuals deal with discomfort and pain differently. In later years frequent complaints of pain are associated with the common physical problems of arthritis, angina pectoris, rheumatism, and other periodic, nonspecific aches and pains. The personality, cultural background, and nature and severity of the pain determine how the elderly deal with pain. Every person has an individual pain threshold that varies depending on the extent and intensity of pain.

Social Losses

The loss of a marital partner or other significant persons can be profound since, in later life, it is difficult to find substitutes for such losses. The elderly experience grief, guilt, loneliness, depression, and anxiety as a result of such losses, as do people of every age. However, there is a unique quality to the character of these feelings in old age.

Grief reactions may include numbness and inability to accept loss; there is a sense of shock at the reality and implications of the loss. The elderly person may experience delusions and obsessive preoccupations with the image of the lost person and may continue daily activities as if the deceased person were still present. The survivor may attempt to keep the possessions of the deceased and even entire rooms intact, as they were before the death of the loved one, or may even avoid new contacts that might replace the role of the deceased.

Some indications of disorganization of normal response patterns are anxiety, inability to work, aimless wandering, depression, and hopelessness. Insomnia and digestive and bowel disturbances are also common symptoms of depression. Acute grief usually lasts from 6 months to 2 years, although further loss may reactivate depressive symptoms.

More serious depressive reactions may occur with the prolongation of unresolved anger, rage and ambivalence toward the deceased and other relatives. Other symptoms may develop, such as somatic illnesses, manic activity, and disturbed interpersonal relations over an extended period of time. A loss of significant persons for the elderly is a crucial factor contributing to the decline or development of problems in physical and emotional functioning. Futhermore, a combination of losses at one time (e.g., of meaningful loved ones, health, employment, and possessions) or changes in appearance can be significant precipitating factors in stress and illness.

In anticipation of the death of a spouse or a relative who has had a long illness, depressive feelings may lead an elderly person to try to adjust before death occurs. It can cause problems of premature disengagement from the dying person, who is then left alone, feeling rejected and isolated.

PRESSING ON

An example of successful aging is characterized by the life of Andrés Segovia, who at the age of 87 reined as the master of the classical guitar. Segovia believed he had achieved the goals he set for himself when, in his teens in his native Andalusia, he committed himself to becoming a professional musician. His ensuing years were occupied with the task of taking the guitar out of the realm of flamenco and elevating it to the concert stage.

In 1938, after the outbreak of the Spanish Civil War, Segovia left Spain solely to escape the turmoil. This loss of his home and familiar surroundings, noted in his autobiography, caused him intense sadness. Home became a variety of places—Montevideo, Uruguay, and New York City. His philosophy was characterized by the statement "We go on."

When asked "How long do you envision yourself on the concert stage?" he responded, "It will continue for as long as my fingers are obedient."

EMOTIONAL REACTIONS OF THE AGED

There are common emotional reactions that are manifested in old age; some of them are reflective of the life events of older people. However, almost all of the emotional reactions and mental disorders found in younger persons persist or recur in old age.

The elderly frequently reflect and reminisce about the past, this can evoke a resurgence of previous hurt, anger, conflict, and regret. Guilt may emerge to haunt elderly persons. They may reflect on actions that should have been taken; words that were intended but were left unsaid; and "sins that were committed" (or omitted) for which individuals blame themselves and that may weigh heavily in the light of approaching death. Elderly individuals who find themselves with such feelings may want to make restitution, seek forgiveness, and resolve differences. Such feelings should not be taken lightly or overlooked; they should be confronted seriously. Direct handling of guilt is an essential part of the final acceptance of later life adjustment and approaching death.

Loneliness

The concerns of the elderly include the fear of surviving alone in a threatening, hostile world and the fear of being emotionally isolated, unable to relate effectively to others to obtain emotional warmth, support, and caring.

In the later decades of life the fear of being abandoned is real. Finding themselves unable to provide for physical sustenance is a continual source of anxiety for the elderly. They are often isolated in apartments or houses where the rent and taxes are low; they fear being mugged, robbed, and victimized, even in their own homes and neighborhoods.

In addition to threats that emanate from the environment, the elderly also suffer a fear of loneliness, of having no one available to relate to. Significant relatives, friends, grandchildren, and children, if they exist, may live far away. There are also fewer persons to offer emotional support previously provided by close family ties. The limited involvement with religion, hobbies, pets, television, and other interests are often not enough to satisfy emotional needs. The emotional burdens of the elderly at critical times in their lives, with weak and fragmented networks of communication, render them vulnerable to depression and other emotional reactions.

Manipulation

Elderly people may attempt to use the changes in their lives and bodies to manipulate or control others for their own purposes. An older person, like any individual at any stage of development in the life cycle, may exploit illness, disease, and impairments by manipulating others in order to capitalize on alleged and real helplessness and incapacity. Manipulation in any form is an attempt to influence the behavior of others for one's own gain and can result in angry, ambivalent feelings between the elderly person and other persons. Elderly individuals with a personality pattern of controlling others can use illnesses, symptoms, or impending death to manipulate people for their own benefit at the expense of others. For example, an older person may behave tyrannically from the sick bed, commandeering personal services from family and others and acting helpless and incapacitated while appearing physically and mentally sound and capable to others. People react with anger, resentment, and retaliation when they feel they have been manipulated. The use of manipulation is destructive in that it eventually decreases cooperation and causes problems in interpersonal interaction.

Depression

Depressive reactions increase in degree of severity and frequency with old age. The highest rates of suicide occur among older persons. The sense of impotence and helplessness of elderly individuals who were once powerful and influential significantly affects self-esteem and contributes to grief, anger, guilt, and depression (see Chapter 7).

Anger

Anger is another emotional reaction often characteristic of old age. Some of the irritability may be an appropriate response to the treatment and neglect of old people by society and family, but other feelings of anger and indignation may be the result of the frustrations in dealing with the aging process and its debilitating effects. Anger, rage, and hostility are often expressed in aggression, which can be constructive when used appropriately in problem solving. When anger, however, is non-problem solving, unrealistic and the outcome of unresolved emotional conflict, it can be self-descructive and pathological.

Anxiety

In the elderly anxiety becomes intensified and pervasive as these people are confronted with accelerating changes in body, mind, relationships, feelings, and environment; and they are expected to adapt to these changes. Anxiety may be manifested in relation to the task at hand, the resources available to deal with it, and the feeling of confidence or failure elicited in coping with the task.

Symptoms of anxiety may appear in many forms: a fear of aloneness, paranoid ideation, and unpleasant and often vague feelings of apprehension that are accompanied by one or more recurring bodily sensations. Anxiety warns of impending danger. The threat or danger may be unknown and internal. Anxiety may produce motor restlessness, or agitation. Anxiety ususaly leads to some action to reduce the threat, but excessive anxiety may result in panic reactions in the elderly and cause disorganization of ego functioning, repression, or nonadaptive defenses (see Chapter 7).

DEFENSE MECHANISMS COMMON IN ELDERLY PERSONS

Elderly persons have acquired individual patterns of handling anxiety, anger, frustration, and the pressures of life. Such techniques are known as defense mechanisms. These are internal, automatic, and unconscious ways in which the personality protects itself against the threat of danger, shame, guilt, loss of pride in the midst of emotional needs, tension, and stress. *Defensive patterns* in the elderly persist throughout life, taking on different emphasis at various stages of the life cycle.

Repression

In some ways repression is the most basic of the mechanisms because it is present to some degree in several other defenses. The elderly frequently fail to recall many past events that are relevant to the present *repression*. This process is unconscious and undeliberate.

Not all forgetting is due to repression, but repression is motivated forgetting with a motivated continuation not to recall. The threat of anxiety leads to and causes repression. Some events may not upset the elderly at the time the memory occurs but, soon thereafter, the person becomes anxious, and threatening memories are repressed.

Denial and Emotional Withdrawal

Denial appears in many forms. It is used widely in all stages of life and is a basic defense of the elderly. It can be a useful component for maintaining a sense of stability. However, it can also seriously interfere with the developmental tasks of old age. It may refer only to the feeling associated with a particular idea or event, or there may be massive denial of the experience itself or of its memory. It may be manifested by the older person pretending to be young and refusing to deal with the realities of aging. An elderly person may deny illness and refuse to take medication, be treated, or be hospitalized.

Withdrawal is closely related to denial. The individual may withdraw by refusing to become emotionally involved or to interact with other people because of previous painful experiences. In extreme cases, withdrawal may be total, and reality may be avoided by apathy, or resignation. Denial and withdrawal may be at work when an elderly person asserts about a painful experience that ''It hasn't happened to me,'' or ''I will shut myself in my room and it won't happen.''

Projection

In the mechanism of *projection* individuals attribute their feelings and wishes to others because of an inability to assume responsibility for these feelings or to manage the painful effects they evoke. Some elderly persons attempt to allay their anxieties by projecting feelings outward onto someone else. They may verbalize feelings of suspicion, fear, and complaining: ''I am being cheated,'' ''My children prefer other relatives,'' and ''I am being neglected.'' In modern urban society the elderly have legitimate complaints and fears about situations that exist because of the high delinquency rates and criminal assaults on older people; it is therefore often difficult to distinguish between denying the reality of life and projection. However, projection as a defense from anxiety is apparent in the elderly population and signifies internal stress, which can become pathological unless the stress is alleviated.

Regression and Fixation

Through the mechanisms of *regression,* the elderly person attempts to return to an earlier phase of functioning in which gratification of need was assured in order to avoid the tension and anxiety at the present level of development. Regression is a normal phenomenon at all developmental stages. When it is used to describe the behavior of the elderly, it often implies a destructive, unhealthy, maladaptive retreat from the present into childish behavior. In old age the stress of physical, economic, and social problems places undue strain on the healthiest personalities.

In *fixation* the elderly person persists in a behavior pattern or stage of development and is unable to go to a more advanced level of functioning. For example, temper tantrums, oral dependency, and sibling rivalry are not outgrown in fixation. The elderly person may want to stop such behavior yet refuses to change.

Displacement

The mechanism of *displacement* consists of directing an emotion of anxiety or discomfort toward a safe or acceptable object or circumstance as a substitute for a threatening or unacceptable object. For example, an elderly woman may rage at her husband when, in reality, her son has offended her. Frequently the emotion in displacement is anger, which is directed toward a scapegoat in an overt action, attitude, or fantasy.

Rationalization

In *rationalization* elderly persons attempt to bolster their self-esteem by advancing rational explanations, which may or may not be valid, in an attempt to hide from themselves and others the actual motives for their behavior. Many individuals may try to justify their own behavior and prove that others are wrong; such attempts are found in both disturbed and relatively undisturbed people at all stages of development. Defensive behavior is motivated primarily by anxiety and guilt and drives an individual to be overemphatic, impatient, angry, and easily frustrated. A defenseless person could not cope with emotional and social pressures. When the defenses of the elderly are no longer adequate to manage unacceptable impulses and anxiety, psychopathological symptoms may emerge and intensify.

In summary, most aging persons are able to *cope* fairly well with the anxiety, frustration, and stress encountered in their lives; however, when barriers and obstacles are placed between an individual and satisfaction of needs and achievement of expected goals, there is a heightened probability of anxiety, stress, and frustration. Individuals may react to debilitating situations in many ways. They may manifest destructive and maladaptive behaviors such as aggression, hostility, and argumentativeness. They may attempt to manipulate the lives and emotions of those around them by becoming physically or verbally abusive toward others, overly self-protective, demanding, or dependent. Other destructive manifestations may be directed toward the self in feelings of inordinate *guilt,* remorse, indifference, and depression. They may resort to physical harm to themselves, disregard personal bodily needs, or indulge in alcohol or drug abuse.

SUCCESSFUL COPING

Old age need not be marked by unresolved grief, total frustration, and helplessness. It can be an emotionally healthy and satisfying time of life, with a minimum of physical and emotional impairment. Many elderly persons have adapted to old age with little stress and a high level of purposefulness, direction, and morale. The ability of the elderly to adapt and thrive is contingent on health, personality, earlier life experience, and *social roles*. If, therefore, elderly persons are to have an emotionally healthy and satisfying old age, they must develop and change in a flexible manner. The recognition of one's individual strengths, abilities, and potentials should be encouraged, reinforced, and supported.

Because their lives are changing does not preclude that the elderly must be programmed for failure or defeat. The loss of a spouse and other changes are unquestionably severely stressful events, but the potential for continuing adjustment, new relationships, and growth exists. Elderly persons do draw for strength from a lifetime of gathered experiences and a rich potential for spiritual, emotional, social, and intellectual growth.

In the process of successful coping and adjustment, elderly individuals may direct their energies toward constructive, appropriate outlets. They may concentrate on the development of self-awareness to understand their needs, behaviors, and problems and to mobilize their energies in the management and resolution of their problems and conflicts. Also, they may expend large amounts of energy in the pursuit of enjoyable work, physical exercise, social programs and projects, group participation with interpersonal contacts, education, and the management of themselves and their personal affairs.

Successful coping strategies may often be facilitated by positive interaction with friends, relatives, and religious and social institutions. Temporary emotional support by a close friend or another meaningful person during a period of stress may provide the needed aid toward an eventual positive adjustment.

Some basic coping strategies that may be helpful in facilitating emotional well-being among the elderly are considered next. These guidelines may also be relevant for persons who work with older adults who may have encountered adjustment problems or who may be confronting formidable circumstances and difficult demands in their lives.

Self-Esteem

One of the most important factors affecting personal adjustment and interpersonal communication is an individual's self-concept.

How people view themselves is the frame of reference, the personal reality that affects how they see, hear, evaluate, and understand everything else. An elderly person's *self-concept* determines how an individual will perform, react, and communicate with others. A positive self-concept is necessary for successful adjustment and satisfying interaction, whereas an inadequate or negative self-image often generates feelings of inferiority and insecurity. An elderly person with a healthy self-concept will not have difficulty expressing ideas and feelings but will be able to converse with others, sharing or accepting constructive criticism without ego collapse. The elderly who have a positive self-concept will not be subject to the destructive feelings of insecurity or inferiority that can hamper the ability to communicate and to adjust but will feel that they and their ideas are as interesting and important as anyone's and they they can be as open and friendly as is consistent with their basic personality.

The *self-image* of elderly individuals is reinforced by the way they are treated by important people in their lives. From personal interactions with others, they determine whether they are liked or disliked, accepted or unaccepted, respected or disdained, competent or disabled. Generally, persons with a positive, realistic, unexaggerated self-image are accepted and often liked, and the aged are no exception. To enhance self-esteem, everyone needs love, caring, respect, acceptance, and positive interactions with others, and these are critical factors in an elderly person's ability to cope and adjust successfully.

Self-Expression

Many elderly individuals find it difficult to say what they mean or to express their feelings. They often assume that others understand them and know what they think and feel. This assumption is a difficult barrier to effective communication.

An elderly person who has experienced dramatic change and significant loss must be encouraged, in an accepting, empathetic atmosphere, to verbalize thoughts and feelings. It is important to provide opportunity for individuals to cry and to talk about their feelings of hurt, hate, and anger and their disappointments and problems. This can do much to dispel anxiety, tension, and frustration.

Very often the expression of emotion may be unpleasant and cause embarrassment or discomfort to other people. When this happens, there may be a tendency to discourage any open expression of feelings. Friends and relatives who mean well may attempt to change the subject to divert attention from deep emotion or its display. This forces the stress-laden individual to keep feelings inside and to repress emotion. When anxiety and emotion are bottled up and spontaneous expression is frustrated, destructive and nonproductive behavior may be manifested in order to release tension. The buildup of tension, restlessness, and dread may have serious consequences for the elderly. The encouragement of self-expression is essential to effective communication and adjustment.

Friends and relatives can facilitate successful coping for the aging person by providing an accepting attitude through the encouragement of self-expression and self-disclosure. This would enable persons in a crisis to share their thoughts, feelings, judgments, and values and expose their fears and frustrations, triumphs and failures without condemnation. If this is not possible in the immediate network, various other resources may be able to provide a therapeutic environment of trust and good will in which the open sharing of emotion is encouraged to alleviate anxiety and tension; examples include the various professionals, such as psychologists, social workers, clergymen, psychiatrists, and other mental health workers.

Coping with Anger

The ability of the elderly to manage strong emotions such as anger frequently results in breakdowns in interpersonal interaction and effective communication because many people feel that communication of anger or any negative emotional reaction is unacceptable; however, if negative irritation is kept in, it may result in an overcharge of reactions and represent a failure to cope with anger.

Elderly individuals need to express their emotions in order to relate effectively to others; to influence, affirm, and redirect their goals; and to grow. They must learn how to express and manage angry feelings constructively.

Some helpful steps in this direction include recognizing and admitting the existence of the emotions, accepting responsibility for it, exploring the reasons for it, and checking whether what is being expressed matches the motives. Such steps require self-honesty but, if persisted in, can bring relief and positive action through seeking alternative ways to express the emotions appropriately; determining a plan of action to manage the emotions; and evaluating the results of these efforts.

New Directions and Goals

The pursuit of substitute *goals* may be highly effective in facilitating successful coping adjustment for persons in stress. Participation in activities such as hobbies, sports, travel, interaction social groups, work, and self-*actualization* may help to direct energies constructively. An elderly person who has experienced severe stress may be reluctant to engage in any new activities and may verbalize resistance to any suggestion, but such negative attitudes and withdrawal of information severely reduce the effectiveness of planning and consideration of substitute goals, which are greatly needed by the elderly. The refocus of energy in a new direction should be encouraged to develop in the elderly a sense of personal interest, commitment, and motivation for self-growth and the development of relationships.

Although elderly persons should not be coerced into new goals and activities during stress periods, an active and judicious encouragement of participation in meaningful pursuits and relationships may bring about a change in attitude and prove to be emotionally beneficial and satisfying.

New activities and undertakings should be encouraged, but elderly persons in periods of severe stress should avoid making major life changes. It may be advisable to maintain a relative status quo instead of aggravating life changes that may increase emotional pressure. Major changes made under duress in periods of stress may bring later regrets.

The elderly who have experienced acute stress or frustration should be expected to assume responsibility for the self-management of personal and financial affairs and life direction wherever possible. Some support may be needed for a reasonable amount of time. To remove all responsibility for a prolonged period of time may be counterproductive and may negate feelings of adequacy. The rapid assumption of responsibilities, with the reassurance that help is available if it is required, may help to facilitate successful coping with stress and the maintenance of a realistic attitude toward oneself and others.

Summary

The process of aging may be regarded in various ways. Many individuals accept aging and maintain some control over their life. Others are less able to cope with aging and the problems of aging successfully. Society has expectations about what is acceptable behavior for the elderly. When roles change, repercussions may result for the elderly. The ability to adapt is contingent on an individual's attitude, physical health, personality, societal and familial support systems, housing, and adequate health care.

Maslow's (1970) theory of a hierarchy of needs is valuable in understanding the behavior of the elderly. The basic needs for physiological satisfactions, food, survival, and safety are important considerations. Only when these needs are met can the aged attain the achievement of higher needs and attainments.

There are life changes imposed on the elderly that are specific sources of stress, such as emotional losses, death of a spouse, loss of a job, loss of physical capacities, and social losses. These stress-provoking experiences may occur suddenly and must be endured for extended periods of time. They may occur when individuals are in poor health and have reduced control over their environment and circumstances, rendering them more vulnerable to the negative effects of change. The critical prolonged nature of many stress situations encountered by the elderly may precipitate psychological and physical problems and reactions.

The frustrations of needs in the elderly person may give rise to anxiety and symptoms of loneliness, depression, anger, agitation, or recurring bodily sensations. These symptoms can be unpleasant and may cause panic. To ward off and reduce the perceived disabling threat of anxiety, defense mechanisms of repression, denial, withdrawal, projection, regression, fixation, and rationalization are used. These unconscious psychological processes persist throughout life and are used at all stages of development. Among the elderly, certain defensive patterns used to cope with anxiety become more prevalent and characteristic of adjustment to stress factors. When the defenses of the elderly are no longer adequate to manage anxiety, psychological pathology may emerge.

Most aged individuals manage and cope with anxiety in life situations exceptionally well. In order to facilitate the process of successful adjustment in periods of severe stress, certain coping strategies are recommended: to acquire and maintain a positive self-esteem; to encourage self-expression of ideas and feelings; to manage anger and conflict in constructive ways; and to develop new directions in life and work toward the implementation of these goals.

Persons trying to help the elderly may encourage the growth of these strategies in an empathetic, supportive atmosphere. They should recognize that professional help might be needed to facilitate the adjustment process in some individuals.

FURTHER READINGS

Jacobs, R., and B. Vinick, *Re-Engagement in Later Life,* Greylock Publishers, Stamford, Conn., 1979.

Kalish, R. *The Later Years: Social Application of Gerontology.* Brooks/Cole, Monterey, Calif., 1977.

Maslow, A. H., *Motivation and Personality* (2nd ed.), Harper & Row, New York, 1970.

Monk, *The Age of Aging: A Reader in Social Gerontology,* Prometheus Books, Gainesville, Fla., 1979.

Neugarten, B., R. Havinghurst, and S. Tobin. "Personality and Patterns of Aging," in *Middle Age and Aging,* University of Chicago Press, Chicago, 1964, pp. 173–177.

Watson, W., *Stress and Old Age: Race Relations and Minorities,* Transaction Publishers, New Brunswick, N J , 1980.

7

Mental Health and the Aging Process

Society is slowly moving toward a better understanding of the nature of mental health. Recent fact-finding task panels created to review the mental health needs of the nation recommended future courses for public policy. These recommendations suggested a wider dissemination of knowledge on the nature and treatment of mental disabilities; more comprehensive, high-quality care with special emphasis on under-served populations; greater responsiveness to the diverse racial and cultural back-grounds of people; and expanded personnel and more adequate financing of ser-vices. These goals reflect changing viewpoints of mental health. Who is treated and what problems they are treated for have changed as the definitions of mental health have expanded to include both more appropriate responses to mental health prob-lems and the increasing recognition and acceptance of mental health treatment services. However, despite concerted efforts to incorporate current knowledge about the biological, psychological, sociological, and environmental factors in men-tal health to underserved populations, many elderly go unserved or inappropriately treated.

The wide range of *mental disorders* prevalent in the elderly are explored in this chapter in order to emphasize the need for appropriate evaluation and treatment. Over 85 percent of those over 65 years old are mentally healthy and, of those who are not, many can be helped with appropriate treatment. Factors influencing dis-turbed patterns of behavior in old age are considered, as is the relationship between aging and the dysfunction in emotional response, thinking patterns, and daily functioning. Certain organic mental disorders observed in elderly persons are explored. They are described according to the specific nature of the disorder and its pathophysiological process.

In our society the use of certain substances to modify mood or behavior under certain circumstances is generally prevalent. Among the elderly, there are variations in the use of alcohol and of certain substances often used medically to alleviate pain, relieve tension, or suppress appetite. This chapter discusses substance use disorders—behavioral changes in the elderly associated with regular use of substances that affect the central nervous system.

Some elderly persons manifest features of *schizophrenic disorders* that involve multiple psychological processes and deterioration from a previous level of functioning. These disorders are considered along with their impact on the level of functioning in the daily life of the older person.

Paranoid disorders with persistent persecutory delusions or delusional jealousy are described; common manifestations of the disorders as observed in the elderly are presented. The emotional and behavioral effects of the disorder are also discussed.

Affective disorders combined with a mood disturbance can color the psychic life of an older person. Depressive or manic episodes may be severe and intense and may seriously affect the individual's functioning.

The group of disorders in which anxiety is the predominant disturbance experienced by the individual—the anxiety disorders—are described. These recurrent periods of anxiety that can occur in the lives of the elderly may be unpredictable and cause discomfort.

Specific personality disorders are observed in elderly persons just as they are in the rest of the population. Various personality traits are seen in older persons; they encompass enduring patterns of thinking about the environment and oneself. When these significant personality traits are inflexible and maladaptive and cause significant impairment in social functioning and distress, they constitute personality disorders.

Although most old people cope with stress effectively without outside help, many are unaware of how to obtain professional evaluation and treatment for emotional disturbances. The attitudes of the elderly toward psychiatric treatment are becoming more accepting, and many agencies are attempting to understand and meet the needs of the elderly.

INCIDENCE OF MENTAL ILLNESS IN THE AGED

The prevalence of mental disorders in older persons is difficult to document. Research in the area has been neglected, and many professionals have considered the mental disorders of the elderly inevitable and intractable; however, most disorders and dysfunctions are treatable and reversible.

The American Psychological Association has estimated that at least 3 million elderly persons (15 percent of the older population) need mental health services.

There are at least 7 million elderly persons who live below or near the poverty level in social and environmental conditions that contribute to emotional stress and breakdown. The feelings of isolation and neglect and the effects of institutionalization frequently precipitate further emotional problems already in existence. At least 2 million other older persons living in the community have serious mental disorders with associated emotional reactions that require care.

The elderly have the highest incidence of acquired brain disorder. The American nursing home population of 1.2 million people (5 percent of persons over age 65) is estimated to have a 50 to 75 percent prevalence of intellectual impairment. About 3 million Americans over 65 are afflicted with dementia, and 67 percent of them live in the community.

It is likely that at least 300,000 elderly persons in the United States can be restored to useful living by appropriate evaluation and treatment. Once diagnosed, most mental impairment in the elderly is reversible with treatment. The crucial step for health workers is to recognize that many treatable psychological disorders in the elderly produce symptoms of mental impairment that are hard to distinguish from the impairment of irreversible diseases of the brain.

WHAT CAUSES DYSFUNCTIONS OF THE PERSONALITY SYSTEM?

The manifestations of mental disorder are the outcome of complex biological, sociocultural, and psychological interacting forces. The *personality* of an individual refers to the sum total of the unique patterns of thought, feeling, and behavior that one habitually employs in adaptation of life. Adaptation to the environment is a complex process that involves the individual's memory, cognitive processes, psychological processes, physiological processes, hereditary predisposition, and social interaction. These processes are constantly undergoing change, yet one must continually strive to maintain or bring about an adaptation to the environment.

Adaptation is the series of changes occurring within the self as one fulfills needs in relation to personal satisfactions and to the realities of the environment. A breakdown in the adaptational process represents an inability to maintain a reasonably satisfactory pattern of interactions between the self and the environment and could occur for various reasons such as extreme pressures, emotional loss, and physiological, psychological, or environmental changes that disrupt emotional gratification. If these stresses are so overpowering that the personality system cannot adjust to them or maintain effective functioning, the breakdown of the personality system may emerge as disorders of thought, feeling, and behavior.

ORGANIC MENTAL DISORDERS

Organic mental disorders are psychological or behavioral disturbances of abnormal behavior that reflect brain damage or dysfunction. The organic cause may be a disease of the brain or another systemic illness that affects the brain. These mental disorders may also be caused by a substance or toxic agent that has disturbed or impaired brain tissue or by withdrawal of a substance on which an elderly individual has become physiologically dependent.

Some symptoms of organic mental disorders are impaired orientation for time, place, or person; disturbance or loss of memory; impaired judgment and intellectual function; constantly changing emotions; and changes in personality and behavior. They need not all occur at the same time or with the same severity and, of course, not to most of the elderly. Organic mental disorders may be accompanied by emotional symptoms and behavioral disturbances.

The individual's basic personality and the environmental situation affect the severity of the symptoms. They may occur suddenly if the cause is acute or develop slowly if the cause is a degenerative disease; the course may vary from a progressive, episodic, or static evolution to one that evolves rapidly or gradually, depending on the underlying pathology. Temporary brain dysfunction caused by metabolic disorders, substance intoxications, or withdrawals and some systemic illnesses may end in full recovery.

Even if permanent damage has occurred, such changes do not cause gross impairment in some older people. In others, however, symptoms such as self-centeredness, irritability, difficulty in assimilating new experiences, insomnia, and physical weakness may appear; there may also be marked exaggeration of common losses in the elderly such as decrease in memory of recent events, altertness, and a change in adaptive functioning. Deterioration and regression of personality can occur. Many persons become untidy and careless and lose control of bladder and sphincter muscle. Personality disturbances echo tendencies and characteristics of the individual's previous personality. Older people may become anxious, depressed, confused, and paranoid, experiencing *delusions* and hallucinations of a persecutory, erotic, or grandiose nature.

Emotional reactions may respond to treatment, and some functioning can return or improve with proper support even though the physical loss is irreversible. In planning, consideration should be given to the elderly remaining in their own residence, if possible. Psychological, social, medical, or nursing support services may be needed to provide adequate assistance.

Various organic mental disorders are briefly described in the following pages; the list and details may be depressing at first reading, but remember that they are a survey of possibilities, not a list of unavoidable disasters for the aged and, like medical reference works, contain information, not each individual's fate.

Primary Degenerative Dementia, Senile Onset

Alzheimer's disease has been referred to as a senile *dementia* because it is a neurological disease in which the age of onset is over 65 and it involves loss of memory, judgment, and abstract thought and changes in personality and behavior.

Only a small percentage of the elderly (2 to 4 percent of those over 65) develop senile dementia. The disorder progresses steadily and gradually. In early stages memory impairment may be apparent, but subtle personality changes may also appear, such as apathy or withdrawal, although individuals usually remain cooperative, neat, and well groomed. As the disease progresses, the symptoms become more apparent and serious until, in the late stage, individuals may be mute, inattentive, and incapable of caring for themselves. From the onset of the disorder to death is about 5 years. It is more common in women than in men.

Multiinfarct Dementia

Although the main feature of multiinfarct dementia is deterioration of intellectual functioning, unlike senile dementia, the onset is abrupt and the course is stepwise and fluctuates with rapid changes. *Infarct* simply means a localized area of tissue (in this case, brain tissue) that is dying or dead because it was deprived of its blood supply. Vascular disease is always presumed to be present and to be responsible for the dementia. When the blood supply to the brain is altered or reduced, insufficient oxygen and nutrients reach the brain, deterioration of cerebral tissue results, and symptoms appear. Hemorrhage, thrombosis, and embolism may occur. The causes of the vascular problem itself are still unclear; factors such as heredity, diet, smoking, pollution, and lack of exercise have been suggested as contributory. Many elderly persons, however, show no signs of this dementia even in their seventies, and others are not affected at all. There is, moreover, wide variance among affected individuals in symptoms and course of illness. Many retain considerable capacity for several years, and good remissions are possible.

The onset can occur between 50 and 70 years of age; its pattern of deficits is patchy, leaving some intellectual functions relatively intact and others impaired, depending on which region of the brain is involved. Memory, abstract thinking, judgment, impulse control, personality, and behavior can be disturbed, and neurological manifestations including weakness and a stepped gait appear in many. If new attacks follow, each one does additional damage (see the following case). This disorder is more common in men.

ORGANIC MENTAL DISORDER

Paul, a 75-year-old retired professor, widowed and with three married children, was determined to live alone and independently. He lived in a small house on a small retirement pension. His house was cluttered with books, newspapers, plants, and memorabilia. He continued to read and write in his field of interest. He sometimes forgot to shop for food and reportedly had gone a few days at a time without eating.

One of his daughters visited and found him lying in bed, confused disoriented. He was not feeling well and was unable to care for himself, prepare food, or eat. Neighbors reported that he played the radio very loudly, and it was disrupting to everyong in the area. He was also seen wandering aimlessly at odd hours when he was mobile.

Since he seemed to be dehydrated, he was admitted to the hospital. He was found to have an organic mental disorder with impairment in intellectual functioning, memory, judgment, and orientation. Focal neurological signs and symptoms gave evidence of significant cerebrovascular disease related to the disturbance. Since he was unable to care for himself at home and living with relatives was not feasible, arrangements were made for him to be admitted to a nursing home.

Organic Brain Syndromes

Organic brain syndrome is the term used to describe a constellation of psychological or behavioral symptoms without any reference to the cause of the syndrome.

Delirium. Generally temporary, this disorder may last about 1 week or persist for 1 month; recovery is usually complete if the underlying cause is attended to. It can occur at any age but is especially common after the age of 60. It develops over a short time, but sometimes occurs abruptly, after a head injury.

Dementia. Found predominantly in the elderly, the course of dementia depends on the underlying cause and can be arrested and reversed when the causative disorder can be treated. It may begin suddenly, but it remains for a long time. In primary degenerative dementia, however, the onset is usually insidious and progresses slowly to death after several years. The symptoms include memory impairment— the sufficient loss of intellectual abilities to interfere with functioning, abstract thinking, and judgment. Personality change, irritability, anxiety, and diminished social participation may be present.

Amnestic Syndrome. Amnesia may result from any pathological process that causes brain damage. The onset is usually fairly sudden, and the essential characteristic is impairment of short- and long-term memory. Elderly persons with amnestic syndrome may remember details of a decade ago but have no awareness of where they are presently residing.

Organic Delusional Syndrome. Delusions are the predominant feature of this syndrome. They occur in a normal state of consciousness and are due to a specific substance such as amphetamines, cannabis, and hallucinogens. The types of delusion vary, but the most common are persecutory. Individuals may be dangerous to themselves or others when reacting to delusions, and care must be taken to prevent harm. Organic syndrome delusions can occur at any age and are not more prevalent in the aged.

Organic Hallucinosis. A current persistent *hallucination* with no clouding of the consciousness is the major manifestation of an individual with organ hallucinosis. It can occur at any age. Prolonged use of alcohol is one of the most common causes. Hallucinogens, blindness, and deafness can also produce hallucinations that, depending on the underlying cause, can last from a few hours to several years. Individuals with this syndrome manifest no significant loss in intellectual abilities or any apparent disturbance in mood. The hallucinations range from pleasant to those causing severe anxiety and depression.

Organic Affective Syndrome. The essential characteristic of organic affective syndrome is a disturbance in mood resembling a manic episode or a major depressive episode that does not occur in a clouded state of consciousness. It is usually caused by toxic or metabolic factors and can occur at any age in mild to severe form. An elderly person with organic affective syndrome in a depressed mood may show fear, anxiety, suspiciousness, brooding or, in a manic mood, may manifest restlessness and irritability.

Organic Personality Syndrome. A change in behavior or personality occurs in this syndrome, usually due to brain damage from a head trauma or, most likely in the elderly, vascular disease. A common pattern is explosive temper outbursts, sudden crying spells, impairment in impulse control, poor social judgment, and sexual indiscretions. Another pattern is to show an apathy or indifference not characteristic of the individual.

Intoxication. Maladaptive behavior because of the recent use and presence in the body of a specific substance such as alcohol or amphetamines is the common manifestation. In elderly persons excess ingestion of the substance may cause a fall or involvement in accident and in coma or death if the substance has a depressant effect on the nervous system.

Withdrawal. This substance-specific syndrome occurs after the cessation or reduction in use of a substance that has been regularly used to induce intoxication. It varies according to the substance used. Common symptoms are unpleasant and include anxiety, restlessness, insomnia, impaired attention and, with some substances, nausea and vomiting; an individual may continue to use the substance to avoid these symptoms.

SUBSTANCE USE DISORDERS

These disorders refer to the maladaptive behavior associated with the fairly regular use of substances taken to alter mood or behavior. Many elderly persons manifest behavioral changes associated with regularly taking substances that affect the central nervous system; examples are alcohol, barbiturates, sedatives, opiates, cocaine, amphetamines, hallucinogens, cannabis, tobacco, and caffeine. Some of these have legitimate medicinal purposes but, when used without supervision, may cause extremely undesirable behavioral changes.

Substance Abuse

This term describes a pattern of pathological use that causes interference with social or occupational functioning in a disturbance that has lasted for 1 month (but is not necessarily manifested continuously throughout this time). Frequently individuals who develop *substance abuse* disorders also have preexisting personality problems or problems in personal and social interaction.

Substance Dependence

In this severe form of substance use disorder the user is physiologically dependent and develops a pattern of pathological use that causes impairment in functioning. Markedly increased amounts of the substance are required to achieve the desired effect and, in withdrawal, a specific syndrome follows. Some persons, the elderly included, inadvertently become physiologically dependent on a medicinal use of an opiate prescribed by a physician for relief of pain.

Alcohol Abuse

This pattern of pathological use of alcohol is the most common and widely recognized example of substance abuse and dependence that causes impairment in functioning. There are three main patterns: regular daily intake of large amounts, regular heavy weekend drinking, and long periods of sobriety interspersed with binges of daily heavy drinking for weeks or months. Once regular drinking is established, usually abuse develops within the next 5 years, but the elderly may be involved because many alcoholics begin drinking young and live to old age. In San Francisco a study of arrests of persons 60 years of age and older indicated more than 80 percent were for drunkenness. Behavioral changes, manifested in excessive use of alcohol, are often detrimental to interpersonal relations and to physical and mental health. Alcohol abuse is characterized by a loss of control when drinking begins and by a self-destructive attitude in relationships and situations.

THE FLESH IS WEAK

Ray N. was a 70-year-old Norwegian immigrant who had worked as a carpenter and was still working part-time on selected jobs. Because he was ambitious and conscientious and considered efficient and reliable, his services were still in demand. He lived with his wife who was arthritic and had two married sons who lived out of state. Having become confused and disoriented, he was picked up by the police while wandering along a major highway. He was unable to remember his name and address; his face was flushed; his speech, slurred; and his gait, unsteady.

After a medical examination he was diagnosed as having organic substance use disorder, alcohol abuse and was hospitalized briefly. He regained his abilities and continued to work part-time. His wife recalled that he recently had been having complaints of dizziness, headaches, and decreased physical and mental vigor. He had been consuming increasing amounts of alcohol over the past 2 months and reported to have been irritable and depressed. Referral was made to an alcohol treatment center for medical and psychological evaluation and treatment.

Alcoholism. No simple cause by itself appears sufficient to produce an alcoholic. Alcoholism, which is attributed to various physiological, social, physical, and cultural influences, is said to result from a disturbance and deprivation in early life. Or it is proposed that the alcoholic identifies, from some basic physiochemical responsiveness, with significant others who deal with life through habitual excessive use of alcohol. Also, some sociocultural influences creating inner *conflict,* anger, ambivalence, and guilt may result in the abuse of alcohol. Yet despite uncertainty about causes, the extent and effects are clear. After heart disease and cancer, alcoholism is the third leading health problem in the United States. Most deaths caused by alcoholism are due to cirrhosis of the liver. However, alcoholism can also cause heart disease and brain damage.

The most notable and dramatic effects of alcohol are those of behavior that are attributed to the action of alcohol on the brain. These effects are related to the concentration of alcohol in the blood and not necessarily to the amount consumed. At high levels of blood–alcohol concentration, greater brain depression occurs, resulting in lack of coordination, confusion, disorientation, stupor, anesthesia, coma, or death.

Malnutrition is one of the most serious consequences of alcoholism because the chronic alcoholic does not eat regularly or properly. Hence many alcoholics develop liver disease, which is related to poor diet, malnutrition, and possibly protein and vitamin deficiencies. If treated in the early stages, the individual can recover. However, if untreated, liver disease may become severe and irreversible (cirrhosis of the liver), causing death in approximately half the cases. Other physical disorders frequently seen in alcoholics are peripheral neuritis, requiring lengthy vitamin B treatment, gastritis, skin manifestations, and cardiovascular disorders.

Alcohol Withdrawal. Cessation of or reduction in alcohol consumption, following a prolonged spree in a chronic alcoholic, usually results in delirium. Delirium, which begins 2 to 7 days after the cessation of heavy drinking, is most likely related to metabolic disturbances and vitamin deficiences. It is characterized by restlessness, agitation, confusion, disorientation, vivid and frightening visual and auditory hallucinations, irritability, insomnia, tremors, dilated pupils, rapid pulse, and convulsive seizures. The prevailing mood is one of frightful apprehension and feelings of being watched and threatened—paranoia. The individual may experience terrifying visual hallucinations of animals, bugs, rats, or snakes. Serious in nature, delirium can be modified with hospitalization and treatment. Tranquilizers are most effective in lessening the anxiety, but death still occurs in some individuals, largely as a result of other illnesses present at the same time.

Alcohol Idiosyncratic Intoxication. Occasionally, a mentally unstable person, particularly one who has had brain injury or is hysterical or epileptic, will suffer from a transitory mental episode on drinking even a small amount of alcohol. The symptoms are more severe than ordinary drunkenness.

Alcohol Hallucinosis. This is a frequent complication of a persistent excessive indulgence in alcohol, characterized by vivid auditory hallucinosis following cessation of or reduction in alcohol ingestion. Symptoms are fear, apprehension, and auditory hallucinations, which are usually accusatory and threatening. Some individuals also have delusions and visual and olfactory hallucinations and may panic, become angry and depressed, arm themselves in self-defense, or attempt suicide. Recovery from alcohol hallucinosis usually occurs in less than a week, but occasionally, the episode continues for weeks or months or perhaps even as a chronic form. Recurrences are common if the individual again imbibes alcohol excessively.

Wernicke's Syndrome. This syndrome includes varying degrees of eye dysfunctions, inflammation of nerves, clouded consciousness, and a confused mental state. Wernicke's syndrome mainly occurs in chronic alcoholics but has also been described in persons with other diseases. The prevalent treatment is intensive vitamin therapy, particularly the administration of thiamine.

Korsakoff's Syndrome. This is a *confabulatory* (fictitious memories) amnesia syndrome (individual invents details to compensate for memory loss) with or without periphera neuritis. Usually associated with chronic alcoholism, it is also seen in individuals suffering from head injury, arteriosclerosis, and toxic reactions. Koraskoff's syndrome results from a vitamin B deficiency. There is permanent impairment and a degree of intellectual and emotional deterioration in some instances. Treatment of Korsakoff's syndrome involves hospitalization, abstinence from alcohol, and vitamin therapy. If irreversible structural damage has already occurred, it cannot be remedied by vitamins.

Dementia Associated with Alcoholism. The majority of the numerous alcoholics who consume excessive quantitites of alcohol over a long period of time, and who will not accept treatment or treatment has failed, suffer disintegration of personality and physical and mental deterioration. Deterioration of personality can be permanent and the dementia irreversible if the alcoholic continues the use of alcohol.

The "skid row" areas of cities represent a waste of suffering humanity, and treatment facilities must be found and made available to prevent alcoholics from deteriorating to the level of utter helplessness and death.

Treatment of Alcoholism. The difference between excessive drinking and becoming an alcoholic depends on the personality and other intangible characteristics of the individual rather than on the quantity of alcohol consumed. All excessive drinkers do not become alcoholics, but many do.

Alcoholics need help-treatment to overcome their problems. With an uncontrollable compulsion to drink, they are unable spontaneously to give up drinking, even though they are aware of doing great damage to themselves and their family. They manifest problems in mental and physical health, interpersonal relationships, and economic and social functioning–not being able to hold a job, suffering from malnutrition, cirrhosis of the liver, or other tissue damage, and alienating relatives and friends. Alcoholics may abstain from alcohol for a few days or longer, but inevitably revert to drinking, for they suffer from a type of withdrawal syndrome, physical and mental in nature, when drinking is halted for a period of time. The alcoholic is dependent on alcohol to relieve unbearable tensions, face problems, and seemingly, to function at all. However, with alcohol causing impairment of the ability to function, alcoholics may be quarrelsome, neglectful, demanding, often verbally abusive, and physically violent and a disruptive force in family living.

Early recognition of the symptoms of alcoholism facilitates treatment and recovery. The sooner the individual admits he or she has a problem and seeks help and treatment, the better will be the opportunity to solve the dilemma and face life realistically.

Treatment for the elderly alcoholic does not differ from that for the young alcoholic, including both medical and psychological care. A period of hospitalization that is sufficiently long to include a comprehensive treatment program may also be necessary. Such programs combine various therapies in a total team approach to a multifaceted problem to incorporate medical and psychological evaluation, treatment and psychotherapy, both individual and group sessions, family sessions, social rehabilitation, educational sessions on the nature of alcoholism, and attendance at Alcoholics Anonymous meetings.

SCHIZOPHRENIC DISORDERS

Newly developed schizophrenic disorders rarely occur in an older person, but some, who developed types of *schizophrenia* in earlier years, carry them into old age. Schizophrenia, one of the most common of the serious mental disorders, is the least understood. It represents a group of disorders characterized by fundamental disturbances in reality, difficulty in interpersonal relationships, and disturbances to varying degrees in affecting behavior, intellectual formulations and functions, and personality organization. The schizophrenic is recognizable by odd behavior and suspiciousness, immaturity, and emotional disharmony. He or she often makes unpredictable, inappropriate, emotional responses, and may suffer from *delusions* and hallucinations. There is an apparent deterioration in habit, social expectations, and personal self-regard and care in the severest forms of schizophrenia.

Some elderly schizophrenics have been hospitalized for several years, receiving only minimal treatment other than custodial care. In contemporary psychiatry, efforts are being made to provide treatment and rehabilitation promptly and to return the patient to the home and community as soon as possible. Outpatient treatment may be provided over an extended period.

AFFECTIVE DISORDERS

The most common disorders of old age are the affective disorders. These comprise a group of emotional disturbances, ranging from periods of mild *depression* to incapacitating illnesses. Mood disturbance may be one of elation or depression—even a full or partial manic-depressive syndrome. Recurrent periods of depression that may last from a few minutes to a few days or longer are common among the elderly. Typical symptoms of depression are discouragement, worry, fear, self-accusation, pessimism, diminished self-esteem, apathy, and indifference about the present and future.

Major Depressive Episode

A major depressive episode may occur when general depressive symptoms are magnified in intensity, extent, and duration. Some of the symptoms the individual may experience nearly every day or for a period of at least 2 weeks are: poor appetite or significant weight loss, insomnia or hypersomnia, psychomotor agitation or retardation, loss of pleasure or interest in usual activities; decrease in sexual drive, loss of energy, feelings of worthlessness, self-reproach, guilt, complaints of an inability to think or concentrate; indecisiveness; recurrent thought of death, and suicidal ideation. Depression may occur in response to significant losses, decline in physical vigor and mental agility, retirement, decline in income, and social isolation. The loss of spouse, relatives, and friends through death or separation may be the most difficult experience of all. The withdrawal of narcissistic nurturance by loved ones may result in depression, with the older person feeling everything is lost and there is nothing worth living for. However, the impact of events in life depends on the individual's personality, previous life experiences, and present circumstances. Anger and hostile impulses are usually an important element in all depressions and may become self-directed in the form of self-accusations and guilt. Depressive symptoms may persist without relief, and severe anxiety may manifest itself in body tremors or agitation, pacing, hand-wringing, clawing at clothing, and possible attempts at self-mutilation or suicide.

One of the highest rates of suicide in the United States occurs in the elderly (about 8000 yearly, aged 65 years and older). Doubtless, varying degrees of depression may contribute. Any threat of suicide by a depressed individual, young or old, should be taken seriously.

Effective treatment should be obtained to alleviate the depression and to provide the elderly with meaningful activities, friendships, relationships, interests and a sense of purpose, usefulness, and direction for daily living.

Psychotherapy, drug therapy, and hospitalization have been effective in the treatment of depression. Antidepressant drugs can be very useful in treating older persons, but they must be monitored closely for side effects, which may affect the central nervous and cardiovascular systems.

Manic Episode

Although the depressive episodes predominate among the affective disorders in older people, manic episodes do occur in old age. In a manic episode the individual manifests manic symptoms exclusively, characterized by a predominant mood of excessive elation, optimism, irritability, talkativeness, and hyperactivity, with euphoria, accelerated speech, and motor activity. Brief periods of depression may occur, but the euphoria returns quickly with a flight of ideas. The hyperactivity often involves excessive planning of and participation in activities.

Psychotherapy and institutionalization are helpful in the treatment of manic illnesses. The use of lithium carbonate in drug therapy in the last decade has been effective but requires careful monitoring in old people because of caridac, renal, and other complications that may contraindicate its use.

PARANOID DISORDERS

Persistent delusions, with either persecution or jealousy as essential features, are frequent in old age and are manifested in disturbances of mood, behavior, and thinking.

Acute paranoid disorders are usually of short duration, often less than 6 months, and tend to occur under adverse social conditions such as isolation, imprisonment, and solitary confinement. In the elderly, deafness, sensory defects, and blindness can create isolation and are thought to contribute to the development of paranoid disorders. When vision or hearing decline, older persons may perceive their surroundings as vague, hostile, and threatening, and compensating for the deprivation, they may create a new world to fill the void. Paranoid projections are often of hostile intent. The elderly often blame others close to them for their problems, thus providing an excuse for their own failures. "They" are responsible for my problems. "They" are plotting against me. "Someone is spying on me"; "the neighbors are stealing from me"; "relatives are trying to poison me." These paranoid persons can be dangerous. Common associated features include resentment and anger, which may lead to violence.

Several theories have been suggested to explain the development of paranoid disorders. One theory that seems more acceptable than a single factor approach is that paranoid disorders are the result of family and interpersonal distortions and a deep-seated sense of insecurity. Perhaps older paranoid persons, unable to experience intimacy in relationships in earlier years, may have manifested personality characteristics of insecurity, sensitivity, fearfulness of a threatening environment, and uncertainty. Some may be considered as angry or suspicious types, cranks, eccentrics, and thus, being difficult to get along with, encounter more hostility and fewer opportunities than others to develop relationships.

For the elderly person in contemporary society, however, life in many urban areas is inimical and dangerous. Muggings, robberies, assaults, and murder are commonplace. What may appear to be paranoid behavior, therefore, could well be a reaction to fearful and unbearable anxiety resulting from physical, emotional, and environmental stressors. Professional evaluation could help to ascertain the severity of the disorder.

Treatment of Elderly Paranoid Patients

These individuals rarely seek treatment and are often brought for care by relatives or governmental agencies. Reducing anxiety is an immediate treatment goal with paranoid persons. Psychotherapeutic intervention, combined with drug therapy and minimizing the threat of the environment, may assist in achieving a more favorable adjustment for the individual.

Treatment may also be directed at restoring the patient's self-esteem. A therapeutic relationship and empathetic understanding of the individual's life situation may be most helpful. Exploration should be made to provide the elderly with safe, adequate housing, which is relatively familiar and uncomplicated. Checking for eyeglasses to correct visual defects and/or hearing aids to improve auditory losses is also necessary wherever possible. Other elderly paranoid individuals may require other medical care, physical or activity therapy, financial assistance, social service, or additional forms of concrete assistance.

ANXIETY DISORDERS

Excessive and disabling anxiety, evoking in certain persons emotional and behavioral disturbances, is the predominant characteristic in this group of disorders. The anxiety represents persistent fear that arises from known and unknown sources but may be related to emotional conflicts, frustration, or impending threat. Patterns of response, designed by the individual to manage subjective feelings of discomfort arising from anxiety, may significantly disrupt or incapacitate daily functioning. Inordinate amounts of energy, expended in attempts to cope with anxiety, may be ineffective. Certain anxiety disorders are more common among the elderly. Emotional responses to problems that give rise to stress and conflict tend to become intensified for older persons.

Generalized Anxiety Disorder

The essential characteristic feature of generalized anxiety disorder is pervasive, persistent anxiety of at least a month's duration, yet impairment in social functioning is rarely more than mild and recovery is likely. Although specific manifestations vary, the individual is usually tense, frequently expresses physical complaints, and generally has signs of motor tension, autonomic hyperactivity, and apprehension.

The anxiety may occur under any circumstances and is not restricted to specific situations or objects. This disorder must be distinguished from normal apprehension or fear, which occurs in realistically dangerous situations. Anxiety disorder is an exaggeration of reasonable fear. It may be described as a fear of impending disaster, heightened by feelings of insecurity, and a fear of death that may result from any situation that may threaten the personality, or any frustration or crisis related to areas of adjustment, such as vocation, marriage, or sex. With apparent minimum of effective defensive processes, the person with severe anxiety usually feels inadequate to meet the demands and to cope with the problems of life. Many of these individuals are characteristically overly sensitive to the opinions of others, fearful of making mistakes, scrupulous, and prone to feelings of inferiority. If the anxiety becomes increasingly perturbing, it may be expressed in a rapid pulse rate, headaches, fatigue, as well as panic states, suicidal ideas, loss of interest and motivation, difficulties in focusing attention, and outbursts of aggressiveness.

The indicated form of treatment is psychotherapy, focusing on the evaluation of the person's personality and the situations that create frustration and *tension*, in order to uncover the underlying and unrecognized sources of anxiety. Tranquilizing medication may be administered to provide symptomatic relief from the distressing anxiety.

Depressive symptoms that are most common in elderly persons and often associated with incapacitating or painful physical disease may be related to the anxiety state. Symptoms may also be precipitated by a situation such as a grief or a loss sustained by the person or possibly associated with deep-seated guilt feelings for past failures or misdeeds. The extent of the depressive symptoms depends on the person's ambivalence toward the loss (person or object), as well as on the realistic circumstances of the particular loss. Individuals most prone to depressive symptoms have usually had feelings of inadequacy prior to the situation precipitating the depression. Some may unconsciously use their symptoms to elicit sympathy from others.

Panic Disorders

Recurrent *panic attacks* that may occur unpredictably at nonspecific times characterize panic disorders. Usually occurring frequently and not precipitated by exposure to a life-threatening situation, this condition is common in the elderly. Older persons tend to find these attacks quite frightening and upsetting. The attacks are manifested by a sudden onset of intense apprehension, fear or terror and generally last for minutes or a few hours, but in some cases, for several months. If they have recurred frequently, the individual becomes fearful of being both left alone or in public places.

Obsessive Compulsive Disorders

The manifested characteristics of an obsessive compulsive disorder are recurrent obsessions and compulsions, persistent ideas, thoughts, images, and impulses. These thoughts are not voluntarily produced and attempts to evade or suppress them may be futile. Often, these obsessive ideas are repugnant and illogical, the most common being iteration of thoughts of infection, contamination, and harm or violence inflicted on or by another person. Obsessions represent unconscious attempts to control anxiety by the intrusion of repetitive thoughts. Compulsions are acts or behaviors that are ritually performed repeatedly in an attempt to prevent some future calamity. The behavior, senseless, and unpleasant, may provide a temporary release of tension, and thus may diminish anxiety somewhat. Individuals may go to great lengths to avoid objects, places, or people, and certain items or materials may be perceived as a source of contamination to be avoided.

Much of the content of obsessions and compulsions of the elderly is morbid or irrational, a significant source of distress to the individual, and tends to interfere with social functioning. Those affected may constantly think that some physical harm awaits them or that others are ''watching'' their house, apartment, mail, or garden for malevolent purposes. These obsessions and compulsions are likely to persist as long as the older individual is unable to understand and manage the underlying cause precipitating the anxiety.

Phobic Disorders

Phobias are persistent irrational fears of specific objects, activities, or situations that result in an intense desire to avoid the dreaded object, activity, or situation. The individual, although possibly recognizing that the fear is unreasonable and excessive and may grossly interfere with functioning, may avoid the situation in which he or she would be exposed to possible criticism or humiliation by others. If the object of the *fear* is an integral part of daily interpersonal interactions, the individual may be unable to function successfully. For example, if the older person's relationship with a spouse becomes highly stressful and anxiety becomes unbearable, a phobia toward the object (the spouse) may appear. The phobia may represent a symbolic way of dealing with the real source of anxiety. When exposed to the phobia stimulus, after avoidance, the individual may become overwhelmingly fearful and experience symptoms similar to those described in a panic attack.

The impairment to the older person may be minimal if the phobic object is easily avoided. However, if this is not possible, the incapacity may be considerable.

SOMATOFORM DISORDERS

This group of disorders as manifested in the elderly suggest physical symptoms for which there are not demonstrable organic findings or known physical causation. There is positive indication that the symptoms are related to psychological factors or conflicts. The major somatoform disorder observed in the older population is hypochondriasis.

Hypochondriasis

Hypochondriasis is frequent among older people, particularly the women, and is manifested in a preoccupation with one's own body and fear of presumed disease or malfunctioning of various organs. An elderly person may be overly concerned and acutely sensitive to any irregularities in physical and mental functioning and may go to extremes to safeguard his or her health.

The predominant disturbance of hypochondriasis is an unrealistic interpretation of physical signs or sensations that lead to a preoccupation with and persistence of the fear or belief of having a serious disease, despite medical evaluation, and which may cause social malfunctioning. These individuals generally shop around for a doctor who can provide a proper diagnosis and treatment. Frustration and anger at medical professions are common feelings when continued evaluation does not support a diagnosis of physical disorder.

Hypochondriasis in the elderly also may be a means of social interaction and communication with others who can provide attention, care, and interest. It represents a withdrawal of psychic interest from other objects and persons to a focus on self—one's own body and its functioning. An older person who has experienced anxiety over the loss of spouse, job, financial security, status, and prestige may find it more acceptable to show concern over bodily processes and functioning.

A treatment approach that can provide an opportunity for the older person to share anxieties and concerns in an understanding, *empathetic* atmosphere can be most helpful. It may also be conducive to directing the individual to examine the real reasons for the intolerable anxiety and to develop insight into his or her situation. Although the individual may gradually lose the intensity or the bodily preoccupation as a result of therapy, symptoms may be exacerbated when critical life situations mount.

PERSONALITY DISORDERS

Personality disorders are a broad group of disorders in which inflexible and maladaptive personality traits are exhibited that cause personal distress of significant impairment in functioning. These traits demonstrate a lifelong pattern of perceiving and relating to oneself and one's unique environment. The maladaptive behaviors that are deeply ingrained and generally recognized in adolescence continue throughout adult life. Elderly persons with personality disorders may express dissatisfaction with their inability to function effectively and the effect of their behavior on others.

Personality disorders can be classified by the specific features that adequately describe the individual's disturbed personality functioning. A wide group of personality disorders such as paranoid, schizoid, schizotypal, histronic, narcissistic, antisocial, avoidant, dependent, compulsive, and passive-aggressive personality disorders, serve different adaptive functions for the individual.

The essential characterisitics of persons with a passive-aggressive personality disorder is a resistance to demands made on them in performance and functioning. Resenting and opposing such demands, they express their resistance indirectly through behaviors such as procrastination, stubbornness, purposeful forgetfulness, and passive resistance. Individuals with this disorder are often dependent and lack self-confidence. The passive-resistant behavior seriously impairs both social and interpersonal functioning.

PROFESSIONAL EVALUATION AND TREATMENT

An elderly person who seems depressed, withdrawn, and exhibits any of the symptoms of mental impairment in social or emotional functioning for an extended period of time without improvement should be encouraged to seek professional help for evaluation of the problem. Elderly persons may be defensive and angry at the suggestion that they need help and may insist that they can work it out by themselves. Perceiving outside assistance as an indication of personal weakness, they may believe that with time they can mobilize their physical and mental resources to cope with their problems. Very often, individuals who are experiencing manifestations of intense stress and anxiety are unaware of their irrational behavior and the effect and consequences of their actions on others. Denial involving the refusal to admit or accept the existence of erratic and maladaptive behavior may prevent a person from seeking and obtaining professional evaluation and needed treatment.

In some cases elderly people are more willing to accept physical illness than mental disorders. A stigma attached to mental illness and psychiatric treatment seems to persist in some segments of society. Many people do not readily understand individuals with emotional problems and may tend to become fearful, impatient, and annoyed with their patterns of maladjustment. Although many older people may not hesitate to seek medical help for a suspected physical illness, they are unaware, misinformed, and suspicious of psychiatric evaluation and treatment.

A person in need of help, however, has a number of resources available, for some mental disorders can be cured. Individuals with emotional problems can receive assistance from professional mental health workers to manage and cope with fear and anxiety effectively and to live meaningful, satisfying lives. There has been a steady growth in theory and practice in the treatment of mental disorders in the elderly, with emphasis on the rehabilitative possibilities. Comprehensive evaluations of older persons suffering from emotional distress is gaining wider acceptance, and genuine therapeutic efforts on their behalf are being accepted as needed and worthwhile activities.

Mental Health Evaluation

A mental health evaluation should provide information on the diagnosis of the mental disorder, the cause of the illness, the complications to be expected, the extent of impairment of the disorder, the predisposing factors, and a recommended plan of treatment.

A comprehensive evaluation should also consider an understanding of the total person and the problem, for an emotional disorder may have multiple ramifications. The problems older persons present are often not their major ones. They may be unaware of the actual problems. In order to plan effectively for treatment—whether for crises intervention, brief service or extended service, or referral for other evaluative tests—comprehensive evaluation should be undertaken.

The gathering of information should be made so that it ensures comprehensiveness and at the same time is flexible. A spontaneous, harmonious responsiveness is most conducive to the establishment of an effective therapeutic relationship. Rapport between the elderly person and the therapist should not be underestimated.

Psychotherapy

The goal of therapy is to help an individual to improve his or her behavior and functioning. Through the treatment process, the person may develop an understanding of self and thus be able to cope more adequately with anxiety and stress. The dynamic therapeutic process can release emotional energy for developing and maintaining relationships and help to remotivate the person. Mobilization of the individual's inner resources toward a healthy pursuit of interests, work, and activities commensurate with their unique intelligence, skill, and capacity is a primary objective of therapy. If psychotherapy is recommended for the older adult, there are several modalities of psychotherapy that could be considered: individual therapy, group therapy, family therapy, and environmental therapy.

Individual Therapy. Individual psychotherapy can be most helpful to older people, who need the opportunity to talk on a one-to-one basis and to have an objective, empathetic listener. Also a therapist can be supportive to a person in old age who may be experiencing frequent, profound multiple crises. The elderly can be receptive to psychotherapy and often are strongly motivated to diminish incapacitating anxiety and to resolve their problems. The capacity to find satisfaction in old age can be demonstrated in the therapeutic process, for the elderly gain from insight and knowledge, reevaluating some of the patterns of their life.

Group Therapy. Group therapy, which is becoming more widely used in institutions, nursing homes, hospitals, and outpatient services, can be a valuable experience. It utilizes psychotherapeutic principles and techniques as well as group process dynamics. Group therapy has its own applicability and is a powerful psychotherapeutic technique in itself. Usually, sociability and emotional ventilation are main objectives in group therapy, but management of behavior and adaptation are also major considerations for the elderly in institutional settings. Imparting information, developing socializing techniques, interpersonal interactions, and group cohesiveness are other important objectives of group therapy for older people. The role of the therapist in group therapy may be active or passive and involves various functions, from active listening to questioning, explaining, interpreting, supporting, reassuring, and confronting. Some see the role of the therapist as a catalyst to facilitate emotional interchange, and to deal constructively with anger and anxiety.

Family Therapy. The family of an elderly person, if available and interested, should be considered in any therapeutic plan unless for any reason it would seem to be contraindicated. It is not unusual for a son or a daughter to bring a parent in for evaluation of a mental disorder or emotional disturbance, some problems in functioning and disturbed family relationships may have prompted the family to seek help. The therapist may decide to see the family together, particularly if decisions must be made that will affect the entire family or if there is conflict among family members and if there is a need for the individual's continuing care and involvement. The therapist may bring together those residing in the same household as well as family members living separately. Family therapy can be very helpful in providing elderly family members with an opportunity to verbalize their concerns about themselves, their children, and grandchildren in a therapeutic forum with an objective therapist present.

Environmental Therapy. Environmental therapy is the term used to encompass the various activities that may be necessary to mobilize and influence social and community resources in behalf of an adult client. Mental health workers may become actively involved in advocacy programs and employment services or in causing political organizations and consumer groups to support the needs, grievances, and rights of the elderly. Actively seeking objectives through political and social participation can be a source of satisfaction and increased self-esteem for older people.

Summary

Most elderly people are able to function effectively and do not exhibit maladaptive patterns of thought or behavior in late maturity. However, the incidence of mental disorder does increase in the period of old age. Mental disorders refer to the constellation of psychological or behavioral symptoms and patterns that occur in an individual. They are associated with distress or impairment in functioning and are manifested by disturbances in behavior, thought, mood, and biological dysfunction.

The mental disorders are grouped descriptively by the manifestations of the specific mental disorders according to the classification in the *Diagnostic and Statistical Manual of Mental Disorders* (3rd ed.), *DSM-III*. The descriptive approach consists of presenting the characteristic features of the disorder and the identifiable behavioral signs of symptoms that may be observed in older people.

Individuals with organic mental disorders manifest symptoms of psychological or behavioral abnormalities that are associated with transient or permanent dysfunction of the brain. By means of a history, physical examination or laboratory test, the presence of a specific organic factor may be demonstrated to be related to the mental state. Differences in clinical manifestation reflect the localization, mode of onset, progression, duration, and nature of the underlying pathological process. The organic factor responsible for an organic mental disorder may be a primary disease of the brain or a systemic illness that secondarily affects the brain. A toxic agent or a substance may also be a factor that is currently disturbing brain function or has left some long-lasting effect.

Organic mental disorder encompasses a wide range of organic brain symptoms. Some of the important disorders related to aging, primary degenerative dementia and multi-infarct dementia, are characterized by a loss of intellectual abilities of sufficient severity to interfere with social functioning. The deficit involves memory, judgment, abstract thought, and a variety of other functions, including possible changes in behavior and personality. Dementia may be progressive, static or remitting. The reversibility of a dementia is a function of the underlying pathological process and the availability, effectiveness, and timeliness of treatment.

The substance use disorders are those mental disturbances that result in behavioral changes associated with more or less regular use of substances that affect the central nervous system. The behavioral changes include: impairment in social functioning as a result of substance use; inability to control use of or to stop taking the substance and the development of withdrawal symptoms such as "shakes" and malaise after cessation of or reduction in substance use. Personality disturbance and disturbance of mood are often present and may be intensified by the substance use disorder. Five classes of substances are associated with both abuse and dependence: alcohol, barbiturates or similarly acting sedatives or hypnotics, opiates, amphetamines, and cannabis. Some of these and other substances, such as amphetamines, barbiturates, opiates, and tranquilizers are used medicinally. Many long-term users become physically and psychologically dependent without realizing it. Clearly, elderly persons need help to avoid the misuse of substances.

The schizophrenic disorders are a group of disorders in which the characterisic symptoms involve multiple psychological processes and deterioration from a previous level of functioning. Schizophrenic disorders always involve delusions, hallucinations, or certain thought disturbances. The delusions have no basis in fact and may be somatic, grandiose, or religious in content. Persecutory delusions may be accompanied by hallucinations. Also, auditory hallucinations may be present in which two or more voices converse with each other. The individual with a schizophrenic disorder may be incoherent and illogical in thought with a marked poverty in speech content. Other prominent symptoms are: social isolation or withdrawal, marked impairment in role functioning, inappropriate affect, and marked impairment in personal grooming.

Paranoid disorders are marked by the presence of persistent persecutory delusions or delusional jealousy in an individual. Other associated features include anger and resentment. Often there are social isolation, suspiciousness, seclusiveness, and complaint about injustices with threats of legal action. Intellectual functioning is usually preserved, but social and marital functioning is often impaired.

Affective disorders are a group of disorders in which there is a disturbance of mood, accompanied by a full or partial manic or depressive syndrome, each with characteristic symptoms. The manic episode is manifested by distinct periods in which an expansive, elated mood is prominent. During this period there may be a significant increase in activity, restlessness, excessive talking, and flight of ideas. The depressive episode may be characterized by a depressed mood that is relatively persistent. Other symptoms associated with the depressive episode may include: appetite disturbance, sleep disturbance, psychomotor agitation or retardation, and fatigue. Thoughts of death are common. Typical depressive expressions of an elderly person might include "I have nothing to live for," "life is over for me," or "I wish I were dead." There is a loss of interest and pleasure in activities and there may be a withdrawal from friends, family, and other social contacts. Also, a sense of worthlessness and guilt may be present. The elderly person may complain of difficulty in concentrating and of a loss of memory. Major depressive episodes are common mental disorders in the older population.

In the group of anxiety disorders, anxiety is the predominant disturbance. In elderly persons who suffer from these disorders, there exists an intense fear of a specific object, activity, or a situation that may result in a compelling desire to avoid the threatening object, activity, or situation. The fear may be recognized as excessive, but the individual is unable to cope effectively. The fear and anxiety have a significant effect on life adjustment. Phobic disorders represent an irrational fear that may be far from the actual threat or danger of the specific object, activity, or situation. Panic disorders are recurrent attacks of anxiety that are characterized by intense apprehension or terror. Common symptoms experienced during the attack may be heart palpitations, choking, chest pain, dizziness, faintness, and trembling. The elderly person during the attack may feel tense or helpless, with a loss of control.

Obsessive compulsive disorders are marked by recurrent obsessions and compulsions. The common repetitive thoughts or impulses (obsessions) may be senseless and uncontrollable. Compulsions, repetitive behaviors that are performed according to certain rules, are an attempt to provide a release of tension. When an individual attempts to resist a compulsion, there is an increased feeling of stress. Such disorders are a significant source of distress to the individual and may interfere with social and role functioning.

Somatoform disorders are a group of disorders in which there are physical symptoms suggesting physical disorders, but for which there is no evidence of organic causation. The essential characteristics of the somatoform disorders are recurrent and multiple somatic complaints of several years duration. The complaints are often presented in a dramatic, vague, or exaggerated manner or are part of a complicated medical history with physical evaluation considered without organic findings.

Manifestations of personality disorder are recognized by personality patterns that are inflexible, maladaptive, and cause distress and significant impairment in social functioning. The personality disorders, characteristic of an individual's current and long-term functioning, are grouped according to the essential features of the disorder.

If emotional problems and symptoms of mental disorder persist beyond a reasonable period of time, a mental health evaluation should be considered. An evaluation would provide a method for approaching the problems of the elderly, arriving at decisions as to what is happening, and what can be done to solve the problems or to alleviate the distress. The older person and the mental health worker together try to discover whether the problems are from personality factors, mental disorders, personal reactions to situations, or environmental stressors in the individual's life experience. The person's historical data and current physical, social, and psychological functioning, gathered together, can provide necessary material for assessment and evaluation. On the basis of an evaluation, effective decisions can be made for reasonable, achievable treatment plans.

FURTHER READINGS

Birren, J., and J. Renner, "Research on the Psychology of Aging," in J. Birren and K. W. Schaie (eds.), *Handbook of the Psychology of Aging,* Van Nostrand Reinhold, New York, 1977.

Birren, J., and B. Sloane, "Manpower and Training Needs in Mental Health and Illness of the Aging." A Report to the Gerontological Society for the Committee to Study Mental Health and Illness of the Aging, for the Secretary of the Department of Health, Education and Welfare, 1977.

Butler, R. N., and M. I. Lewis, *Aging and Mental Health,* C. V. Mosby, St. Louis, 1973.

Diagnostic and Statistical Manual of Mental Disorders (3rd ed.), American Psychiatric Association, Washington, D.C., 1980.

Havighurst, R., B. Neugarten, and S. Tobin, "Disengagement and Patterns of Aging," in B. Neugarten (ed.), *Middle Age and Aging: A Reader in Social Psychology,* University of Chicago Press, Chicago, 1968.

Kalish, R. *Late Adulthood: Perspectives on Human Development.* Brooks/Cole, Monterey, Calif., 1975.

Kimmel, D. *Adulthood and Aging,* Wiley, New York, 1974.

Kuhlen, R. H. "Developmental Changes in Motivation during the Adult Years," in B. Neugarten (ed.), *Middle Age and Aging: A Reader in Social Psychology.* University of Chicago Press, Chicago, 1968.

8

Family and Friendship Networks of Older People

Older people experience change in important areas of their lives, and a growing number of workers in the field of gerontology have begun to pursue the question of how changes in aging affects the personality. Can regularities of change be discerned? If so, are they to be regarded as developmental or as the result of environmental and social situations that occur at successive points in the life cycle? This chapter examines some of the changes that occur in the elderly and the effects of these experiences on the personality.

Early relationships within the family mold personality structure in ways that affect future behavior. The personality structure takes form in early interaction within the family and tends to develop according to patterns established in childhood. The dynamic elements of personality are reflected in interpersonal relationships within the family and subsequently with significant others. This chapter examines some of the factors in the dynamics of the relationship between the self and others.

This chapter focuses on some major life events such as grandparenthood and widowhood to examine them in regard to precipitating changes. With new intergenerational family relations emerging in the United States, the new roles of grandparents, adult children, and grandchildren are manifestations of companionship within an area of social life. The vitality and meaning of family relations to the older person is evident when consideration is given to the loneliness of the widowed, especially those lacking the emotional support of their children.

It has been found that certain personality traits are powerful assets to adaptation. The personality of an older individual, self-concept, and social interaction can be pivotal factors in successful aging and coping well. This chapter looks at how social intervention can enhance the psychological well-being of the elderly.

It is through the family that the unique process of *socialization* first takes place. In our society the family is for almost all persons a valued possession. There are many characteristics of the family that make it a cherished social group to family members. Emotional support through a mutual expression of love and affection is usually first obtained in the family. American society places a high value on love and caring, and people enter relationships expecting to find and maintain love and affection. Also, the family provides an environment in which members engage in interdependent activities, share experiences, and enjoy mutual companionship. The family can be viewed as the most significant primary group with a discernible structure. It is a network of intimate interpersonal face-to-face relationships where informal communication takes place. In the family, individuals are significant to others and are loved and treated compassionately. It is within this environment that the unique process of socialization of the individual comes into existence.

SOCIALIZATION

Each individual is a social being, and as such engages continually in complex interpersonal and intrapersonal processes. The process by which one learns to share in the culture of society where values and expectations are transmitted by one generation to the next to make society ongoing is called *socialization*. In this dynamic process the individual learns what society expects, accepts, and demands and what role behaviors are appropriate. This complex socialization process is as yet only partially understood, but through a gradual development process, the individual learns to acquire skills; to use and understand objects in the environment; and to identify, respond, and communicate with people.

The acquisition of language, communication, and thinking processes enables the person to participate in intimate social interaction and to develop awareness of self. Communication permits subtle and influential interaction between persons and is a major factor in the development of a self. The new human being experiences an external process or authority that controls and compels the actions of others, thus becoming conscious of others. In this learning process the individual, who discovers in the early stages of development that there is also a self, gradually, responds to this self, even as he or she responds to other persons. To respond to, evaluate, approve or disapprove of self, requires an ability to look at the self as an object. This capacity develops through social interaction and a growing ability enables the individual to view the self from the persepctive of another—to imagine how the self appears to others. This concept formulation was one of the first efforts to understand the development of the self as a consequence of social interaction, language, and mind and has profoundly influenced our understanding of the relation of the elderly person to society.

Mead postulated that the *interaction* between the child and a significant other, such as the mother, involves learning the attitudes that are expressed in words that convey emotional responses of liking and disliking, approving and disapproving. Language opens up the complex world of symbolic communication; the child learns to speak like others, to use language to convey ideas and feelings, and to respond in a similar fashion. For Mead, this meant that, by taking on the roles of others in particular, such as mother or father, the individual learns how they respond to objects around them. These responses are internalized. By assuming the roles of significant others, the individual learns to feel and think as they do. Later on in the developmental process the person takes on the role(s) of "generalized others" and has general expectations of performance for others and the self. This capacity for self-judgment indicates that the individual now has a self that developed through the individual's social interactions and constitutes a pattern of personal actions and responses that may be called the self-concept.

Self-Concept

The self involves those human processes by which an individual internally answers the questions: Who am I? What do I want? How will I attain my desires? The self refers to an awareness of what one shares with and how one differs from others. The self arises only by human social interaction through communication and experience. Development of the self is a dynamic process that begins in early infancy and remains an important influence throughout the adult years and continuously develops and changes, providing a source of continuity and creativity for the person. The network of interactions and the relationship to the self are especially useful for understanding the individual in adult years and old age.

Social Roles

An adult's self may be characterized by a diverse range of social roles, that the individual enacts because, in the process of the development of the self, the person learns to perform various social roles. The concept of role is related to the person's social position and the expectations of the society (norms). A role can be described as the set of behaviors expected from a person occupying a particular social position. An individual learns the expected role behaviors of mother, father, sister, brother, son, daughter in the social interaction that takes place in the family or with significant others. This learning process arises from taking the attitude of another and internalizing it toward one's own behavior. Thus as life progresses an individual enacts many roles in the course of a day, assuming possibly the behavior of a father, a husband, a son, a grandfather, a professional worker, and a student. Each role involves expected norms and differs in expectations of behavior at different age periods. Role behavior is an integral part of any individual or family, and society prescribes appropriate roles for each family member and relative. Each has a position or status in the family, and the family as a whole has a status in the community. Role expectations change through the developmental life cycle. What is expected of the father role when offspring are in the infant stage of development would not be expected of the father when the infant is in the adolescent stage. Role changes in which certain roles are added, expanded, changed, or dropped are particularly relevant to a discussion of old age where there are significant role modifications and role shifts. An elderly woman may have experienced a range of role changes in the family and, at the same time, have another set of role shifts in work and other activities. For example, a woman may have been a teenage daughter, unmarried single, wife, mother, grandmother, and widow, while in her career she may have been a student, teacher, retired worker, and part-time author.

Social roles form the basis of an individual's identity and are essential to the maintenance of positive feelings toward the self. As an individual approaches later maturity, there is a tendency, not always through choice, to become disengaged from those activities and social roles that have become a critical component of self-identity. It is rather common for the aged to go through a period of adjustment after retirement, with the loss of an important social role, which often means a shift to a lower status, a downward mobility. Similarly, divorce or widowhood may bring about a shift in social status, leading to a change in norms and expectations for the new role. Therefore, to maintain positive feelings toward self, an elderly person must adopt other meaningful social roles to replace those that have been lost. An involvement in new activities, interests, and relationships may provide opportunity for the development of new roles necessary for a continuity in feelings of a positive self identity, but to do so these activities must call for a degree of personal commitment and offer gratification. To a great extent most older people do avoid the profound devastation that frequently accompanies loss or disengagement of significant roles.

Interaction processes continue through the adult years, socialization is never complete, and personality is never fixed. As individuals and families move through periods of the life cycle, older people continue to grow and fill different social roles and tasks that relate to family, friendship, and community. As role configurations change in the second half of the life cycle, these changes affect interrelationships among the individual, the family, and the sociocultural environment.

THE FAMILY LIFE CYCLE

Interpersonal relations of husband and wife and of older parents and their married children can be viewed from the perspective of the family life cycle. This method permits a description of changes in marital roles from marriage in the early years through the middle and later years. This analysis also reveals some of the critical situations faced by individuals at different periods in the life cycle.

The developmental approach emphasizes the sequences in the family life cycle, of which the most systematic and widespread use is formulated by Evelyn M. Duvall (1971), who provided a clarification of the developmental-task concept. Developmental tasks will arise during certain periods in an individual's life. Successful achievement of a certain group of tasks results in success with subsequent tasks, but failure to achieve them may lead to unhappiness, subsequent disapproval by society and probably difficulty in handling later ones. These tasks have two primary origins: physical maturation and social pressures and privileges.

Duvall (1971) contended that, like individuals, families also have tasks that arise at a certain stage in the life cycle. The family's developmental task may be described as a growth responsibility that emerges at a particular stage in the life of a family. Successful achievement will result in satisfaction and will lay the groundwork for success with later tasks in the family, but failure in the developmental task may result in failure and unhappiness in the family unit. With concomitant societal disapproval there may be difficulty in achieving later developmental tasks. Therefore in order for families to continue to grow as a unit, they need to satisfy biological requirements, cultural imperatives, and personal aspirations and values at a given stage. The family developmental tasks are numerous and complex.

Duvall's family cycle consists of eight stages: married couples without children, childbearing families, families with preschool children, families with school children, families with teenagers, families as launching center (first child gone to last child leaving home), middle-aged parents (empty nest to retirement), aging family members (retirement to death of both spouses).

Every family, however, does not fit into this pattern because there is no smooth progression from one stage to the next. Many situations, such as death of spouse, divorce, disability, or other events may arise that might interrupt progress; moreover, there are overlapping stages and many variations in families.

Although this scheme of family development has limitations, it serves as a method of study and a frame of reference, indicating that all family groups have roles, which change over time. It emphasizes the basis idea that tasks are essential for families to exist and function and that change in any part of the system brings about change in other parts of the system. It shares with other points of view the importance of positions, roles, and interaction processes.

Middle Age and the Transition to Old Age

Middle age in our society had been frequently delineated as between 30 and 60 years; 45 to 65 years has been found more useful for demographic purposes. Middle age is, also, to a great extent, defined by functional position in life, a time when most people are engaged in providing a livelihood for a family and completing the task of raising children. People in the middle years are often in commanding positions in our society in terms of power, influence, norms, and decisions. Constituting 40 percent of the population, they carry some responsibility for the population over 65 and the half of the population under 25.

The middle years usually start around the time of the departure of the children from the home and continue until the beginning of retirement. The average married couple has a period of approximately 14 years between the departure of their last child and the death of the spouse. In our society a couple who had children while in their twenties or early thirties will have about 20 years or more of active life to anticipate and to plan for after the children are grown.

Two themes that appear to predominate in midlife are the growing awareness of personal aging and the changes in life pattern that occur as children grow up and leave the home, parents grow old, and the middle-aged assume new personal and social roles.

Developmental Tasks of Middle Age

These tasks may vary with sex, class, age status, social structure, age norms, age expectations, marital status, and family size (if any). Very different life-styles are possible, given variables in these major areas.

Important middle-aged tasks that seem to cut across these variations are: maintaining and contributing to cultural institutions; maintaining generational bonds and boundaries (with children, parents, and relatives); maintaining interpersonal relationships; redefining one's self; coming to grips with a changing body and declining physical capacities; and formulating and implementing a philosophy of life based on older experiences. Those who age most successfully in midlife are those who begin to use their minds and to achieve mental-based values in their self-definition and behavior.

Another major issue in the middle years seems to be the ability to master experience and to achieve a degree of detached perspective, using them as provisional guides to the solution of new problems. Many, however, may appear to grow increasingly inflexible, set in their opinions and closed to new ideas—a tendency that becomes a critical issue by the middle years.

Developmental Tasks of Later Life

The developmental tasks of later life are more difficult to fulfill than those of middle years. Even the elderly see late life adjustment as a subjective state of mind related to past successes and failures. Studies have shown that the elderly who live to over one hundred years recall a period of threat and emotional reorganization during their 70s and that, in studies of adult development up through 65 years, increasing concern in advancing age was found with regard to health, relationships with

spouse, friends, and children, attitudes toward self, resignation to the disappointments of life, and shifts in time orientation. Neugarten (1975) describes an increased inferiority and personalization of death as marking the transition from
midlife to old age.

All older people must face and accomplish new tasks and roles appropriate to
this stage of life in which some do well and others fail. Some roles and tasks are
now greatly reduced while others are intensified. As one's children grow up and
move away, as aging parents grow old and feeble, as physical abilities decline, as
death takes away loved ones, as retirement eliminates work, it becomes imperative
that new satisfactions and activities replace the old ones. The major challenge
therefore of the later years is a crucial shift in values to maintain a sense of integrity
and self-worth, with new identities and directions emerging despite a growing
awareness of personal aging and eventual death. This adjustment can be achieved
through developing new anchorage points and deriving security and satisfaction
from new activities and social relationships, for the goal of a satisfying adaptation in
these years is to see life as more than a brief bodily sojourn. A major determinant of
successful adjustment is probably how one has accomplished change in the preceding stages of life. An additional determinant is the nature of emotional commitments
to people and productive endeavors.

HOUSEHOLDS AND THE AGING

In contemporary American society the main emphasis is on the challenges of ur-
banization, industrialization, youth, progress, productivity, and the nuclear family.
Unlike other cultures of the world, limited value has been singled out for old age,
which manifests itself in the attitudes of American children toward aging parents.
Thus far, the mutual support networks of the extended family, applied to older
people living with adult children and their families, have not been generally accepted in the American view of family life, although it does occur as a solution for
aging parents. Nevertheless, before such arrangement takes place, much satisfaction
is derived in intergenerational familial relationships in the changing American family.

Separate Households

The emerging pattern of family life is one of separate households for all but the very
old or sick, while in varying degrees maintaining a complexity of family relationships that can be viable, supportive, and meaningful. In American society the
nuclear family, consisting of father, mother, and children may necessarily be isolated, mobile, self-sufficient and self-sustaining either because of employment or
preference. If this is the situation, older parents and grandparents may be a part of
an extended kinship family system. This kinship system may be highly integrated

within a network of intimate, warm, affectionate, social relationship, with mutual assistance operating over several generations, and for an older person may include sons, daughters, grandchildren, great grandchildren, assorted in-laws, and friends. Some older people have never married and have no immediate family of children or grandchildren or even kin, whereas others have an assortment of near or distant kin or adopted kin to whom they are not related but to whom they relate closely. The significance of meaningful, personal interrelationships for the elderly should not be underestimated.

In many instances regular activities link the members of the kin family network. Visiting is facilitated by modern transportation and interaction among members by up-to-date communication systems. The role of the kin family network is to provide supportive services to old persons, such as giving or supplying physical care, providing shelter, escorting, shopping, performing household tasks, and sharing leisure time. These acts are performed voluntarily for the most part and can be a major source of aid and service when elderly family members become increasingly infirm.

The importance of parent–child relationships in the development of physical, emotional, intellectual, and psychological and social well-being is given considerable attention in society. It is widely accepted from the standpoint of mental health that physical and emotional sustenance by loving and caring parents is desirable and absolutely necessary for individuals to reach mature adulthood. However, only limited research material is available on the importance of adult children–parent relationships and the continued need for ties of affection, emotional caring, and sustenance for the elderly. As an individual goes through the aging process, the need for family, kinship, and friendship remain necessary (if not accentuated) for the emotional and social well-being of the elderly.

Most elderly enjoy and desire contact with significant family members, but nevertheless choose to be independent, maintaining separate households. Approximately two out of every ten older people in the United States live alone. Most are single, widowed, or divorced and a large proportion are women. In 1977 only one out of three women 65 years and over was married and living with her husband. Fifty-two percent of the women were widowed, and over one in three women was living alone. Among women 70 years and over, almost 70 percent were widows.

Many of the elderly have children but prefer to live apart from them in separate households. A greater portion of the very old, over 80 years, either live with family members or in institutions because of declining capacities. Apparently, the majority of older people choose independent living arrangements with a spouse or alone as long as possible. The question remains as to what plan is feasible and mutually acceptable when independent living is not practicable. A conflict arises when the older person expects to move in with family members, but it is not mutually agreeable with all concerned.

Although a majority of the elderly and their families desire separate households, four out of every ten older unmarried people with children live in the same household with at least one child. An additional three out of every ten are 10 minutes or less distance from their nearest child. In all, 82 percent of all unmarried old parents in the United States who have children are less than 30 minutes distance from at least one of them.

It seems that most older parents turn to adult children for help in time of illness and need and expect their children to be available to help them.

Three-Generation Households. In the United States 8 percent of families consist of three generations living together under one roof. There are also increasing numbers of a fourth generation of relatively frail elderly people who are being cared for by middle-aged children. A 60-year-old woman faced with the problem of caring for an infirm mother in her eighties or older is not an uncommon situation. Frequently, middle-aged children have to look after an elderly widowed parent or even two sets of parents if the children are married and to provide adequate care and financial support and in many instances take them in because they are too infirm or impoverished to live alone any longer. A typical pattern in the United States is one of an older mother moving in with her daughter and family. In three-generation households the problems of maintaining individual freedom and independence can be only one of a myriad of areas of potential conflict, but older parents often find a role in their childrens' lives. Managing conflict in interpersonal interactions is critical to the success or failure in such arrangements, because there are many areas of possible difference and disagreement. However, multigenerational families (more than two generations) are not an uncommon entity in American society. Longer life spans have increased the likelihood of families consisting of three, four, or five generations.

A MULTIGENERATIONAL FAMILY

At a recent birthday party for Mrs. H., a widow, age 80 years, the following individuals were present: her daughter, who was 58 years and her husband, 60 years; her granddaughter, 30 years, and her husband, 32 years; and her great granddaughter, 3 years, plus more friends of each. Multiple generations can and do mix socially. Mrs. H. lives in her own one and a half-room apartment in special housing for senior citizens provided by the county at a reduced rental. She is active in senior citizen groups at the center located on the premises of the housing project. Once a week she takes a bus trip to a shopping mall with other senior citizens and has lunch at a nearby restaurant. At the housing project a mobile unit provides medical and dental care weekly for the residents. She volunteers twice a week to be a companion aide at a local nursing home. Mrs. H. is a regular member of a local church group and attends ladies aid society meetings once a month, making quilts to send to missionary groups in other countries. In a nonchalant manner Mrs. H. announced her plans to attend a sleep-away camp for a 2-week period, which was sponsored for senior citizens at a nominal cost in a church-related camp. She asked to borrow her granddaughter's duffle bag and flashlight for the trip.

Change of Residence

The issue of an elderly parent "moving" with adult children has profound implications and should not be minimized.

"Home" usually means where individuals have felt most comfortable to be themselves, but the comcept of "home" can have various meanings for the elderly—for some it is a place to love and to stay, for others, a terrifying place to leave as soon as possible, and for every individual, something different based on personal experience. For many, "home" is associated with independence and some measure of control over their own decisions and destiny, free from the manipulation and restraint of others. Home represents an expression of one's own personality, surrounded by friendships, plants, pictures, pets, memorabilia. For those who may have lived at the same residence for many years, home is being located in familiar surroundings amid what may seem to be a threatening, hostile, changing world outside. Personal possessions, daily routines, and habits carried out often for many years, are difficult to relinquish or even modify to fit into another family's schedules and behaviors. Home can also include neighbors and friends, social groups, church, shopping, and a community network, which for an elderly person provides a sense of belonging and security as well as an opportunity to socialize and yet be alone when desired. However, home can also have strongly negative aspects, for some. Fear, crime, theft, muggings, loneliness, and isolation are also a stark reality associated with "home" for large numbers of urban elderly confined to small apartments with cheap rents.

The transition from one's own home to another residence can be a difficult, frightening experience, which may present threatening changes that can also trigger a major depressive episode or an affective disorder. An older person may show signs of bitterness and remorse or be quiet, somber, and withdrawn. They may seem overly polite and ingratiating but rarely take initiative or seek responsibility in activities. They may seem readily prone to tears, dejected with little or no spontaneity. As a result of change, some older individuals may have multiple and persistant somatic complaints, loss of appetite and an inability to sleep soundly. Most eventually recover, but for others the duration of the emotional reaction may be longer.

Living in three-generation households is not always satisfying because relationships among the generations can be problematic. The waning of physical and mental powers can affect the older person's motivation and capacity to carry on customary social roles and responsibilities. The contrast therefore between them and the younger generation(s) may alter the balance of power, and authority may be relinquished by the older person or seized by younger, more vigorous adults.

The potential for conflict between generations is ever present. Role reversal and its consequences can affect an older person's wish to preserve independence while desperately seeking the approval, love, and support of the children. Moreover, when the needs of the elderly parents are visible and apparent, their offspring may be deeply involved in their own marital, parental, and occupational obligations. Time and energy are scarce resources in the three-generation household and when an individual feels the pressure of several role responsibilities, priorities may take precedence, and ties to spouse and children may have greater immediacy and urgency. Although many families manage these problems fairly well, the multiple-generation household presents real problems. For this reason the majority of the elderly population try to maintain separate households as long as possible to protect each generation's independence and privacy and to minimize conflict between parents and children, as well as to avoid becoming subject to their children's authority.

Separate residences between the generations have been made possible by the individual's economic resources, public programs, health care services, and housing for the elderly. In turn, children have been to some extent relieved of the responsibility of caring for their aging parents. As long as the aging couple remain, in fact, in reasonably good health and can rely on their own resources, they may not make onerous demands on their adult children. However, when parents grow older or widowhood becomes a problem, with inadequate resources, increasing demands may be made on the adult children to help in the care of an aging parent.

Some fulfill their material obligations and out of a sense of duty maintain contact with aging parents, but their own independent, separate existence, friends, interests, and familial and occupational demands lessen intimacy and closeness between the generations. The poignant preparation between the generations during the time span when they live apart and develop along different paths may help to explain why relations with children rarely counteract the trauma and desolation of retirement or widowhood.

INTERPERSONAL RELATIONSHIPS

Adaptation to changing familial and friendship network roles confront the elderly. Today the aging parent is apt to be a grandparent, to have an aging spouse or to have lost a spouse by divorce or death, and even possibly to have found a new partner. The elderly are likely to see fewer old friends but may find the opportunity to develop new ones. Although some of these roles may bring difficult problems, some can have positive and supportive effects that provide energy and motivation for continued functioning.

Grandparenthood

The role of grandparent introduces a newly increased social role in our culture. In the United States 70 percent of the older people now have living grandchildren and

32 percent of persons over 65 are great grandparents; these figures are likely to grow significantly by the year 2000. Although research has not clearly defined roles for grandparents, five differentiated styles of enacting the role of grandparent have been identified: the formal, in which grandparents maintain a constant interest in the grandchildren but are careful not to interfere or offer advice to childrearing; the fun-seeker, characterized by informality, playfulness, "having fun," with emphasis on the sharing of satisfaction; the surrogate parent, in which actual caretaking responsibility for grandchild (or grandchildren) is assumed; the reservoir of family wisdom, which is an authoritarian patriarchal relationship; the distant figure, who emerges on holidays and special occasions but whose contact with the children is infrequent and fleeting. These types of grandparenting may reflect the age of the grandparent. The "formal style" occurred significantly more frequently in those who were over 65 years, whereas the "fun-seeking" and "distant figure" styles occurred significantly more frequently in the younger group (under 65 years).

Not all older people want the role of grandparent, although most experience some satisfaction with it. Some elderly feel exploited by their children and express negative feelings in this regard, but positive satisfactions in the role of grandparent can provide feelings of self-fulfillment through teaching and helping in various ways. Such satisfactions, moreover, depend on a series of factors: the amount of contact; the relationships among grandparents, parents, and children; the child's perception of the older people; and the grandparents in particular. However, the role of grandparent can be a meaningful, openly affectionate one, a sharing of activities, enjoyment, and experiences and resources with one's own grandchildren. It can be a time when past remembrances and future aspirations merge into the present. This life stage can give older people a new sense of the tie between generations and the ongoing force of life.

Marital Conflict in Later Life

Emotional gratifications are strongly expected in the marital relationship of older couples. The needs of a couple, however, may change from those of the early and middle years of life, and each person has had an individual life experience as well as a joint relationship in the marriage. They may have become more responsive to the needs, hopes, and aspirations of each other or become increasingly different, leading separate lives and existences.

With the additional adjustments called for by the aging process, conflict and difference is inevitable in any mature relationship. The opportunity for unmanaged, unresolved conflict between the individual can intensify or dissipate with more time spent together as a couple. As they age, some people become more irritable; stressful; insecure; losing confidence in self and others; and changing in health, endurance, and identity; all of which can seriously affect the marital relationship. Many elderly persons, who have experienced a level of mature adaptability learned through healthy adjustment during the various phases of the life cycle, expect and accept change and loss and eventually respond constructively. However, others manifest deleterious effects from personal and environmental influences or deterioration of physical and mental health that adversely affect the marriage. Research has shown disenchantment and deterioration in up to one-third of the elderly marital relationships.

However, most older marriages are broken by death rather than by divorce, which is more likely to happen in youth or middle age when resources and options are greater. Some of the more common difficulties in such marriages are precipitated by the consequences of physical or emotional illness. It can be an emotional and financial drain on the spouse who attempts to care for a seriously ill husband or wife, with limited help from outside sources. Frustration, anger, and despair in the caretaker spouse may develop into physical and emotional symptoms. Very often this role can be arduous, continuous, and overwhelming for one person. Depending on the severity of the illness, other arrangements for proper care and treatment for the ailing spouse, such as home care, a nursing home, hospitalization, a skilled nursing facility, or a home for the aged, may have to be found. These will be explored in a later chapter.

In old age the mutual support in a marital relationship can be a vital factor in the emotional and physical health of each spouse as well as the sharing of mutual interests, friends, aspirations, and affection, which can be maintained throughout life. For most married elderly people the sharing and companionship facilitate coping with crises and aid in successful adjustment.

Widowhood

Death of one's spouse is a traumatic event and may have serious effects on the attitude and morale of the surviving spouse. A marriage represents a relationship based on a bond of love, caring, solidarity, often over a long period of time. Losing a spouse to death causes grief at the end of a love relationship.

Fifty-six out of every 100 of the elderly become widowed; three out of four are women. The loss of a spouse is a major problem of old age because the period of bereavement is aggravated by the need to undertake other necessary emotional decisions—living arrangements, personal possessions, deceased spouse's personal effects, relationships with relatives, in-laws, and friends. Widowhood can have isolating effects on the bereaved individual who may feel abandoned by friends and relatives as well as by the loss of a companion. The death of one spouse may also tend to destroy the basis of a relationship between the surviving spouse and those married friends with whom the couple had jointly associated. Patterns in relationships are forced to change, and very often the widowed person may feel excluded in both conversation and contact so that these social contacts may become less frequent or discontinued altogether.

A widowed woman may also be seen as a threat or potential rival by married women and therefore previous friendships with married couples often wane. She may either remain isolated or establish contacts and cultivate friendships with others in similar situations: the widowed, separated or divorced, or single.

Often friends and relatives feel uncomfortable with the bereaved and may tend to ignore or socially ostracize such a person. The widowed, with a change in marital status, are forced to seek out new friends for companionship or to fall back on what may be their own limited, individual resources.

Remarriage and Divorce

Very few elderly persons marry or become divorced. In 1975 only 1 percent of the brides and 2 percent of the grooms were 65 years old and over. Recent statistics on divorce by age show that only 1 percent of those who became divorced in that year were over 65 years of age. Sixty-seven percent of those who married were previously widowed, and three of every four of the remainder were previously divorced. The marriage rates per 1000 eligible population were quite low; for persons 65 and over the remarriage rate for widowers was 20 and that for widows, only two. The corresponding rates for divorced men were 31 as compared with only nine for divorced women. American culture offers little impetus for the elderly to marry; instead, they are encouraged to protect their estate for their offspring. Although marriage may be considered desirable for older people for several reasons, there appears little likelihood that marital union will rise above the present low levels.

At present there are 4.3 million older couples in the United States, reflecting the continuing increase in the proportion of people who survive until they reach old age and demonstrating the continuing preferences for the married state among today's great majority of the elderly.

According to the extension projections made by Glick and Norton (1977), however, there is likely to be a large increase between now and the year 2000 of elderly women who eventually become divorced. The proportion of women age 65 to 75 years who eventually become divorced is expected to approximately double, from about 12 percent in 1975 to 22 percent in the year 2000.

The multitude of social changes in the United States, including more education and employment of women, provide increased available options for them. These forces have affected the rising marital dissolution rates of women at all ages.

Friendship Networks

In contemporary society in the United States people form many acquaintances over a lifetime, but few are close and enduring friendships. The lack of genuine intimacy and commitment in many relationships makes little difference as long as the aging individual and the associate both continue to perform adequately in their major work or social roles. Many friendships are connected with a role and maintained while the elderly person enacts that particular role, such as in a work situation or in marriage. But such relationships end when the role is over or when the occasion for contact diminishes, and consequently, the bond of interest on which the friendship was based fades.

As long as older people are married or working, morale remains high, regardless of the extent of social participation. Also, marriage can be a buffer to protect morale in old age even if the spouses have few social resources or contacts outside the marital relationship. The extent of social participation and friendship networks become critical issues after widowhood or retirement, and evidence reveals incidence of low morale among the retired and widowed who do not maintain an active social life.

The number of social roles in which an individual engages at a given time increases the likelihood that the individual is needed either because of the services the person has to offer or the individual's personal qualities that are of value to others. Participation in a number of social roles tends to make older people less dependent on any single role to sustain morale and a sense of well-being; therefore those with extensive social ties do best, even though certain roles may cease.

The roles of marriage, parenthood, and work represent the social resources most individuals have possessed that have meaning and significance for their lives. These roles have provided differing levels of satisfaction for each person, some have found more satisfaction than others in their work, whereas others have experienced more gratification in marriage and parenthood. Although friendships may be of less significance in adulthood than work and marriage, in old age friendship networks become an important means to replace the previous work, marital, and/or parental roles.

After retirement or widowhood, friendships with one's peers becomes vital for an individual. Friendship can be a significant factor in morale, which is established in mutual sharing, mutual needs, and a voluntary exchange of sociability. To share interests and experiences in common with others at a similar stage in life helps to sustain an older person's sense of identity, usefulness, and self-esteem. Therefore older people need opportunities to meet and associate with individuals of their own generation. Even a single, intimate friendship can be effective in preventing depression, isolation, and demoralization in the face of major losses for the elderly. Intimate friendships are usually not made quickly; they need time and considerable propinquity, both of which are increased necessities and decreased possibilities for an older person. Finding an intimate friend can be a difficult task, for opportunities and an individual's capacity for intimacy can greatly influence the likelihood of success in this endeavor. To give and receive affection, support, and sustenance, and to be sensitive to the needs of others, are qualities needed to cultivate friendship at any age. Friendship networks, however, not necessarily intimate, can complement kinship ties by relieving some of the burden of care from relatives. In later years friendship patterns will change. Friends of long standing may continue to be extremely important to the elderly person, but new ones should be sought and cultivated. Large groups may rely entirely on friendship networks for social interaction for those who are without or geographically inaccessible to relatives. Such groups might include bachelors who never married, or who were widowed, long-time singles who have reached old age and are without "blood" relationships, and "childless" couples. If friendships are desired, concerted effort toward achieving this objective must be pursued. The more characteristics neighbors and friends have in common, such as socioeconomic status, marital status, and religious and value orientations, the more integrated will be the friendship network; and the more involved older people are in social networks, such as family, friendship, leisure, work, religious and other groups, the more likely they will achieve successful aging despite major critical life changes.

Summary

It is increasingly accepted that psychological, social, cultural, and eocnomic elements all affect an older person's sense of well-being and physical and mental health. The interdependency of biological and social factors is also well recognized in fostering health and adding to both the quality and the duration of life.

The majority of older persons prefer to live in separate households and are engaged in a wide range of social roles, actively participating in the community.

Most of the elderly are not isolated from family and friends or from neighborhood and friendship networks, but at the same time, social isolation, age segregation, and inadequate social participation characterize substantial numbers of others, particularly the very old in American society.

The experience of change and the response to it are not uniform among older persons. Life transitions and drastic changes of later life are often associated with physical and psychological deficits and with the loss or modification of central life roles. Negative and deleterious manifestations that do occur seem to be significantly affected by the timing of the event in the life cycle, by previous experiences and patterns of coping behavior, and by the social resources, activities, and interactions available to the individual. Chronological age alone is a relatively weak predictor of adaptation patterns.

The family is a primary social group and remains a social network of interpersonal relationships for the elderly. The family continues to be characterized by intimacy, affection, and supportive behavior among family members. In the family there is usually an emphasis on informal unrestricted communication.

This chapter shows the influence of the developmental process on behavior in later life and clarifies the understanding of that behavior. Role behaviors are an integral part of any family because appropriate roles are prescribed for husband and father, wife and mother, son, daughter, children, and relatives. Each family member has a position in the family.

Major social processes occur in the family. Socialization is the process by which an individual learns the norms and the expectations of society in the framework of learning to perform a range of social roles. The process is a dynamic one in which communication and interaction takes place. According to George Herbert Mead (1934), the self emerges through the use of language and the development of the capacity to reflect on oneself in social interaction.

The self-concept constitutes all those characteristics that one sees in oneself, as well as those aspects of the self that others may see when interaction occurs with other people. There is a significant relationship among the self-perception of an individual, the physiological state, and social competence. The extent and nature of this relationship in the face of profound changes needs further study. One important implication is that there are multiple patterns of successful aging, and if society is to improve the quality of life for older persons, public policies should provide a wide range of options with regard to living arrangements, housing, opportunities for work, education, leisure, health and social services.

FURTHER READINGS

Duvall, E. M., *Family Development* (4th ed.), Lippincott, Philadelphia, 1971.

Havighurst, R. J., "Life Style and Leisure Patterns," in R. Kalish (ed.), *The Later Years: Social Application of Gerontology,* Brooks/Cole, Monterey, Calif., 1977.

Kerchoff, A. C., "Family Patterns and Morale in Retirement," in I. H. Simpson and J. C. McKinney (eds.), *Social Aspects of Aging,* Duke University Press, Durham, N.C., 1966.

Lopata, H. Z. *Widowhood in an American City,* Schenkman, Cambridge, Mass., 1973.

Neugarten, B., *Middle Age and Aging,* The University of Chicago Press, Chicago, 1975.

Peterson, J. A., and M. Briley, *Widows and Widowhood,* Association Press, New York, 1977.

Peterson, J. A., A. E. Larson, and T. A. Hadwen, *A Time for Work, A Time for Leisure: A Study of In-Movers,* University of Southern California Libraries, Los Angeles, 1967.

Peterson, J. A., and B. Payne, *Love in Later Years,* Association Press, New York, 1975.

Pineo, P. "Disenchantment in the Later Years of Marriage," in B. Neugarten (ed.), *Middle Age and Aging,* The University of Chicago Press, Chicago, 1975.

Streib, G. F., "Social Stratification and Aging," in Robert H. Binstock and Ethel Shanas (eds.), *Handbook of Aging and the Social Sciences,* Van Nostrand, New York, 1976.

Shanas, E., and G. Streib (eds.), *Social Structure and Family Intergenerational Relations,* Prentice-Hall, Englewood Cliffs, N.J., 1965.

Sussman, M. "The Family Life of Old People," in R. Binstock and E. Shanas (eds.), *Handbook of Aging and the Social Sciences,* Van Nostrand, New York, 1976.

Treas, J., "Aging in the Family," in D. Woodruff and J. Birren (eds.), *Aging: Scientific Perspectives and Social Issues* Van Nostrand, New York, 1975.

U.S. Bureau of the Census, Census of Population: 1973, Subject Reports. Final Report PG(2). 4B, Persons by Family Characteristics.

Warren, R. *The Community in America.* Rand McNally, Chicago, 1972.

CHAPTER 9

Retirement, Work, and Leisure

Separation from the work world with the intention of making it permanent is an experience of considerable social and personal significance in American society, because people to some extent are regarded and measured by occupational success. Individual effort and perseverance are meritorious qualities to be rewarded, and in the work environment, the individual has established certain expectations and patterns of behavior that are difficult to relinquish.

Although more and more people expect to retire, and retirement is becoming an acceptable stage of life, the transition from work to *retirement* becomes an extremely important step and one not without problems. To a large extent, retirement is giving up a role and status by which an individual has been identified, but all too frequently there is no new role or other status for the retiree to acquire. A basic problem of retirement, moreover, is that it is mostly a status change, in which one is deprived involuntarily of a meaningful, gratifying role, rather than a voluntary relinquishing of a role. Instead of providing an opportunity to retire, American society has demanded and insisted on retirement. Even many older workers have been convinced that they ought to retire because jobs are limited in the struggling economy.

However, retirement can also be a new beginning, taking on another, new role and perhaps a different career or a change of job. The process of retirement, including preparation for retirement, the transition itself, and the individual's adjustment to it, influence the success or failure of the retirement experience.

142

This chapter looks at major trends in retirement and discusses factors affecting adjustment to retirement. The present arbitrary widespread system of mandatory retirement is frequently based on an arbitrary nonfunctional definition of old age. This abrupt withdrawal of an older person from the work force may deprive the individual from the opportunity to be productive and to earn what may be essential income for reasonable existence. Such abrupt deprivation may present a complex problem to the maintenance of self-esteem, health, and well-being.

In the United States many individuals accept retirement and expect and antici-pate the change; they have some plans for retirement, although often times vague. They have given consideration to financial arrangements, pension, social security benefits, health insurance coverage, housing, and may have even thought about what immediate changes may have to be made in their life-style.

WHAT IS RETIREMENT?

Retirement is the separation from remunerative employment. It may be a relatively informal or a formal transition, but it is an important step in most people's lives and may signal a crucial stage in the life cycle from middle age to the period called old age. For some individuals retirement represents a passage in life from productive maturity and involvement in work and career to the unproductive period of old age.

Retirement is always accompanied by change. When work ceases, the amount of time available increases. Some individuals are able to use the time productively and to engage in leisure activities with enthusiasm. Thus changes may occur in an individual's self-identity, financial status because of decreased income, interper-sonal relationships, and personality.

TRENDS IN RETIREMENT

The number of persons retiring by age 65 has steadily increased over the years. In 1900 more than 67 percent of all men age 65 or over remained in the labor force; by 1970 only about 25 percent continued working; and by 1990 the forecast is for less than 20 percent. Recent evidence suggests retirement is becoming a more acceptable concept. The proportion of voluntary retirees, although small, has doubled over the last 12 years, and rapid growth has occurred in development of retirement plans. Despite this trend, however, the actual retirement experience is viewed by many older workers as a crisis, although usually little planning or preparation for the change is made and exposure to information about it is minimal. To some extent, those who are interested and anticipating retirement, may seek out information, whereas those who are dreading the experience may ignore the inevitable. There are two kinds of retirement: the completely voluntary and the forced. The latter is caused by poor health, company policy, or similar constraints.

Voluntary Retirement

Studies in retirement preferences suggest that four major factors affect retirement plans: employment income, expected retirement income, state of health, and the physical demands of the job. Research indicates that when retirement income is adequate, there is a growing trend for workers to retire early, although some call health the reason. But where retirement income is inadequate, workers are more likely to delay retirement even if acute problems persist. In addition, education appears to be a differentiating variable related to retirement; generally the higher the degree of education is, the more likely the individual is to keep on working. In 1970 16.5 percent of men with 4 years or less education were in the labor force; as well as 38.6 percent, who had completed college, and 54.9 percent, who had education beyond college. Retirement, therefore, is less prevalent among those who have more education and who presumably have had higher incomes during their working lives. Such individuals are likely to have a greater sense of commitment to their occupation, having invested considerable education and training in preparation to enter it. However, adequate retirement income, high employment income, in addition to good health, are most often associated with the high occupational status correlated with later retirement.

Work status differences in occupation also have an effect on determining attitudes during retirement. High occupational status is frequently associated with adequate retirement income, high employment income, and good health. Individuals in high-prestige occupations are least enthusiastic about retirement, choosing later retirement, whereas those in low-prestige occupations are most enthusiastic. Unskilled workers with retirement plans are most likely to take advantage of early retirement.

The retirement process itself is often a critical period, for the highly trained professional invested considerable time and energy in education, preparing for the career. Yet studies show that after retirement these individuals who have high-prestige preretirement occupations adjust better than unskilled workers who were most enthusiastic at first. However, professionals who work as long as they can, at some point, must confront the fact that in retiring they are relinquishing a status, which makes the period of transition less smooth. Whereas, unskilled workers who retire because of unrelated criteria, such as mandatory retirement age, may more easily accept the retirement transition.

In the case of women the extent of their participation in the labor force has increased in the last century. There is a tendency on the part of most women workers to work hard and steadily and to hold on to paid employment as late in life as possible.

There is a wider variance in the attitudes of women toward retirement. Socioeconomic factors and occupational status are important variables in affecting a woman's decision to retire. As in the case with men, reluctance to retire usually increases with higher education, and occupational status and better pay, with self-employment.

Many older women are heavily concentrated in those occupations where pensions are nonexistent or inadequate. These positions have low wages, thus low social security payments. These conditions present serious economic problems for the older woman facing retirement. Also, many who are divorced, widowed, or married to men with low incomes usually opt for later retirement to put off the drop in income that accompanies retirement.

Forced Retirement

Most persons who retire in the United States leave the work stiuation at about the same time in the life cycle, over 60 years of age, for various reasons. Many elderly persons give poor health as the main reason for leaving the work force, but others are removed from the work force more or less unwillingly by established retirement procedures. What may be considered a right to retire, to withdraw from the work force and still receive income, shifts suddenly to an obligation to retire at the time retirement pay becomes effective.

The transition to the retirement role arouses concern for the aged and creates problems regarding adaptation to retirement, morale, purposefulness, and productive, creative ways of spending time. Some of the elderly may feel ambivalent about separating from work, but feel that it is mandatory or strongly encouraged in order to allow the young to enter the labor force and to advance in their career. Forced retirement, however, is seen in the labor market as an alternative to layoffs in times of economic recession, to which the elderly person may react bitterly at such inhumane, unfair treatment after long and faithful years of service.

There has been a shift in emphasis in retirement policies. The values that originally influenced the acceptance of retirement policies were viewed as a social necessity. In the United States, in the 1930s, the depression made the problem of the aged overwhelming. They were the group most likely to be unemployed and there was no governmental provision to assist them. The Social Security Act addressed this problem to provide a plan for social insurance. It was originally assumed that every worker would continue working as long as he or she was able, but subtle inversion of emphasis has been made from the provision of aid at a time when workers are unable to work to the attitude that whenever a worker can have full benefits, they should retire. This shift in emphasis has come to mean that the age of 65 is the inviolable demarcation point between work and retirement.

Many industrial companies accept 65 as the age of withdrawal from work, and expect persons reaching this age to retire. (See the case on ''Planning for Retirement''.) Recent changes in the law have raised the mandatory retirement age to 70 years in certain positions in the labor force, which may have far-reaching effects on the economy.

RETIREMENT PROBLEMS

The problems at retirement are many, but the economic and employment situation and health head the list. If sufficiently provided for, the older person has a good foundation for successful retirement; however, that is not always the case.

Economic Considerations in Retirement

The most immediate effect of retirement for the worker and the household are of an economic nature. Although the incomes of older people have improved during recent years, they remain significantly low in relation to the present economy. With respect to work and retirement, there are emerging more flexible patterns for the elderly such as shorter work weeks, 2½- and 3-day weekends, and expanded annual vacations.

Planning for Retirement

Robert K., 65 yers of age, was retired from the utility company by which he had been employed for the past 30 years. He was an active, energetic man and was ill prepared for retirement.

He and his wife, without visiting South Carolina, decided to move there near his wife's sister to get away from the cold northern winters.

Mr. K. and his wife were both dissatisfied with their lives in South Carolina. She missed her other family and friends, and he was unable to find any part-time work and was not interested or content with gardening, fishing, golf, swimming, or puttering around the house, activities that seemed to occupy the lives of so many in that community. He reported depressed feelings in response to varied stresses during his life. He wished he had more hobbies. His planning for retirement and old age and the future had been incomplete.

After much deliberation, they decided to return north but were unable to locate an apartment in their old neighborhood. They were temporarily living in a furnished room until they could find suitable and affordable accommodations. Mr. K. felt retirement was forced although it appeared to be ostensibly voluntary. He regrets his decision.

The emotional impact of retirement is a function of economics, temperament, health care, vigor, range of interests, and planning. Many organizations, firms, and private enterprises are making efforts to assist older workers in preparing for retirement. Also, many firms are opening up employment possibilities for older and retired employees.

SALLY E.

Mary and Sally Evans, sisters, had long discussed what to do when Mary had to retire from the communications company where she had worked for many years as a supervisor, while Sally, whose health was less hearty, had done what she could over the years by doing part-time work. They were unmarried, had no close relatives, but did have some savings to add to social security and Mary's pension. They knew that very careful plans must be made because their combined income would drop considerably at retirement. They had listed their needs, drawn up budgets, including the rent at housing for the aged and retirement homes in the various locations where they took their modest vacations. The sisters also considered their tastes: Both enjoyed people and craftwork. Eventually, they found a convenient apartment in a housing development for the elderly in a town where they had made a few friends and had grown to like during vacations.

On the waiting list for an apartment for several years, shortly after Mary retired, they were notified that one was available. They moved and found congenial people and nearby craft programs and have made a good adjustment. Although the rising cost of living may threaten their solution, they consider themselves more fortunate and only hope they will be able to stay.

This case demonstrates evidence of intelligent forethought and action in retirement, along with modest resources.

In the late 1970s there were 7.2 million families headed by persons over 65. The median income was under $7300. One 25 percent, or about 1.8 million, had incomes in excess of $9000 per year. The median income for persons over 65 years of age was about $3000. About 16 percent (3.4 million) of all elderly were at or below the poverty level. Among the very old, incomes were particularly low; $2700 for men and $2200 for women aged 73 years and over who were living with relatives.

Since Social Security adjustments have not kept pace with the rise in the cost of living, inflation has been increasingly severe on fixed incomes and the poor are poorer. Economic deprivation is a major and frightening problem for the aged, and one that threatens to persist.

Poverty is a typical condition associated with old age. Many people who are employed during their working years become economically poor, with meager incomes, when they get old. Although the elderly represent 10 percent of the total population, they constitute 20 percent of the poor in America. In late 1970 half the elderly (10 million) lived on less than $75 a week. In this present economy, with increasing costs for food, shelter, and medical expenses, older people are living on bare subsistence incomes. Most of their money is spent for the basic essentials and for the most part, they are unable to afford much money for clothing, leisure, transportation, or recreation.

The sources of income for the elderly vary. Two percent of their income is earned from continuing employment: 46 percent comes from retirement; 4 percent, from public assistance programs; and the remainder, from investments (15 percent), veterans benefits (3 percent), and contributions from relatives (3 percent). The benefits from social security and medicaid, moreover, have not met the needs of the elderly, and many jobs were not covered until recently.

The social security program justified a transfer of income claims from workers to nonworkers. The prevalent attitude in the United States that supports a reluctance to apportion larger percentages of the nation's income to retired persons results in a marked difference between the income of the worker and that of the retiree, even including their savings and part-time earnings.

Some thought has been given to revise social security benefits, to safeguard the cost of living and periods of inflation. A central issue remains as to what offsets can be made available to keep retirement incomes in line with those persons still at work. Some ideas under consideration have been the following: to permit continuance of work at least on a part-time basis for persons beyond 65 years, to increase their capacity to save during work life, or to raise the social security benefit by transferring larger income claims to the elderly through the taxation-benefit scheme. The present generation of retirees, however, are dependent on increased incomes in order to raise their eligible retirement benefits.

Employment in Retirement

One way of offsetting inadequate retirement income and economic needs is for the elderly to continue employment as long as they are willing and able. At present, people over the age of 65 earn about 29 percent of their income. The ability to earn money to supplement their income is hampered by two factors in American society: (1) social security ceiling on earnings and (2) age discrimination in employment.

Social Security policy provides for reductions in the benefits of individuals who exceed designated earnings limitations. Each beneficiary may earn a designated amount per year without any reduction in benefits. However, if a beneficiary exceeds this limit, the benefits are reduced by $1 for every $2 of annual earnings. This practice has received marked criticism, because it is complicated and difficult for the average person to understand and also because it penalizes those who show incentive to supplement their incomes. In addition, it forces others to seek employment where income is ''off the books'' so that their incomes will not be jeopardized.

The direct factor of age discrimination in employment prevents many older persons from seeking or successfully finding employment. Age discrimination is apparent in arbitrary retirement when an individual reaches a certain age and is prevalent in practices against promoting or hiring older workers. The worker over 50 has more difficulty finding another job during economic recession or fiscal austerity, when cutbacks in employment, layoffs, industrial shutdowns, or relocations occur. Management may even encourage the older worker to leave, because younger workers can be hired at less pay.

Unemployed older persons usually remain without employment for longer periods of time than other age groups. They also tend to be underemployed and their abilities underutilized. All too often they are forced to accept salary cuts under the threat of possible job loss. Such practices reveal age discrimination in employment, which puts considerable constraints on an elderly person's option to work. The Age Discrimination in Employment Act of 1967 is an attempt to prevent and eliminate age discrimination. However, it has not been enforced adequately and applies only to persons under 65 years of age. The elderly over 65 remain unprotected by law.

Health Issues in Retirement

Older people have a larger incidence of illness than the young or middle aged. In 86 percent of the elderly population over 65 years there are chronic health problems that require more frequent visits for medical care, and more and longer periods of hospitalization as well as more illnesses at home. Furthermore, the elderly have more physical and emotional disability than the rest of the population.

Many of their diseases, illnesses, and ailments are possibly preventable and usually treatable, but a main problem is that the majority of the elderly cannot afford proper medical care, and health professionals and personnel are inadequately trained to deal with the unique problems of the aged.

In 1968 the per capita expenditure by the elderly for health care was $590, more than that required by other persons in the United States. By 1975 the expenditure had risen to $1215, of which Medicare paid only $463. Medicare covers only 42 percent of the health expenses of the elderly. The rest is paid for out of their incomes. By 1980 medical costs had soared for everyone and problems were compounded. Other essential items not covered by Medicare include: hearing aids, glasses, dental care, podiatry, and various pharmaceutical supplies.

Health care costs place an overwhelming burden on older persons in retirement. Retirement benefits that are very meager must also include payment for essential medical care services, not covered by Medicare.

OPPORTUNITIES IN RETIREMENT

With retirement, opportunities arise that may have been limited by previous responsibilities. More time for new endeavors can open the way to leisure activities and the pursuit of new fields of learning.

Leisure

If leisure activity is to be meaningful for the elderly, the retired person must choose activities that are appropriate in terms of personal and cultural values, taking into consideration economic and physical constraints. In anticipation of retirement with its departure from an occupational role and social identity of work relationships, individuals may, either alone or with family or friends, pursue activity that is interesting, enjoyable, and meaningful to them. It is also helpful in the case of the retiree if the activity affords the person the opportunity to develop a social identity and to enhance self-esteem and self-concept.

A society that emphasizes efficiency and productivity will define the value of the individual in terms of ability to perform in the system. Thus acting on the myth that the elderly must become incompetent, society assumes that they must be removed and replaced, putting them at a particular disadvantage because they are subject to limitations that necessarily reduce their capacity to fulfill roles and expectations. Hence there is a carryover in the world outside of work that the opportunity to engage in some form of leisure provides enjoyment and compensation from repetitive tasks.

Some activities, however, offer hope for better health and emphasis on action and the need for physical exercise to keep the body in condition. Older people are participating more in physical activities that are respected in general by others as well as by those of their own social category or group. These include golf, jogging, folk dancing, physical exercise classes, walking, swimming, and fishing.

The older person who has an interest in some activity is less likely to feel nonfunctional, useless, ineffectual, or worthless than one who has disengaged from work and leisure activities. It does appear that meaningful leisure has the potential to reduce the repercussions of social loss to which the aged are subject, particularly after retirement, and may also facilitate adjustment. Leisure activities may provide an opportunity for the older person to establish an identification with older groups in society that are respected by others.

Some people choose participation in groups created for and comprised of older people, such as senior citizen groups, Golden Age clubs, Gray Panthers, and Retired Professional Action groups. Others may not choose to participate in groups that offer an old age identity because they feel the older person is set apart from younger people. The leisure activity of the retired and elderly must be appropriate in terms of personal and societal values applicable to the aging and acceptable, in general.

For many individuals the elements and characteristics of work are interwoven in leisure activities. Hobbies and activities become participation in an activity with acceptable goals and a rationale of being useful, justified, and economically productive in some way and not simply participation in an enjoyable action. Some activities are even focused on the investment and monetary value of the leisure. Many elderly offer their leisure time to volunteer activities and feel useful working in subordinate auxiliary roles. Individuals participating in such activities may feel they are a part of a larger work system that offers them a measure of status, prestige, and authority and other meaningful satisfactions. The extent and variety of leisure participation will differ with each person, and to some extent is affected by family, economic, and health circumstances.

Some older persons choose not to participate actively. The reasons offered for nonparticipation include health, financial inability, and lack of transportation. However, their attitude may be reflective of a basic feeling of inability to cope with the demands of socialization and interpersonal interaction. To be an active participant, one needs certain commitment to a role to meet the requirements and expectations of others. If an elderly person believes that difficulty or discomfort physically or emotionally will be experienced in attempting to meet those expectations, he or she may opt not to participate to avoid a threat to self-identity and self-esteem.

RETIRED WIDOWER

Harvey L., a retired widower alone for a number of years, was persuaded by an acquaintance to go to a "Senior Citizens" leisure group. He went reluctantly because it was a long time since his wife died and since he had socialized at all. He had been a minor contractor, had few interests, and was diffident in company. But during their sing-a-long session Harvey remembered all the old tunes and their words, although he had paid no attention to this ability before, assuming it was a common one, and had not really made use of it. To his surprise all were impressed and pleased so that he also felt pleasure and thus returned the next week. Everybody said "Here comes Harvey! What a memory! Ask him" and from this little success a door opened to friendships and even an opportunity, though limited, to do what he used to enjoy.

One of the most challenging problems of aging in contemporary society is to find functional roles in the social system that are meaningful and satisfying to the older individual and that can help to replace the social role loss accompanying occupational retirement. It is important that the roles have intrinsic value for the individual.

Retirement can be a welcome anticipated change. At the same time, it is one of the most profound changes that occurs in one's lifetime. The transition process is difficult. Careful planning for retirement may help the elderly individual to make better decisions about the future and to try to minimize major alterations in life-style, effecting gradual changes during the middle and later years.

Educational Opportunities for Senior Citizens

Many institutions of higher education, refocusing their thinking about education, have begun to see education as helping people to continue to grow throughout their lives. This broadened perspective is illustrated by programs for the elderly, established in a wide range of institutions. Colleges and universities are offering prime locations and mechanisms for organizing educational programs, as well as for holding a primary responsibility for providing continuous educational opportunities in a learning society, including arranging access to programs for older persons outside the full-time pattern.

The recent White House Conference on Aging defined four categories of needs: coping, expressive, contributive, and influence. Educational institutions of higher education are beginning to look at the extent to which they are attempting to meet these needs. It is apparent that opportunities available through colleges and universities can play a major role in bringing about the successful adjustment of older people to changes in their life situation.

Various types of programs throughout the United States include reduced tuition rates and nonrequirement programs for senior citizens. A nationwide program is offered each summer under the auspices of Elderhostel Inc. at colleges and universities in the United States and Canada. Founded in 1975 at the University of New Hampshire, it combines intellectual stimulation and informality in living arrangements that resemble youth hostels, adapted to meet the needs of older people. Elderhostel is based on the belief that retirement does not mean withdrawal and that the college experience provides an informal opportunity to enjoy learning.

Under the program, "hostelers," age 60 years or older, spend a week on a college campus attending classes, living in dormitories and taking part in a variety of extracurricular activities. Age is the only criterion. Participants may also be spouses of individuals 60 and over. Lack of a formal education is no barrier. In 1979 13 percent of the participants nationally had never gone beyond high school. Scholarships called "hostelships" are available for those who cannot afford the price of $130 a week. In 1980 Elderhostel accommodated nearly 20,000 participants at over 300 colleges. Some colleges offer 1 or 2 weeks, whereas others run the program all summer; some are considering offering the program year round. Interspersed among courses in engineering, the family, creative writing, are field trips, a play, a trip to a state park, physical exercise seminars, dancing classes, and other social events. Participants in the program are encouraged to use the available campus facilities, swimming pool, tennis courts, library, and dining rooms.

There are special programs in colleges and universities for senior citizens. Lehman College, a Senior College of The City University of New York, has a liberal policy that senior citizens, 65 years and older who enroll in credit courses as nondegree students, pay $25. There is no other tuition charge. These programs offer older persons the opportunity for new experience, growth, and intellectual development.

SUCCESSFUL ADJUSTMENT TO RETIREMENT

• The particular role(s) and patterns assumed by the retired person to a large extent are influenced by the personality of the individual. The needs, interests, values, and motivations of the individual affect how one moves toward retirement and old age. Persons who are fairly well adjusted, able to accept themselves realistically, and who have found satisfaction in life pursuits and interpersonal relationships, are likely to draw on established coping strategies to deal with retirement and its changes. Individuals who have learned how to manage anxiety appropriately with a functioning system of defense mechanisms are better prepared for the emotional upheavals that may occur in retirement. If a person has adjusted well throughout other periods of the life cycle, there is a strong possibility that such a person will adjust successfully to retirement.

There are different perceptions of what constitutes satisfaction in retirement. One individual might find contentment and happiness in living alone, with a daily routine that involves extensive gardening, which can be an exhilarating experience for some! Priming the soil, planting, weeding, mulching, watering, pruning, gathering the harvest are necessary activities for a serious gardner. Every season has its chores, if the garden is to be productive and bear fruit. However, this activity would not bring pleasure to all elderly people, for the vast majority live in urban metropolitan areas where caring for a pet or potted plants may be a more realistic and satisfying endeavor. Recognition of individual differences is an important factor in determining successful adjustment to retirement, and one can expect to see a wide range of behavior manifestations that may be indicative of successful adjustment to retirement. If a person is in good health, has an adequate financial income, is able to maintain a positive self-concept, and is capable of engaging in meaningful activities and relationships, an adjustment to retirement is generally successful. For these older persons, retirement and its inconsistent changes are likely to present less overwhelming stress.

Summary

Mandatory retirement as a result of certain retirement policies can present a complexity of problems. The abrupt withdrawal from employment can deprive many older persons of the opportunity to earn essential income and to be needed and productive. A large number of persons as a result of retirement experience receive an automatic cut of their income, between 50 and 67 percent of what they had previously earned. Many are thus forced into poverty, even though they may be able and willing to work. Some 3.3 million elderly live in households with incomes below the official poverty level.

The majority of older persons in America who are physically and mentally able to work bring in one-third of their income through their own employment. The reduction in Social Security benefits for those who earn a certain amount is an important issue. Better ways must be explored to distribute education, work, retirement, and leisure over the course of the life cycle. The fixed requirements of many retirement programs do not provide the elderly with choices and options if they should want to continue working. Social trends, however, are making it imperative to reconsider retirement practices. As the proportion of old to young in the population increases, the cost of financing the care of the retired will fall more heavily on the employed middle aged and young. The employment of older persons who want to work and are able to remain in the labor force might do much to improve the ratio of an increasingly smaller number of workers supporting an increasingly larger number of retired beneficiaries.

It is recognized that remunerative employment has a positive impact on self-esteem and interpersonal relationships with others. The impact of the loss in earnings and possible loss of self-esteem brought about by retirement can have serious consequences. Formal organizations and primary groups such as the family must work together closely to help older people through the difficult transition to retirement.

The unique problems of women and retirement must be considered, because the life expectancy rate is different for men and women—women generally live an average of eight years longer than men. The tendency for women to marry men on average of 3 years older than themselves has resulted in women facing about 11 years of widowhood. Widowhood is often characterized by poverty, loneliness, and isolation.

Economic issues are crucial in determining the need for change in retirement policies. Some individuals might consider alternatives to mandatory retirement, such as staged or phased retirement, to cut down their hours and taper off work, rather than to stop entirely when one reaches a given age. Flexible retirement policies offer more options as to when a person leaves the work force.

FURTHER READINGS

Harris, Louis, and Associates, Inc. "The Myth and Reality of Aging in America," A Survey for the National Council on the Aging, Washington, D.C., 1976.

Hemistra, R., "New Career Opportunities in Gerontology for the 1980's! A Crystall Ball," in M. Seltzer, H. Sterns, and T. Hickey (eds.), *Gerontology in Higher Education: Perspectives and Issues,* Wadsworth, Belmont, Calif., 1978.

Miller, S. J., "The Social Dilemma of the Aging Leisure Participant," in A. Rose and W. Peterson (eds.), *Older Persons and Their Social World,* F. A. Davis, Philadelphia, 1965.

Murray, J., "Family Strucutre in the Pre-Retirement Years," Retirement Study Report No. 4, U.S. Department of Health, Education and Welfare, Washington, D.C., 1973.

Newcomes, R., "Housing Services and Neighborhood Activities," paper presented at the Twenty-Sixth Annual Meeting of the Gerontology Society, 1973.

Peterson, J. A., "Factors Involved in the Adjustment of Retired Faculty," research monograph, Andrus Gerontology Center, University of Southern California, Los Angeles, 1976.

Regnier, V., "Neighborhood Planning for the Urban Elderly," in D. Woodruff and J. Birren (eds.), *Aging: Scientific Perspectives and Social Issues,* Van Nostrand, New York, 1975.

Riley, M., and A. Foner, *Aging and Society,* Vol. 1, *An Inventory of Research Findings,* Russell Sage Foundation, New York, 1968.

Rosow, I., *Social Integration of the Aged,* Free Press, New York, 1967.

Shanas, E., *Old People in Three Industrial Societies,* Atherton Press, New York, 1968.

Seltzer, M., H. Sterns, and T. Hickey (eds.), *Gerontology in Higher Education: Perspectives and Issues,* Wadsworth, Belmont, Calif., 1978.

CHAPTER 10

Housing, Living Arrangements, and Services for Older People

There are presently about 23 million people over 65 years of age living in the United States. The living arrangements of these people have become of increasing concern. This chapter explores the following questions: With whom do elderly people live? Where do they live? Are they isolated apart from family and friends? Do they live in substandard housing inadequate for their means? This chapter looks at the economic conditions among the elderly and the factors influencing housing in old age. The poor, minority disabled, and rural aged are particularly in need of more adequate housing that meets their economic and health needs and is located in desirable areas. Many old people prefer to remain in their own homes, in familiar surroundings, although sometimes these homes may be deteriorating and located in decaying urban neighborhoods. Urban elderly who live in apartments, paying moderate rents or benefiting from rent subsidies, may be forced to move because of the location, inadequate services, and the fear of crime. Such barriers often hinder the mobility of the elderly in freely going shopping, visiting neighbors, and traveling to places of interest. The fear of crime among older people is a deterring factor in their participation in activities. Those living in large urban areas appear to be more fearful of robbery and mugging than those in smaller cities, suburbs, and rural areas, with some elderly persons refusing to leave their apartments after dark.

The location of apartments in neighborhoods without access to appropriate public transportation for the elderly presents serious problems for maintaining their independence. Transportation facilities, moreover, are not always conducive to use by older persons because of serious questions concerning the availability, access, safety, and cost of public transportation. Elderly people are dependent on transportation to participate in cultural, social, and religious activities, but the lack of transportation often hinders their active participation. Some cities and suburban communities have developed transportation programs to help meet these needs.

There has been a shift away from institutionalizing older people in mental hospitals. Only about 5 percent of persons over 65 live in institutions such as nursing homes, extended care facilities, or homes for the aged. This chapter looks at some of the issues and attitudes regarding institutionalizing old people. It also discusses alternatives to institutionalization that are presently available to the elderly, thus giving them a choice to remain in their onw homes, where some prefer to be rather than to move into nursing homes or other types of institutional settings. Many services and programs have been developed to respond to the growing needs of the present aged and the increasing number of future aged.

HOUSING THE ELDERLY

The kind of housing and living arrangements in which the elderly reside reflects various factors, such as the older individual's state of health and sources of available income. Some of their possible living arrangements are: his or her own home, an apartment, specially built housing and age-oriented environments for the elderly, a home of one of their children, a home for the aged, a nursing home, a health-related facility, or a hospital. Age is often an important determinant, in that persons in their sixties are likely to be living in different arrangements from individuals in their nineties.

Living Arrangements of the Elderly

The distribution of living arrangements for the elderly in the United States, according to census figures, shows that the majority of them live in families, either maintaining their own households with a spouse or living with relatives in their own or the relative's (usually adult children's) home. Among those 75 years of age and older, compared to those aged 65 to 74, almost twice as many live with relatives. As a result of widowhood, there is an increasing number of older people living alone, many of whom are women, because there is a higher incidence of widowhood among aged women.

Institutional living arrangements are on the increase in the United States but represent a comparatively small proportion of the elderly; only about 5 out of every 100 old persons live in institutions. Many of these have never married or are widowed or divorced and thus are more often in institutions than older persons who have a spouse or children to care for them. Nursing homes contain only 5 percent of persons age 65 and over. For individuals over 75, it is 9.4 percent, and for those over 85, it is still only 19 percent.

Increasingly, it is recognized that despite profound changes in the roles of family members, grown children are the ones who bear primary responsibility for the well-being of their parents and who are involved in the planning of their living arrangements.

Elderly parents want an intimate relationship, but with independence. They prefer to live near, but not with their adult children, who want to help their parents with the tasks of daily life and to serve as a buffer against isolation and loneliness. It is estimated that 85 percent of the elderly who have children live within an hour's travel of at least one child and that 50 percent live within walking distance. About 80 percent of the care provided to the elderly comes from adult children and in many families one child, usually a daughter, may be tacitly appointed as the caregiver. There are differences based on ethnic, family, economic and social characteristics as well as on individual personalities, but the sense of obligation toward parents is strong, persisting even when the emotional ties in the family have been weak. Many of the elderly are as impaired as some in nursing homes, but the difference is that they have families or adult children who take care of them. Placing an elderly parent, is usually done at the point of desperation. The caregivers may be too old or frail themselves, because there is a growing phenomenon of people in their sixties or seventies caring for 80- and 90-year-old parents respectively.

With the life span increasing, there are several distinct age categories among the elderly that affect living arrangements. The "young–old" are 60 to 75 years who want to be independent, but expect phone calls and visits, want interpersonal contact, and expect advice on major decisions. The frail elderly have difficulty with daily tasks and require others to do more of the shopping, cleaning, and driving to the doctor, as well as to provide socialization. The final category is the very sick, those who are bedridden, disoriented, and incontinent. The families struggle to keep them at home as long as possible but eventually may have to place them. The case of the H. family exemplifies the strong emotional ties within the family.

A LIVING ARRANGEMENT

Gertrude H., 75 years old, took care of her 74-year-old husband who has Parkinson's disease until she incurred a serious heart ailment last winter. The H.'s went to live with their daughter, Lillian M., 49 years old, and her husband, Arnold, 54 years old. Mrs. M. works part-time so that she can be home when they need her.

Mrs. M. is the mother of two children and the grandmother of three. She refuses to consider institutionalizing her father, who is nonambulatory and must be lifted out of bed into his wheelchair. His mental attitude is much better at home. In the hospital he is depressed and his body is rigid. Mrs. M. does most of the housework; her mother helps with some light chores. The father must be lifted in and out of the wheelchair. Mrs. M. concedes, "At times I do feel very tired and somewhat resentful. I have no life of my own. I do it because I love them; because for my whole life they did for me."

Mrs. H. seems aware of the burden her daughter has undertaken, but she does not see any other possible living arrangement. "At times you feel guilty, like you are imposing on their lives and their home."

It is estiamted that almost a majority of all persons 65 and over live in their own home. This housing pattern may include a variety of different types of dwellings: a single-family dwelling, apartment, mobile home, retirement community, room, boarding house, or hotel.

Life-styles and Living Accommodations

The lives of older persons can be characterized by diverse patterns and life-styles. Most of the elderly who enter into friendships, marriage, and work find these choices tend to be satisfying. The intimacy of the marital relationship offers old people warmth, affection, and sharing. Emotional ties that have been developed during the middle years tend to continue to be meaningful during old age.

When a husband or wife dies, the remaining spouse may feel lonely and abandoned. Most old people who are in comparatively good health manage to handle bereavement, loneliness, and widowhood, dealing with it through their own resources. Some individuals may choose to remarry; others, to live together without the contract of marriage if marriage penalizes them financially or if they prefer it. Society must reevaluate legislative and pension policies that tend to penalize widows who remarry by cutting pension and Social Security benefits.

American women, who often marry older men, generally live longer than their spouses. Nearly 67 percent of women over 65 are widows. The likelihood of older widows and divorced women remarrying is not significantly great and decreases with each year, so that at older ages there are increasing numbers of unmarried women.

Older women and men in America are a diverse group, with their life patterns reflecting their varied life experiences as well as their ethnic, cultural, geographic, economic, and educational differences. These factors all influence the type of living arrangement they will choose.

Geographical Distribution

Old people in the United States are primarily residents of urban areas. About 73 percent of all elderly persons reside in either cities or towns, with 2500 or more populations, or in the suburbs. Fifty-five percent of the elderly population, who live in cities of 50,000 or more or in the neighboring suburbs, are primarily home-owners. Approximtely 70 percent own the homes they reside in, most of which have been purchased when the couple was much younger; therefore the houses are more likely to be older, substandard, and in older neighborhoods in central cities than the housing occupied by younger persons. If the elderly are renting, unless it is subsidized housing especially built for them, it is particularly apt to be substandard because older persons often cannot afford higher rents.

Relocation Necessities. To relocate the elderly is not easy. They are tied to their older homes by attitudes and feelings toward the familiarity of objects, the nostalgia of neighborhood, friends, neighbors, church, and long-established patterns that are difficult to duplicate or replicate in other surroundings. Many of the older homes were suitable when the children were living at home, but often the elderly remain alone in a house that is underoccupied and in need of repair. Because the old person may be unable to provide for the required upkeep, maintenance, and care, living in older large homes can present as serious and difficult problems as other living arrangements.

Preferences. Some older persons place considerable emphasis on the degree of independence afforded them in housing and would prefer to live in a house or apartment in an age-integrated neighborhood where they have the most independence and no special services are provided. However, with increasing age, when physical strength wanes and other changes take place in the bodily systems, old people may be required to relinquish some degree of independence. Specialized retirement apartments, hotels, and other living facilities in which certain services are provided may meet the needs of these older persons. Centralized dining facilities, laundry, and health and dental services on the premises may be available for elderly residents who have difficulty shopping, preparing meals, or doing housework.

Types of Arrangement. Congregate living arrangements for the elderly vary from adult group homes for the healthy aged who require a sheltered environment to health-related facilities, where skilled nursing care is provided on a 24-hour basis, or to nursing homes and hospitals. There are many older people with differing needs who may benefit from protective care in a congregate living arrangement that provides many services in a therapeutic environment. Some elderly from varied ethnic, religious, cultural, occupational, and socioeconomic backgrounds may not have available family members, friends, or other resources. They may also have different levels of bodily energy, health, types of illness, interests, and physical and mental functioning.

Presently, a well-organized system of comprehensive care for the elderly, which includes planning for housing, health care, and service delivery programs, is nonexistent. The existing programs have been fragmented, with little coordinated planning among the federal, state, and local governments to develop a coherent plan to provide for the multifaceted problems of the elderly.

For the most part, old persons would like to be and should be helped to remain in their own homes for as long as possible, but some older persons live in the homes of family members. This is an acceptable arrangement if it meets the needs of the individuals without undue conflict among family members resulting in the destruction of family and interpersonal patterns and relationships. For many physically and mentally ill older persons, attempts to keep them at home or in a relative's home are unrealistic. It may be an overwhelming burden on the caretaker(s) physically, emotionally, and financially, and be impractical in providing care for the individual. In such instances congregate residential settings may provide beneficial care for the older person. Many families make herculean efforts to care for their elderly relatives and consider institutionalization as a last resort. Home care of the mentally impaired, chronically ill, or severely disabled old person may be provided by the family but often only at a cost of debilitating the energies and abilities of the family unit to perform other essential tasks. It may also place serious stress on those individuals in the family who are trying to provide adequate care.

There are many elderly ill, impaired, and disabled who have no protective family. The family members may be deceased, ill, infirm or unable or unwilling to provide appropriate care. Such persons may find their way into institutions to obtain protective care and necessary treatment. It should be recognized that there are increasing numbers of homeless men and women in contemporary society, many of whom are seen on the streets of some large cities.

NOWHERE TO LAY HER HEAD

Ellen, a thin, gray-haired woman, 74 years of age, lost her husband a year ago. He died in a municipal hospital in New York City of emphysema. Mrs. G. had cared for him while he was sick during the last several years. They had no children. She was unable to grieve openly and felt her life was over when he died. He left her penniless, with his small disability pension stopping at the time of his death. She was unaware of any financial aid programs for which she was eligible. When Mrs. G. did not pay the rent for 3 months, she was evicted from the small apartment she had shared with her husband. Her furniture and possessions were set out on the street. She put what she could carry in shopping bags and donned several pieces of clothing. She carried her possessions around with her and slept in a park for 6 months. When the weather got too cold, she slept in an abandoned car. One day when she returned from a walk, the car had been towed away. She then began sleeping at Grand Central Station. There are passageways under the station where homeless men and women found shelter. At least she was out of the cold.

Increasing numbers of the urban poor are old people who live in barely minimal conditions: park benches, train and bus stations, or who drift from shelter to shelter with no established residence and no place to lay their heads.

New Trends in Housing and Living Arrangements

Various housing and residential arrangements are being developed for the elderly in the United States, some sponsored by voluntary organizations such as churches, religious organizations, and fraternal groups; others, designed and established by private commercial investors. The federal government, the Department of Housing and Urban Development (HUD), has assumed an active and involved interest and role in housing construction for the elderly. These new types of housing include: planned communities, retirement villages, high-rise apartments, hotel projects, mobile home communities, and other types of congregate developments.

A recent innovation is the retirement village, a planned community in which the sale of housing is age-restricted. The housing may be high-rise apartment buildings, hotels, mobile homes, combinations of independent housing units, or large congregate living facilities. These planned communities offer standard housing at a somewhat lower cost than comparable housing in other communities and appear to be of good value. Some retirement villages have the quality of a resort, offering golf, swimming facilities, other recreational facilities, and transportation. Often the houses provide some architectural concessions to assist older people, as for example, helper bars in the bath, a gradual rise on stairs, or placement of electric outlets higher on the wall for easy reach. Residents are expected to be independent and able to take care of their physical needs, although maintenance of grounds is often provided by the developers. Often a planned community will also offer its residents medical centers. These communities are most successful when church, shopping, and transportation are readily accessible. Location in a metropolitan area often provides the older person nearness to family and friends; such communities are most satisfying to older people who enjoy the companionship of others at the same stage of life with whom they can share common interests. However, many old people prefer to remain integrated with people of all age groups, social classes, and ethnic groups.

High-rise apartments for the elderly have been on the increase in recent years, sponsored by local housing authorities, churches, fraternal and voluntary organizations, and private investors. They usually offer services and amenities such as a common dining room, medical facilities, and varying degrees of recreational activities. They may be located in central cities or in suburban areas, offer companionship with an age-peer group, and provide ready access to social interaction. Also, they give a sense of security from the muggings, robbery, and assault that are commonplace in large urban areas. High-rise apartments as presently designed have been criticized because they can be potentially hazardous in the event of a power failure, making the elevator system unusable and thus isolating the elderly.

Retirement hotels for the elderly are similar to the high-rise apartments, because they bring together large numbers of old people, usually of the same economic level. Retirement hotels generally offer meals and maintenance of living quarters as well as access to medical care and some minor supervision and care as needed.

Mobile homes are another form of housing for old people, especially popular in mild climates such as Arizona, California, and Florida. Their appeal is the reasonable cost of purchase and financing and the ease of continued maintenance. The mobile home park provides elderly residents with independent living yet gives access to their age peer group for social interaction. No special services are provided in these complexes and the elderly residents are expected to be physically able to take care of themselves, but it may be difficult for them to leave the home they had known for many years. This was the case in the following situation:

A HUMAN TOUCH

Wedged between the mountains and a meandering creek, this tiny coalfield community, Matoka, once had rows of houses set side by side. This was a flourishing coal-mining country 30 years ago. Although the Organ mine shut down, some of the people remained. Even though the houses did not belong to them, Matoka was their home. This year, the land company that owns the town decided to tear down the row houses.

Mattie, an 80-year-old widow and one of the few residents left, had fond memories of the string of coal camps where she reared her eight children. "Back in the 20s the coal miners and their families were so close. If you needed help they'd be there in a minute. It's like a ghost town now." Most of the houses around Mrs. T. are vacant. Their windows are gone and the lumber is being hauled away. Here and there remain signs of a human touch, a patch of flowers poking through the rubble. Mrs. T. must leave, but it is very painful because its the only home she has known for 22 years.

Chafin, D., 78 years old, a disabled coal miner who lived in Matoka for 28 years, said that it hurts him to pass his former home. He and his wife had treated the house as their own, planted trees, painted walls and fences. "It's all over now. When they say move, you've got to move." The D.s moved into a crowded trailer park. Their former home was torn down. Mr. D. said sadly, "But it hurts. It really hurts."

Other congregate forms of housing for the elderly are being developed. In some, certain services may be taken care of by the institution, such as household chores, and meals may be provided if desired. Residents of independent units have access to health facilities as needed, a service most reassuring to a frail older person who is fearful of being alone if a catastrophe strikes. This type of arrangement can be particularly suitable for older couples or an individual who prefers independent living with privacy, in combination with the provision of certain services of the institution as desired.

The attitudes and economic resources of the elderly will have a decided influence on the type of housing facilities that are developed in the future. Separate, independent housing where the elderly are homeowners will be affected by their income level. Therefore an increased demand is likely for housing patterns in congregate facilities that provide combinations of living arrangements where a person might initially retain a small house or apartment but could progressively move into less demanding units or health care facilities as needed within the same institutional complex. Living arrangements for the elderly that respect the desire for independent living are apt to continue to gain in popularity, provided that ready access is available to nearby network services. The older person cannot function in a vacuum, and the housing and living arrangement as well as the immediate environment are important in helping the elderly to meet their social, psychological, and physical needs.

INSTITUTIONAL CARE

The term *institutional care* refers to a variety of types of services for the elderly. It has commonly referred to the inpatient services rendered by long-term care psychiatric facilities, but it may also refer to homes for the aged, skilled nursing facilities, and health-related facilities as well as to foster homes, retirement homes, and senior citizen hotels. Very often these places are counted as places of institutional care because they service a population whose needs and problems are similar to those who become institutionalized.

Over one million elderly, of the approximately 23 million in the United States over 65 years, are now in institutions. It is intimated that many more of them need protective care in hospitals, nursing homes, or congregate living arrangements.

Most of the elderly in institutions are considered poor economically. A higher proportion in institutions is dependent on welfare aid at the time of admission. Although there are many private patients in commercial and nonprofit homes, about 80 percent of the payment for the care of the elderly in institutions is from government funds, such as *Medicare* or *Medicaid*. The average age at the time of application to long-term care settings is about 80 years, and the average age of elderly residents of long-term and nursing care facilities is over 80 years.

Older persons in congregate settings require comprehensive care, which includes medical, psychiatric, social, and other therapeutic services.

Old persons in institutions for psychiatric conditions have a wide range of disorders. The largest group have organic mental disorders, which may be accompanied by physical illness or physical impairment. Active disease of the cardiovascular, renal, pulmonary, musculoskeletal, or central nervous systems are common among elderly people in institutions. Some mental disorders have existed prior to old age and are complicated by changes during the aging process. Many of the elderly in institutions are, moreover, poor and would be unable to afford indepen-

dent living even if this were an available alternative. Other psychiatric manifestations of older persons in institutional care are the affective disorders and thought
disorders. These emotional disturbances may be accompanied by other brain
changes that result in memory and mental impairment. The psychiatric disorders
common to the elderly are discussed in more detail in Chapter VII.

Approximately 50 percent of the elderly in long-term institutional care are
nonambulatory, and as few as 10 percent of old people in such places are fully
ambulatory. Over 70 percent of these old persons suffer from organic brain disorders and have symptoms to some degree of confusion and disorientation as to time,
person, place and of memory defect, including both recent and remote memory. In
many of the institutional facilities over 30 percent of the elderly population have
severe confusional states, and from 25 to 40 percent of the elderly residents are
reportedly incontinent.

The majority of the aged living in institutions enter when they are in their late
seventies or eighties. The immediate factors leading to institutional care include
age, debility, multiple impairments of sight, hearing, ambulation, mental functioning, and self-care ability. Other factors are: lack of financial resources or of family
who are willing and able to provide care. Women tend to outnumber men in
institutions by two to one because women generally live longer than men and
usually outlive their spouse.

A PLACE TO CALL MY OWN

Mrs. H. is 79 years old, widowed, who lives alone with a small dog in a
six-room house in an inner city area in New York City. The house is much in
need of repair. The roof leaks, and two windows were shattered by children
playing ball in the streets and have never been replaced. She tenaciously clings
to living in the house despite its hazards and dilapidation. Her health is waning.
She is frail and has been seeing a doctor irregularly for diabetes and other
ailments. Mrs. H. becomes frustrated when he prescribes medication that she
cannot afford. Her income is a meager $125 a month Social Security from her
husband's retirement benefit. This money must pay for taxes on the house,
food, utilities, and fuel to heat the house. She has long since had the telephone,
which was her only means of communication with the outside world, removed.
To save on the fuel bills, she lives in one room of the house during the cold
winter months and keeps the thermostat as low as possible.

Mrs. H. and her husband worked hard to purchase and maintain this
house. She worked as a houseworker, cleaning homes of other people. Her
husband was a night watchman for a neighborhood bank. They scrimped and
saved to pay off the mortgage. He died 5 years ago of a heart attack.

Mrs. H. has no living relatives. They had one son, unmarried, who is
deceased. She feels all alone and has no significant friendships. Neighbors
have invited her to a local church women's group, but she feels uncomfortable

with those people who seem "well to do" and have their own families. She feels depressed at times and finds herself frequently crying. She feels the loss of her husband and son deeply, and says she has "nothing to live for." Robbed twice, with little of value left, she is afraid that the house will be vandalized when she leaves. Walking the streets is also threatening, because teenagers have been stealing the pocketbooks of old women in her neighborhood. Fearful to go out into the streets, she only ventures out to buy food.

Cognizant of her increasing physical and mental disability, she said repeatedly, "What will become of me?"

Her doctor suggested selling the house and moving into Meger Home, which is an adult home for elderly people.

Mrs. H. refuses to leave the only home she has ever owned. She insists that the only way they will get her out of there is to "carry her in a box."

Many sick elderly are maintained at home by their children despite the burden of care because institutionalization is an abhorrent step to many families. Other ailing elderly remain in nursing homes or homes for the aged, only being institutionalized when all other means are exhausted. Symptoms that frequently signal a need for psychiatric hospitalization include suicidal attempts, dangerous wanderings, and confusion. The loss of spouse or other protective persons by death, the threat to security in the change of neighborhood or residence, or the fear of waning health and a need for protective care may lead to application to homes for the aged, but the waiting period for admission to such facilities may take from three months to three years.

Nursing Homes and Related Facilities

Most nursing homes are commercial, proprietary facilities that tend to provide a level of care different from homes for the aged, but reimbursement formulas and requirements are resulting in closer resemblance between their services.

Nursing home care is generally obtained by referral through hospitalization because of impairment from acute illness, accident, or other crisis circumstance. Nursing homes serve a large number of relatively ambulatory, physically well, but moderately to severely mentally impaired aged. Although the hospital and the nursing home provide many of the same services, they are not alike in terms of goals and objectives. The special average length of stay for the hospital patient is seven days or less, whereas the nursing home resident can be expected to remain for a period of 1 to 3 years. Both institutions provide medical and nursing care with food and housing in an appropriate health care environment; however, the long-range health care needs are different.

There are wide variations among nursing homes in the selection and retention of patients and in size, staffing, programs, quality, and cost of care. Many long-term care facilities appear to be moving toward the provision of skilled nursing care, general care and residential care through the development of one facility with differently staffed areas resulting from federally established reimbursement formulas.

Medicare provides money for the elderly for 3 to 4 months of posthospital care in specified nursing homes. The concept of "skilled nursing care" areas attempts to maintain standards of nursing home care for the long-term as well as the short-term elderly patient. Patients in these facilities are entitled to reimbursement by Medicare. Elderly patients who need less skilled nursing care are assigned to "intermediate care" areas. The extended care facility may be considered a "halfway house" or place for convalescence after acute hospital care. There is considerable misunderstanding and confusion about the various types of facilities, the complex admission procedures, and the plans for financing care for the elderly. This often leads to mistaken ideas by families in planning for elderly relatives.

Nursing homes are under the jurisdiction of state and municipal departments of social welfare, hospital, or health departments for supervision and licensing, because over 80 percent of the residents in nursing homes are recipients of welfare assistance. Thus the welfare departments have some supervising responsibility over such facilities, holding them accountable for monies allocated and also for maintenance of a quality standard of care.

In nursing homes, medical care and services are obtained and provided by private physicians or physicians assigned by welfare agencies through group, hospital, or team health care providers. In acute illness, elderly individuals would be transferred to a local hospital. Nursing homes are required to have a physician medical director or staff to coordinate and be responsible for maintaining quality medical services.

Nursing care varies with each facility, from minimal care and services given to an excellent quality of care and services. Special nursing care can be provided if required for individual elderly patients beyond the usual care of the institution, if the patient or the family wishes the care and can financially afford it.

In the vast majority of nursing homes nursing care is limited and all too frequently inadequate. Care is often thought of as custodial, and the needs of the elderly for social, psychological, and other meaningful dynamic therapeutic services are ignored. Acquiring and maintaining personnel for these facilities presents problems: Aides are frequently poorly trained and ill equipped for the positions; staff turnover in all areas is considered high in nursing homes; and abuses are common.

Skilled nursing facilities are presumed to provide quality nursing services. The definition and standards of adequate nursing care is vague and open to question, which often results in abuse. Because psychiatric services are usually not provided, elderly individuals manifesting such symptoms are excluded from most nursing homes, thereby bypassing large groups of older people in need of nursing home care.

In many nursing homes social services are rarely provided although they could be most helpful in applicant screening, as well as in ongoing counseling and continued liaison work with family and significant others.

The length of stay in nursing homes is decreasing, with many being converted to skilled nursing facilities, and increasing in intermediate care facilities according to standards and regulations, with continued maintenance of patients who would otherwise be transferred.

The size of nursing homes generally ranges from 15 to 300 or more beds. The services provided are usually limited but as intermediate care facilities are added, nursing homes are gradually beginning to include other services, usually those reimbursed by Medicare.

In the past the admission policies into nursing homes have been fairly liberal, with no waiting period and, if it became necessary, the patient was transferred to a hospital facility. However, with Medicare reimbursement, nursing homes that have moved into the provision of skilled nursing facilities or extended care facilities are more likely to be selective of the kind of patient who fits the services offered. Medicare rulings, however, encourage admission of a hetergeneous population of all economic backgrounds.

HELP IS AVAILABLE

Mrs. G. was a widow, living in her own home, with no living relatives. She had increasingly poor eyesight and was unaware that she qualified as being "legally blind." She did not know that arrangements could be made to use her property value at sale to help to keep her until death. She lived on very little food, "the tea and cracker" meals of many an oldster because they could not get about easily. Unaware that there were services to remedy this situation, she struggled on bravely, but frightened and depressed. With old neighbors gone and new ones who spoke another language, she had little contact. An old neighbor who happened to "drop by," grasped the situation and saw what the suffering Mrs. G. was experiencing. She elicited some pertinent information from Mrs. G. and without raising false hopes, contacted The Society for the Blind. A worker visited Mrs. G. and was able to ascertain that she qualified for help from the agency. An explanation was given as to what could be done and arrangements were made to provide the assistance.

Mrs. G. was surprised, relieved, and grateful and said, "I thought no one cared."

Homes for the Aged

Old age homes are usually nonprofit, voluntary, and sectarian (religious). They are sometimes under the auspices of benevolent and fraternal organizations or associations. The private, nonsubsidized homes for the aged may resemble the nursing home in such areas as admissions policies and the patient population. Homes for the aged differ as to the size of the home, the level and extent of care provided, and the method of financing the facility.

Homes for the aged are under the supervision and licensure of the departments of social service in residential areas or by the state departments of health in hospital catchment areas. Welfare departments usually have some supervision of old age homes because a large percentage of their residents are welfare supported.

The medical care services vary in homes for the aged, ranging from minimal to fairly comprehensive and from fair to excellent. If surgery, radiotherapy, or care in an outside hospital is necessary, it is paid for by Medicare in most instances. Old age homes have the option of employing physicians. Social services are often available in homes for the aged and can be used extensively in helping the patient adjust to the change in residence and in providing concomitant services for the family as needed.

Patients in homes for the aged usually plan to stay for the remainder of their lives. The rate of mortality in these homes ranges from 20 percent in those that select the healthy to about 40 percent in those that are more like hospitals or nursing homes. The number of beds in old age homes range from 20 to 500 or more, and a variety of services may be provided, some of which may include: social services, psychiatric consultation, occupational and recreational therapy, sheltered workshops, podiatry, barbers and hairdressers, shops, chapel, dentistry, clinics, clubs, libraries, dramatics, and music. Homes for the aged depend on voluntary contributions, patient's own savings and income from Social Security and other pensions. It is therefore difficult for them to offer a wide range of services to meet the medical and psychiatric need of the elderly.

The admissions policies in the past for homes for the aged were selective, thus the population tended to be homogeneous with regard to socioeconomic, cultural, and religious background. Patients who were acutely or mentally ill were excluded. The relatively healthy were given preference for admission. Contributions from the patient's family, religious groups, and churches were invited. The waiting period for admission varied anywhere from 3 to 6 months to 1 to 3 years. In recent years, as the age of applicants and residents has increased, there has been a relaxation and liberality in admissions policies to admit older, sicker persons with some level of psychiatric behavioral disturbance.

Since the passage of the amendments to the Social Security Act of 1965, filial responsibility for aging parents is no longer necessary or required; therefore the maintenance of older people in old age homes is seldom paid for by families. If the funds of the patient are exhausted or insufficient to meet the monthly rate of the home, referral can be made to the department of social services for old age assistance or medical aid for the aged to make up the difference. The state department of health of the department of social services establishes a reasonable monthly rate for domiciliary care, which is much less expensive than infirmary or hospital care.

In addition to nursing homes and homes for the aged, some multi-institutional arrangements are being tried successfully to provide more comprehensive care for the elderly. Such facilities can include: residential apartment buildings; several small units, intermediate boarding facilities; a day care center for the elderly living in their own homes in a community; a geriatric outreach program providing community social services, "meals on wheels," "drop-in" centers with recreational services; and at the main centers, intermediate care, health-related facilities, and skilled nursing facilities. In addition, a 300 to 500 bed accredited chronic disease hospital can become available for the elderly who require these services at the central site. Middle income housing projects located in the same complex can accept as many as 300 elderly residents.

These exemplary efforts to provide the elderly with comprehensive services that approximate a type of campus living arrangement have met with successful results. These larger complexes offer flexible utilization of an integrated care system that provides for the progressive need for care of the elderly persons who may need help from social institutions because of physical decline, mental impairment, or emotionally disturbed behavior.

Planning facilities for the aging must take into account that the majority will need the facility for the remainder of their lives. Therefore the environment should be protective and emotionally and psychologically supportive. The ideal institution is one that provides protective services in a supportive environment, with general medical care and special medical and social services that cover a wide spectrum to meet the different needs and levels of functioning of the aged.

Administrative Issues

The essential services that administration must provide in any residential facility for the elderly are food, lodging, and basic medical care. The objectives of these services can be interpreted broadly to cover a wide range of physical and psychological needs and can include a conglomerate of professional therapeutic efforts. In psychotherapy, some goals are to increase in the individual a sense of worth and value; to foster self-sufficiency, independence and self-fulfillment; to promote social integration and social relations while allowing for individual needs for privacy and independence; to encourage involvement in the decision process in areas relevant to self; to encourage the use of self within a helpful setting; to encourage personal creativity, interests, and self-actualization wherever feasible; and to provide support against the fears, anxieties, and apprehensions that are common to the elderly.

Quality care medical services should also be provided, including counseling, social work services, individual and group therapy, and activities therapy needed by all institutionalized persons. More than 50 percent of the population in institutions need special medical care, such as podiatry and dentistry. Approximately 10 to 40 percent of the elderly in institutions require intensive care for cardiovascular disease, infections, and acute illnesses. Because there are varied needs, the services provided must be expansive—medical care services must monitor the changing, fluctuating, and unstable state of health of a large number of the aged. With common conditions of old age, such as diabetes, hypertension, cardiovascular disease, emphysema, anemia, and arthritis, prompt attention is required with follow-up care. Medication, appropriate diet, health education, exercise or rest, and continued treatment are important aspects to maintaining and restoring health. The multiplicity of symptoms and the chronicity of illness demands the provision of quality health care services of an alert, responsive professional health team of persons knowledgeable in gerontological problems.

Administration of a facility should take into account individual preferences for privacy. Some elderly individuals prefer social interaction with an opportunity for interpersonal relationships but desire private, unshared rooms, whereas others may prefer to share rooms. A common dining room can be an opportunity for social interchange. Often helpful in the adjustment to a change in residence is to provide an atmosphere as homelike as possible and to avoid the starkly clinical, even in intensive care facilities. Rugs, lamps, beds, and furnishings should be appropriate for the needs of the elderly.

The interpersonal relationships with staff and personnel in the institutional facility is of the greatest importance in giving optimal care. Staff attitudes toward, and interest in, the care of the elderly should be given priority attention. Staff members often need help in providing a structured but flexible program without unduly subjecting the elderly to embarrassment, failure, or confrontation with their deficits and impairment. Staff conferences, continuing and in-service educational programs, and team collaboration can favorably influence staff attitudes, behavior, and morale in the care of the aged.

Attitudes Toward Institutionalization

The low quality of institutional care in the past has tended to reinforce negative *attitudes* about the use of such facilities. Institutions have been so poorly staffed, inadequately equipped, and lacking in skilled management that the elderly and their families regard them as undesirable sites. Moving into such residences, moreover, may tend to affect an individual's self-esteem, worsen an already present disability, and intensify other physical and emotional disorders. Some institutions, however, have demonstrated new and useful approaches in community living for the aging, providing therapeutic activities and services, pleasant accommodations, and a competent, well-motivated staff, all having a positive effect on the adjustment and morale of the aged person, and thus counteracting and preventing institutional deterioration. If elderly persons or their relatives are contemplating long-term care in a nursing home or a home for the aged, many factors should be considered in the selection of a quality facility. The following list of questions may be helpful:

Is the facility licensed? (Ask to see the license)

Is the facility approved by Medicare and Medicaid?

What other insurance plans are acceptable?

Are there additional charges for personal services?

Are residents allowed to furnish their room with their own furniture?

Can residents have their own radio and television?

Can a husband and wife share the same room?

Can residents have alcohol or smoke in their rooms or lounges?

Are there restrictions on making or receiving phone calls?

What are the visiting hours? Is the resident allowed to visit friends and relatives outside the facility?

Where is the resident's money kept? Is there provision for personal banking?

Does each resident have a separate closet and chest of drawers?

What is the capacity of the facility? How many residents presently reside at the facility?

Is the size of the staff adequate for the facility?

How often do firedrills occur? Are there ceiling sprinklers, available extinguishers, and exits?

What types of activities are available for the residents?

What medical and social services are available?

Is the staff professionally competent?

What are the dining arrangements? Are special dietary services available?

SERVICES FOR OLDER PEOPLE

Significant advances have been made in the last decade in developing and making services available for the elderly. Perhaps more than any other group in society, the aged rely heavily on health and welfare services and resources. The lengthening postretirement period has exacerbated the problems of providing adequate health and social serivices and the abilities of the elderly to function in society. Older people depend on complex public and private institutions and a considerable number of available programs to provide services ranging from simple information to direct aid during a crisis. In some instances these programs are less than adequate because policies for the aged are affected by economic, political, and social trends in society.

Home Health Care Services

Many people require some form of institutionalization, but large numbers of the elderly could avoid being institutionalized if other services were available. A recent report of the General Accounting Office estimates that about 25 percent of the patient population is treated in institutional settings that offer services exceeding patient needs because a complete range of other health services do not exist and health care has been oriented primarily toward treatment of acute illness. This is a costly form of health care and not always the most effective. Alternative health services that could be considered are: home health care, friendly visitors, and a variety of services in the community.

Home health care has been cited as a means of health care delivery for reducing hospital costs. Besides being less costly than the daily rate in a general hospital, home care services have other outstanding advantages over institutionalization. Most older people prefer to be at home in familiar, comfortable surroundings that are reassuring and supportive, thus ensuring their morale, which is an important factor in treatment. Home health care can be very beneficial for the acutely or terminally ill and the convalescent by using the family instead of strangers as a resource for ongoing patient care, supplying certain patient needs and desires. Some elderly people prefer the greater freedom of receiving health care at home to the regimen at a hospital or institution. An example of a positive experience in home health care is the case of Mr. C.

HOME HEALTH SERVICE FOR MR. C.

Mr. C. had been a frequent patient at the local general hospital. In the past year he had been hospitalized for as long as 3 weeks to a month for each stay. His condition was diagnosed as chronic emphysema. Mr. C. strongly disliked hospitals, preferring to be at home surrounded by his family and his numerous plants, and he enjoyed watching sports events on TV.

After one week during his last hospitalization his physician arranged for the patient to be discharged to home health care for 1 month. Arrangements were made for a weekly visit by a visiting nurse to monitor his condition. A portable respirator was ordered to be delivered to the home, and the patient and his wife were taught how to use it. Mr. C. and his family were pleased with this alternative health care plan and the resulting benefits, including watching the Superbowl without interruption.

Providing home health care is not satisfactory in all situations. Some families may find caring for an elderly relative burdensome and do not feel they have the skills to give adequate care. Others, however, having small children or family members requiring significant attention do not have adequate time to devote to the older person, although their intentions are good. Effective planning for such care should entail physicians', nursing, and home health services.

Physicians' Services

Physicians are not always available or willing to make house calls. In most cases they prefer to provide evaluation and treatment in the office or hospital. Getting to the physician's office may be difficult or impossible for some older persons, thus complicating the problem. Using physician's assistants—a new category of health care professional, who may function as a physician extender—in home health services, may offer possibilities in geriatric medical care. Trained in certain technical skills, physicians' assistants may carry out routine patient tasks and diagnostic and therapeutic procedures assigned by and under the responsibility of a physician.

Nursing Services

Nursing services have traditionally offered home care provided by Public Health nurses who work for city or county health departments or Visiting Nurse associations. Some of their duties may include: visiting families in their homes to give direct nursing care for patients with acute and chronic illnesses, providing health education to patient and families, and exploring community health and social resources for the patient or family.

Homemaker-Home Health Aide Services

Homemaker or home health aide services may be provided to offer a range of needed homemaking activities such as laundering, shopping, and preparing meals. They may also include taking vital signs, giving baths, and assisting with certain medical and physical care tasks. They can serve an important function in helping to keep families intact or enabling an older person to return home after receiving specialized care. Homemakers and home health aides receive training from a hospital or community agency to carry out assigned tasks under the supervision of a professional, who is responsible for the plan of care.

Friendly Visitors

Many communities have friendly visitor service programs available. Well-trained visitors are usually employed by welfare agencies to provide companionship and other services to the homebound elderly. They may help with shopping and securing health, nutritional, and other needed services for their clients.

Nutritional Services

The federal government has provided funding for nutritional services for the aged. The U.S. Department of Agriculture, under the Food Stamp Act passed by Congress in 1964, provided to eligible people the opportunity to purchase stamps at less than face value, to be used to purchase food in local food stores. This program presently services large numbers of the elderly. Government action on food stamps changes periodically, however.

The U.S. Congress passed the Comprehensive Services Amendments to the Older Americans Act in 1972, which provided a national program for one nutritionally planned hot meal a day, 5 days a week, to people 60 years and over. Congregate dining sites have been established for impoverished and isolated elderly people in the 50 states. The programs now provide over 270,000 meals daily to senior citizens. Transportation and escort services for the elderly are also provided where needed between their homes and the dining site.

Meals on wheels programs, established in the 1960s in some communities as a part of nutrition programs, provides portable meals for homebound elderly persons. A minimal fee may be charged for this service. This program services about 12,000 people annually.

Day Care Services

Geriatric day centers have been developed in the United States in recent years to make available to older people supportive care and services. These centers may be open 8 hours a day, 5 days a week, providing several types of day care facilities: medical day care centers, where daily medical care services are given to individuals who may be recovering from an illness but no longer need to be hospitalized; health-related day care centers that provide health care services to chronically ill individuals, requiring continued nursing services and other health care supports; psychiatric day care centers with a supervised, therapeutic environment for the individual with a history of mental disorder and who could benefit from a protective environment that offers psychosocial day care; senior citizen centers that provide appropriate social day care experiences for the individual who is capable of independent social functioning but requires no custodial care.

Social Services

The need for more services for the elderly has intensified, but at the same time, difficulties have emerged in assuring that the services already provided are cost effective. Moreover, many assumptions used in developing social service programs were simplistic and not always in keeping with the needs and nature of the clientele. There is a major need to understand how improvements can be made in defining what services are necessary and in structuring, implementing, and in ensuring, that they aid the intended population.

Social services programs for the aged should only be created with an understanding of how they are affected by the age, sex, ethnic group identification, and socioeconomic status of those to be served and the differences between urban and rural life. Clearly, incomplete comprehension of the characteristics of a target population results in an underutilization of services and an inability of services to reach their intended population. Another factor influencing the use of social services is the lack of agreement between the needs of the elderly as perceived by the elderly and those as perceived by workers in the field of gerontology, yet programs for the aging have frequently been developed without any documentation on this problem. There is a necessity for impact and outcome assessment to supply information on the effectiveness of current methods of providing services for the elderly.

Foster-Family Care of the Elderly

Some states have established foster care programs for elderly adults who are in need of care and protection in a substitute family setting for a planned period of time. The goal of such services is to enable the socially, physically, or mentally handicapped or isolated adults to resume or continue life within a family unit in their own community, near friends and relatives. This arrangement may eliminate or postpone the need for institutional care. The individual who chooses to accept service under the foster family care program may expect a wholesome family life in which one can hope to participate within limits of the older person's and the family's desires. Usually, the state department of social services and local social service districts share responsibility for the approval and supervision of foster family care homes and family-type proprietary homes for adults.

The decision to place an elderly individual in foster care is based on the individual's potential for adjustment in such a setting, level of social integration, desire and capacity for this level of independence, availability of other placement options, and the motivation of the elderly person and the foster family.

In addition to the close ties possible in the family setting, there are the advantages of stimulation and interaction to be found in foster care for the elderly. Also, opportunities may exist for social activities and recreational diversions in accordance with the interests and needs of the individual. A foster family can serve to facilitate integration and help to restore identity for elderly persons who have been released from institutions. In order to promote personal relationships and family atmosphere, the homes should be small, with possibly four residents the upper limit. The attempt should be made in the selection of the home to achieve the best possible match among the older person, the family, and the environment.

The use of foster family care for the elderly is a viable living arrangement for some persons when they can no longer meet the demand of an independent setting but do not need the higher levels of care offered in a nursing home or hospital.

Emergency Alarm Response System

Emergency Alarm Response System (EARS) is a personal electronic device that helps older people maintain independence in their own homes and neighborhoods with the greatest possible security, confidence, and dignity. Developed by Lifeline Systems, under a HEW grant, EARS is sponsored by the Metropolitan Jewish Geriatric Center and is the first program of its kind in the New York metropolitan area. EARS provides immediate 24-hour access to health, social, and protective services in an emergency situation and is designed to put isolated and disabled elderly persons in touch with concerned family, friends, neighbors, and professionals in the community when help is needed. Making users more confident about living alone in their own homes, saving on the cost of expensive medical care, and preventing the need for placement in a nursing home are major benefits of the system.

As people grow older, some may feel isolated, suffer from chronic poor health, be partially disabled, and have difficulty in performing daily tasks, and are especially vulnerable to falls, household accidents, and heart attacks. EARS can help to reassure the elderly that they are never alone and can get help when necessary!

EARS costs a minimum amount a day and can easily be connected to most phones without extra cost, although there may be a one-time charge by the telephone company for a special phone jack.

Protective Services

Traditional approaches to caring for the helpless or dependent, including family arrangements, community services, institutionalization, and legal protection, have not been adequate for the needy. The number of aged persons requiring support or protection in the United States today exceeds two million. More than twice this amount would likely need assistance if the support systems of relatives, friends, or social service agencies were to cease.

Some elderly are frail and infirm and have no one to care for them and nowhere to go. They are seen wandering at large, unkept, rummaging through garbage cans for a piece of paper or clothing. Many keep to themselves, afraid to go outside. Others are confined to nursing homes or mental hospitals, or they live in conditions of decay.

Most older persons who need assistance in daily living activities accept it eagerly. Family, friends, and social service agencies support them in finding a place to live, an adequate diet, part-time employment, and social opportunities. Services that assist a physically or mentally infirm older person in carrying out the normal activities of living are termed "protective services." They could be health or social services, psychiatric, or legal services. However, when the intervention is significant or resisted, there may be a need for legal intervention to authorize the necessary services. In most states legal intervention can be authorized in one of several ways; commitment to an institution; guardianship of the person, which transfers control over personal decisions; conservatorship of property, which transfers control over one's property and financial affairs; or temporary intervention and protective placements.

On one hand, protective services involve complex questions of personal choice, individual freedom, and respect for individual differences. On the other hand is the principle that society has a responsibility to protect those unable to care for themselves from dangerous and destructive situations.

A NEED FOR PROTECTIVE SERVICES

Mr. T., 75 years of age, was referred for consideration of protective services. He was described as "living under physical conditions of an abhorent nature" and was the object of concern and despair of the neighbors and of sanitation and health officials. Mr. T.'s style of living for himself, his 15 dogs, and a cat was obnoxious to everyone but himself. He was a diabetic, with ulcerated legs. He resisted medical care, ate improperly, and was described as "filthy." He kept the animals confined to the house, and both he and they were starving. He barely maintained himself in a ten-room house, begging food from neighbors.

Mr. T., who had lived alone for almost a quarter of a century in the old, increasingly neglected house, was the last survivor of a large family. He had worked as a carpenter until the age of 68. Mr. T.'s social deterioration was of several years standing, and his grave financial limitations undoubtedly contributed to neglect of himself, his home, and his animals. The ownership of the home and his tenacity about keeping it, complicated his eligibility for public assistance. The accumulation of filth in the home and the denial of the existence of this state of affairs were destructive. He fought any steps toward temporary guardianship. A social worker visited him and discussed the possibility of selling the house, providing for the animals, and moving into a residential care facility. Mr. T. seemed relieved that someone else would take care of these arrangements for him, and was placed and cared for.

Summary

For the next several decades the United States will have an increasing population of the elderly, in which females will out number males. The effectiveness of the policies designed in response to these changes in population will depend on an understanding of the aged individually and in groups. Incomplete knowledge and erroneous assumptions may lead to policies and legislation that result in inadequate and disappointing outcomes.

The support systems available to much of the population in the United States are frequently unavailable to the aged. Obtaining housing arrangements, protection from crime, economic security, transportation, and a full range of services presents serious problems to them. The aged can be divided into the "old" (60 to 75 years), who are usually retired, healthy, active, and able to undertake meaningful activities, and the "very old" (75 years and over), many of whom can manage if provided with a support system, and a small number requiring sustained support. It is important to recognize in the consideration of housing facilities and services that the elderly are a diverse group with individual differences and needs.

The inability of some aged persons to cope successfully with intellectual and social tasks is usually due to stresses associated with aging rather than caused by aging itself. Some physical or mental declines in the elderly are often caused by manageable impositions that are only partially related to age, such as disease, poor diet, economic plight, social isolation, or inadequate housing, rather than solely to the biological process of aging. It is possible to prevent such problems by providing services that enable many of the aged, given the opportunity, to lead independent, self-sustaining, satisfying lives.

Institutionalization is limited to a small portion of the elderly. The vast majority are living in their own homes, intellectually and socially able, productive when given the chance, interested in their surroundings, and eager to participate in the social life of family, friends, and community. Specially designed housing and age-oriented environments also often benefit the elderly.

However, because many elderly own their own homes (70 percent of the housing occupied by older persons), maintaining and improving the homes can be a serious problem.

Available transportation that is safe, economically viable, convenient, and designed to meet the special needs of the elderly is less than adequate. Therefore persons with physical disabilities and failing health are unable to use most forms of public transportation, mainly because of infrequent service, numerous steps to climb, fear of personal safety, long distances from residences and destinations, and sometimes, inclement weather.

Where the appropriate option is institutional care, efforts should be made to help the elderly and their families cope more effectively with institutionalization. Continued concern must be widened to assess and assure the quality of institutional care.

In order to meet the transportation needs of the elderly, many communities are offering programs, such as "Dial a Ride," in which older persons can arrange a taxi ride for a reduced fare. Free bus service is available to the elderly in some cities, and senior citizens' groups in other areas have a minibus system to assist older people, but improved transportation experiments offering ways to link people and services are needed.

There is a wide range of services for the aged in the United States, but it is necessary to make them available to the aged. Older persons need an effective network of available facilities, programs and services to help them survive short-term crises and to meet long-term requirements. Without these supports many needlessly lose their capacity to live independently in their own homes. Given the varied and changing needs of older persons, programs of health and social care must be comprehensive to be effective.

Although many services are available to the elderly in large metropolitan areas, they are only accessible to those residing in the immediate geographic vicinity. Society must strive toward finding, maintaining, and promoting adequate quality and accessible services for the elderly.

FURTHER READINGS

Bengtson, V., and D. A. Haber, "Sociological Approaches to Aging," in D. Woodruff and J. Birren (eds.), *Aging: Scientific Perspectives and Social Issues,* Van Nostrand, New York, 1975.

Bengtson, V. L., et al., A Progress Report: USC Study of Generations. Andrus Gerontology Center, University of Southern California, Los Angeles, 1976.

Bengtson, V. L., and K. D. Black, "Intergenerational Relations and Continuities in Socialization," in P. Baltes and W. Schaie (eds.), *Personality and Socialization,* Academic Press, New York, 1973.

Black, K. D., and V. L. Bengtson, "Solidarity Across Generations: Elderly Parents and Their Middle-Aged Children," paper presented at annual meeting of the Gerontological Society, 1973.

Brotman, H., "Analytical and Summary Reference Tables: The Older Population Estimates for 1975 Projecting through 2000," prepared for the National Institute on Aging, January 1976.

Hill, R., N. Foote, J. Aldous, R. Carlson, and R. MacDonald, *Family Development in Three Generations,* Schenkman, Cambridge, Mass., 1970.

Kerckhoff, A. C., "Nuclear and Extended Family Relationships: Normative and Behavioral Analysis," in E. Shanas and G. Streib (eds.), *Social Structure and Family: Intergenerational Relations,* Prentice-Hall, Englewood Cliffs, N.J., 1965.

Schwartz, A., *Survival Handbook for Children of Aging Parents,* Follett, Chicago, 1977.

Weg, R. B., "The Old: Who, What, Where, How?", mimeographed report, E. P. Andrus Gerontology Center, University of Southern California, Los Angeles, 1977.

CHAPTER 11

Death and Aging

Whatever the circumstances at this phase of the life cycle, the elderly cannot avoid the fact of ultimate personal death. In approaching death, older people must either make a healthy adjustment or build up defenses to shield themselves to some extent from facing reality. Thus the awareness of death and its personal meaning to the aged is a crucial aspect of the aging process, affecting the behavior of all concerned.

This chapter assembles available knowledge and ideas on death with the main emphasis on understanding how people reportedly face personal death and its impact on the bereaved. Some common notions about death that affect both the dying and those concerned are examined. With a brief discussion on the causes of death, the focus is on the ways people cope with the difficulties of dying and how the bereaved deal with the challenge of altered life patterns.

Research itself on these matters is a problem because of difficulties in conceptualizing death and arriving at operational definitions suitable for valid research. Investigators, moreover, have used diverse methods so that comparisons among findings are difficult, and some procedures may be inadequate to measure accurately the meaning of death for different people. In addition, data are taken at only one point in time, although serial interviews over a span of time might be useful. Research is in process but much remains to be done.

A major aspect of dying for the aged is the separation of the physical from the psychological. According to Fischer (1971), death of our physical self is a problem insofar as we identify the self with our physical body. Death, then, is a problem of identity. The more constricted the identity is to a sense of worth based on the physical aspects of life, the more vulnerable it is to destruction; whereas death, known and accepted as part of the life process, increases the resistance of the person to total destruction of self-esteem based on bodily changes that may accompany the end of life.

BIOLOGICAL DEATH

Death over the centuries has been commonly viewed as occurring when the heart stops and breathing ceases, but science has established more specific criteria. Scientists now agree that the brain, which continues to function for a short time after the heart stops (less than 10 minutes) is the key to human life. Once the brain stops functioning, the person is medically and in some states legally dead. Brain death is characterized by: no movement or breathing, no reflexes, and most reliably, no trace of electrical activity of the brain. Most states either have adopted or are considering legislation that defines death in this way.

Causes of Death in the Elderly

The 20 most common causes of death in the elderly are listed in Chapter 3. From age 65 and over, disorders of the vascular system take the lives of an increasing proportion of older people. However, there are considerable data available from which it can be determined how many years the average person can expect to live, depending on the particular terminal disease. Although malignancies claim many lives after 65 years, vascular system disorders kill many more. Arteriosclerotic heart disease is the most important cause of death in all age ranges, with brain hemorrhage second, especially for people over 75 (about 10 million and the fastest growing group of elderly). Blood vessel disease is involved in the majority of deaths over 75 and remains an important cause for those over 85, although outranked by arteriosclerosis, cerebral thrombosis, and embolism. A number of vital functions often decline rapidly and simultaneously.

Other factors such as occupational backgrounds, sex, and geographical location can be used to predict death more accurately and may tend to differentiate the individual from the average. Women, for example, may be expected to live longer than men, and the married person is less likely to die than a single person of the same age. Some acute conditions, including violent death, are more common in the unmarried. Living conditions for the aging can also alter the likelihood of developing fatal disorders and even in a comparatively small geographic area the mortality rates of the elderly vary between different areas, generally higher in urban than in rural areas. The life-style associated with different occupational groups, and their exposure to potential disease-producing factors in the working place, is an important factor in mortality rate. There is also some variation in the types of illness for different social classes.

Fear of Death and Dying

Without a doubt, conditions affecting physical health do affect feelings and increase the fear of approaching death, thus stirring thoughts about the meaning of life and death and the tenets of religion.

Death is commonly represented as an ominous figure, yet, surprisingly, many people dread the pain of illness more than death itself. Nursing homes report that most geriatric patients indicate they see death as preferable to continued illness or chronic disability. According to Kalish, (1966, 1976) they have become "socially dead," often viewing death as timely and welcome. It is obvious in everyday life that adults often avoid the mention of personal death or if people speak of their own demise, they are often hastily reassured. This may bring temporary but not wholly successful ease of a painful subject. Cameron et al. (1973) in measuring the consciousness of death throughout the life-span found that youth thought about death on the average every 2 days, whereas old people only think about it once a week, thus concluding that the elderly largely repress thoughts of death. Moreover, the use of euphemisms and continued evasion of the reality of death may contribute to greater stress when the threat of death is undeniable. In recent National Institute of Mental Health (1981) surveys of healthy older people, overt fear of death judged by onlookers was present in about 30 percent. Butler (1977) points out that even though many older people may not show any obvious fear, when confronted with the reality of it, they may react otherwise.

Fear of the Dead

Another sort of fear apparent in the phenomenon of death concerns the death of one's own body. This is much less evident than the fear of dying but is regularly expressed by those faced with personal death as dread or even horror over the altered state of the body in dying. When one's own physical being has been disfigured by death or injury, people appear to shrink from dismay at the change in what is so closely related to one's identity. Unfortunately, the dead or dying body is still treated as though it were the person. Because the body is held in such high regard in American culture, changes in appearance may be viewed with fear and deep concern.

Other Fears Displaced on Death

Most people will experience normal fears about death, when either symptoms or a particular situation holds a fatal threat or a significant person or goal might be lost in one's life.

It is easy to comprehend why anxiety is focused on death and dying for people who are aware of physical changes in response to stress, such as labored breathing and faster heart beat, and for those in whom it means separation, rejection, and isolation.

[Older people have expressed that the fear of death is tied up with prolonged illness, dependency, and pain, all of which may bring severe threats of rejection and isolation, loss of social role, self-determination, and individual dignity]

As mentioned, another important aspect of death is fear of the prospect of imposed separation. Where there is undue emotional dependence, morbid fears of death can also rise. Dependency may be manifested as anger or frustration at the loved one. In this emotional climate there are both excessive fears for the safety of that individual, and underlying anger at him or her and the situation itself.

Along with the fear of dying, people might be overwhelmed by the impulse to commit suicide. Considering the suffering and pain involved in the stress of aging and dying and the accessibility of means, surprisingly, suicide is not more prevalent. It is probably more common among the old than it once was. Suicide remains a difficult problem for Americans who continue to picture it as immoral or a sign of severe emotional disturbance. Many clergymen still refuse to officiate at public ceremonies for people who have committed suicide. For some of the dying and their families suicide is often seen as the only rational decision. In others it seems that an uncivilized element in one's nature has emerged in the form of thoughts of death and self-destruction. Current research indicates that suicide resulting from concern with death tends to occur more in persons with neurotic conflicts, who have depressive symptoms, rather than in those who are either normal or psychotic.

With so many sources of anxiety over death, dying appears to be a time of great fear. It is true that when dying, people are influenced by their previous attitudes and fears whether they are normal or irrationally abnormal. However, the most uncomfortable thoughts on death may not necessarily come forth at that time. Often people reach a courageous serenity in accepting the inevitable that Koestenbaum (1964) argues is an achievement of final integrity. It is often the mark of the adult who sees death as a completion of a pattern and can accept death at the end of a productive life.

Philosophies of Life and Death

In the United States we have often inherited ways of perceiving aging, death, and dying that are rooted primarily in a Judeo-Christian heritage and are both an affirmation of and denial of life. Attitudes are programmed into our thinking and behavior from infancy by our homes, churches and synagogues, and society—influences sometimes open and direct, often subtle. Religious beliefs may affect or determine attitudes of personal identity and worth and the way the aged perceive death and dying.

The principle source of authorative Judeo-Christian thinking is the Bible, which is accepted in part or whole or with added writings by Jews, Christians, and Moslems. These religious bodies with which individuals align themselves are the conveyors and interpreters of the biblical concepts that are the nucleus of religion in mainline American churches and are based on texts considered divinely revealed. Hence supernatural authority is given to principles, values, and attitudes implicit in the sacred writings and affirmed by expositors. The Bible is thus used as a source book and interpreted to support a variety of divergent opinions.

Most of the religious systems include the concept of "God's will" and teach that all events occur for a purpose and that certain forces are beyond individual control. Such beliefs may encourage a "what will be" attitude toward infirmity and death. There are some who are convinced that human life span is limited by divine decree, and they support their belief from the Bible. A psalmist wrote "Our life span is seventy years or, if heaven decrees, eighty" (PS.90:10).

In Hebrew thought, longevity was a reward for obedience to divine instruction, but this belief encounters difficulty when the good die young, when suffering comes to the obedient follower, or when the wicked enjoy longevity and good health. Today a believer enjoying good health and longevity might feel rewarded for adherence to the faith. On the other hand, disability, pain, and loss might induce guilt and a search for a reason for the curse of divine wrath.

For some, promises of blessing in a future life may make infirmities more bearable and the thought of death tolerable, but beliefs about suffering and eternal life vary. Some Jews do not believe in life after death. Others (Orthodox) believe in an afterlife with rewards and punishments. For Christians, there is judgment in the life after death, with heaven and hell as possible alternatives and purgatorial cleansing interposed for Roman Catholics.

Personal Meaning of Death

If our present society were predominantly Christian as it is often considered, the general conviction would be that death had been vanquished, but in fact, about one-fourth the population disclaim any religious belief and about a half do not believe in life after death.

When older people were asked in the Duke studies (Busse, 1977) what death meant to them, although some replied it would be the beginning of a new life, others looked on death as the end. It might appear that such findings are atypical of the general population; however, these two dominant outlooks have been reported in other studies, particularly in one where less than 45 percent of the elderly viewed death as the beginning of new life (Trelease, 1975).

Most of the subjects who believed in an afterlife expressed confidence that there would be reunion with loved ones and usually viewed death as a transition to a better life, as a reward for a life well lived. Only seldom were there direct expressions that death meant punishment.

These and other recent inquiries into current views of the end of life reflect the mixed views that are held. The belief that eternal life after death is determined by a personal relationship with God established in this life is fading, with some notable exceptions, and fantasies or uncertainties about life after death seem to hold greater sway than religious teachings.

TERMINAL ILLNESS

Awareness in the individual that this illness may indeed be final and that death is approaching, evokes both fears of physical distress and a set of anxieties specific to this last period of life. Dying is often feared as a time of bodily distress. Reassurance is often sought concerning three aspects of terminal illness; How long does it take to die? Will there be severe pain? Can it be relieved?

Length of Terminal Illness

Much of the information on the course of fatal illness is biased toward chronic illness, but the majority of men and women beyond 65 die in the hospital from malignancies, pneumonia, and heart disease. Although men are subject to greater mortality than women at every stage of life, death from cerebrovascular disease in the older aged begins to equalize between the sexes. The majority of these deaths occur in the wards for the chronically ill geriatric patient, but even with chronic illness, the terminal period is usually short. A national survey (Hinton, 1976) found that between 75 and 80 percent of terminally ill patients died within three months of their last admission to the hospital. For patients with cancer the terminal, painful part of the illness lasted about six weeks. Those crippled with arthritis or other chronic disease, illness, or handicap may live for years.

The nature of the illness is important in determining the length of the terminal phase. On the whole, it is the sudden, serious disorder of blood vessels that kill most quickly.

In summary, although some elderly are struck down suddenly and a small proportion have months of personal illness, the majority will have a terminal period lasting a few days to a week and, occasionally, depending on the disease, exceeding three months.

Pain in the Dying

Pain is the symptom that many people fear will accompany a terminal illness, and although it is often inherent in some illnesses, it is not inevitable. Distress and pain is very subjective and therefore difficult to assess or measure. Subjective accounts indicate that when morale is high and the person is occupied with other tasks, the sensation of pain may cause little distress.

In most surveys of people who are mortally ill, when significant pain is reported, it usually refers to the degree of pain that distressed the patient. In many reports from geriatric settings where the elderly die, a surprisingly small percent, about 15 percent, had pain that was not adequately relieved. These results should dispel the fear that death is inevitably painful. Although about 25 percent of the patients dying of cancer are liable to have pain, it can be controlled if needed by powerful drugs. That fatal illnesses were often less painful to the elderly as compared to the young has been noted in a number of studies. About 20 percent of those over 70 reported pain compared to 50 percent of the younger with similar diagnoses of terminal illness. In hospital settings, surveys show that with proper care and avoidance of unnecessary concern about how much drugs were used, pain in terminal cancer (Hinton, 1976) was always possible to alleviate.

Other Physical Distress

Pain is not the only discomfort to the dying. Other common physical problems are: nausea and vomiting, breathlessness, loss of control over excretory functions, unpleasant odors, and sometimes disfigurement. Acute breathlessness can be relieved by morphine and unpleasant odors by ventilation arrangements, but for these discomforts in the final stages, loss of full consciousness usually intervenes. In most terminal illness, depending on the type of disease and drugs used, the majority of people become increasingly drowsy, perception is clouded, and the sharp awareness of pain is lost. In the later stages of terminal illness, full awakening with alertness becomes less and less common. On the day of death, a majority of terminally ill are not conscious, and few awake again before death. The moment of death, therefore, is seldom a crisis because most of the vital functions have failed and full consciousness had been lost earlier (Kavanaugh, 1974).

Reactions to Terminal Illness

How people cope with death reveals a variety of adaptive approaches, reflecting a host of emotions—pleasant and unpleasant, some visible and clear to see, others more hidden. When people die gradually, their moods are not often constant, and sudden changes in temperament may occur. Sometimes the disease causes alteration in brain function, resulting in out-of-character behavior and emotions of the dying.

A considerable proportion of patients dying in a hospital are observed to be anxious, showing symptoms of distress—looking tense and fidgeting. These an-

What are the causes of anxiety? An important aspect may be that time drags for many of the terminally ill, especially in the hospital setting. People prepare emotionally to die, and then when nothing happens, must begin preparing again. Moreover, those who surround the dying also create anxiety because they represent the world of life that the dying no longer share, and because they seem to be mourning before the person is gone. Most people do not laugh or talk normally to the dying. Some pretend that the past will continue, whereas others seem to wander in and out overcome by pity or guilt, affecting their comments and appearance.

Given a chance, most dying will willingly talk to anyone prepared to listen to what they fear. Frequently, anxiety is heightened because the dying feel alone, more so probably than any other time in their lives. The opportunity to share their thoughts can give them a sense of purpose, thus making them less anxious. However, many are fearful that their willingness to talk may trouble loved ones or that these verbalizations may not be accepted but instead may reflect on the dying persons as lacking depth, thoughtfulness, or faith.

Frequently, death that seems unreal to the living now becomes a frightening reality for which the dying feel unprepared. Although dying people are apprehensive about the pain of dying, it is not always easy for others or even for them to know the main source of their fear. The worst fears seem grouped around the process of dying, actual death, the idea of life after death, and the collective associations that surround dying.

Dying is also distressing because of fear of becoming a burden to others. As strength recedes, dying people realize that being lifted, washed, fed, even toileted, ties those they love to the growing burden of the dying's needs. The whole environment of dying arouses fear of indignity in people who have learned to get satisfaction from cleanliness and modesty. The depths of indignity from loss of body function and control are often indescribable. A sense of pride and decency and control, make the dying feel naked, embarrassed, ashamed and out of control of life. Visitors become intruders, peeking at falling hair, peeling lips, bleary eyes, and thinning, yet disease-bloated bodies.

Other consequences of fatal illness that bring anxiety are the separation from loved ones and the fear of being replaced by new and better love objects.

Another fear occurring near actual death is the troubling awareness of the incompleteness of life. The dying recite their failures and omissions; their faults in marriage or family relationships, the lost opportunities, the unfinished tasks. It is failing to finish little things that seem to bother the dying most. Such thoughts increase their anxiety and awareness of a road that will never be traveled again.

In reflecting on fear, the dying also describe fears connected with afterlife. No matter how illogical, the dying find it difficult to divest themselves of the thought that they are only where their bodies are. They become preoccupied with what will happen to their bodies even though they are gone. Their fear of loss of self-identity is tied up with thoughts of decay, cremation, and surgery.

Some are not comforted by faith; there is dissatisfaction in many believers who are dying. Many expect to meet God but are baffled by the feeling that this is unattractive compared to what they know of life. It is possible that faith, for them, is attractive because it helps solve and define some of life's ambiguities, but many may find some notions of the joys of heaven as fearfully strange as the fires of hell.

It is often difficult for the dying to distinguish whether such apprehensions are the echoes of a frightened past or the tugs of a conscience so steeped in sin that it cannot feel forgiven.

As people decline physically, they seem more conscious of the atmosphere of death, probably one of the most terrifying things the dying face. The entire hospital to the dying, reportedly smacks of hopelessness, reflected in people's whispers, appearance, and approach to the dying.

Another fear described by the dying is the horror of rejection by others. Any hint of rejection seems to intensify the fear of dying alone, abandoned, isolated, and in terror.

WAYS OF COPING WITH DEATH

This section attempts to summarize what is known about the emotional reaction to terminal illness. Kübler-Ross (1973) analyzes five typical responses seen in the terminally ill patient: (1) denial and isolation, (2) anger, (3) bargaining, (4) depression, and (5) acceptance. Whereas these emotions are typical, they do not always occur in this full sequence or necessarily in this order. These insights into the emotions of the dying person hopefully will sensitize those working with aging people to be more aware of their human needs.

Denial and Isolation

Among the many studies of dying patients, most reacted to the awareness of terminal illness with denial. Although denial is truer of those informed abruptly, it is done partially by all patients at first and also from time to time. Most are reluctant to know the full truth of their condition. Thus denial acts as a buffer, allowing the dying to mobilize themselves and, with time, turn to less radical defenses against the shock of the news.

The following brief case of Mrs. T. is an example of an elderly person who used denial for an extended period of time.

DENIAL

Mrs. T. was 72 years old, black, and a Protestant. After examination at a medical clinic, she was told that she had lung cancer. The family reported the patient had difficulty accepting her diagnosis. A friend encouraged her to attend a healing service where many people reportedly had been healed, but because of her condition she had great difficulty in even getting to the services. The patient reported that "she immediately felt healed" and had no problems even returning home.

In the weeks that followed she was brought to the hospital by the family, as directed by the clinic. The patient told the staff that she had come "to show the doctors that she had been healed.'' Medical tests revealed that her condition had not changed. She was a difficult patient and refused to follow directions, take medications, or see a psychiatrist. She denied her illness almost completely and claimed, ''God would perform his miracle,'' until her death several months later.

Anger

When the state of denial cannot be maintained, it often gives place to a state of anger, with which it is usually difficult for family and staff to cope. Anger is usually displaced into the environment, often apparently at random. Sometimes it is reflected in anger at the level of concern by the staff or boredom at the routine. It is most difficult when anger is turned on loved ones because they represent life and a fading world of children, love, work, and laughter. The whole milieu of dying arouses indignity in people who are experiencing loss of both function and mastery over their body and their lives. The result is that many people will avoid the dying at this stage and shorten contacts to avoid confrontations. When such withdrawal is perceived by the dying, it may reinforce their feeling of loneliness. Avoiding others, however, may also represent an attempt to withdraw from interactions in which they no longer will be a part so that they will not be missed so badly by the dying.

Bargaining

A third response, the phenomenon of bargaining, is less well known but may be helpful to the patient for brief periods. It is a familiar reaction of children who become angry, then consider the approach of being nice to get what they want. Bargaining in the dying is really an attempt to postpone the inevitable. Their wish is most always an extension of life, followed by the desire for a few days without pain or physical discomfort.

JUST ONCE MORE

A patient, Mr. J. was a 68-year-old retired steel worker with a malignancy, who asked ''to be home with his family if he felt better.'' With great effort and therapy he would prepare for weekends and be quite comfortable for several days. Each Sunday night he would return to the hospital, tired and exhausted. Each weekend for several months, he would leave the hospital happy to be with his family, saying he felt better every time.

Bargaining also characteristically sets a self-imposed deadline (''one more weekend'') and often includes implicit bargains with God or others (the medical staff) if their life is extended. When the terminally ill are no longer able to handle illness with denial or bargaining because of surgery, hospitalization, or more drastic symptoms, they usually respond with shock and deep depression.

Depression

Depression is probably the most common form of emotional distress in the terminally ill, reflected in loss of interest, incapacity to enjoy things, and dulled emotion. It is wrong to assume that this is entirely due to the physical disease process, although steady deterioration, unpleasant exhaustion, and increasing discomfort can contribute to depression and the realization that life will shortly end.

An understanding loved one will have little difficulty in alleviating some of the unrealistic shame or guilt described by some patients as the source of depression. When patients can find a rewarding person-to-person intimacy, depression can be alleviated by communication. However, when depression is a tool to get away from someone (also themselves) to be left behind, then encouragements and reassurance are not meaningful. The withdrawal by the dying is understandable because both the living and the dying have to cope with the anticipation of losing the person they know and love. If allowed by a therapist to express sorrow at such loss, the dying will often find final acceptance of death much easier.

In the fatally ill, acceptance and resignation to the inevitable seems appropriate. In about 25 percent of the dying, such resolution and positive composure is manifested (Butler, 1977).

Acceptance

If the dying have had some time before death and have been given some help in working through the previously described feelings, they usually reach periods during which they are neither depressed nor angry about their condition. They will often have talked about the loss of meaningful persons, places, and activities and will be able to discuss the end of their life with a quiet acceptance. They are often weak and appear tired, dozing at brief intervals in this phase.

This stage is a period almost devoid of the intense feelings of other stages and should not be mistaken as a happy time. Visitors are generally not wanted at this point, and the person's interests seem to diminish. The following case of Mrs. B. is a brief summary of such an event.

ACCEPTANCE OF DEATH

Mrs. B., a married 68-year-old woman, was hospitalized with a malignancy and circulatory complications that gave her intense pain and discomfort. She complained rarely and impressed the staff with her cheerfulness and calmness in the face of impending death. A few days before her death, it was obvious she was tired and ready to die. She talked about her grandchildren and wondered how they would carry on without her. She felt her life had been good, and there was little left that anyone could do that she had not done. She suggested that the family come later the next day as she was very tired. Early the following morning she died, just before visiting hours.

Hope

Through all the reactions that come and go in endeavoring to cope with death successfully, hope is an important factor. Defined as an expectation of something that is desired, hope is often manifested in patients desire for an eventual cure, or recovery. Usually, in long illness it becomes a hope that they may die with less pain and resolution of some important issues with family and loved ones. This is often evident when the terminally ill have talked to someone seriously about their feelings and, after gaining some promise that they are not forgotten or rejected, may find that life has not been meaningless.

The following interview with Mr. H. illustrates a typical range of emotions in response to illness and yet displays the phenomenon of ever-present hope.

ALL OVER

Mr. H. was a 68-year-old black man, hospitalized with lung cancer after years of intermittent hospitalization and increasing circulatory disorders and disabilities.

He was first really disabled about 5 years before with breathing difficulties (emphysema) that were so bad, he could not catch his breath. ''I didn't want to go to the hospital, but I couldn't even shave without resting. When I went, they said I wasn't getting enough oxygen, and that's why I couldn't do anything. I also met a doctor that I liked and he did some other tests. I figured he would be able to help because I heard about new machines and medicines and I read a lot about it in the papers. He asked me whether I had ever been burned in the lungs and then I knew what he was getting at. He even looked sad because I guess we both realized we knew what it meant. I asked my son what it meant, and I appreciate him telling me the truth, that there was a growth and they couldn't operate. I guess I felt sorry for myself for a few days. Then I came to my senses and said, Well, you have to die of something.''

The worst part he said was, ''we were just beginning to enjoy some of the things we always wanted to do. We had a little vacation out West and I knew I'd never get back there again. There are nights I think about things, and I even start laughing. Lately though you get to a place where the pain is so bad you can't sleep and you're fighting it. I even pray, but I'm getting so I can't see the use. I told them last week, don't let's keep it up, it's no good. They talked about taking the legs off, but I just want to go. I used not to sleep, but whatever they give me, my lungs don't bother me a bit any more, but I think the legs are what's going to get me. You hear talk and I don't let on, but these legs are awful looking now, and I kind of wish it was all over.''

After all his years of struggle, his children were grown-up, he had a little house and was able to travel. He acknowledged that his hopes were gone in that area, and his energy was focused on his pain. As he became weaker, his expectations decreased and he lived from one moment of pain-free time to the next. He no longer maintained false hopes but seemed to be buoyed by an enchanced ability to talk to his loved ones about his thoughts and feelings. As his illness progressed, he began to hope that death would take away the pain because he no longer perceived life as bearable under these circumstances.

Emotional Barriers to Coping

In general, a lack of flexibility and an inability to cope with past or new experience are usually present in those cases where facing the threat of death has been difficult.

Denial (already discussed), an attempt to avoid clear awareness of painful threat, is considered to be a major obstacle to overcoming the threat of death. Other defenses that serve the purpose of exclusion from awareness include suppression, rationalization, and externalization, which are frequently seen together.

Some aged attempt to cope with death by retreating from anxiety. This pattern may be aimed at protecting the dying against the later pain of loss of loved ones. More often it is a pattern manifested by the living to protect against the loss of significant others. In the void of social isolation, a wish for attention may be manifested in bodily complaints.

Among the less socially approved mechanisms employed against death fears is that of withdrawal or escape by way of alcohol and drugs. Because it is a more hidden condition, it cannot be ascertained as to what extent this mechanism is used by older people in relation to death. However, elderly widowers have the highest rate of alcoholism of all age groups.

A third category of coping behavior is characterized by attempts at mastery and resolution at the threat of death. These include defenses such as intellectualization, counterphobic dress and behavior, and excessive activity. Butler (1977) cites counterphobic behavior as a coping style in which inappropriate dress and mannerisms are used in an effort to appear young. Hyperactivity can be interpreted as a desperate attempt to hold on to aspects of life that reflect past achievements or plunging into activities such as art, hobbies, travel, or community endeavors that curtail thoughts of death.

Butler also suggests that many older people indulge in critical reminiscence or critical life review. For those who cannot face themselves, such reviews appear repetitious, are misrepresentations of reality, are escapes into the past, and seem to focus on past guilts and unhappy memories rather than on the pleasant or positive.

Coping with Death: Adaptation

In most instances of successful adaptation to dying, a number of factors appear to be involved. Those that determine ability to cope include: distance from death, physical and mental health, religion and other socioeconomic factors, family, personal experience with death, and psychological integrity and maturity. A major determinant appears to be previous adjustment to crises of life. Erikson (1968) suggests that adaptation to death involves predominantly a satisfaction with life as it has been lived and with death as a completion of this pattern.

In patients who are dying, religious beliefs can serve as a bolster against the threat of death. In what ways is faith helpful during illness? Of those who had firm religious faith, only 20 percent were apprehensive about death and 77 percent said they, "were sure" of life after death. Clearly, for them death was made acceptable by religious belief.

One of the most satisfying adaptations to the end of life seems to be a close relationship with children and grandchildren, which provides a feeling of affection and belonging while providing a source of satisfaction in having contributed to the future through the family.

Involvement in planning and meaningful preparation for death has also been indicated as signifying a realistic and personal acceptance of death and dying. Also, those who wholly accept dying are not always concerned with weighty thoughts about the subject. Some even show a quiet relaxation, as the struggle of life begins to end.

Given sufficient emotional and physical help, it is probable that most of those moving toward death would drift into permanent unconsciousness. The factors that favor calm acceptance of death include flexibility, self-awareness, and prior success in coping with the crises of life. Some, based partially on personality and life experience, wish for death because they are suffering.

ADJUSTING TO THE DYING PERSON

Thus far, the focus has been mainly on the dying and their problems, attitudes, and ways of coping. However, all those involved, such as family or others close to the dying person, also have problems. Seeing a loved one fading and suffering, those close to the dying person are faced with their own problems; how to care for and to relate to the dying, what to do about financial problems, and for a spouse, how to deal with the isolation already looming.

The Effects on the Family

It is not possible to help the terminally ill without including the family in a meaningful way because serious illness and hospitalization usually bring about profound changes in a household. As the spouse's death approaches, women may worry about financial insecurity, but survivors of either sex will often have to take on new roles and adjust to new and increased demands. Along with concern for a dying spouse, increased loneliness and often resentment occurs. Expected help from children or relatives may not come or may not be satisfactory, and the advice of friends and neighbors may add to rather than decrease one's burdens.

A husband's sense of loss may be even greater because of dependence in regard to coping with meals and household tasks. This sense of loss may appear as soon as a wife is bedridden or limited in function, and he may resent these changes no matter how necessary they become.

The family's needs will change from the onset of illness and continue until long after death has occurred.

Problems of Communication

It is often the elderly spouse who is first told about the seriousness of the illness and is left with the decision as to when and how to share it with the dying partner, children, relatives, and friends.

During these crucial days much depends on family structure and unity, the ability to communicate effectively, and supportive friends to ease the pain of facing certain death.

It is important for both the living and the dying to help one another meet death. One way to do this is to share feelings with one another. Discussing feelings and fears gives family members an opportunity to work out their grief.

Guilt in the face of death is often disabling. Relatives are often guilt-ridden because of their anger in life's experiences with the dying person. Such feelings should be faced openly and the realistic reason for guilt determined. It is understandable that people are reluctant to speak about personal death; however, freely discussing the matter does not lead to alienation and isolation. Couples able to talk intimately about impending death find themselves communicating in a deep and meaningful sense.

The most tragic death perhaps is that of the very old. Death often requires a family to mobilize all available money for final care and if medical complications occur, the expenses can be so astronomical that the family may wish for a quick and painless death. That such wishes bring strong guilt feelings is obvious.

Another aspect that is frequently not considered is the kind of fatal illness. The person with cancer typically faces a lingering pain-producing illness, whereas the heart attack victim often dies quickly. It is sometimes easier to talk with a cancer patient, because of fears that undue anxiety brought about by discussing important issues may cause death in the heart patient. Having more time, the family and the cancer victim have more opportunity to prepare in a meaningful way for death.

The Hospice Concept

The word "hospice," comes from the concept of a house or shelter kept by religious orders for travelers or strangers in the Middle Ages. Today the term is used as a concept for care of the terminally ill. First started in England, a number of centers have been created as community-based systems of care for dying persons, especially those who cannot be aided by modern hospital technology (Stoddard, 1978). The general model of hospice care may be characterized as follows.

First, a hospice is conceived as a caring community of health care professionals who share in a common task; promoting the physical, emotional, and spiritual well-being of the dying and their families.

Second, the staff of a hospice must be highly trained in conventional discipline and also in awareness of the special concerns and needs of the dying. Particular emphasis is on control of pain, dignity of the individual, and freedom of choice. For example, many patients are given control of their own medication to avoid the fear of spending their days in physical discomfort and pain. The typical medical practice of sparing use of drugs and fear of addiction are irrelevant to the dying. In addition, the patient receives attention in as pleasant and free an environment as possible. The person's own physician ordinarily continues medical aid and the person is free to enter the hospital for medical treatment. Many of the patients return to their homes after severe pain is under control and frequently regain much of their ability to function independently. Assistance is always available whenever needed on a 24-hour, 7-day-a-week basis.

Third, the hospice offers its services to the patients as well as to their families, aiming to create an environment where the person need not be alone or have to hide his or her illness from others. Visiting hours are usually all day from early morning to early evening, with few limits on numbers. Close attention is given to the social, physical, and psychological needs of both patients and their families so that death, while acknowledged, is treated more as a famililar reality than something to be forestalled or denied. The thrust of the hospice is to help the patient and family and also friends at the time of death, as well as in the bereavement period that follows. Counseling and follow-up services are offered for as long as they are required, and families are often contacted for 6 months to a year.

Fourth, the hospice is a community operating on its own principles, which are different from those of a hospital or nursing home. Hospices have sought to be autonomous in developing procedures and approaches that are innovative and relate to the special needs of the dying. Many of the medical and social concepts of the hospice are different from the conventional and medical attitudes in American society. In America the majority of hospices are now part of hospital inpatient and outpatient programs. Typical programs provide: medical supervision and consultation; nursing care; pain and symptom control, use of medical and nonmedical techniques; patient and family counseling; nutritional care; spiritual support, social services; recreational therapy; emergency telephone and volunteer services; bereavement follow-up; and 24-hour coverage. Studies need to be done on hospices and findings will be important in evaluating the benefits of hospice service as compared to conventional hospital care. It is apparent that the hospice provides one way in which some of the fear and terror of death can be reduced, and dying made a more fully human and humane process (Holden, 1976).

BEREAVEMENT

The shock of death, even if long expected, has repercussions in the family and particularly in the spouse. There are many and varied responses: initial stunning grief; a number of not unusual, perhaps surprising feelings such as anger, guilt, relief; or even more extreme emotional disturbances and physical reactions. The compulsion somehow to survive brings most bereaved through the funeral and finally to make the adjustment and to continue with their own lives.

The Family

After a death, those who knew and loved the deceased still suffer, for even if death is anticipated over time, there is a resurgence of grief. However, a host of emotions will be aroused, which contributes to wide variations of behavior in different people. Grief, a common emotion of mental suffering or distress, is displayed over the loss, but it is a subjective experience and can be associated with other feelings such as guilt, helplessness, despair, anxiety, restlessness, and regret. Mourning usually refers to the outward manifestations of sorrow, whereas bereavement is a term usually used to connote the feeling of desolation or deprivation resulting from loss due to death.

Grief has a different meaning for the bereaved spouse than even for close relatives or friends. For children of the aged, it is usually the cutting off of only one of numerous relationships, but for the bereaved spouse, it is experienced first as shock or numbness, with a lack of feeling due to the enormity of the pain. Misery and despair only break in slowly. During this initial period, the bereaved's attention begins to turn inward because of the struggle with actualities of burying the dead and the more or less unconscious insistence of wishes and habit against acceptance of the facts of death. Apathy may inhibit efforts and movements are often slow. From time to time, waves of yearning for the dead and fears of loss of control are brought back by memories of the lost loved one. The survivors begin to face memories they cannot block out and to realize how lonely they are going to be and the depth of their feeling for the departed, knowing that closeness with that individual is gone forever. Grief may be manifested as physical tension, tightening in the chest, shortness of breath, and weakening strength.

Usually, following the immediate reactions at the instant of death, there are some rapid adjustments, often stimulated by the recognition of the things that must be done. Five types of responses may commonly be noted in the postimmediate stage, in which the funeral can also be included. The first type of behavior may be called acquiescent, which is being as near to usual as possible. The facts are recognized and conventions tolerated or fulfilled with self-direction in a responsible manner. The second may be called, agitated, which is characterized by overstimulation and constant activity with strong interest in the formalities. The apparent self-control seems artificial and betrays a defense against inner turmoil. The third response may be called defensive, which is characterized by violent protestations and the "why" of cause and purpose. Such persons show little self-control and have a tendency to blame others for the death. Although offering little support to grieving others, they are preoccupied with anger at their personal loss. The apathetic, a fourth type have another reaction. They seem impassive or indifferent and go through the motions of the funeral without direction in what appears a disoriented fashion. Finally, some react in a depressed manner, where despondency rather than active weeping occurs. There is an evident inability to talk about feelings but a self-centered style of withdrawal with minimal participation and loss of sleep and appetite. Other patterns of behavior may be apparent, such as periods of shift into different manners or mood swings encompassing varied styles. All these are commonly evident in the immediate bereavement period. Although such modes of behavior may differ, all reveal an agitation of mind and body in the overwhelming throes of grief. Such grief is often accompanied by painful self-doubt, the bereaved frequently blaming themselves for not having shown more appreciation to or doing enough for the deceased.

The suddenness of death may leave some people, who had little contact with others before, stranded together. Perfect strangers may begin to talk to one another, especially in the urban setting where they live in close proximity or commute together over several decades. Although a natural catastrophe touches everyone similarly, the death of an aged man or woman leaves the spouse (particularly a widow) in isolated prominence. The bereaved (especially a woman) becomes the target of sympathy, well-intentioned over familiarity, and morbid curiosity. Immediately after death, people begin to visit and call. Some bereaved resent this intrusion and respond with anger and withdrawal, especially at what may seem a marked concern for details about the specifics of how, what, and why of the death. Others may say things and reveal feelings that they would never reveal normally. They may talk to strangers at length in an attempt to make contact with them or possibly to release pent-up emotions generated by death. People, too, seem to ask questions that otherwise would be left unsaid on matters such as finances or remarriage. Perhaps the grieving have not thought about them yet or are not interested in them at the time of death. There is, in even these earliest contacts with others, the potential for conflict. For relatives and friends, the network of relationship may be less significant and thus they appear to mend more quickly in a somewhat impersonal way, saying and doing things that the bereaved spouse or family cannot accept. Sudden death has a different meaning for the bereaved spouse; it is a tearing up of one's whole life. Because of the initial shock, the bereaved seem unable to function and some relatives and friends trying to be helpful may seem to be taking over the whole household. People may offer to stay with the bereaved or to take them "home," as they put it. Although most bereaved appreciate having someone bring them a meal immediately after death, many prefer to stay at home from the very beginning. Often they will neither go anywhere or have people come in. Many bereaved spouses, particularly, feel they have to be in command of their lives and managing a home can help them to maintain that control.

Three Common Reactions

There are three common reactions at bereavement: The mourner may feel anger or relief or show a tendency to idealize the dead. Anger at others and criticism is one way in which some of the mourner's grief and overwhelming emotion is discharged.

    In our society we do not tend to accept such anger or even to accept i;s place in mourning, but at the time of death, there are many convenient targets for the anger of the bereaved—against the hospital staff who did not seem to have done all that they could or even to care and against relatives who appear anxious to receive a possible legacy.

    In studies of bereavement, Schulz (1978) found that the picture of distress often included hostile feelings. For the bereaved to express such feelings was not considered wicked or unusual. Doctors, too, are an easy target for accusations of neglect or incompetency for failing to prevent a loved one's death. The displacement is not very different when it is directed at the clergy or the family denounce God for permitting the death. At funerals, anger is often directed indiscriminately. The bereaved frequently add to the burden of other mourners by their anger. It is not unusual to see deflected anger directed at old feelings and past relationships, even going back to childhood frustrations. Evidently, the child in every adult, feeling bewildered and left alone, talks about past circumstances in which these feelings were first aroused.

    Similarly, there may be accusations against relatives whose loved ones have died, asserting that the in-laws did not show sufficient care of their dead relative, or against other relatives, claiming that they did not help enough or never visited the deceased, particularly the aged. Apparent good intentions of those who attempt to console the bereaved may be met by angry remarks of neither understanding nor caring enough for the dead. Thus funerals often mark the opening of old wounds and the beginning of new familial rifts.

    Anger occasionally centers on the person who has died. The bereaved feel rejected and left alone. Yet the adult mind knows that the dead did not die willfully and anger at them usually is unthinkable. Most say they did not think they felt anger at the dead but can see in the anger of others some of their own anger at the dead for their life-style or carelessness that permitted death to occur. Occasionally, the deceased are openly criticized, but it is usually expressed more covertly by not attending the funeral or by some other act of displeasure. If the bereaved are not visibly distraught yet display anger at the deceased, other mourners in being horrified may quickly idealize the dead.

    In contrast to anger, often some sense of relief is expressed when death comes.

The bereaved may feel that death was a release from pain and suffering for the dying, having watched the dying over a long period.

Relief may be felt by those who had some unpleasant relationship with the deceased, living together but unhappy because of domination or some continuous dissatisfaction. For children who looked after their parents, there may be relief at an end to responsibility for the loved one.

As mentioned earlier, part of the anguish of the bereaved in their sense of failure is exacerbated by the tendency to idealize the dead. From the funeral eulogy to the recollection of friends and relatives, the tendency is to remember only the good things about the dead.

Memories may ameliorate the hurt; however, the danger lies in a retreat into memories, resulting in the avoidance of new relationships. Probably everyone who experiences loss may indulge in fantasy in which the dead are miraculously restored, perhaps only to gain a few minutes of peace, but can readily stop such fantasies when it goes too far. Morbid preoccupation with and idealization of the past, making future contacts with others unsatisfactory by comparison, may necessitate recalling the dead as they really were and realizing at some point that the deceased were human and had faults. Putting a loved one on a pedestal may seem to make life easier, but it is misrepresentation, deceiving no one, and is not helpful. Verbalizations of feelings such as anger, hostility, relief in the bereaved are often opposed by others who consider such expressions cold, but they often enable the bereaved to control themselves at first.

Other Emotions

The emotions discussed so far may seem quite understandable. The sense of relief is often recognized and even sympathized with if moderately expressed, but some may not be inclined to accept anger and resentment as appropriate to the period following death. However, most people, in considering their experience and that of others around death and dying, will discover these feelings exist. There are, also, many less common reactions to death that are either exaggerations of normal emotions or more disturbed reactions.

Continued incapacitating grief is the most common variation from the usual pattern. Although the period of sorrow varies, severe stress usually eases after the first week or two and most distress is largely diminished within six months, with notable periods of loneliness in the first year quite probable.

Another reaction is the exaggeration of shock and lack of feeling in the initial responses to death. Usually, the apparent paralysis of feeling and inability to realize the extent of loss and sorrow lasts only hours or at most a few days, but some bereaved continue in an apparent daze for weeks and act as if nothing had ever happened. Although signs of sorrow may develop, some people never show their distress at loss. However, hidden grief may be released much later. Often pain of bereavement is manifested at a time of the loss of a much less important love object. Sorrow in these circumstances will appear excessive and inappropriate to observers but may reflect a delayed grief for the initial bereavement.

Some of the more immediate emotional reactions to loss can create fears and anxieties that become reflected in neurotic manifestations. Illogical fears may arise from being left alone or undue concern with illness, death, and dying may occur. People who were unstable before may feel a sense of unreality or depersonalization as a result of the death of a loved one. Others describe obsessions or recurrent thoughts.

Although emotional disturbances are often seen after death, many aged who have suffered loss focus on physical complaints. Fatigue, irritability, bowel irregularity, insomnia, and loss of energy are all marks of depression. Even though they do not talk about their sorrow, some may focus on the physical symptoms that are a reflection of and bodily reaction to the stress of grief, especially in the elderly.

The Causes of Severe Grief Reactions

Severe grief reactions occur more often in women, probably because there are more widows than widowers. Although the widow may be relatively capable of being alone after a husband's death, loss of a spouse can utterly disrupt her emotional and social life.

Gradual death does not eliminate eventual distress. However, knowledge that a person is going to die and having a longer period of time to prepare for it can help alleviate the pain when death does come, whereas sudden death tends to produce greater trauma and emotional disturbance. The existing personality of the survivor affects his or her reactions. Those who have manifested depressive symptoms in the past are particularly vulnerable to breaking down again as a result of the death of a loved one. Such depressions seem to be linked, with the loss of "narcissistic supply," the bereaved feeling that they have lost everything—there is nothing to live for (Hinton, 1976). Moreover, it is evident that the nature of the relationship with the deceased is significant in determining how distressed or disturbed the elderly will be in bereavement. For a full discussion, see Chapter 7.

Funerals and Readjustment

The funeral is an ordeal for most families, and many deplore its elaboration for status and competitive display, yet it does appear to have sociopsychological value. The family itself is traditionally and symbolically represented at a funeral, which gives everyone the opportunity to do something for the deceased. If a funeral goes well it can be a source of satisfaction, and enables people to communicate on other matters besides death. Also, in this way death is publicly recognized and thus made more real. The funeral marks the start of acceptance of death and to that extent the bereaved may begin to adjust. The value of rituals (rites of passage) at passages from one life stage to another has long been recognized as filling human need.

Mourning and Readjustment

In the period after the funeral the process of mourning gives way in most people to a time of recovery. During mourning, survivors tend to recall the loved one, but with episode after episode they come to realize that actuality has changed. Gradually, pent-up emotions and energies habitually attached to the deceased are released and transferred to other objects or constructive activities.

As Sullivan (1956) describes the process, the first days after a death, because intimacies interpenetrate so much of life, it is impossible not to be reminded of loss by every little thing. But each time it happens, the power of that association to evoke the image of the lost is decreased. This is what the bereaved describe when they talk about blocking associations that hurt and then letting just a little float up into consciousness. For example, shopping together will hit the bereaved as something they once enjoyed with the deceased, but by performing the task alone, or with others, it becomes less painful. This process allows people to remember associations or actions that used to be part of their interaction with the dead, and eventually enables the bereaved to face them alone or with someone else. The rehashing of memories and reorientation of roles during mourning has been called "grief work," which is necessary for healthy adjustment (Glaser and Straus, 1968). Mourning also permits a time for the relaxing or releasing of resentment toward the deceased and the expiation or handling of any guilts felt in the past.

In this period there are often strong impulses to be alone, yet responsibilities have to be resumed; decisions must be made or life and family will drift. The behavior of the bereaved is often shaky and tentative. The depressed person may start out without real interest or old enthusiasm, but by habit or the necessity of finding work, he or she will be drawn into participation in a new life. It is at this time that family contacts and the support of friends is critical.

Our culture tends to give men more opportunities to resume normal roles and duties, whereas a woman who has experienced life vicariously through the spouse rather than having a distinct identity may have difficulty in handling bereavement. For friends and relatives, sudden death is a crisis to be met; many are filled with the urge to help but also have definite expectations of what should be done. Men especially will attempt to assist in applying for social security or boxing up a household. Even though they may mean well, friends will have no qualms about criticizing if expectations (norms) are violated. An inexpensive funeral, a closed casket, cremation, will cause neighbors, even practically strangers, to make critical comments. If a widow, particularly, violates expectation, society, in the form of friends and relatives will reprimand her; she must perform the role of widow.

When people are dependent on others at a time of death, they may often find others ready to take over the whole household. However, it is important, especially for those who have been dependent on the deceased, to begin to maintain control of their own lives and households. This can be true for the widower as well as the widow. It is important to have confidence in one's own judgments in spite of the expectations of family and friends. People often receive satisfaction from getting attention rather than from taking personal action. Without the survivors verbalizing such a purpose, bereavement itself can make people feel sorry for them. Nevertheless, taking action and assuming responsibility for one's own life and not seeking or requiring the approval and services of others, is important in overcoming bereavement.

RECOVERY AND STABILIZATION

Mourning has its place, but there comes a time when it is over. The convention of mourning, besides giving some guide to acceptable behavior, may also help by indicating that there is a time to begin to participate actively in life again. Mourning periods seem to have a purpose, as seen from the 3 days common in American society, or the 7-day period of the Jewish tradition. The period for Jews is well defined, called a period of shieveh or intensive mourning for the dead and special prayers throughout the day. Visitors come to the home where the family "sit" and comfort them by talking of the deceased and of other matters. The dead are buried usually within 24 hours and more normal life is resumed after this week, although, of course, there are still prescribed mourning rituals observed. In America most other religious groups do not give such a clear guideline to the mourning period, and social conventions that dictate procedures are vague and varied.

There is so little ceremony in America that each widow or widower has to find a point at which life takes precedence over the dead past. Intimate relationships are often most easily renewed through children or grandchildren, but many people have a difficulty in relating closely to anyone for a while after death of a spouse or loved one. Older people in grief will seem to do things with children and grandchildren without real feeling. Part of this, however, may be the need to maintain self-control, not showing warmth or real feeling from fear of being hurt again, but the spontaneity and warmth of children and concerned others can break down the sense of isolation older people describe. Those who have lost, in death, a parental figure may seek someone they can relate to in this manner and may even come to regard a child, relative, or friend in this light.

Other broken relationship needs may be reestablished in new ways. Those who found meaning in a family role may move in with divorced children and act as father and mother to this family. Emotional conflicts are common as adjustments are made in such relationships, but mutual strength can result for both the older person and the "new" family.

It is not easy and sometimes impossible for the bereaved to replace the sort of affection they have lost. Older people, especially, cannot transfer to others the quality of feelings or shared activities that existed with a spouse, and therefore death of an aged spouse in a family unit as small as a couple has a severe impact on the surviving partner.

In some societies, it is accepted practice that the widow automatically be incorporated into one of her children's families, but in ours, widows may have considerable difficulty in even relating to children who tend to feel little sense of interest or obligation in opening their homes to the bereaved parent. Many in-laws have highly conflicted relationships with their families, particularly daughters-in-law, and cannot consider this a viable possibility. In our society the bereaved do not find new intimates and affection easily and usually it is some time later before an older person could open again to such a relationship. However, despite the severe impact of death on the surviving partner, some eventually do find new intimates or partners.

Besides the need to replace bonds of affection, the aged person may need financial and practical help. Although widowers are likely to be financially independent, widows are often economically hard pressed and, wishing to preserve their independence, are forced to readjust their standard of living far below even retirement levels. Even older widows must either obtain support from children or relatives or go to work. Consequently many widows may find themselves living in poverty. (For fuller discussion, see Chapter VI.)

The woman who loses her husband, in our society, has a considerable problem in social readjustment. Older widows are much less likely to remarry than younger women or widowers whose children or relatives usually support plans of older people to remarry. The remarriage of older women, particularly, is commonly regarded as one of convenience in the face of familial and societal opposition.

Most bereaved widows remark in retrospect that grief is overcome through the necessity of practical considerations, reinforced by the changing attitude of people who finally realize that the bereaved have shown enough sorrow and the time has come for them to be more independent and less in need of assistance.

In the later stages of mourning, formerly submerged aspects of the surviving spouse may begin to emerge. Where the self was not totally dependent on a spouse for self-esteem, abilities and interests are reactivated. Moreover, relatives and friends contacted in the period of mourning may help to renew old acquaintances. Where social links are avalable through the family, often new avenues of relationships for the future are made available.

Most mourners are usually relieved when grief at last begins to dissipate. The aged look forward to being their old selves again. Although there will be periods of continued pain, many people are relieved to be happy again and to feel that they can still have a meaningful life. The interest in the world, friends and the like are renewed and gone are the feelings, of complete loss.

Intellect helps in dealing with grief in a positive rather than in a negative sense.

In those who have successfully faced death of a loved one it is observed that in fulfilling their life's own needs—in working and maintaining contact with others—the bereaved can be made to feel whole again. Experiencing life and all it has to offer is enough to make the healing heart glad once more.

Even in a basically satisfying relationship there are some facets of ones life, interests, and talents that do not fit the pattern of life evolved and consequently are wasted. In part because these are aspects that do not carry memories, and partly because these aspects of the self can surface now, these long dormant interests and abilities may be reactivated.

Everything that is achieved—even conducting one's day-to-day business after a tragedy is an accomplishment—will act as a stepping stone to any future endeavors. For some persons the period of adjustment is long; for others, it is short, depending on individual needs and circumstances. Many find comfort in old friends, in new friends, in work, in family, in past little pleasures.

After a period of time, facing the activities of living life again and alone begins to take on new meaning. Strength gained from children, relatives, friends, religion, and from the realization that one is managing alone provides the impetus to venture forth to seek new activities, new social relations, and a new life.

An understanding and acceptance arises for those who live that there is still a future and that life can be what you choose to make of it. By recognizing and understanding what one feels in facing death, one can also better understand oneself. In a sense, through death one acquires a new trust in the self. Confidence and trust in our own actions is based on self-esteem, in knowing what we feel and being able to trust these feelings. The emotions of grief, hurt, and anger that are commonly expressed in the face of death are as much a part of us and our response to life as the more acceptable ''good'' feelings. As we learn to cope with these supposedly unacceptable feelings, we can better understand ourselves and thus can use and develop our sensitivities as a gauge in gaining new understanding for living the rest of our lives.

We have to accept the pain of life along with the pleasure. Yet as we mourn our losses, we can enrich our lives by no longer hiding our true emotions. Most important, as we finally accept our past losses, we will not be hindered in facing current loses. With such acceptance, therefore, feelings of grief and anger will often dissipate.

As long as we live, there will be sorrow for those who have died. But life goes on for the living, with feelings of pleasure and happiness to look forward to in the future.

Summary

Death and dying are the appropriate concern of gerontology because the probability of death increases with age. A major task of older people in relation to dying is to confront existential anxiety about nonbeing and to ponder about the meaning of life. Erikson's eighth stage of development defines the issues of healthy aging in the later years as a struggle to experience an acceptance of life and a belief that it has meaning. It appears that the fear of pain and disability are more common concerns for the aged than the fear of death. Studies reveal that attitudes toward death are also influenced by factors other than age, for example; personality, ethnic background, and religion.

The ways in which people cope with death reveal a variety of approaches used to adapt to this life-threatening situation. All individuals do not pass through an orderly sequence of adjustments.

The characteristic responses of denial, anger, bargaining, depression, acceptance, and hope can often be noted among terminally ill older persons. They provide helpful clues to understanding the reactions of individuals who are facing death.

Following the death of the loved one, the bereaved reacts in a number of ways that almost parallel the responses of the dying. This process of mourning lasts about a year. As with the dying person, the expression of feelings and review of events surrounding death are often helpful. The funeral itself and visiting and extending comfort to the bereaved during the time of mourning can reaffirm the social character of the experience of death. Accepting death and coming to grips with feelings of grief and anger during bereavement can facilitate a shift in roles, resocialization, and recovery of stability. In dealing with grief over death, and in learning to cope successfully with another's death, we are preparing for the eventuality of our own demise. Thus we can experience a mode of optimum growth so that we can learn to live the rest of our lives more fully.

FURTHER READINGS

Birren, C., et al. (eds.), *Human Aging: A Biological and Behavioral Study,* Public Health Service Publication, No. 66, U. S. Government Printing Office, Washington, D. C., 1963, 1981.

Busse, E. W., and E. Pfeiffer, *Behavior and Adaptation of Later Life,* Little Brown, Boston, 1977

Butler, R. N., *The Life Review in Behavior and Adaptation in Late Life,* E. W. Busse and E. Pfeiffer (eds.), Little Brown, Boston, 1977

Butler, R. N., and M. Lewis, *Aging and Mental Health: Positive Psychosocial Approaches,* Mosbey, St. Louis, 1977.

Cameron, et al., "Consciousness of Death Across the Life Span," *Journal of Gerontology,* January 1973, *28*(1) 92–95.

Eliot, D., *Adjusting to the Death of a Loved One,* in R. S. Cavan (ed.), *Marriage and Family in the Modern World: A Book of Readings,* Crowell, New York, 1974.

Fischer, G., "Death, Identity and Creativity," *Omega,* 1971, *2,* 303–306.

Glaser, B. G., and A. L. Strauss, *Time for Dying,* Aldine Press, Chicago, 1968.

Hinton, J., *Dying,* Penguin Books, Baltimore, Md., 1976.

Holden, C., "Hospices: For the Dying, Relief from Pain and Fear," *Science,* 1976, *193*(4251), 389–391.

Kalish, R. A., "A Continuum of Subjectively Perceived Death," *Gerontologist,* 1966, *6,* 73.

"Death & Aging in a Social Context," R. H. Binstock and E. Shanas (eds.), *Handbook of Aging and the Social Sciences,* New York: Van Nostrand, 1976.

Kavanaugh, R. E., *Facing Death,* Penguin Books, Baltimore, Md., 1974.

Koestenbaum, P., "The Vitality of Death," *Journal of Existentialism,* 1964, *5,* 139.

Kübler-Ross, *On Death and Dying,* Macmillan, New York, 1973.

Schulz, Richard, *The Psychology of Death, Dying and Bereavement,* Addison Wesley, Reading, Mass., 1978.

Stoddard, S., *The Hospice Movement: A Better Way of Caring for the Dying,* Vantage Books, New York, 1978.

Sullivan, H. S., *Clinical Studies in Psychiatry,* Norton, New York, 1956.

Trelease, M. L., "Dying Among Alaskan Indians: A Matter of Choice," in E. Kübler-Ross (ed.), *Death: The Final Stage of Growth,* Prentice-Hall, Englewood Cliffs, N. J., 1975.

CHAPTER 12

Health Care for the Aged

The recent large increase in the number of the aged, over 65, over 75, even over 85 years of age has brought many health care problems; individuals, society, and government have been scrambling to find, formalize, and enforce solutions. This ongoing struggle in many ways has fallen behind. Nevertheless, the number of professionals in geriatric health care, the number of researchers now studying the aged, the growing number of programs for older people's nutritional needs, the founding and development of Medicare, Medicaid, and other health insurance plans all reveal increasing attempts to cope with this recently new phenomenon. Dismay at the high costs of care and the obvious lacks in some areas must be viewed against the positive growths in geriatrics. The faster and sooner the old age problem is dealt with, the better; however, any progress, even gradually is welcome.

It is true that more health care is needed, that the elderly need help in obtaining this assistance, that health care professionals have not been strongly motivated or well informed for geriatric care, and in addition to preventing, diagnosing, and treating illness, the system is inadequate for delivering health services that consider the individual's nutritional, social, psychological, financial, and educational status.

This chapter looks at some of the complex intertwinings of health and social concerns in the following areas: the assessment of health and illness; the management and delivery of innovative health services for geriatric health care through an interdisciplinary team approach; and a wide range of health care programs and services provided in a variety of settings in the context of family, community, and cultural life patterns. Because the problems of the elderly tend to be intricate and multifaceted, health care cannot be the responsibility of any single health or social profession or of any single facility or program. This chapter presents an overview of Medicare and Medicaid programs as they relate to the elderly, their benefits and gaps, as well as the growth of health care delivery systems and problems that exist despite them.

ASSESSMENT OF HEALTH

Later life has its own special rewards and gratifications, but also health hazards and problems for which there are many health services yet serious gaps and deficiencies exist. A coordinated system of comprehensive health care and services is needed to provide continuity of care that understands and responds to the whole person and to all facets and roots of that person's condition. Such an approach must concern itself with public and professional education and attitudes toward aging, as well as biological, psychological, and social factors affecting health.

Health has subjective as well as objective aspects. Assessment should include two important views, evaluation by professionals, based on the presence of pathology, as well as on the attitude of the older person about his or her own condition. These views may not always agree because self-health evaluation is based on factors other than medically verified illness. Some old people with various impairments or diseases from mild to serious, think they are "well," or "as well as can be expected," whereas others with similar conditions think they are "sick."

Other crucial factors in health assessment by the elderly may be related to degree of incapacity and to social and cultural determinants. The ways in which elderly persons have utilized their resources to cope with such experiences as physical illness, social and economic hardships, family losses, personal frustrations and disappointments, without being overwhelmed in earlier years, will influence their attitudes toward health and disease in later years, as well.

When an individual equates activity with health, even minimum impairment or restriction on activity may evoke an attitude of complaint about poor health and sick health status. Therefore important considerations in health care of elderly patients require an evaluation of the whole person by a team of professionals, such as physicians, nurses, social workers, physical and occupational therapists, nutritionists, dentists. When an elderly person seeks help for a particular problem or illness, a comprehensive evaluation should include, in addition to findings: physical examinations and diagnostic tests, information on the reasons the individual seeks help; the way the person expresses attitudes toward the "illness,"; the kind of life experience, changes in status, family situation, or personal relationships this person has or has had. A viable, realistic plan of treatment for the whole person should then be feasible.

Because the problems of the elderly may be either emotional, physical, social, or any combination thereof the individual's symptomatic response may also reflect a complexity of converging forces and factors, which only a team approach can ascertain and act on.

Despite attention given to the health problems of the elderly and related factors of poverty and deprivation, the images that older people have of themselves and of their ability to cope with their problems is far less dependent on outside circumstances than on their own existing attitudes.

Studies reveal that if older citizens perceive themselves as healthy, participating in a satisfactory, intimate, interpersonal relationship, and able to meet their minimum economic needs, they are more likely to have an optimistic attitude toward the future. Of those who participated in the survey, it was found that 67 percent always felt useful, that 65 percent had strong self-images, and that 61 percent believed that life was worthwhile. The majority indicated that good health was the factor that most strongly influenced their sense of well-being and their ability to function in the face of hardship. Studies indicate that the elderly are extremely courageous, and that if they see themselves as healthy they manage to maintain their faith despite other problems. Other factors that contribute to optimism are related to health to some extent: 56 percent noted that having a healthy intimate spouse was important to their general outlook, and 41 percent indicated the extent of their economic security related to their degree of optimism. Of course, deprived circumstances can, in themselves, affect health in a multitude of ways from diet and exercise to availability of medical and health care help.

PROFESSIONAL RESPONSIBILITIES IN HEALTH CARE FOR THE ELDERLY

Although the elderly comprise 10 percent of the population, they utilize a significant amount of the available health resources: 33 percent of the nation's hospital beds, 95 percent of the long-term beds, 70 percent of the home-health services. Despite these figures, crucial problems prevail in the delivery of health services for the elderly, particularly with respect to the quality and availability.

Physicians and Geriatric Health Care

Recruitment in the field of geriatrics has been hampered by a number of factors, including: a lack of prestige associated with the specialty and the attitude on the part of physicians that it is a less rewarding area of practice. The lack, furthermore, of training in geriatrics also leads to problems in dealing with elderly people in health settings. There is a tendency on the part of many physicians to be impatient with older patients and their detailed recitations about physical infirmities, and some physicians also incorrectly use the aging process to explain a variety of complaints without providing a thorough assessment of ancilliary problems.

Medical students' attitudes, however, toward geriatrics seem to be changing. In eight medical schools 75 percent of the students indicated a desire to have a full course in geriatrics, and 72 percent wanted to take an elective course on the elderly at some time during their clinical practice. Also, more interest in geriatric residencies was expressed. These kinds of exposures can have a significant impact on attitudes toward geriatric medicine. Geriatrics is a field that will continue to expand. Physical resources, choice of accessible health care facilities, and funding sources are improving.

The elderly are often overmedicated. It is well recognized that older patients are more likely to have adverse drug reactions than younger patients. The elderly are at increased risk of complications from drug therapy for two main reasons: they often have multiple medical problems requiring multiple drugs and with age, there are changes in physiology that sometimes lead to changes in the ways in which drugs affect the body. Physicians must understand the patient's pharmocological profile in order to avoid negative interactions and overdoses.

Nurses in Geriatric Health Care

In the past the nursing profession has shown limited interest in geriatric nursing practice, but the situation appears to be changing. Gerontology and geriatric courses are being added to nursing curriculums. Continuing education programs will be important for retraining nurses from other specialties, as well as updating and improving the skills of geriatric personnel. Many administrators are encouraging training programs within long-term care facilities to include courses for nurses in social gerontology, social services, nutrition, and drug usage as they relate to the elderly.

More direct involvement of nurses in primary health care can result in better services to older individuals and their families. Geriatric nurses, moreover, are becoming more actively assertive in their professional roles in caring for patients without the constraints of the medical stratification system.

Geriatric Social Workers

A social worker in geriatric health care assumes responsibility for intake and admission procedures, ongoing casework and groupwork with patients and families, community referrals for necessary services, and discharge planning. They should also know the human resources available to aid an older person in planning for financial resources, transportation services, nutrition programs, legal services, home health services, and other therapeutic programs. A professionally trained social worker can offer therapeutic services, working with the patient and the family, helping them to cope with and adapt to a variety of stressful situations.

Physical, Occupational, and Speech Therapists

Therapists working in their area of specialty can bring about significant improvements in elderly patients' conditions.

The physical therapist works with people who need intensive rehabilitation, the disabled who need exercise to keep functioning, and the physically slow and unsteady in need of general exercise. Tangible aspects of care should be accompanied by sensitive concern for the individual patient, flexibility, patience, and psychological reinforcement for achievement; all are important in helping to restore an older person's self-confidence.

Occupational therapy seeks to maintain the elderly person as a functioning individual after a condition has been observed that involves sensory loss, visual disturbances, loss of muscle function, impaired cognition, balance, coordination, strength and other areas that affect the ability to perform productively. The primary function of the occupational therapist is to develop a plan of action to improve an individual's adaptive skills and performance capacity.

Speech therapy is being increasingly used in geriatric care. Some conditions can cause speech disorders that may affect the person's mental well-being, self-image, and independent function, with success often dependent on the individual's physical status and motivation to regain the lost capabilities.

Accurate evaluation, realistic goals, and interaction with other members of the health care team are essential components for physical, occupational, and speech therapists to develop and maintain an understanding of the geriatric patient.

Other Personnel in Geriatric Health Care

Changes have occurred in the methods and delivery of health care that have created the need for increasing numbers of new health workers, such as health administrators who plan, organize, and direct geriatric health care facilities and services; health educators who can provide educational services to professionals, nonprofessionals, patients, and their families and can also help dispel indifference about geriatric health needs; nutritionists who can provide sound nutritional principles and clinical applications, relating them to geriatric health care, and train other health workers concerned with the nutritional base of health; geriatric aides who work in nursing homes and long-term care facilities and are responsible for most daily patient contact; spiritual counselors who may be clergymen of the patient's religious faith and can provide spiritual counseling and support; recreational therapists who can establish a well-organized plan of recreational activities for the needs and interests of an elderly group in a particular setting.

A team approach to geriatrics can provide a comprehensive quality program for the aged, while providing a satisfying, collaborative atmosphere for the various disciplinary practitioners who make up the team.

WHAT IS TEAMWORK?

The concept of "team" and "teamwork" as currently used in health services has a variety of meanings. The meaning of "team" is often unclear and confusing. Some so-called teams work separately, with minimal contact, communication or coordination. An individual may see many different professional specialists who may be referred to as a team who never meet together to collaborate. In such a situation the "team" may consist of the services of persons that patient needs: internist, dentist, podiatrist, opthamologist, social worker, or nurse. The term "team" has also been used to refer to an array of professional, paramedical, and ancillary personnel who are working together under the direction of a physician. These varied uses of the term have created such a loose concept of the term that for some, the term "team" has become too loose and innocuous to be meaningful. However, many health care organizations find the term "team," in spite of its drawbacks, a descriptive mechanism to provide for health services for individuals and families. The following definition of "team" includes some of the general principles that are basic to all teamwork, and are especially pertinent to the combined efforts on behalf of the elderly.

A team is a group of people, each of whom possesses particular expertise and is responsible for individual decision making. Together they hold a common purpose and meet together to share ideas, communicate, collaborate, consolidate information and knowledge out of which plans are made, actions determined, activities coordinated, and future decisions considered (Brill, 1976).

It should be pointed out that teamwork may not necessarily be the preferred mode of health service delivery in all situations of care for the elderly. However, when the patient health system is highly complex, and problems appear to be multifaceted, team effort is critical to effective patient care. In order to determine appropriateness of team action, as part of an initial assessment, a process evaluation may be provided to ascertain the patient's physical, emotional, and social problems, desires, needs, and the health care delivery system that can best meet the patient's need for service. This is provided in relation to treatment for illness or disease, maintenance of health, education and prevention of illness, and improvement of living conditions on comprehensive health care for older people.

A case situation of an elderly couple illustrates multi-faceted problems that can best be helped by an interdisciplinary team approach.

TEAMWORK

Cora W., a 77-year-old married woman, was seen at a local neighborhood health center for evaluation of complaints of constipation. She was mildly confused, depressed, and crying intermittently. She had paranoid ideas about the electric company, which had resulted in her not paying the bills for several months. She had been threatened with having the electricity turned off, which would leave her without lights, heat, and electricity in midwinter. She lived with her husband, who was 81 years old, was arthritic, and had been a stroke victim a year earlier. He had a partial paralysis. Although he could walk, he had not left the house since the stroke and spent most of his days sitting in a chair doing nothing. Before he had the stroke he was active and worked part time as a gardener and handyman. He had retired from working as a security guard at a local bank at the age of 65. He had a meager Social Security pension that he and his wife were unable to live on. Therefore he had continued to work for many years to supplement their income. Since the stroke, he had not worked, and there had not been sufficient funds for food, bills, and other necessities.

The couple had a son who lived in another state. The mother and daughter-inlaw had never gotten along and couldn't tolerate talking to each other. The son, caught in the middle between the two women in his life, visited infrequently. The couple did not want to depend on them.

Mrs. W. had a poor appetite, and was reportedly unable to sleep. She had been active in a women's sewing group at a church, but in the past year had lost interest in her usual activities. She described feelings of fatigue and a loss of energy. She felt worthless and was unable to think or concentrate. At times she felt that she might as well have been dead, because she felt useless.

A presentation of this case at an interdisciplinary team conference elicited an evaluation and treatment plan that included the following disciplines: a psychiatric evaluation for medication and psychotherapy and social services to determine whether this couple could remain at home with home health services and homemaker services. Social services had planned a further evaluation of the financial resources of the couple. Community resources available for Mr. and Mrs. W. in the community were to be explained: medical services were to be provided for Mrs. W.'s physical complaints. Also, a nurse planned to make a home visit to assess Mr. W.'s condition and possible need for medical care, nutritional services, and physical and recreational therapy.

Immediate arrangements were made by social services to avert the shutoff of the electricity. Because there were no funds available for an immediate payment, protective services made a partial payment of the bills and arranged with the electric company for the woman to pay the rest later. The couple qualified for Supplemental Security Income and other benefits, and their monthly income was increased. Continuing contact with the social worker enabled the woman and her husband to continue to live in their own home with homemaker service provided a few hours daily. Arrangements were made for visiting nursing services to make regular home visits to provide services for the husband. A physical therapist made arrangements to provide rehabilitative service for Mr. W. in a local hospital where the necessary equipment was available. The physical therapy was beneficial and helped to relax muscle tension and to improve Mr. W.'s circulation. With medication and psychotherapy, Mrs. W.'s affective condition was greatly improved.

Each of these various disciplines provided special skill and expertise to help Mr. and Mrs. W., for indeed the problems of the elderly are often complex and multifaceted.

NUTRITION AND THE AGED

Diet is important to people of all ages, but older people in particular may have questions about what they should eat to maintain their health. Because many health problems of the elderly are the result of poor nutrition, the following guidelines may help older people plan a healthy diet.

Most people gain weight more easily as they grow older because they are less active, but they need the same amount of most nutrients (vitamins, minerals, and protein) as younger people. This means that the elderly in particular should eat nutritious food and cut down on sweets, salty snack foods, high calorie drinks, and alcohol.

Exercise is also important in keeping off extra pounds. With regular exercise, a person can eat more without gaining weight than a person who sits most of the day.

Eating too little can be harmful as well. People who do not eat enough may have less energy and may become lonely and depressed. In addition, a diet containing too few calories is also likely to be lacking in vitamins and minerals.

Good nutrition is an important requirement for the elderly, but many do not give adequate attention to their nutritional needs in later maturity. The diets of older people are often below standard, both in quantity and quality, and are frequently low in minerals and vitamins. The reasons for this have been cited as lack of funds, lack of motivation, loss of mobility, changing health status, lack of information, and long-standing food habits.

Nutritional Needs of the Elderly

According to the National Research Council of the United States Academy of Sciences, for those age 55 and over a diet of 1650 to 1825 calories, with 55 grams of protein daily would be good for women, while 2000 to 2200 calories with 65 grams of protein daily would be required for men. These requirements, however, are highly individual, according to personal activity and need. As far as calorie needs for everyday activity, a most significant factor is the common decrease of physical activity in the elderly. There may be some variation in physical activity, depending on age, inclination, occupation, recreational participation, and the state of health of the individual. Many elderly take a more sedentary approach to leisure and recreational opportunities. The reduction in the need for calories is approximately 7.5 percent for each decade past 25 years of age. Obesity because of overeating or a poorly balanced diet is a major problem among the elderly, can complicate other problems, and may contribute to decreased physical activity.

Adequate protein is an essential need for a prudent diet and an important nutrient for the elderly for tissue building or rebuilding. Protein sources that contain low animal fat, low cholesterol, and are low in calories are more conducive to good health than are sources that are high in animal fats. cholesterol, and calorie levels. It is recommended that protein sources that contain high levels of fat such as eggs, dairy products, and meats be reduced and that when animal fats are eaten, sources low in fat can be selected, such as chicken, turkey, and fish. Vegetable protein sources are found in food such as grains, beans, and nuts, which are low in fat. The body's need for fat does not change with age. It is recommended that in a balanced diet, fats not constitute more than 20 percent of the total caloric consumption.

A well-selected mixed diet with a wide variety of foods should supply all the essential vitamins and minerals in normally needed quantities for everyone. Increased therapeutic needs should be evaluated on an individual basis. The three important minerals that may present problems are iron, calcium, and potassium because the elderly may have poor diets. Calcium is especially important for building and maintaining strong bones and teeth. Food rich in calcium include milk and cheese, as well as dark leafy greens. Some legumes and nuts also supply good amounts of calcium. Encouragement and education may be needed to ensure adequate dietary sources of these minerals among their daily food selections.

Two additional dietary considerations that play an important role in proper nutrition and bodily function are water and dietary fiber. Water is important for proper elimination and water balance in the body. Many elderly people have significant problems with constipation and dehydration. It is recommended, therefore, that elderly people drink six to eight glasses of water a day. Fiber, which is contained in bran or wholegrain cereals, adds bulk to the diet, aids in intestinal motility, and may also help control constipation.

Factors Affecting Nutritional Health

Food often means more than merely the satisfaction of hunger; people eat for pleasure. Food choice may be associated with an expression of personality and may be influenced by emotions, occasions, habits, life-style, and a multitude of other factors. It is difficult to change the food habits of the elderly, but gradual change is possible with nutritional education, and many times easily accepted changes may be all that is necessary to make an elderly person's diet nutritionally sound. Most people of all ages look forward to meals, but good nutrition may be neglected in old age for a variety of reasons: periods of depression, of sickness, of bereavement, or practical difficulties in shopping for the ingredients for meals, steep stairs, or a neighborhood that is dangerous for shopping. If people live alone, after sharing meal-time with others for many years, they may feel little motivation to prepare food and eat alone. Some of the most serious nutritional problems occur among elderly widows and widowers. A widower who lives alone may have never cooked for himself, and may be hesitant to undertake this task in later life. The elderly widow may find herself with low funds, and little motivation to shop, cook, eat, remain active, or in some cases to go on living. Emotional stress and deprivation associated with changing roles, isolation, disease, and disabilities can lead to a loss of appetite and to nutritional deficiencies.

Physical problems of aging may seriously affect eating habits, with poor nutrition resulting. Certain biophysical changes affect the choice of foods to be eaten. The loss of teeth or the existence of denture problems can lead an individual to dietary modifications involving less chewing. Chewing problems can be very real and complicated by decreased salivary secretion that may make swallowing difficult. In some elderly individuals there is a diminished sense of smell and taste caused by a declining number of taste buds, which can affect the appetite. Previously enjoyed foods may become less attractive and may precipitate negative changes in eating habits. Neuromuscular problems often lead to inability to handle utensils, cooking appliances, and food. If individuals are home alone with Parkinson's disease, chronic arthritis, or a similar disability, they may be unable to prepare certain foods, which may lead to an inefficient use of food and the elimination of some foods. In addition the presence of chronic disorders may require modified diets that may be expensive and difficult to follow. A program of education and counseling may be needed to help elderly patients realize the nature of their problems and cooperate with the diet regimen that may be prescribed.

Income status of the elderly can also be a major factor in determining diet. Income, which is greatly reduced in old age, affects what items elderly shoppers can or cannot purchase because the budget for food must compete with necessary expenditures for rent, utilities, health care, and medication. The constraint of insufficient funds for food may lead an individual to buy cheaper foods, which may be less nutritious.

Because there are numerous factors that operate in situations where the elderly do not get sufficient amounts of food to eat, a nutritional assessment of the elderly individual to ascertain the adequacy of diet, is an important component of health and well-being.

Nutrition Education and Programs

Educational programs for the elderly on nutrition must deal with problems to which they can relate and must consider the social, economic, and cultural circumstances of the individuals involved. Proper nutrition among the elderly can be further encouraged and promoted in a number of ways. Because eating in pleasant surroundings with the opportunity for social interaction can be conducive to the enjoyment of food, some programs have been designed both to provide adequate nutrition to older people and to help combat loneliness by providing other social activities.

"Meals on Wheels," These programs have been established by local groups with technical assistance and, when necessary, funds are received from the Administration on Aging, the federal government, and the Department of Agriculture. Local groups provide daily meals and group dining to many aged who need them and to the homebound who require "Meals on Wheels." Such programs help to meet the nutritional dietary needs and also provide social interaction for older people. Meaningful employment and voluntary services may also be provided. In 1972 the Nutrition Program for the Elderly provided for fairly low-cost nutritious meals at conveniently located settings for older people, 60 years of age and over. Older people are encouraged to pay a small fee for the program, yet this amount may be difficult for many elderly persons.

Food Stamps. The food stamp program initiated through a federal act of 1964 has assisted many elderly persons to obtain adequate food essentials. The bureaucratic red tape in the application process for food stamps and transportation difficulties to and from the sites, as well as the degrading, embarrassing experience of using them, has prevented many eligible older persons from utilizing food stamps.

Supplemental Security Income (SSI). SSI is another available resource for elderly people who have inadequate incomes or difficulty in obtaining food. Passed in 1972, SSI provided a national uniform system of benefits for the needy aged, blind, and disabled and provides a guaranteed annual income for all needy older Americans. It is administered by the Social Security Administration and financed out of general tax revenues.

Some of the requirements for eligibility were obstacles in getting indigent older people to apply. For example, many states required recipients to cash in life insurance policies worth more than $200, yet for many older persons such a policy represents a meager protection for the family for funeral expenses. Moreover, although the SSI is an attempt to guarantee income for the elderly indigent, the federal government has continued to provide income at levels below the official poverty line established by economic advisors of the government itself.

Pension reforms and Social Security reforms are needed to establish and maintain adequate income levels for older retired people, and in addition, improved health care services for the elderly are vital. If these changes are not effected, an increasing number of the old will be condemned to poverty, poor health, and despair.

Special Health Care. These programs have been established in some communities to help meet specialized needs. They include the Heart Association and the Diabetes Association, which conduct activities related to these special needs of older persons.

The Senior Citizens of America and the American Society for the Aged, Inc., provide programs in larger urban centers to involve elderly people in a variety of activities. These programs include leisure time, recreational, and educational activities and volunteer programs. Nutritional support programs to meet physical needs are also available and promote improved dietary habits.

SELF-CARE AND SELF-HELP GROUPS

Today there appears to be a reawakening of the ''self-care,'' ''self-help'' approach. Highly specialized technical care has been criticized by some for being too impersonal, too costly, and not without dangers. Consequently, individuals are asserting their right to treatment, demanding a greater part in deciding what treatment should consist of, and accepting responsibility for their own health.

''Self-care'' is the term given to actions that individuals perform on behalf of themselves, their families, or their neighbor's well-being.

Most individuals perform some self-care activities as a matter of everyday living; good nutrition, dental care, routine first aid such as cleaning cuts, treating of minor burns, and flushing a speck of dirt out of the eye are common practice. Self-care has come to involve taking over tasks usually relegated to a professional such as measuring heart rate and blood pressure, obtaining throat cultures, testing urine, or giving one's self or a family member insulin injections for diabetes. It has been found that these tasks and others can be performed well by nonprofessionals. A number of organizations, both public and private, now offer classes to teach self-care skills and many programs teach the layperson how to make self-care judgments wisely. The best known are the ''activated patient'' courses. The activated patient become deliberately involved, accepts responsibility for his or her own health, and works cooperatively with the physician.

''Self-help'' groups are clusters of people who share a common problem and goal and come together to offer one another the benefit of their experience and mutual support. Self-help groups have been established to meet a variety of needs. There are groups for smokers, stutterers, alcoholics and their families, individuals who have had open heart surgery, and the widowed. It is estimated that there are half a million self-help groups, and more are formed every year.

Self-help health groups are begun by patients themselves or their families. Most self-help groups are formally organized and hold regular meetings that commonly include group discussions where members share experiences. Almost all such groups are nonprofit. Some stress medical care and rehabilitation, while others target self-improvement as the primary goal. One of these groups is SAGE (Senior Actualization and Growth Explortion), which calls itself ''a growth center for people over 65.'' SAGE was founded by a psychiatrist and is based on the premise that ''old age should be a rich, creative culmination.'' Weekly meetings incorporate breathing exercises, massage, exercise to music, biofeedback, and counseling.

SAGE participants reported often the development of relationships with one another and their families. They claimed that the techniques that they learned helped them control some of their symptoms such as headaches, or the techniques reduced blood pressure, improved depression, cured insomnia, and limited dependence on medications.

There are also several organizations that address the need of older persons, which include a number with health-related components. The Gray Panthers are a coalition of older persons, organized to support the rights of those who have been excluded from power and influence by the prejudices of ageism. Their chapters have taken on social concerns, health care, reforms in nursing homes, and consumer protection. In addition, there are approximately 5000 Senior Centers in the United States, some of which provide extensive health services and health education. The National Council of Senior Citizens regularly publishes *Senior News* to activate their members to health issues, health legislation, and other matters that affect their lives.

Self-care efforts and self-help groups have special appeal for older adults. Observing healthful practices can significantly enhance their sense of well-being, as well as their ability to lead active lives.

FINANCING HEALTH CARE FOR THE AGED

Health care is an expensive commodity for older persons, especially where private practitioners and private hospitalization are involved. The high cost of health care is beyond the budget of most elderly.

The Federal System of Old Age Benefits for Retired Workers was passed in 1935. This legislation grew out of the climate of destitution and poverty of the Depression. The Social Security program was intended to prevent destitution by maintaining an income for retirees when employment ended. Retirement benefits were made available to those persons 65 years of age and over. Provisions for mandatory retirement and payments to the retired worker were instituted to provide a means to open up the labor market for younger unemployed workers. The Social Security Act was intended to include health insurance provisions for the people of the United States, but there was such strong opposition from organized medicine that the health insurance component was abandoned. There have been attempts to establish a national health insurance program since 1935.

Private health insurance was established in America through Blue Cross and Blue Shield, Aetna, Metropolitan, and Connecticut General during the decade 1940 to 1950, to pay for medical expenses. There were large groups of people who were considered high-risk medically and were excluded from coverage. The private insurance method of financing health care was largely unavailable to the elderly in America.

In 1965 the Social Security Act was amended to provide health insurance for the aged in the United States, which is known as Medicare. It represents the inauguration of national financing of individual health services in the United States.

Medicare—Part A

The *Medicare* program is directed exclusively to institutional providers of care: hospitals, extended care facilities, and home health agencies. Every person in the United States who has attained the age of 65 years, and has appropriate health needs, is entitled to inpatient hospital services and home health services.

Medicare consists of two basic components. Part A is a compulsory hospital insurance plan that covers a bed patient in a hospital, and under certain conditions, in a skilled nursing facility or at home after leaving the hospital.

Under social security, workers, their employrs, and self-employed people pay a contribution based on earnings during their working years. At age 65 the portion of their contribution that has gone into a special Hospital Insurance Trust Fund guarantees that workers will have financial assistance in paying hospital bills. An individual who has not been previously covered under the Social Security Act may apply for a health insurance benefits card on presentation of proof of age. Reimbursement to providers of services is based on reasonable cost of the services provided. The provider must be qualified to participate in the health insurance program and must agree to abide by the set forth conditions of participation for hospitals, extended care facilities, and home health agencies. The details of the provisions are specific and can be found in the code of federal regulations.

Part A is financed by employer-employee contributions and a tax on the self-employed. Part B is a voluntary program of supplemental medical insurance that helps to pay for physicians services, outpatient hospital benefits, home health services, and certain medical services and supplies.

Part A hospital insurance benefits are measured by periods of time known as benefit periods. A benefit period begins when a patient enters the hospital and ends when the individual has not been a hospital bed patient for 60 consecutive days. Medicare will help to pay covered services for a patient for up to 90 days of inhospital care, for up to 100 days of extended care in a skilled nursing facility, and for up to 100 home health visits in each benefit period. There is no limit to the number of benefit periods to which an individual is entitled. If an individual extends a period of hospitalization within a benefit period, there is a lifetime reserve of 60 additional hospital days. Use of the reserve permanently reduces the total number of days left in the lifetime reserve.

A Medicare patient is financially responsible for various components of the hospital insurance plan. The individual must pay a fixed deductive of money in each benefit period before Medicare coverage begins. Part A of Medicare pays for covered services for the first 60 days of hospital care. If the patient requires beyond

60 days of hospital care in a benefit period, there is a required copayment to be made by the patient. The copayment is a fixed rate per day in excess of 60 days of care. If the patient needs beyond 90 days of care in a benefit period, an increased copayment is required in accordance with the lifetime reserve days.

Hospital Benefits. The kinds of services provided by Medicare, Part A, while a patient is receiving hospital care are listed here. Only services provided by participating facilities are eligible for Medicare reimbursement. There are services that are not covered under Medicare.

Hospital Benefits, Medicare, Part A[a]

Medicare, Part A, will help to pay for:
1. A bed in a semiprivate room (defined as one having two to four beds) and all meals, including special diets.
2. Operating room charges.
3. Regular nursing services (including intensive-care nursing).
4. Drugs furnished by the hospital.
5. Laboratory tests.
6. Radiographs and other radiology services.
7. Medical supplies such as splints and casts.
8. Use of appliances and equipment furnished by the hospital such as wheelchair, crutches, and braces.

Medicare, Part A, will not pay for:
1. Personal comfort or convenience items (such as charges for a telephone, radio, or television furnished at the patient's request).
2. Private-duty nurses.
3. Any extra charge for use of a private room unless the patient needs it for medical reasons.
4. Noncovered levels of care such as custodial care.
5. Doctor's services (medical insurance helps to pay for these).
6. The first three pints of blood received in a benefit period.

---

[a] Compiled from information in U.S. Department of Health, Education, and Welfare, Social Security Administration Medicare Handbook.

Skilled Nursing Facility Benefits. A patient can receive Medicare coverage for services rendered in a skilled nursing facility. Before a patient can receive Medicare coverage in a skilled nursing facility, there are requirements that the facility must meet. Some of the requirements that must be met are listed as follows:

1. A physician must determine that the care is necessary.
2. Care received in the facility must represent further treatment of a condition for which the patient was treated in the hospital.

3. The patient must have been in a hospital for 3 consecutive days before the admission (not counting the day of discharge).
4. The patient must have been admitted within 14 days after leaving the hospital (or 28 days if no bed is available before then).
5. A utilization review committee or a professional standards review organization must approve of the stay.

Extended Care Benefits. Extended care benefits are provided under Medicare Covered Services for the first 20 days in a benefit period are included. After the first 20 days the recipient must pay a daily fee for up to 80 days in the benefit period. Extended care benefits provided for under Medicare are listed as follows.

Extended Care Benefits, Medicare, Part A[a]

Medicare, Part A, will help to pay for:
1. A bed in a semiprivate room (defined as one having two to four beds) and all meals, including special diets.
2. Regular nursing services.
3. Drugs furnished by the skilled nursing facility.
4. Physical, occupational, and speech therapy.
5. Medical supplies such as splints and casts.
6. Use of appliances and equipment furnished by the facility such as a wheelchair, crutches, and braces.

Medicare, Part A, will not pay for:
1. Personal comfort or convenience items (such as charges for a telephone, radio, or television furnished at the patient's request).
2. Private-duty nurses.
3. Any extra charge for use of a private room unless the patient needs it for medical reasons.
4. Noncovered levels of care such as custodial care.
5. Doctor's services (medical insurance helps to pay for these).
6. The first three pints of blood received in a benefit period.

---

[a] Compiled from information in U.S. Department of Health, Education and Welfare, Social Security Administration Medicare Handbook.

Home Health Benefits. There are certain services that are covered under Medicare for home health care. Home health benefits include 100 visits within a benefit period and can be paid for up to a year after the patient's most recent discharge from a hospital or extended care facility. Benefits are counted on a per visit basis. Home health benefits provided under Medicare are listed as follows, as well as those services that are not paid for.

Home Health Benefits, Medicare, Part A[a]

Medicare, Part A, will help pay for:
1. Part-time skilled nursing care; physical or speech therapy.
2. If the patient needs any of the preceding services, the following services are also covered:
   (a) Occupational therapy.
   (b) Part-time services of home-health aides.
   (c) Medical social services.
   (d) Medical supplies and appliances furnished by the agency.

Medicare, Part A, will not pay for:
1. Full-time nursing care.
2. Drugs and biologicals.
3. Personal comfort or convenience items.
4. Noncovered levels of care such as custodial care.
5. Meals delivered to one's home.
6. Homemaker services.

[a] Compiled from information in U.S. Department of Health, Education and Welfare, Social Security Administration Medicare Handbook.

There are certain stipulations under Medicare that are required for reimbursement of benefits.

Home Health Benefits, Medicare, Part A[a]

1. The patient must have been in a hospital for three consecutive days (not counting the day of discharge).
2. The visits must represent further treatment of a condition for which services as a bed patient in a hospital or extended care facility were received.
3. A physician must order and set up the program within 14 days after discharge from a hospital or skilled nursing facility.
4. The patient must be confined to his/her home.
5. The agency providing the services must participate in Medicare.

[a] Compiled from information in U.S. Department of Health, Education and Welfare, Social Security Administration Medicare Handbook.

Medicare—Part B

The second part of the Medicare Program (Part B) is entitled Supplementary Medical Insurance Benefits for the Aged. This program is a voluntary program. Approximately 93 percent of the eligible elderly have elected to participate in the program.

It helps to pay for doctor bills, outpatient hospital services, medical supplies and services, home health services, outpatient physical therapy, and other health care services, as well as for many of the costs of illness not covered by hospital insurance.

Doctors' Services Benefits. Certain doctors' services are covered by Medicare, Part B.

The medical insurance (Part B) program is a voluntary one, and an individual must pay a monthly premium in order to be eligible for coverage. In addition, the subscriber is responsible for an annual deductible before coverage begins. Once the deductible is met, the enrollee must pay 20 percent of the remainder of charges for covered services.

The services provided for and excluded from coverage are indicated as follows.

Doctor's Services, Medicare, Part B[a]

Medicare, Part B, will help to pay for:
1. Medical and surgical services by a doctor of medicine or osteopathy.
2. Certain medical and surgical services by a doctor of dental medicine or dental surgery (only when surgery of the jaw or facial bones is involved).
3. Certain podiatric services (except for routine foot care).
4. Certain chiropractic services (manual manipulation of the spine but not diagnostic services or radiographs).
5. Services ordinarily furnished in the doctor's office and included in the doctor bill, such as:
   (a) Diagnostic procedures and tests.
   (b) Medical supplies.
   (c) Services of the office nurse.
   (d) Drugs and biologicals that cannot be self-administered.

Medicare, Part B, will not pay for:
1. Routine physical examinations.
2. Routine foot care.
3. Eye refractions and examinations for prescribing, fitting, or changing eyeglasses.
4. Hearing examinations for prescribing, fitting, or changing hearing aids.
5. Immunizations (unless directly related to an injury or immediate risk of infection such as a tetanus shot given after an injury).
6. Cosmetic surgery unless needed because of an accidental injury or to improve functioning of a malformed body part.

---

[a] Compiled from information in U.S. Department of Health, Education and Welfare, Social Security Administration, Medicare Handbook.

Outpatient Hospital Benefits. Medicare will help to pay for certain outpatient hospital services. The outpatient hospital services that are covered and excluded from Medicare coverage are listed as follows.

Outpatient Hospital Benefits, Medicare, Part B[a]

Medicare, Part B, will help to pay for:
1. Laboratory services.
2. Radiographs and other radiology services.
3. Emergency room and outpatient clinic services.
4. Medical supplies such as splints and casts.
5. Other diagnostic services.

Medicare, Part B, will not pay for:
1. Tests given as a part of a routine checkup.
2. Eye refractions and examinations for prescribing, fitting, or changing glasses.
3. Hearing examinations for prescribing, fitting, or changing hearing aids.
4. Immunizations (unless directly related to an injury or risk of infection such as a tetanus shot given after an injury).

[a] Compiled from information in U.S. Department of Health, Education and Welfare, Social Security Administration, Medicare Handbook.

Home Health Benefits. Under Medicare, Part B, certain home health benefits are covered for reimbursement. The home health benefits that will and will not be paid for under Medicare, Part, B, are listed as follows.

Home Health Benefits, Medicare, Part B[a]

Medicare, Part B, will pay for:
1. Part-time nursing care, physical therapy, or speech therapy.
2. If the patient needs any of the above services, the following services are also covered:
   (a) Occupational therapy.
   (b) Part-time services of home health aides.
   (c) Medical social services.
   (d) Medical supplies and appliances furnished by the agency.

Medicare, Part B, does not pay for:
1. Full-time nursing care.
2. Drugs and biologicals.
3. Personal comfort or convenience items.
4. Noncovered levels of care such as custodial care.
5. Meals delivered to one's home.

[a] Compiled from information in U.S. Department of Health, Education and Welfare, Social Security Administration, Medicare Handbook.

Before an individual may receive benefits for services or supplies delivered in the home, certain stipulations must be met. These requirements are listed as follows.

As with Part A, certain stipulations must be met before an individual may receive benefits for services delivered in the home. These stipulations are:

---

1. The individual must need part-time skilled nursing care or physical or speech therapy services.
2. The individual must be confined to the home.
3. A physician must determine that home health care is needed.
4. A physician must set up and periodically review the plan for home health care.
5. The home health agency must participate in the Medicare program.

[a] Compiled from information in U.S. Department of Health, Education and Welfare, Social Security Administration, Medicare Handbook.

Other Medical Services and Supplies. There are a variety of other services and supplies that are reimbursable under Medicare, Part B. The services and supplies that are covered and those that are not covered for reimbursement are listed as follows.

Other Medical Services and Supplies, Medicare, Part B[a]

Medicare, Part B, helps to pay for:
1. Diagnostic laboratory tests furnished by approved independent laboratories.
2. Radiation therapy and diagnostic radiographic services.
3. Portable diagnostic radiographic services furnished in the patient's home under doctor's supervision.
4. Surgical dressings, splints, casts, and the like.
5. Rental or purchase of durable medical equipment prescribed by a doctor to be used in the individual's home such as wheelchair, crutches, or oxygen equipment.
6. Devices (other than dental) to replace all or part of an internal body organ; this includes corrective lenses after a cataract operation and certain colostomy equipment and supplies.
7. Certain ambulance services.

Medicare, Part B, will not pay for:
1. Prescription drugs and drugs that one can self-administer such as insulin injections for a diabetic condition.
2. Hearing aids.
3. Eyeglasses.
4. False teeth.
5. Orthopedic shoes or other supportive devices for the feet except when shoes are a part of leg braces.

[a] Compiled from information in U.S. Department of Health, Education and Welfare, Social Security Administration, Medicare Handbook.

Medicaid

Medicaid, or Title XIX of the Social Security Act, was also passed in 1963 and became effective July 1, 1966. Medicaid represents a medical assistance program for certain groups of low-income people including the aged poor. In this joint federal–state program the federal government contributes 50 to 83 percent of the funds, depending on the wealth of the state, with eligibility for the program varying from one state to another.

With respect to its elderly recipients, Medicaid is designed to pay for medical expenses that are not covered by Medicare. Qualifying for Medicaid may follow an eligibility requirement process, which is complicated and difficult for most people. Elderly persons may find Medicaid a resource only after they have depleted all or most of their resources.

Title XIX of the Social Security Amendments of 1965 required that each state desiring to participate in Title XIX must establish and enact a state plan for medical assistance, setting forth the method of administration consistent with the law, the eligibility of an individual's benefits to be received and in the case of inpatient hospital services, the method of payment for such services.

Eligibility under Title XIX was extended to the following groups of people.

1. Families with dependent children.
2. The aged.
3. The blind.
4. Permanently and totally disabled individuals who are medically indigent.

The benefits provided under Title XIX are a fairly inclusive list of health care benefits. They range from inpatient hospital services to prescribed drugs, dentures, eyeglasses, prosthetic devices, and "other diagnostic, screening, preventive and rehabilitative services." Title XIX is financed by general tax revenues of the federal government and of participating states. The cost of the program is shared on an equal basis between the states and the federal government. For the most part, states reimburse providers for services either in accordance with a fee schedule, established or under a cost reimbursement method developed by the state.

The program paid for with federal, state and local tax funds is Medical Assistance for Needy Persons, generally called Medicaid. This help is available through local departments of social service throughout the state to all who qualify.

Medicaid seeks to protect and promote the health of children and adults who need help.

Medicare and Medicaid Benefits and Limitations

The Medicare program has made available to many people various medical services, which may not have been possible otherwise. Older people living on a limited, fixed income may not have had access to a physician, hospital, skilled nursing home, home health program services without Medicare. There are some major benefits from the program.

There are, however, serious problems that have become evident since the enactment of Medicare. About one million of the elderly are not eligible for Medicare, and those who are, find that the program covers only 44 percent of their average annual health care expenditure. Medicare has no limit on out-of-pocket expenses and does not cover catastrophic protection. For a variety of reasons the elderly spend more out-of-pocket money than they did before Medicare was enacted.

There are deductibles, copayments, coinsurance requirements, and limitations in services provided. Medicare only pays approximately 40 percent of the medical care expenditures of the elderly, which results in 60 percent to be paid for by other sources, such as by personal out-of-pocket payments or by Medicaid for those who are eligible. The charges Medicare users must pay have soared. When Medicare went into effect, a patient paid $3 a month for coverage for doctor bills. In 1981 the patient had to pay $9.60. In 1966 a patient paid $45 deductible on admission to a hospital. The deductible has risen to $180 and is expected to be increased. As the hospital stay is extended, Medicare requires patients to pay more. After 60 days patients must pay $45 a day, then $90 a day after 90 days. They must pay everything in those few cases where hospitalization is extended beyond 150 days.

Medicare does not cover most out-of-hospital services, whose costs have risen dramatically. It does not pay for prescription drugs outside the hospital, eyeglasses, hearing aids, dentures, or routine dental care. It covers no preventive care, including flu shots or a medical checkup.

Medicare covers a smaller part of doctor bills than it did in 1966, the first year the program went into effect. At the outset, it paid 80 percent of what the doctor charged. The physician could bill the patient for the rest. But when program expenses spiraled, Medicare established cost controls. These controls changed reasonable charge to a percentage—roughly 75 percent—of what all doctors charge in a locality. That reduced what Medicare paid each doctor and left more costs for the patient to bear. For example, if a doctor charged $100, Medicare now established $75 (instead of $100) as the reasonable charge. It pays only 80 percent of $75— or $60. This means the patient now has a bill of $40 instead of $20. The program allows doctors to be paid directly by the government if they wish. This is called accepting ''assignment.'' By doing so, the doctor agrees to accept Medicare's reasonable charge as full payment and not bill the patient above that amount. But fewer doctors—just over 50 percent in New York—are accepting assignment as the years pass.

Perhaps the most crucial failing is the fact that the program does not pay for most nursing home care, a critical need for elderly patients crippled by stroke, cancer, or heart disease. After hospitalization, many need only custodial care—help in eating meals, bathing, toileting. But because Medicare pays only for "skilled" nursing home care, these claims are denied. The result is that these sick people must see their life savings depleted until they fall to the poverty level where Medicaid, a program for the poor, can cover them.

The fact that Medicare pays for only skilled nursing care also means there is little coverage provided for home health aides. The result is that frail elderly people, who might recuperate in their own home, must call on their relatives for help or seek expensive nursing home care.

A typical example was an 80-year-old widow who was paralyzed by a stroke. She saw her life's savings of more than $30,000 completely eroded, even money she had earned working as a secretary until she was 75 years old. All her savings went to cover expenses for 2 years of nursing home care then for a home health aide when she was discharged. The health care services were not covered by Medicare.

It would appear that although Medicare has provided health services for many people, it does not meet the health needs of the elderly population today. Health care costs have increased astronomically. The necessity for and extent of long-term care was not taken into account in the planning and development initially of Medicare legislation. Government Medicare expenses have increased from $3 billion in 1966 to $33 billion in 1980. For many of today's elderly, Medicare does not meet their health needs.

Psychiatric care is limited under the Medicare program. An individual has a lifetime limit of 190 hospital benefit days for care in a psychiatric hospital, and a limit of $250 annually for outpatient psychiatric coverage. This represents a totally unrealistic scheme of reimbursement for this kind of health care.

The thrust of emphasis in Medicare focuses on illness, acute care, medical care, and medical necessity. Therefore health care needs of the elderly must be considered from a broader perspective of health. Health maintenance, prevention of illness and many aspects of personal care and rehabilitation are important aspects of health care. The elderly population are often in need of such services.

Only about 50 percent of the nation's poor are enrolled in Medicaid. Many of the elderly poor are excluded as a result of unrealistic state eligibility levels. The right requirements of many states discourage the elderly from even filing an application.

Private Health Insurance Plans

Over 50 percent of persons 65 and over have some form of health insurance in addition to Medicare. An elderly enroller may find the hospital deductible is covered and some plans provide cash payment for hospitalized days, eye examination, prescription drugs, or physical checkups. Most elderly persons on a low, fixed income find insurance premiums are not a viable solution. These policies are expensive and do not fill in the gaps already indicated in Medicare. These deductible and coinsurance features to Medicare may actually be a barrier to health care. There is evidence that they increase the eventual expense of treatment for the patient and for society by not supporting preventive measures and maintenance of health care.

National Health Insurance

If the health needs of the elderly are to be served, and if suitable health maintenance and preventive programs are to be developed, it would appear that a financing system must be developed and implemented that is comprehensive in nature. Many people are looking beyond the inadequacies of existing Medicare, Medicaid, and private insurance programs toward a national health insurance plan. Many plans have been proposed that cover a range from providing partial health insurance for catastrophic illnesses to total comprehensive health insurance coverage for all the financial arrangements for each differ. It is apparent that providers and consumers alike are dissatisfied with present health insurance coverage and many are advocating major innovative changes toward quality, efficient health service system to meet the needs of elderly and the entire population as well.

FUTURE HEALTH CARE NEEDS

Between 1980 and 2000 the growth of the older population will produce significant increases in demand for all kinds of health services. The rates of utilization will increase the demand for space in acute-care hospitals and nursing homes. Demand for physician services will increase with the expanded use of ambulatory services by an older population. Periodic examinations, accident prevention efforts, better nutrition, and more exercise are all important ways to promote better health among older people.

Summary

The health of individuals in the 65 and over category differs significantly. Most older people consider themselves to be in reasonably good health and are not limited in their activities by illness or injury.

Although the health of many older persons is good, there are many whose health is so impaired that they require various services. We are beginning to deal with some of the problems of old people through vigorous efforts on the part of the health profession, in geriatric services working together in interdisciplinary team approaches, government agencies, volunteer organizations, and special community services.

The health status of an elderly individual is influenced by a variety of factors: biological and psychological changes and impairment; attitudes toward health; socioeconomic characteristics of the individual; nutritional status; availability, accessibility, and quality of health care and geriatric health services; and the attitudes and skills of health providers in understanding the geriatric patient.

With the advances in technology, increased medical knowledge, and techniques are available to ameliorate many of the illnesses of later life, but all too frequently existing health care systems are organized primarily to deal with acute, episodic illnesses in hospital settings. Institutional health care systems are usually not linked to community-based systems for primary, preventive, rehabilitative or supportive care. The lack of coordination among health delivery systems has compounded the problems of health care for the aged. Some of the elderly require maintenance care over a long period of time; others require supportive services during periods of crisis; and some are in need of sophisticated rehabilitation services. No single professional facility, service, or institution can provide the medical care necessary for such a mix of patients and individual needs.

For the independent elderly, obtaining a healthful and satisfying diet depends fundamentally on what food is available and what food the individual chooses to eat. Where income is a factor in obtaining nutritious food, certain governmental programs have been established to assist the elderly, such as "food stamps," and "meals on wheels." Services in areas of nutrition and health care are mostly preventive in nature. Older people often need help with weight control, diabetes, and other chronic disorders that require dietary therapy, diet counseling, or nutritional education. With physical health problems, and the psychological affects in the loss of family and friends, the elderly may have increasing difficulty and lack motivation in preparing food. Support services have been developed in some communities to meet the needs of the elderly, including: shopping assistance, home-delivered meals, and homemaker services. Important areas of future concern in nutritional surveillance of the elderly include: a careful monitoring of the impact of economic conditions on society; identification of nutritionally vulnerable groups; policy recommendations to broaden food assistance and service programs; education programs in nutrition for the elderly appropriate to sociocultural life-styles, food technology, and consumer marketing practices; direction for setting standards for nutritional status in various geriatric health care settings.

The high cost of health care for the aged, the problems related to its access and inefficiency are some of the most noted aspects of American health care. The United States has Medicare and Medicaid programs for certain of its citizens, the elderly and the indigent poor, respectively. Medicare as a form of national health insurance has provided some financial access to medical services for the elderly. Other national health insurance plans are presently being considered to provide broader access for people of all ages. Accessible services for the elderly should include primary health care services with continuity and maintenance of care, an integrated, interdisciplinary team approach to geriatric health care delivery, expanded home health care services, and a variety of convalescent care centers. If a national health insurance program is developed with consideration given to these needs, the health care system of the elderly will be significantly improved.

There are elderly people living in poverty, and any programs for them must address this group of people. One of the areas most needed is to increase the minimum benefit for Social Security that would raise people above the poverty line. Elderly individuals who have meager financial assets and low incomes are less likely both to have feelings of well-being and to make use of the positive supports that would enhance morale. They are more likely to suffer from poor health and to be alone without any other intimate companions, after losing a spouse.

Aging is not an isolated event. Rather, it is a continuation of the circumstances that have determined all an individual's prior life. The time to begin to prepare for old age is in youth.

Everything that has happened in a person's life has a bearing on how well he or she will cope with the aging process.

This chapter places major emphasis on legislation that will provide for preventive and maintenance systems in health care. If prevention and continuity of health care are available through the life cycle, more people will approach old age with fewer problems of the kind that lead to loss of independence, loss of confidence, and loss of a healthy self-image.

FURTHER READINGS

Bell, W. G., "Community Care for the Elderly: An Alternative to Institutionalization," *Gerontologist*, 1973, *13*, 3.

Birren, J., and B. Sloane, "Manpower and Training Needs in Mental Health and Illness of the Aging." A Report to the Gerontological Society for the Committee to Study Mental Health and Illness of the Aging, for the Secretary of the Department of Health, Education, and Welfare, 1977.

Bonner, C. D., *Hamburger and Bonner's Medical Care and Rehabilitation of the Aged and Chronically Ill* (3d ed.), Little Brown, Boston, 1974.

Brill, N. E., *Teamwork: Working Together in the Human Services*, J. B. Lippincott, Philadelphia, 1976.

Brody, S. J., "Comprehensive Health Care for the Elderly. An Analysis. The Continuum of Medical, Health, and Social Services for Aged," *Gerontologist*, 1973, *13*, 412-418.

Insel, P., and R. Moos (eds.), *Health and the Social Environment*, D. C. Heath, Lexington, Mass., 1974.

Kahana, E., "The Human Treatment of Old People in Institutions," *Gerontologist*, 1973, *13*, 282-289.

Keller, W., "Care and Treatment of the Aged and Chronically Ill," in H. P. Von Hahn (ed), *Practical Geriatrics*, S. Karger, Basel, 1975, pp. 42-54.

Shanas, E., and G. L. Maddox, "Aging, Health and the Organization of Health Resources," in R. H. Binstock and E. Shanas (eds.), *Handbook of Aging and the Social Sciences*. Von Nostrand Reinhold, New York, 1976, pp. 592-618.

U. S. Department of Health, Education and Welfare, Social Security Administration, Medicare Handbook. Superintendent of Documents, U. S. Printing Office, Washington, D. C.

CHAPTER 13

Successful Aging

This chapter is prescriptive in its orientation because little research has been focused on happy or successful aging. In examining this topic, we consider behaviors, orientations, and attitudes that appear to be helpful to physical, emotional, and social well-being in the aged. The emphasis is on the relationship among positive attitudes, psychological functioning, and successful aging, and the importance of assuming personal responsibilities, which is highlighted as a key factor in those who cope successfully with the stresses of this stage of life. Finally, the preparation for aging begins in behaviors and practices that must begin now to prepare for later life well-being.

DEFINITION OF SUCCESS

Until very recently, most empirical studies of well-being (happiness, morale, life satisfaction, success) in old age involved testing for associations between some measure of psychological well-being and one, or at most a combination of three or four, of their presumed determinants. Successful feelings of well-being in old age are the product of social, psychological, and physical factors. Well-being does not come naturally. Successful aging is an achievement by people who expand time and energy in this stage as they have in other stages of life. For many of the aged, attitudes, practices, and principles conducive to success in aging are commonsense behaviors that have been learned and practiced in previous years, but regardless of whether behaviors leading to life satisfaction have been followed or ignored earlier, success in aging appears dependent on more attention to healthy attitudes and activities in later life (Wilker and Cantor, 1980).

ENVIRONMENTAL AND HEALTH FACTORS

People who age most successfully are those who are able to remain healthy and vigorous and able to accept the increase in physical problems and changes in appearance that are encountered at this stage. Those who are healthy in their attitude toward aging accept these physical changes and limitations as physical problems that can affect a person at any age. One such example follows.

IN TOUCH WITH YOURSELF

Mr. M. was a retired lawyer who was seen following a prostate operation. He had a prominent social and financial position in the community, was well regarded professionally, and had many friends and colleagues. He had a wide range of interests in addition to his professional field. His relationship with his wife and family were excellent, and his physical status was superior. He had great work capacity and was seldom bored but also seldom expressed marked emotion or talked about feelings.

His only difficulty arose in relation to a prostatectomy for which he was not emotionally prepared. He admitted later that he and his wife had never faced the possibility of growing old. He reported that the necessity of talking about aging had put him in touch with a part of themselves that he and his wife had never discovered. He stated he was probably happier now and put much less pressure on himself and others than at any time in his life. He also indicated that he had begun to wear glasses that he reportedly "needed all my life."

In those who have felt a sense of satisfaction in old age, physical problems are not ignored or tolerated. Although declines in physical stamina may be expected, the healthy person does not relinquish those aids that are available to compensate for sensory decline.

On the other hand, people need to know that they can expect to feel physically well in old age except in time of illness. Memory, learning ability, sexuality, capacities for relationships, and potential for enjoying life last in the majority of older, healthy aged until the end of life. Aging has no effect on the self, and when the self is "old," one will probably feel no different from how they felt in youth.

Clearly, there is a hereditary component involved in health and length of life, but hereditary factors are probably best seen as potentials that may only be realized to the fullest extent in a supportive environment. For example, Jones (1980) estimates that external factors such as rural living or marriage increase the average life expectancy by five years. It has also been noted that survival age of parents and grandparents and presence or absence of disease can be used in predicting longevity, and therefore are variables that are external and uncontrollable but do relate to healthy aging. Long, healthy life does indeed run in families; moreover, living in an economically privileged country, the average person has a good chance of reaching an age between 70 and 90 or higher.

Apart from accidents, pollution, disease factors and life-styles, most people die of age-dependent diseases. Those who are healthiest can alleviate some of the concern of aging by attention to diet. Specifically, reduction of fat in the diet can decrease arteriosclerosis, and it is known that persons with ideal lipoprotein concentrations (which reflect the ability of the body to metabolize fats) enjoy increased health and longer life. Although this process appears to have elements of heredity, it also seems possible to affect this condition by attention to eating habits and exercise. In addition, control of disease such as diabetes can add significantly to the chances of a longer, healthier life.

Three factors have been identified that are significantly related to health that can and should be avoided in the elderly (Palmore, 1974). People who smoked tended to be significantly at risk in terms of health and damage to their body. Although some 25 percent of those who saw age as a satisfying time in the Baltimore study (Shock, 1978) (see Chapter 2) were overweight, people who are overweight do tend to have more health difficulties in old age. In addition, it was found that activity and exercise were significantly correlated to high morale in the aged.

Exercise

The most successful aged do not abandon activities because they are perceived as inappropriate to old age. In a study done for the Administration on Aging, De Vries (1975) found that after a one-year exercise program, a class of 70-year-old men displayed increased cardiovascular and other bodily reactions comparable to men 30 years younger. The elderly men also reportedly looked and felt better. The effect of self-rated health provides significant increments to feelings of well-being that are important to older people of all ethnic backgrounds (Wilken and Cantor, 1979).

Sexual Activity

In later maturity those persons who are among the most satisfied are also those who continue to report they are still sexually active and/or interested in intimate relationships (Duke University, Chapter VIII). Older people who are most satisfied do not abstain from activities because such activities are deemed inappropriate. In essence, elderly persons who are able to decide what is "right" for them and behave accordingly have the highest morale.

SOCIAL FACTORS

People who obtain satisfaction from their social contacts and work, who enjoy higher levels of occupation and socioeconomic status are more likely to be happy at later maturity. Of course, differences in these areas also influence factors such as housing, health, nutrition, and medical care.

The most satisfaction in the elderly was noted among individuals who continued to enjoy and cultivated activities or behaviors that were personally satisfying (Alwin and Hauser, 1975).

Crime

For all elderly, regardless of ethnic background, criminal victimization appears as a growing concern that erodes their feeling of satisfaction and increases their anxieties (see Chapter 2).

Residence

Satisfaction in life among the elderly of all backgrounds in highly correlated to residential environment. This means that activities that are personally enjoyable or emotionally satisfying have been developed and located in a specific geographic area, whereas sudden or frequent disruptions in residence can have tremendous impact on the elderly and should be avoided and recognized as counterproductive and potentially harmful. Encouraging older persons to remain in their own homes and neighborhood with minimal disturbance to life-style is most important for successful readjustment.

Social Contacts

Families have been found to be of great importance to the psychological well-being of many of the elderly, but they evidently are particularly important to satisfaction of the elderly black and Spanish females (H. H. S., 1980). A closer examination of the findings suggests that this is due to the frequency and regularity with which black and Spanish women were able to see their relatives, which in turn evidently was a function of proximity to their relatives.

One of the functions that ethnicity seems to serve in society is the provision for large segments of the elderly population to maintain a fairly positive level of well-being despite low social power and prestige (Abad and Boyce 1970).

Work and Income Satisfaction

Many of the elderly derive great satisfaction from work. Among Spanish males, the work-income domain has the highest direct effect in their description of aging satisfaction (Palmore and Luikart, 1972). For elderly women, the importance of the work-income domain as related to satisfaction is lower than for men, probably due in part to the greater importance and associated satisfaction of work for men. However, for all ethnic backgrounds and both sexes, loss of income becomes an important worry and concern.

The approach of retirement age for older men and women of all backgrounds raises the specter of loss of work and income. All elderly people join an under-privileged minority at this point in life; there is no way of avoiding this at the present time for most individuals. Those who are successful realize that they will be de-prived of half their usual work income in their old age. Some older people, how-ever, become familiar with and actively seek the benefits they can and should demand by rights. Those who are most satisfied with aging prepare for it at a younger age by planning for a second career or line of work to ensure that they stay in paid useful work (Palmore and Luikart, 1972).

PERSONAL CONTROL OF LATER LIFE

In those who experience the greatest satisfaction, old age is envisioned as a normal stage that offers exciting possibilities as an integral part of the life cycle. The manner in which old persons have lived their life will significantly influence later life adjustment. Most researchers agree that feelings of health and well-being are related to the behaviors and attitudes of the individual.

It behooves all of us to try to develop or enhance certain traits that geron-tologists suggest are necessary for a longer and more comfortable life. There are five traits suggested in the research that are worth noting. The first is flexibility and the ability to allow changes to occur. This implies the ability to shift easily from one activity to another within daily life, as well as to be able to prepare successfully and carry out major transitions in life. One example would be the ability to plan success-fully for moving from the period of active work to the retirement years. It is evident that flexibility should be recognized as an important trait, and attention should be given to the cultivation of it and to the planning and preparation of major transition stages.

A second trait is acceptance and awareness of limitations. Self-assessment through the life cycle can become more efficient if one grows confident in one's abilities and realistic about personal limitations. Honest self-assessment is a valu-able asset in later life. A third characteristic of those who seem to age most success-fully is the capacity to keep on learning and growing. Learning is a lifelong activity that increases the range of one's options. Learning institutions are making it easier for older people to return to formal education in later years. The accumulation of knowledge enlarges one's interests and broadens in later years, thus potentially enhancing satisfaction with life.

The fourth trait is developing resources for old age. One can shape future resources at one's disposal by planning ahead. One can often earn money throughout life through part-time work or one's own business. Of course one should prepare during the working career for pursuits and/or employment that one will wish to pursue in the retirement years. Although fairly well understood economically, the concept also applies to mental resources. We have evidence that people who have been active in pursuing their interests preserve their zest for life. An important element of happiness in later life appears to be the ability to face minor losses and changes in life. Through a process of successfully handling the problems of life, coping mechanisms are developed. The ability to cope can make the vicissitude of life experientially rewarding.

The last trait is the ability to achieve a sense of well-being. This should result naturally from the successful development of a mature life-style. The feeling of well-being results from the total interaction of one's personality with the environment. In later years most people will have to get more out of leisure activities, finding in them a greater sense of challenge, accomplishment, and success.

There is virtually no field in which reasonably healthy adults cannot participate in some way, regardless of age. Choices naturally will be influenced by circumstances, economics, education, experience, and health, but one still has a large spectrum with which to work. There are many different levels on which to satisfy your needs. Armed with the proper attitudes and proper forethought, most people should be able to experience the aging years as a positive and rewarding phase of life.

Summary

Life satisfaction in old age is the result of social and psychological factors. It is generally believed that physical activity, nutrition, personal and social relationships, and continuing pursuit of enjoyable activities are important determinants of happiness in later life.

The literature on aging reveals that similar high levels of well-being are attained by different sex and ethnic groups in different ways. It is suggested that psychological well-being is for many elderly largely a function of a person's position in the social system in America.

Other factors besides the person's position in a social reward system also seem to affect satisfaction, namely, a person's health and level of anxiety. However, the effects of these factors are also determined largely by sociocultural factors. In the pursuit of well-being certain behaviors and attitudes are noted in those who display and report satisfaction in aging. Communicating these attitudes is probably the outstanding task of gerontology. Aging as a reflection of physical change is insignificant, compared to the psychosocial adjustments required. The only necessary losses of age (because they occur to everyone) are physical, but most of the losses that we see in the elderly are the unnecessary result of social conventions and do influence the length and quality of old age.

Successful adaption to aging requires the application of certain skills, knowledge, and experience. Recognition of one's aging and the physical and social limits it imposes, acceptance of new perceptions of oneself, and a commitment to meaningful values and goals that can be communicated to and shared in and with others are important focal points in coping with the aging process. Also, the ability to confront conflict and change skillfully can be crucial in effecting decisions about autonomy, interpersonal interactions, and life satisfactions. There is no one pattern to successful aging; the process varies widely from person to person.

Society should recognize that treating old age as a valued stage of life would foster the provision of a broader range of opportunities for elderly persons and would help them to live more productively and to contribute to the world around them.

FURTHER READINGS

Abad, V., J. Ramos, and E. Boyce, "A Model for Delivery of Mental Health Services to Spanish-Speaking Minorities," *American Journal of Orthopsychiatry,* July 1974, *44,* 584–594.

Alwin, D. F., and R. M. Hauser, "The Decomposition of Effects in Path Analysis," *American Sociological Review,* February 1975, *40,* 37–47.

deVries, H. A., "Physiology of Exercise and Aging," in D. Woodruff and J. Birren (eds.), *Aging: Scientific Perspectives and Social Issues,* Van Nostrand, New York, 1975.

Edwards, J. N., and D. L. Klemmack, "Correlates of Life Satisfaction: A Re-Examination," *Journal of Gerontology,* October, 1973, *28,* 497–502.

Elrick, H. M. D., *Living Longer and Better,* World Publications, Mountain View, Calif., 1978.

Johnson, J. L., "Modern Maturity," American Association of Retired Persons, Long Beach, Calif., February-March 1979, p. 4.

Jones, H. B. "The Relation of Human Health to Age, Place and Time," in S. C. McKenzie (ed.), *Aging and Old Age,* Scott, Foresman, Glenview, Ill., 1980.

Leslie, D., and J. McLure, *Exercise For The Elderly,* Iowa Commission on Aging, University of Iowa, Des Moines, 1980.

National Association For Human Development, *Basic Exercises For People Over Fifty,* Washington, D. C., 1976.

Palmore, E., and C. Luikart, "Health and Social Factors Related to Life Satisfaction," *Journal of Health and Social Behavior,* 1972, *13,* 68–80.

President's Council on Physical Fitness and Sports, *Physical Fitness Research Digest,* Series 8, No. 2, Washington, D. C., April 1977.

The American Alliance For Health, Physical Education, Recreation, Dance, "Newskit," *UPDATE,* March and November 1978, March and November 1979, March 1980.

Wilker, L., and M. Cantor, "A Causal Model of Psychological Well-Being Applied to White, Black and Spanish Elderly Men and Women in the Inner City" U. S. Department of Health Education and Welfare, Administration on Aging, Grant No. AA 4-70-089-02, July 1980.

Glossary

Ability Demonstrable knowledge or skill.

Accommodation Adjustment or adaptation; in sight the ability to see clearly objects near or far.

Achievement Acquired ability.

Actualization Process of mobilizing effectively one's resources and potentialities.

Acuity The ability to see small details clearly.

Adaptation Behavior that brings the individual into adjustment with his/her environment; (sight) ability to adjust to dull light.

Adaptive immunity A specific immunity resulting from contact with specific organisms or substances.

Adjustment The process by which a person relates the internal inner self and the external society. It may constitute either an internal or external change process.

Adult development The orderly and sequential changes that occur in personality over time.

Affect An expressed and observed emotion. Common examples of affect are euphoria, anger, sadness. Affect is inappropriate when it is discordant with the content of the person's speed or ideation.

Aggression Forceful, goal-directed behavior that may be verbal or nonverbal. Destructive behavior of any sort.

Ageism A stereotyped attitude directed toward aging, the aged, and the period of old age.

Aging The process of growing older. It may refer to biological, chronological, psychological changes in the course of time.

Agitation Excessive motor activity associated with a feeling of inner tension. The activity is usually non-productive and repetitious. Examples: inability to sit still, pacing, wringing of hands, pulling at clothes.

Amino acid   An organic compound used by the body to build muscle and other tissue.

Aneurysms   Congenital weakness in the walls of arteries (implicated in early age stroke).

Antibody   A molecule that will react specifically with molecules of a single kind. Gamma globulin, a material prepared from blood serum, contains all the antibodies.

Antigen   The particle or organism carrying the antigenic determinants to which the antibody reacts.

Antigenic determinants   Molecular patterns on the antigen to which the antibody reacts.

Anxiety   Apprehension, tension or uneasiness that stems from the anticipation of danger, which may be internal or external. Anxiety may be focused on an object, situation, or activity.

Arrythmias   Changes in the rate and rhythm of the heartbeat usually caused by conduction disorders.

Arteriolosclerosis   A chronic disease process in which the walls of the arteries are abnormally thickened and hardened.

Atherosclerosis   The deposit of fatty substances in the walls of the arteries, causing them to be deformed and sometimes stopping the flow of blood.

Attitude   An orientation toward or away from persons, objects, concepts, or situations. A predisposition to respond in a particular manner.

Autoimmune disease   A disease resulting when the body's immune system attacks one of its own organs.

Autoimmunity theory   Proposes that aging occurs when the various bodily systems begin to reject their own tissues.

Autonomic nervous system   The part of the nervous system that is concerned with control of involuntary functions.

Bereavement   The stage or condition of being deprived of something or someone valued or loved.

Biological aging   Refers to progressive anatomical and physiological changes that take place in cells, organs, or systems of the body over time.

Calorie   A unit of food energy.

Cancer   A disease caused by the uncontrolled multiplication of body, lymph, or blood cells.

Cellular aging theory   (Hayflick) Proposes that aging is due to an intrinsic, finite life span of cells.

Central nervous system   The brain and spinal column.

Chromosomes   Threadlike structures in the nuclei of cells. They carry genetic material that causes a new cell to be like the original.

Chronological aging   Growing older as measured by passage of units of time such as days, months, years.

Collagen   Fibrous protein found in muscles, joints, bones, cartilage ligaments and vessels.

Colon   Portion of the large intestine.

Compulsion   Repetitive behaviors that are performed according to a certain design. The actions are performed with a subjective compulsion that may afford some relief of anxiety or tension.

Confabulations   A fabrication of memory gaps for facts or events not recalled because of memory impairment.

Conflict   The clash of opposing emotional forces, impulses, desires, or tendencies.

Consumer price index   The federal government's official statistical measure of changes in the cost of living.

Coping   The process of managing problems and difficulties by adapting certain behaviors.

Cultural theory   Views aging as reflecting elaborate systems of social norms governing behavior and expectations.

Cybernetic theory   (activity or atrophy of disuse)   Proposes a relationship between aging and deterioration of the neurological control system.

Death   A biological event resulting from cessation of various physical activities.

Defense mechanism   An unconscious defense mechanism in which an aspect of external reality is rejected; refusal to admit or accept the existence of material that is anxiety provoking; at times it is replaced by a more satisfying fantasy.

Delirium   An organic brain syndrome in which there is a clouded state of consciousness with reduced capacity to shift, focus, and sustain attention to environmental stimuli. In addition, there are perceptual disturbances, disorientation, and memory impairment.

Delusion   A false belief based on incorrect influence about reality, despite incontrovertible evidence to the contrary. Types of delusions are classified according to their content: delusions of being controlled by others; delusions bizarre, delusions grandiose, delusional jealousy, delusion nihilistic, delusion persecutory, delusions of poverty, delusion of reference, delusion somatic.

Dementia   Organic brain syndrome manifesting a loss of intellectual abilities, memory impairment, and impaired judgment.

Demographic   Related to statistical aspects of the population.

Denial   An unconscious defense mechanism in which an aspect of external reality is rejected; refusal to admit or accept the existence of material that is anxiety provoking. At times it is replaced by a more satisfying fantasy.

Depression   An affective (mood) disturbance characterized by feelings of sadness, hopelessness, despair, loneliness, low self-esteem, self-reproach, and apathy.

Development   An orderly sequence of changes in behavior or physical attributes.

Disengagement theory   Proposes a relationship between chronological age and a tendency to withdraw socially from the environment.

Displacement   An unconscious defense mechanism by which the affective component of an unacceptable idea or object is transferred to an acceptable one.

Diverticulum   A blind sac branching off from the main cavity, Chapter 3.

DNA (deoxyribonucleic acid)   Acid found in large amounts in the chromosones of all cells; as part of the genetic material determining heredity; it controls development of the whole organism.

Duodenum   The first portion of the small intestine.

Eccrine glands   Sweat glands, which regulate body temperature.

Ego   Self; the concept of self.

Ego development theory   (Erikson) Proposes a progression through sequential stages with accompanying crises in self-concept that characterize aging.

Ego integrity   (Erikson) A concept proposing that a crises requiring the acceptance of one's life as meaningful; occurs in old age.

Elation   Affect characterized by euphoria. It is usually associated with manic episodes and increased motor activity.

Ejaculation   To expel semen in orgasm.

Embolism   The occulsion of a blood vessel by fragments of undissolved material carried in the blood stream.

Empathy   Ability to put oneself in another person's place to understand his/her feelings and behavior.

Enzymes   Proteins in the cells that aid chemical reactions.

Etiology   The cause of a disease or a disorder.

Family   Pairs or groups of persons related by blood or marriage.

Fantasy   Daydream. A fabricated mental picture. It seeks wish fulfillment and immediate solutions to conflicts.

Fear   Unpleasurable affect in response to a realistic threat or danger to one's existence.

Fixation   Defensive persistence of a pattern of behavior or stage of development with failure to move to a more advanced level.

Free radical theory   Proposes that aging may produce by (molecular entities) chemicals that cannot exist alone and combine with almost anything to damage cells.

Frenkel–Brunswik theory   Proposes that the aged life cycle may be understood by perceiving life accomplishments as a reaction to external and biological incidents.

Frustration   The condition resulting from the blocking or thwarting of goal-directed activity. The ability to tolerate frustration and delay gratification; is considered an indication of maturity.

Fulfillment   Satisfaction of needs.

Functional aging   Relates to age-related changes in ability to perform tasks at the same level over time.

Generativity   (Erikson) A concept proposing that a crisis of life expansion of self-interest occurs in middle adulthood (after 30).

Gerontology   Is the scientific study of the phenomenon of aging.

Goal   An end state or an incentive toward which the individual directs behavior.

Granulocyte   A type of white cell that destroys foreign matter found in the blood mainly and forms a first line defense against infection.

Grief   Subjective experiences associated with a major loss or death.

Guilt   An affect associated with self-reproach. Feelings produced when thoughts or behaviors are contrary to moral dictates or standards.

Hallucination   A sensory perception without a concrete external stimulus. It can be induced by emotional and organic factors such as drugs and alcohol. Common hallucinations involve sights or sounds, although any of the senses may be involved.

Hemoglobin   Concentration of protein matter in the blood cells that conveys oxygen to the tissues.

Hormone   A chemical substance formed in one part of the body and carried to another part where it stimulates certain changes.

Hospice   A facility for individuals beyond hope of medical cure.

Hypertension   Abnormally high blood pressure.

Hypochondriasis   Exaggerated somatic concern associated with a fear of having disease. The preoccupation with physical sensations is not based on demonstrable organ pathology.

Hypothalmus   Part of the brain that controls functions such as eating, breathing, sleeping, wakefulness and temperature.

Identity-continuity theory Views the aged as reflecting attitudes, outlooks, and values developed throughout life that have little to do with age.

Impotence Inability to attain erection; can have biological or psychological cause.

Inadequate personality A personality disorder characterized by emotional and physical instability in which the individual feels unable to manage the tasks of everyday living.

Inflexibility Refers to a personality that is characterized by inability to adapt to new situations.

Intelligence Hypothetical mental ability defined by performance.

Interaction theory Interprets aging in terms of interaction between and among the aged themselves and others in society.

Ischemia Impaired vascular functions of minute vessels.

Insomnia Difficulty falling or staying asleep.

Interpersonal skill The ability of an individual to interact effectively with others, to express feelings appropriately, to work cooperatively, to influence, to collaborate, and to be open to change.

Later maturity Term used interchangeably with old age; 65 years and over.

Learning Relatively permanent change in behavior resulting from experience.

Life expectancy An estimate of the number of years an individual may be expected to live based on statistical probability.

Lipofuscin Age pigment. A metabolic waste product that accumulates in the body in conjunction with increased age, ''liver spots.''

Liver spots Accumulations of lipfuscin or age pigment in the skin.

Longitudinal studies Method used to examine the relationship between variables using the same group at different time intervals.

Lymphocytes Type of white cell made in the lymph system and bone marrow that fights infection.

Macrophage One of the two types of white cells that ingest undesirable matter found in the lymph system, especially the lungs and body cavities.

Macula Central region of the retina.

Median income The value that divides the income distribution into equal halves, one-half with income above this amount and one-half below this amount.

Medicaid A joint federal and state program funded from general revenue available to all recipients of public assistance and medically needy to cover the cost of needed medical care.

Medicare Is a federal program that provides Part A for hospital insurance for any person over 65 entitled to Social Security. Part B, is an optional insurance plan to defray medical costs of doctor's bills, medical supplies, outpatient services, and other health services not covered by Part A.

Melanin A brown pigment that colors the skin and protects it from the ultraviolet sunlight.

Mental disorder According to the DSM-III, a mental disorder is manifested by significant behavioral or psychological syndromes that occur in an individual who is associated with distress, or an impairment in functioning.

Metabolic rate The speed at which the body carries out the chemical changes involved with nutrition.

Metabolic rate theory Proposes a relationship between aging and the rate at which the body carries out the chemical changes in nutrition.

Metabolic waste theory   Proposes that a relationship exists between aging and the accumulation of metabolic waste products in the human body.

Metabolism   The physical and chemical processes by which the body converts foods into energy and creates new molecules for body tissue and function.

Middle age   (Peck) Term used to designate those over 30 years of age.

Molecular aging theory   Suggests that aging is caused by errors in various stages of the genetic replication process.

Mood   A pervasive and sustained emotion that markedly affects the person's perception of the world. Examples of mood include depression, elation, anger, and anxiety.

Motivation   Force that pushes an individual's drive toward a specific goal or to act to satisfy a need.

Mutation theory   Poses a relationship between aging and abnormal or atypical cell division.

Near-poor index   The federal government's statistical measure of near poverty or low income. This index is a set of income thresholds comparable to those of the poverty index, but with dollar thresholds set 25 percent higher.

Nephron   The functional units of the kidney.

Nerve   One or more bundles of fibers forming part of a system that conveys impulses (of sensation, e.g.) between the brain or spinal cord, and other parts of the body.

Neuron   A nerve cell.

Neutralization   Binding of an antibody to an antigen so the alien material is no longer harmful.

Nonspecific immune mechanism   A mechanism that keeps foreign matter out of the body regardless of type; e.g. the skin is a barrier for all intrusion.

Normal aging   Inevitable changes that are the result of the passage of time in human life.

Old age   Defined operationally as 65 years old and over.

Oopaorectomy   Removal of the ovaries.

Organ damage theory   Proposes that aging may be due to lack of coordination among body tissue related to damage to particular groups of cells. (e.g. brain).

Orgasm   Climax of sexual excitement.

Osteoarthritis   Most common (90 percent of incidence) form of degenerative join disorder, affecting primarily joint cartilage.

Osteoporosis   A skeletal disorder in which bones become thinner, lighter, and more porous.

Pacing   Rate and speed of presentation in a learning situation.

Panic attacks   A period of intense anxiety, apprehension, or fearfulness. During these attacks there are manifestations of helplessness, palpitations, discomfort, choking sensations, and fear of losing control.

Periodontal disease   Inflammation of the gums and tissues surrounding and supporting the teeth.

Personality   The unique characteristics and ways of behaving that reflect the physical and mental activities, attitudes, and interests of the individual. The sum total of the adjustments of an individual to his/her total environment.

Personality theories   Proposes that aging may be understood as behavior modified by the experience of life.

Phagocytes   One of two types of white cells that ingest undesirable cells.

Plasma   The fluid portion of the blood.

Platelets Elements that cause clotting, part of the solid constituents of blood.

Poverty index The federal government's official statistical measure of poverty or low income. This index consists of a set of 124 income thresholds that are updated annually based on the Consumer Price Index.

Presbycusis Age related learning losses.

Projection An unconscious defense mechanism in which an individual attributes blame on an unacceptable trait or impulse to others instead of self. Projection protects the person from anxiety arising from inner conflict.

Proteins Complex organic compounds containing amino acids as their basic structural units. Proteins are essential for growth and tissue repair.

Psychological aging Age-related changes in the individual's behavior and mental processes.

Psychology The scientific study of behavior.

Psychotherapy A form of treatment for mental disorder and emotional and behavioral disturbances in which a therapist through communication establishes a relationship with a client. The purpose of the contact that attempts to alleviate the disturbance, reverse or change maladaptive patterns of behavior, and encourage personality growth and development.

Pulmonary Of or pertaining to the lungs.

Rationalization An unconscious defense mechanism in which an irrational action, motive, behavior, or feeling is made to appear logical and reasonable. The explanation of the behavior may serve to conceal actual motives.

Red cells One of the three solid constituents of blood.

Redundant message theory (Medvedev) Proposes that aging is due to genes that become active at a predetermined stage of life and introduces error into critical chemical reactions shortening cell life.

Regression A defensive retreat to an earlier pattern of behavior or stage of development.

Repression A defense mechanism in which an impulse or memory that might provoke feelings of anxiety or guilt is denied by its seeming expulsion from conscious awareness.

Respiratory system Pertaining to or serving the process whereby oxygen and carbohydrates are assimilated and oxidation waste products are carried out of the body.

Retirement Mandatory or voluntary withdrawal from formal paid employment.

RNA (ribonucleic acid) Acid that is present in all living cells that play a part in protein synthesis.

Role An organized and interrelated set of attitudes and references prescribed by the social environment. The pattern of behavior that a person takes.

Role activity theory Proposes a relationship between aging and past interactive styles.

Schizaphrenia A group of mental disorders characterized by disturbances in thinking, mood, and behavior.

Self-concept A person's perception of self, values, attitudes and feelings, and appraised self in relation to others and the environment.

Self-image The mental pictures that people have of themselves.

Senility A term loosely used to describe certain pathological brain functions in which the primary manifestations are confusion, forgetfulness, and loss of focus. Not an acceptable clinical term or diagnosis.

Social aging   Refers to age-related changes in an individual or group resulting from socially defined roles or forces.

Socialization   A process of learning interpersonal skills.

Social norms   Social expectation of behavior in a given role or situation.

Social roles   Patterns of activities intrinsic to a particular position in society.

Social Security   Federal program supported by employer and employee payments providing retirement disability and medical insurance programs (Medicare) for persons over 65.

Social status   Rights, privileges, and responsibilities entailed in a position within the social structure.

Society   A defined organization of people and institutions.

Specific immune mechanism   A mechanism that identifies specific organisms or substances and is able to defend against them.

Stenosis   Narrowing of a blood vessel or passage.

Stereotype   A standardized picture or perception of groups, persons, things or events. Often a prejudicial misconception.

Stomach   A saclike enlargement of the alimentary canal forming an organ of storage, dilution, and digestion.

Stress   A state of strain resulting from a perceived or actual presence of threat from situations or conditions, biological or psychological, internal or external that demand very difficult adjustments.

Stroke   Lay term for destruction of parts of the brain as a result of arterial rupture.

Subculture theory   Views the aged as having a sense of group identity.

Subcutaneous layer   The layer of skin consisting of fibrous material and fat that insulates the body from heat and cold.

Substance abuse   A pattern of pathological use of a substance(s) that may produce manifestations of intoxication, with an inability to cut down or stop the use, despite physical disorder or complications, and usually manifests impairment in functioning. Substances associated with both abuse and dependence include: alcohol, barbiturates, opiates, amphetamines, and cannabis.

Substance dependence   A more severe form of substance use disorder than substance abuse and is evidenced by physiological dependence, tolerance, or withdrawal. Usually accompanied by impairment in social functioning.

Supplemental security income (SSI)   Federal program funded by general tax revenues to supplement work income reduced by age, illness, or other medical condition.

Symbolic interaction theory   Proposes a relationship between aging and the effects of social structure.

Symptom   A sign or manifestation of an illness or emotional disturbance.

Synapse   The juncture between two neurons in the nervous system.

Syndrome   A syndrome refers to a group of symptoms that together constitute a recognizable condition. It is less specific than a disorder as it is used in the DSM-III.

Tension   An affect characterized by a marked increase in mental and physical activity.

Thrombosis   Intravascular coagulation of the blood in any part of the circulatory system.

Thrombus   A fibrinous clot that forms in and obstructs a blood vessel.

Tranquilizer(s)   Psychotropic drug(s) that induce tranquility by calming the individual without losing consciousness. Tranquilizers may be antipsychotic or antianxiety drugs.

Unrelated individuals   Persons living alone or with nonrelatives.

Urban/rural   The population that includes all persons living in places of 2,000 inhabitants or more. The population not classified as urban constitutes the rural population.

Vaccination   Producing immunity by injection of killed organisms or natural poisons (toxins) that have been modified to lose toxicity but still have antigenic determinants.

Vascular system   The heart and blood vessels.

White/nonwhite   Self-classifications by people according to the race with which they identify themselves to the census.

Withdrawal   Act of retreating from interpersonal contact and social involvement. May lead to self-preoccupation.

Withdrawal syndrome   A group of physical and emotional symptoms precipitated by withdrawal from the intake of a substance that was previously regularly used by an individual to induce a physiological state of intoxication.

Bibliography

Chapter 1

American Medical Association, "Where Does Aging Begin?", Proceedings of Congress on Improving the Quality of Life in Later Years, 1974.

Anders, R., "The Normality of Aging: The Baltimore Longitudinal Study," National Institute of Health Publication No. 79-1410, July 1979.

Ansel, P. M., and Roth, W. T., *Health in a Changing Society,* Mayfield, Palo Alto, Calif., 1977.

Bergston, V. L., and Haber, D. A., "Sociological Approaches to Aging," in D.S.I. Woodruff and J. E. Birren (eds.), *Aging Scientific Perspectives and Social Issues,* Van Nostrand, New York, 1980.

Bjorksten, J., "The Crosslinkage Theory of Aging," *Journal of American Gerontological Society, 16,* 1968, 408-427.

Bromley, D. B., The Psychology of Human Aging, (rev. ed.), Penguin Books, New York, 1974.

Burnet, F. M., "A Genetic Interpretation of Aging," *Lancet, 2,* 1973, 480-484.

Busse, E., "Theories of Aging," in C. Busse and E. Pfeiffer (eds.), *Behavior and Adaptation in Late Life,* Little Brown, Boston, 1977, pp. 21-22.

deVries, H. A., "Research Review: Fitness After Fifty," *Journal of Physical Education and Recreation, 47,* April 1976, 47-49.

deVries, H. A., "Aging and Health Education—Changing Life Styles," New York State Association, Health, Physical Education and Recreation, Kiamesha Lake, N. Y., March 15, 1980.

Encyclopedia Brittanica, *Gerontology and Geriatrics,* Benton, Chicago, p. 363ff.

Erikson, E. H., *Childhood and Society* (2nd ed.), W. W. Norton, Hogarth Press, New York, 1963, 1976.

Fischer, D. H., *Growing Old in America,* Oxford University Press, New York, 1977.

Havighurst, R. J., Neugarten, B. L., and Tolin, S. S., "Disengagement and Patterns of Aging," in B. L. Neugarten (ed.), *Middle Age and Aging,* University of Chicago Press, Chicago, 1975.

Hayflick, L., "The Biology of Human Aging," *American Journal of Medical Science, 265,* 1973, 432–445.

Hendrick, M. H., and Mrakindan, T., "Nature of Cellular Deficiencies in Age-Related Decline of the Immune System," *Gerontologia, 18,* 1972, 305–320.

Hendricks, T., and Hendricks, C. D., *Aging in Mass Society: Myths & Realities,* Winthrop, Cambridge, Mass., 1977.

Kimmel, D. C., *Adulthood and Aging: An Interdisciplinary Development,* Wiley, New York, 1977.

Kohn, R. R., *"The Effect of Antioxidants on Life Span* in C57BL," *Journal of Gerontology, 26*(3), 1971.

Lowenthal, M. F., *Four Stages of Life: A Comparative Study of Men & Women Facing Transitions,* Jossey-Bass, San Francisco, 1978.

Maddox, G. L., and Douglas, E., "Aging and Individual Differences," *Journal of Gerontology, 29,* 1974, 555–563.

McCay, C. M., "Chemical Aspects of Aging and the Effect of Diet on Aging," in A. L. Lansing (ed.), *Problem Aging,* Wiliams & Wilkins, Baltimore, 1952.

McKenzie, S. C., *Aging and Old Age,* Scott, Foresman, Glenview, Ill., 1980.

Medvedev, Z. A., "Possible Role of Neucleotide Sequences DNA in The Evolution of Life Spans of Differentiated Cells," *Nature, 237,* 1972, 453–454.

Medvedev, Z. A., "Aging and Longevity: New Approaches and New Perspectives," *Gerontologist, 14,* 1974, 381.

Mullahy, P., *Oedipus Myth and Complex: A Review of Psychoanalytic Theory,* Grove Press, New York, 1955, pp. 6–8.

Neugarten, B. L., "Adult Personality: Toward a Psychology of the Life Cycle," in *Middle Age & Aging: A Reader in Social Psychology,* B. L. Neugarten (ed.), University of Chicago Press, Chicago, 1975.

Newsday, "Some New Insights on Aging," June 23, 1980, II-7.

Novikoff, A. V., and Holtzman, E., *Cells and Organelles,* Holt, Rinehart and Winston, New York, 1970, p. 184.

Nylander, M., "Workshop in the Older Woman: Continuities and Discontinuities," *Women and Health, 4*(3), Fall 1979.

Peck, R. C., "Psychological Developments in the Second Half of Life," *Psychological Aspects of Aging,* Proceedings of a Conference on Planning Research, Bethesda, Md., April 24–27, 1955, John E. Anderson (ed.), American Psychological Association, Washington, D. C., 1956, pp. 44–49.

Saxon and Etten, *Physical Change and Aging: A Guide for the Helping Professions,* Tiresias Press, New York, 1978.

Straits, G. F., "Are the Aged a Minority Group?", in B. L. Neugarten (ed.), *Middle Age and Aging: A Reader in Social Psychology,* University of Chicago Press, Chicago, 1975.

Tobin, J. D., "Somal Aging—The Inevitable Syndrome," in S. H. Zarit (ed.), *Readings on Aging & Death Contemporary Perspectives,* Harper & Row, New York, 1977.

U.S. Department of Health, Education and Welfare, *Facts About Older Americans,* 1979, H.D.S. Publication #(80-20006), Washington, D.C.

Von Hahn, H. P., "Failures of regulation mechanisms as a Cause of Cellular Aging," in *Advances in Gerontological Research,* Vol. 3, B. L. Steehler (ed.), Academic Press, New York, 1971, pp. 1-38.

Walford, R. L., and Lui, R. K., "The Effect of Lowered Body Temperature on Life Span and Immune and Non-Immune Processes," *Gerontologia, 18,* 1972, 363-388.

Wigniewski, H. M., and Terry, R. D., "Morphology of the Aging Brain, Human and Animal," *Progress in Brain Research 40,* 1973, 167-186.

Chapter 2

Brophy, A. M., *Facts for Action: The Elderly in the Inner City,* New York City Office of the Aging, New York, 1980.

Butler, R. N., *Why Survive? Being Old in America,* Harper & Row, New York, 1975.

Butler, R. N., and Lewis, M. F., *Aging and Mental Health: Positive Psychosocial Approaches,* Mosby, St. Louis, 1973.

Campbell, A., "Politics Through the Life Cycle," *Gerontologist,* 1971, 12-17.

Carp, F. M., and Kataoka, E., "Health Care Problems of the Elderly in San Francisco's Chinatown," *Gerontologist, 16,* 1976, 30-38.

Collins, W., and Yee, D., Social Forces Within the Seattle Filipino American Community Today: 1972, *Demonstration Project for Asian Americans,* Seattle, Wash., February 1972.

Current Population Reports, "Marital Status and Living Arrangements: March 1975," Series P-20, No. 287, U.S. Department of Commerce, Bureau of the Census, Washington, D.C., March 1975.

Current Population Reports, "Money Income and Poverty Status of Families and Persons in the United States," Series P-60, No. 103, U.S. Department of Commerce, Bureau of the Census, Washington, D.C., March 1975.

Current Population Reports, Special Studies, "Demographic Aspects of Aging and the Older Population in the United States," Series P-23, No. 59, U.S. Department of Commerce, *Bureau of the Census,* Washington, D.C., May 1976.

Current Population Reports, Projections of the Population of the United States, P-25, No. 75, 1977, 2050, U.S. Department of Commerce, *Bureau of the Census,* Washington, D.C., July 1977.

Daum, M. "Selected Demographic Characteristics of Elderly Asian and Pacific Island Americans in New York City," *Facts for Action,* New York City Office for the Aging, January 1977, 9,(1).

Developments in Aging 1976-1977, Part 1, A Report of the *Special Committee on Aging,* U.S. Senate, U.S. *Government Printing Office,* No. 95, 771, Washington, D.C., 1978.

Facts About Older Americans, U.S. Department of Health, Education and Welfare, Washington, D.C., 1975.

Facts and Figures on Older Americans, No. 5, U.S. Department of Health, Education, and Welfare, January 1978.

Fowles, D. G., "Some Prospects for the Future Elderly Population," *Statistical Reports on Older Americans,* January 1978, U.S. Department of Health, Education and Welfare, Office of Human Development Administration on Aging, National Clearinghouse on Aging, No. 3, Washington, D.C., 1978.

Fowles, D. J., Administration on Aging, *Statistical Memo,* No. 33, "Elderly Widows," July 1976, Washington, D.C., 1976.

Fowles, D. J., "Income and Poverty Among the Elderly: 1975," *Statistical Reports on Older Americans,* April 1977, U.S. Department of Health, Education, and Welfare, HEW Publication No. OHD, 77-20286, Washington, D.C.

Hill, R., "A Profile of the Black Aged," Occasional Papers in Gerontology Series, University of Michigan Wayne State University, Ann Arbor, Mich., 1974.

Kalish, R. A., and Moriwaki, S., The World of the Asian American, *Journal of Social Issues, 29*(2), 1973, 187–209.

Lai, H., and Choy, P. O., *Outline History of the Chinese in America,* San Francisco Chinese American Studies Planning Group, San Francisco, 1973.

Lee, D. Y., *Report on the Korean American Community in Los Angeles,* Los Angeles Demonstration Project for Asian Americas, Los Angeles, January 1972.

Nee, V. G., and de Bary, B., *Longtime California: A Documentary Study of an American Chinatown,* Parthenon Books, New York, 1973.

New York City Department for the Aging, *Recent Developments in the Economics of Aging,* June 1975.

New York Times, "Benefits Raised 9.9% Under Social Security," April 27, 1979, p. A16.

New York Times, "U.S. Life Span, 26 Years Longer than in 1900," June 18, 1980, p. A6.

Reinhold, R., "New Population Trends Transforming the United States," *New York Times,* February 6, 1977, p. A1.

Special Committee on Aging, U.S. Senate, *Developments on Aging,* U.S. Government Printing Office, Washington, D.C., 1977.

Statistical Bulletin, Vol. 58, *Metropolitan Life Insurance Company,* New York, May 1977.

Thompson, G. B., "Black-White Differences in Private Pension; Findings from the Retirement History Study," *Social Security Bulletin,* February 1979, *42*(2).

U.S. Department of Commerce: Persons of Spanish Origin in the United States, March 1975. Population Characteristics, Advance Report, *Bureau of The Census,* Series P-20, No. 283, Washington, D.C., 1975.

Williams, B. S., "Characteristics of the Black Elderly and Older American Indians 1980," Statistical Reports on Older Americans, No. 5, April 1980. U.S. Department of Health and Human Services, Office of Human Development Services, Administration on Aging, National Clearinghouse on Aging, DHEW Publication, No. (OHDS) 80-20057, 78-20289, Washington, D.C., 1980.

Chapter 3

Asimov, I., *The Human Brain: Its Capacities & Functions,* New American Library, New York, 1974, pp. 112–188.

Brocklehurst, J. C., "The Large Bowel," in J. C. Brocklehurst (ed.), *Textbook of Geriatric Medicine & Gerontology,* Churchill Livingstone, London, 1973, pp. 346–363.

Burger, P. C., and Vogel, F. S., "The Development of the Pathologic Changes of Alzheimer's Disease and Senile Dementia in Patients with Down's Syndrome," *American Journal of Pathology, 73,* 1973, 457.

Butler, R. N., *Energy and Aging,* U.S. Senate Special Committee on Aging, Washington D.C., April 5, 1977.

Butler, R. N., and Lewis, M. I., *Aging & Mental Health, Positive Psychosocial Approaches,* Chapter 6, "Special Concerns," C. V. Mosby, St. Louis, 1977.

Comfort, A., *A Good Age,* Crown, New York, 1976.

Comroe, J. H., and Dripps, R. D., "The Ten Top Clinical Advances in Cardiovascular—Pulmonary Medicine and Surgery Between 1945 and 1975, How They Came About," Final Report National Heart Lung and Blood Institute, U.S. Government Printing Office, Washington, D.C., January 31, 1977.

Corso, F., "Auditory Perception and Communication," in J. E. Birren, and K. W. Schaie (eds.), *Handbook of the Psychology of Aging,* New York, Van Nostrand, 1977.

Engel, B. T., "Using Biofeedback with the Elderly." National Institute on Aging. M. & H. Publication No. 79-1404, Washington, D.C., July 1979.

Everitt, A. V., "The Hypothalamic-Pituitary Control of Aging & Age-Related Pathology, *Experimental Gerontology* October 1973, *8,* 265–277.

Feinleib, M., and Davidson, M. "Coronary Disease Mortality: A Community Perspective," *The Journal of the American Medical Association, 222,* 1972, 1129–1136.

Fonrose, G. A., "Medical Care in the Geriatric Population," in Monroe Mitchell (ed.), *A Practical Guide to Long Term Care and Health Services Administration,* Panel Publishers, Greenvale, N. Y., 1978.

Gaskowitz, R. W., "Osteoarthritis: A New Look at an Old Disease," *Geriatrics, 28,* June 1973, 121–128.

Groh, D., "Common Disorders of Muscles in the Aged, in A. B. Chinn (ed.), *Working with Older People: A Guide to Practice,* Vol. 4, *Clinical Aspects of Aging,* U.S. Public Health Service Publication #1459, Washington, D.C., 1971, pp. 156–162.

Guyton, A., *Textbook of Medical Physiology,* Saunders, Philadelphia, 1971, pp. 445–447.

Hall, D. A., "Metabolic and Structural Aspects of Aging," in J. C. Brocklehurst (ed.), *Textbook of Geriatric Medicine and Gerontology,* London, 1973, pp. 426–435.

Harris, R., "Special Features of Heart Disease in the Elderly Patient," in *Working with Older People,* Vol. 4, U.S. Department of Health, Education and Welfare, 1971, pp. 82, 83, 86, 87, 89, 90-92, 94.

Hucyk, M. H., *Growing Older: Things You Need to Know About Aging,* Prentice-Hall, Englewood Cliffs, N. J., 1974.

Insel, P. M., and Roth, W. T., *Health in a Changing Society,* Mayfield Publishing, Palo Alto, Calif., 1976.

Jaffe, Jack, "Common Lower Urinary Tract Problems in Older People," in *Working with Older People,* Vol. IV, U.S. Department of Health, Education, and Welfare, 1971, pp. 141, 143-145.

Kahn, A. and Snapper, I., "Medical Renal Disease in the Aged," in *Working with Older People,* Vol. IV, U.S. Department of Health, Education and Welfare, 1971, pp. 131, 133-139.

Kammel, W. B., "Framingham Study and Chronic Disease Prevention," *Hospital Practice, 5,* 1970, 78.

Mitchell, P. H., *Concepts Basic to Nursing,* McGraw-Hill, New York, 1973.

National Advisory Council on Aging, Our Future Selves: A Research Plan Toward Understanding Aging, N.I.H. Publication No. 80-1444, and 45. U.S. Government Printing Office, Washington D.C., January 1980.

National Institute on Aging, "Special Report on Aging: 1979; U.S. Department of Health, Education, and Welfare, N.I.H. Publication No. 80-1907, Washington, D.C., February 1980.

National Society for the Prevention of Blindness, *National Society for Prevention of Blindness Factbook,* New York, 1974.

Peterson, B. A., and Kennedy, B. J., "Aging and Cancer Management Part I: Clinical Observations," *Cancer Journal for Clinicians, 29*(6), November/December 1979.

Rossman, I., "The Anatomy of Aging," in I. Rossman (ed.), *Clinical Geriatrics,* J. B. Lippincott, Philadelphia, 1971.

Ruben, R., *Aging and Hearing in Clinical Geriatrics,* J. B. Lippincott, Philadelphia, 1971.

Russell, R., "Pathogenesis of Primary Intracerebral Hemorrhage," in J. F. Foole (ed.), *Cerebral Vascular Diseases,* Sixth Conference, Grune & Stratton, New York, 1968.

Salter, R. H., Some Aspects of Diverticular Disease of the Colon, *Age and Aging, 2,* November 1973, 225-229.

Seidman, H., Silverberg, E., and Bodden, A., "Probabilities of Eventually Developing and Dying of a Cancer (Risk Among Persons Previously Undiagnosed with the Cancer)," *Cancer, 28,* 1978, 33-46.

Seligman, I., "What Causes Cancer," *Newsweek,* January 26, 1976, in H. Sloan (ed.), *Readings in Health, 1978-1979,* Dushkin Publishing, Guilford, Conn., 1978, pp. 192–197.

Shock, N., *Biomedical Science: Prospects in Aging.* Presentation to Convocation Andrus Gerontology Center, University of Southern California, February 1973.

Shock, N., "Systems Physiology and Aging," Symposium of the Gerontological Society, Biological Sciences Section and the American Physiological Society at the 62nd Annual Meeting of the Federation of American Societies for Experimental Biology, Atlantic City, N. J., April 13, 1978.

Strehler, B. L., *Fine Cells and Aging* (2nd ed.), Academic Press, New York, 1977.

Timiras, P. S., "Diseases of Aging," in P. S. Wimiar (ed.), *Development Physiology and Aging,* Macmillan, New York, 1972, p. 474.

Vogel, F., "The Brain and Time," in W. Busse and E. Pfeiffer (eds.), *Behavior and Adaptation in Late Life,* Little Brown, Boston, 1977.

Chapter 4

Arenberg, D., "Cognition and Learning: Verbal Learning, Memory and Problem Solving," in C. Eisdorfer and M. P. Lawton (eds.), *The Psychology of Adult Development and Aging,* American Psychological Association, Washington, D.C., 1973, pp. 157-219.

Botwinick, J., *Aging and Behavior,* Springer, New York, 1973.

Botwinick, J., "Intellectual Abilities," in J. E. Birren and K. W. Schaie (eds.), *Handbook of the Psychology of Aging,* Van Nostrand, New York, 1978.

Cohen, D., "Sex Differences in the Organization of Spatial Abilities in Older Men and
    Women," unpublished doctoral dissertation, University of Southern California, Los
    Angeles, 1975.
Eichorn, D. H., "The Institute of Human Development Studies, Berkley and Oakland," in
    L. F. Jarvik, C. Eisdorfer, and J. E. Blum (eds.), *Intellectual Functioning in Adults*,
    Springer, New York, 1973, pp. 1-6.
Eisdorfer, C., "Experimental Studies," in C. Eisdorfer and M. P. Lauton (eds.), *The
    Psychology of Adult Development and Aging*, American Psychological Association,
    Washington, D.C., 1973, pp. 71-73.
Eisdorfer, C., "Intelligence and Cognition in the Aged," in E. W. Busse and E. Pfeiffer
    (eds.), *Behavior and Adaptation in Later Life*, Little Brown, Boston, 1977, pp. 213ff.
Eisdorfer, C., and Wilkie, F., Intellectual Changes with Advancing Age, in L. F. Jarvik, C.
    Eisdorfer, and J. E. Blum (eds.), *Intellectual Functioning in Adults*, Springer, New
    York, 1973, pp. 21-29.
Rabbitt, P. M. A., "An Age Decrement in the Ability to Ignore Irrelevant Information."
    Journal of Gerontology, 26, 1971, 133-136.
Schaie, K. W., and Bueck, B. V., "Generational and Cohort Specific Differences in Adult
    Cognitive Functions, A Fourteen-Year Study of Independent Samples," *Developmen-
    tal Psychology, 9*, 1973, 151-166.
Schaie, K. W., and Laborine-Vief, G., Generational Versus Ontogenetic Components of
    Change in Adult Cognitive Behavior, A Fourteen-Year Cross-Sequential Study, *Devel-
    opmental Psychology, 10*, 1974, 305-320.
Shock, N., National Institute of Aging: Baltimore, Md., Reported Surprising Findings in
    The Process of Aging, Science Times Section, *New York Times*, June 19, 1979.

Chapter 5

Butler, R. N., and Lewis, M. I., *Sex After Sixty: A Guide for Men and Women for Their
    Later Years*, Harper & Row, New York, 1976.
Dlin, B. M., "Sex After Ileostomy or Colostomy," *Medical Aspects of Medical Sexuality, 6*,
    1972, 32-43.
Kinsey, A. C., Pomeroy, W. B., and Martin, C. R., *Sexual Behavior in The Human Male*,
    Saunders, Philadelphia, 1948, 1953.
Masters, W. H., and Johnson, V. E., *Human Sexual Inadequacy*, Little Brown, Boston,
    1970, pp. 337-339.
Masters, W. H., and Johnson, V. E., *Human Sexual Response*, Little Brown, Boston, 1966.
McCary, J. L., *Human Sexuality* (2nd ed.), Van Nostrand, New York, 1973.
National Advisory Council on Aging, Our Future Selves: Report of the Panel on Biomedical
    Research, N.I.H. Publication No. 80-1445 U.S. Government Printing Office:
    Washington, D.C., January 1980.
Pfeiffer, E., *Successful Aging*, Duke University Center for the Study of Aging and Human
    Development, Durham, N.C., 1974.
Pfeiffer, E., "Sexual Behavior in Old Age," in E. W. Busse and E. Pfeiffer (eds.), *Behavior
    and Adaptation in Late Life*, Little Brown, Boston, 1977, pp. 130-140.
Rubin, I., *Sexual Life after Sixty*, Basic Books, New York, 1976.

Ryan, K. J., and D. C. Gibson, *Menopause and Aging,* U.S. Department of Health Education and Welfare, N.I.H. No. (NIH) 73-319, Bethesda, Md., 1979.

Chapter 6

Anderson, A., "Excerpts on Black Aged from the Urban League News," in B. B. Hess (ed.), *Growing Old in America,* Transaction Books, New Brunswick, N.J., 1976, pp. 298-516.

Back, K. W., "Personal Characteristics and Social Behavior: Theory and Method," in R. H. Binstock and E. Shanas (eds.), *Handbook of Aging and the Social Sciences,* Van Nostrand, New York, 1976, Chapter 16, pp. 403-431.

Baltes, P. B., and Willis, S. L., "Toward Psychological Theories of Aging and Development," in J. E. Birren and K. W. Schale (eds.), *Handbook of the Psychology of Aging,* Van Nostrand, New York, 1976, Chapter 7, pp. 128-154.

Bardwick, J. M., *Psychology of Women,* Harper & Row, New York, 1971 (paper), Chapter 1, "Psychoanalytic Theory," pp. 1-20; Chapter 11, "Changes in Motives & Roles During Different Stages in Life," pp. 188-205; Chapter 12, "A Summing Up and Some Concluding Remarks," pp. 206-218.

Beeson, D., and Lowenthal, M. F., "Perceived Stress Across the Life Course," in Lowenthal, M. F., Thurnher, M., Chirlboga, D., et al. (eds.), *Four Stages of Life,* Jossey-Bass, San Francisco, 1975, pp. 163-175.

Bengston, V. L., Kasschau, P. L., and Ragan, P. K., "The Impact of Social Structure on Aging Individuals," in J. E. Birren and K. W. Schale (eds.), *Handbook of the Psychology of Aging,* Van Nostrand, New York, 1977.

Bernard, J., "Change and Stability in Sex-Role Norms and Behavior," *Journal of Social Issues, 32*(3), 1976, 207-223.

Binstock, R., "Aging and The Future of American Politics," *The Annals,* September 1974.

Blau, Z. S., *Old Age in A Changing Society,* New Viewpoints, Franklin Watts, New York, 1973.

Block, J., *Lives Through Time,* Bancroft Books, Berkeley, Calif., 1971, Chapter I, pp. 1-19, Chapter VIII, pp. 137-186, Chapter IX, pp. 189-227.

Bloom, M., and Blenkner, M., "Assessing Functioning of Older Persons Living in the Community," *Gerontologist, 10,* 1970, 31-37.

Bronfenbrenner, U., "Toward an Experimental Ecology of Human Development," *American Psychologist, 32*(7), July 1977, 513-531.

Busse, E., and Pfeiffer, E. (eds.), *Mental Illness in Later Life,* American Psychiatric Association, Washington, D.C., 1973.

Busse, E., and Pfeiffer, E. (eds.), *Behavior and Adaptation in Later Life* (2nd ed.), Little Brown, Boston, 1977.

Butler, R. M., "Family Life Style Characteristics and Child Health Care," in M. M. Lewis (ed.), *Social Work Services in Pediatric Hospitals,* USPHS, Department of HEW, Rockville, Md., 1972.

Butler, R. M., *Social Functioning Framework: An Approach to the Human Behavior and Social Environment Sequence,* Council on Social Work Education, New York, 1970.

Butler, R. N., *Why Survive? Being Old in America,* Harper & Row, New York, 1975.

Butler, R., and Lewis, M., *Aging & Mental Health,* C. V. Mosby, St. Louis, 1977.

Coles, R., *The Old Ones of New Mexico,* University of New Mexico Press, Albuquerque, 1973.

Costa, Jr., P., and McCrae, R., "Age Difference in Personality Structure: A Cluster Analytic Approach," *Journal of Gerontology, 31*(5), September 1976, 564-570.

David, D. S., and Brannon, R. (eds.), *The Forty-Nine Percent Majority: The Male Sex Role,* Addison-Wesley, Mass., 1976.

Davison, M. L., Robbins, S., and Swanson, D. B., "Stage Structure in Objective Moral Judgments," *Developmental Psychology, 14*(2), March 1978, 137-146.

Diagnostic & Statistical Manual of Mental Disorders, American Psychiatric Association, Washington, D.C., 1980.

Dickstein, E., "Self and Self-Esteem: Theoretical Foundations and Their Implications for Research," *Human Development, 20*(3), 1977, 129-140.

Dsikszentmihaly, M., *Beyond Boredom and Anxiety,* Jossey-Bass, San Francisco, 1975.

Erikson, E. H., *Life History and the Historical Moment,* Norton, New York, 1975, Part 3, Section III, "Once More the Inner Space," pp. 225-247.

Fiske, M., *Middle Age: Growth, Stagnation and Regression,* Psychology and You Series, Lifetime Books, London, (forthcoming).

Freedman, K. S., *Modern Synopsis of Comprehensive Textbook of Psychiatry,* Williams & Wilkins, Baltimore, 1972.

Friedman, A., Kaplan, H., and Sadock, B., *Modern Synopsis of Psychiatry,* Williams & Wilkins, Baltimore, 1972.

Gargen, K. J., *The Concept of Self,* Holt, Rinehart and Winston, New York, 1971, Parts II & III, pp. 13-64.

Golant, S., "Residential Concentrations of the Future Elderly," *Gerontologist, 15,* 1975, 16.

Gould, R., *Transformations,* Simon & Schuster, New York, 1978.

Gutkin, D. C., "An Analysis of the Concept of Moral Intentionality," *Human Development, 16*(5), 1973, 371-381.

Hayflick, L., "The Strategy of Senescence," *Gerontologist, 14,* 1974, 37-45.

Hendricks, J., and Hendricks, G. D., *Aging in Mass Society: Myths and Realities,* Winthrop Publishers, Cambridge, Mass., 1977, pp. 349-384.

Hogan, R., "Dialectical Aspects of Moral Development," *Human Development, 17*(2), 1974, 107-117.

Huyck, M. H., *Growing Older,* Prentice-Hall, Englewood Cliffs, N. J., 1974.

Insel, P. M., and Roth, W. T., *Health in A Changing Society,* Mayfield Publishing, Calif., 1976.

Jackson, J., "Aged Blacks: A Potpourri in the Direction of the Reduction of Inequities," in B. B. Hess (ed.), *Growing Old in America,* Transaction Books, New Brunswick, N.J., 1976, pp. 390-416.

Kalish, R., and Moriwaki, S., "The World of the Elderly Asian American," *Journal of Social Issues, 29*(2), 1973, 187-209.

Katz, S., Downs, T. D., Cash, H. R., and Gratz, R. C., "Progress in Development of the Index of ADL," *Gerontologist, 10,* 1970, 20-30.

Kiefer, C., *Changing Cultures, Changing Lives: An Ethnographic Study of Three Generations of Japanese Americans,* Jossey-Bass, San Francisco, 1974.

Kiefer, G. W., *Changing Culture, Changing Lives,* Jossey-Bass, San Francisco, 1974.

Klvett, V. R., Watson, J. A., and Busch, J. C., "The Relative Importance of Physical, Psychological, and Social Variables to Locus of Control Orientation in Middle Age," *Journal of Gerontology, 32*(2), March 1977, 203-210.

Kohlberg, L., "Continuities in Childhood and Adult Moral Development Revisited," in P. B. Baltes and K. W. Schaie (eds.), *Life Span Developmental Psychology,* Academic Press, New York, 1973, pp. 179-204.

Lawton, M. P., "The Relative Impact of Congregate and Traditional Housing on Elderly Tenants," *Gerontologist, 16,* 1976, 237-249.

Lazarus, R. S., "Cognitive and Personality Factors Underlying Threat and Coping," in S. Levine and N. A. Scotch (eds.), *Social Stress,* Aldine, Chicago, 1970, pp. 143-164.

Leaf, A., *Youth in Old Age,* McGraw-Hill, New York, 1975.

Leshan, E., *The Wonderful Crises of Middle Age,* David McKay, New York, 1973.

Lifton, R. J., *The Life of The Self,* Simon & Schuster, New York, 1976, pp. 49-81.

Loevinger, J., *Ego Development,* Jossey-Bass, San Francisco, 1976, pp. 413-433.

Lowenthal, M. F., "Summary and Implications," in M. F. Lowenthal, M. Thurnher, D. Chirlboga, et al. (eds.), *Four Stages of Life,* Jossey-Bass, San Francisco, 1975, pp. 233-245.

Lowenthal, M. F., "Toward a Sociopsychological Theory of Change in Adulthood," in J. E. Birren and K. W. Schaie (eds.), *Handbook of the Psychology of Aging,* Van Nostrand, New York, 1976, pp. 116-127.

Lowenthal, M. F., and Chiriboga, D., "Social Stress and Adaptation: Toward a Life Course Perspective," in C. Eisdorfer and H. Powell Lawton (eds.), *The Psychology of Adult Development and Aging,* American Psychological Association, Washington, D.C., 1973, pp. 281-310.

Lowenthal, M. F., and Chiriboga, D., "Respones in Stress," in M. F. Lowenthal, M. Thurnher, D. Chiriboga et al. (eds.), *Four Stages of Life,* Jossey-Bass, San Francisco, 1975, pp. 146-162.

Lowenthal, M. F., and Robinson, B., "Social Networks and Isolation," in R. H. Binstock and E. Shanes (eds.), *Handbook of Aging and Social Sciences,* Van Nostrand, New York, 1976, pp. 432-456.

Lowenthal, M. F., and Weiss, L., "Intimacy and Crises in Adulthood," in J. N. Whiteley (ed.), *Coming of Age: Counseling Adults* (Special Issue of *Counseling Psychology*), 6,(1), 1976, 10-15; also in N. K. Schlossberg, and A. D. Entine (eds.), *Counseling Adults,* Brooks/Cole, Monterey, Calif., 1977, Part I, pp. 19-33.

Maas, H. S., and Kuypers, J. A., *From Thirty to Seventy,* Jossey-Bass, San Francisco, 1974, pp. 132-175.

Maccoby, E. E., and Jacklin, C. N., *The Psychology of Sex Differences,* Stanford University Press, Stanford, Calif., 1974, pp. 349-374.

Maddox, G., and Douglas, E., "Aging and Individual Differences," *Journal of Gerontology, 29*(5), 1974, 555.

Maddox, G. L., and Wiley, J., "Scope, Concepts and Methods in the Study of Aging." In R. H. Binstock and E. Shanes (eds.), *Handbook of Aging and the Social Sciences,* Van Nostrand Reinhold, New York, 1976, pp. 3-28.

McClelland, D., *Power: The Inner Experience,* Irvington, New York, 1975, pp. 30-76.

Neugarten, B., "Age Groups in American Society and the Rise of the Young-Old," *The Annals,* September 1974.

Neuhaus, R., and Neuhaus, R., *Family Crises,* Charles E. Merrill, Columbus, Ohio, 1974.

Norton, D. L., *Personal Destinies: A Philosophy of Ethical Individualism,* Princeton University Press, Princeton, N.J., 1976, pp. 158-215.

Palmore, E., *Normal Aging,* Duke University Press, Durham, N.C., 1974.

Palmore, E., *The Honorable Elders,* Duke University Press, Durham, N.C., 1975.

Palmore, E., The Future Status of the Aged, *Gerontologist, 16*(4), 1976, 297.

Palmore, E., and Manton, K., "Modernization and Status of the Aged," *Journal of Gerontology, 29*(2), 1974, 205.

Pyke-Lees, C., and Gardner, S., *Elderly Ethnic Minorities,* London, 1974.

Rabecca, M., Hafner, R., and Oleshansky, B., "A Model of Sex-Role Transcendence," *Journal of Social Issues, 32*(3), 1976, 197-206.

Rosow, I., "Status and Role Change Through the Life Span," in R. H. Binstock and E. Shanas (eds.), *Handbook of Aging and the Social Sciences,* Van Nostrand, New York, 1976, pp. 457-482.

Rosow, I., "The Social Contest of the Aging Self," *Gerontologist, 13,* 1973, 82-87.

Ryff, C. D., and Baltes, P. B., "Value Transition and Adult Development in Women: The Instrumentality-Terminality Sequence Hypothesis," *Developmental Psychology, 12*(6), November 1976, 567-568.

Sears, R., "Sources of Life Satisfaction of the Terman Gifted Man," *American Psychologist, 32*(2), February 1977, 119-128.

Segall, A., "The Sick Role Concept: Understanding Illness Behavior," *Journal of Health and Social Behavior, 17,* 1976, 162-169.

Simpson, E. L., "Moral Development Research: A Case Study of Scientific Cultural Bias," *Human Development, 17*(2), 1974, 81-106.

Stack, C., *All Our Kin: Strategies for Survival in a Black Community,* Harper & Row, San Francisco, 1974.

Sullivan, E. V., "A Study of Kohlberg's Structural Theory of Moral Development: A Critique of Liberal Social Science Ideology," *Human Development, 20,* 1977, 352-376.

Thomas, H., "Theory of Aging and Cognitive Theory of Personality," *Human Development, 13*(1), 1970, pp. 1-16.

U.S. Bureau of the Census, "Projections of the Population of the United States, by Age and Sex, 1975-2000," *Current Population Reports* (Series P-25, No. 541), February 1975.

Valliant, G., *Adaptation to Life,* Little Brown, Boston, 1977, pp. 193-303.

Wu, T. V. T., "Mandarin-Speaking Aged Chinese in the Los Angeles Area," *Gerontologist, 15*(3), 1975, 271-275.

Chapter 7

Akiskal, H. S., and McKinney, W. T., Jr., "Depressive Disorders: Toward a Unified Hypothesis," *Science, 182,* 1973, 20-29.

Akiskal, H. S., and McKinney, W. J., Jr., "Overview of Recent Research in Depression: Integration of Ten Conceptual Models into a Comprehensive Clinical Frame," *Archives of General Psychiatry, 32,* 1975, 285-303.

Allen, M. G., "Twin Studies of Affective Illness," *Archives of General Psychiatry, 33*, 1976, 1476-1478.

Altholz, J., "The Family and the Older Person," in D. T. Peak, G. Polansky, and J. Altholz (eds.), *The Final Report of the Information and Counseling Service for Older Persons*, Center for the Study of Aging and Human Development, Durham, N.C., 1971.

Altholz, J., "Group Therapy with Elderly Patients," in E. Pfeiffer (ed.), *Alternatives to Institutional Care for Older Americans: Practice and Planning*, Center for the Study of Aging and Human Development, Durham, N.C., 1973.

Ander, S., Lindstrom, B., and Tibblin, G., "Life Changes in Random Samples of Middle-Aged Men," in E. K. E. Gunderson and R. H. Raha (eds.), *Life Stress and Illness*, Charles C. Thomas, Springfield, Ill., 1974, pp. 121-124.

Arnhoff, F. N., "Social Consequences of Policy Toward Mental Illness," *Science, 1975*, pp. 1277-1281.

Baltes, P. B., and Schaie, K. W., "On the Plasticity of Intelligence in Adulthood and Old Age," *American Psychologist, 31*, 1976, 720-725.

Beck, A. T., *Depression*, Harper & Row, New York, 1967.

Bennett, A. E., Psychiatric Management of Geriatric Depressive Disorders, *Diseases of The Nervous System, 34*(5), 1973, 222-225.

Benson, R. A., and Brodie, D. C., "Suicide by Overdoses of Medicines Among the Aged, *Journal of the American Geriatrics Society, 23*(7), 1975, 304.

Blau, D., "On Widowhood: A Discussion," *Journal of Geriatric Psychiatry, 8*(1), 1975, 29-40.

Blenkner, M., "Environment Change and the Aging Individual," *Gerontologist, 7*, 1967, 101-105.

Blenkner, M., Bloom, M., and Nielsen, M., "A Research and Demonstration Project of Protective Services," *Social Casework, 52*, 1971, 483-499.

Botwinick, J., *Cognitive Processes in Maturity and Old Age*, Springer, New York, 1967.

Botwinick, J., *Aging and Behavior*, Springer, New York, 1973.

Bressler, R., and Palmer, J., "Drug Interactions in the Aged," in W. E. Fann and G. L. Maddox (eds.), *Drug Issues in Geropsychiatry*, Williams & Wilkins, Baltimore, 1974, pp. 49-57.

Brody, E. M., Kleban, M., Woldow, A., and Freeman, L., "Survival and Death in the Mentally-Impaired Aged, *Journal of Chronic Diseases, 28*(7/8), 1975, 389-399.

Brosin, H. W., *Discussion, Death and Dying: Attitudes of Patient and Doctor*, Group for the Advancement of Psychiatry, New York, 1965, pp. 642-643.

Brotman, H. B., Who Are the Aged: A Demographic View, *Useful Facts*, No. 42, U.S. Administration on Aging, Washington, D.C., Table 8, August 9, 1968.

Burnside, I., "Loss: A Constant Theme in Group Work with the Aged," *Hosp. Community Psychiatry 21*, 1970, 173.

Busse, E., and Pfeiffer, E., "Functional Psychiatric Disorders in Old Age," in E. Busse and E. Pfeiffer (eds.), *Behavior and Adaptation in Late Life*, Little Brown, Boston, 1969.

Busse, E. W., "Research on Aging: Some Methods and Findings," in M. A. Berezin and S. H. Cath (eds.), *Geriatric Psychiatry: Grief, Loss, and Emotional Disorders in the Aging Process*, International Universities Press, New York, 1965, pp. 73-95.

Busse, E. W., Hypochondriasis in the Elderly: A Reaction to Social Stress. Paper presented at the Tenth International Congress of Gerontology, Jerusalem, Israel, July 1975.

Busse, E. W., and Pfeiffer, E., "Functional Psychiatric Disorders in Old Age," in E. W. Busse and E. Pfeiffer (eds.), *Behavior and Adaptation in Late Life,* Little Brown, Boston, 1977, pp. 158–210.

Butler, R. N., and Lewis, M. I., *Aging and Mental Health: Positive Psychosocial Approaches,* C. V. Mosby, St. Louis, 1973.

Charatan, F. B., Depression in Old Age, *New York State Journal of Medicine, 75*(14), 1975, 2505–2509.

Daniels, R. S., and Kahn, R. L., Community Mental Health and Programs for the Aged, *Geriatrics, 23,* 1968, 121–125.

Davis, J. M., et al., "Clinical Problems in Treating the Aged with Psychotropic Drugs," in C. Eisdorfer and W. E. Fann (eds.), *Psychopharmacology and Aging,* Plenum Press, New York, 1973, pp. 111–125.

Eisdorfer, C., and Fann, W. E., *Psychopharmacology and Aging,* Plenum Press, New York, 1973.

Eisdorfer, C., and Lawton, M. P. (eds.), *The Psychology of Adult Development and Aging,* American Psychological Association, 1973, pp. 74–97, 112–150, 157–219, 220–280.

Epstein, L. J., "Depression in the Elderly," *Journal of Gerontology, 31,* 1976, 278–282.

Epstein, L. J., and Simon, A., "Alternatives to State Hospitalization for the Geriatrically Mentally Ill," *American Journal of Psychiatry, 124,* 1968, 955–961.

Erikson, E. H., *Childhood and Society,* Norton, New York, 1963.

Fann, W. E., and Maddox, G. L., *Drug Issues in Geropsychiatry,* Williams & Wilkins, Baltimore, Md., 1974.

Fann, W. E., and Wheless, J. C., "Depression in Elderly Patients," *Southern Medical Journal, 68*(4), 1975, 468–473.

Felton, B., and Kahana, E., "Adjustment and Situationally-Bound Locus of Control Among Institutionalized Aged," *Journal of Gerontology, 29,* 1974, 295–301.

Friedman, R. J., and Katz, M. M. (eds.), *The Psychology of Depression: Contemporary Theory and Research,* Winston/Wiley, Washington, D. C., 1974.

Gaitz, C. (ed.), *Aging and the Brain,* Plenum Press, 1972.

Gaitz, C. M., and Baer, P. E., "Characteristics of Elderly Patients with Alcoholism," *Archives General Psychiatry, 24,* 1971, 372.

Gaitz, C. M., and Scott, J., "Age and the Measurement of Mental Health," *Journal of Health and Social Behavior, 13,* 1972, 55–67.

Gerber, I., Rusalem, R., Hannon, N., Battin, D., and Arkin, A., "Anticipatory Grief and Aged Widows and Widowers," *Journal of Gerontology, 30*(2), 1975, 225–229.

Goldfarb, A. I., "Institutional Care of the Aged," in E. W. Busse and E. Pfeiffer (eds.), *Behavior and Adaptation in Late Life,* Little Brown, Boston, 1969, pp. 289–312.

Goldfarb, A. I., "Institutional Care of the Aged," in E. W. Busse and E. Pfeiffer (eds.), *Behavior and Adaptation in Late Life,* Little Brown, Boston, 1977, pp. 264–292.

Goldfarb, A. I., "Minor Maladjustment of the Aged," in S. Arieti and E. B. Brody (eds.), *American Handbook of Psychiatry: Adult Clinical Psychiatry* Vol. 3, Basic Books, New York, 1974.

Goldstein, M. S., "Medicare and Care of Mental Illness," *Health Insurance Statistics,* HI-4, March 7, 1968, Washington, D.C., U.S. Department of Health, Education and Welfare, Social Security Administration, Office of Research and Statistics.

Goodwin, F. K., Murphy, D. L., and Bunney, W. E., Jr., "Lithium Carbonate Treatment in Depression and Mania," *Archives of General Psychiatry, 21,* 1969, 486.

Gottesman, L. E., and Bourestam, N. C., "Why Nursing Homes Do What They Do," *Gerontologist, 13,* 1974, 23-31.

Grad, J., and Sainsbury, P., "The Effect That Patients Have on Their Families in a Community Care and a Control Psychiatric Service, a Two Year Follow-Up," *British Journal of Psychiatry, 114,* 1968, 265-278.

Gruenberg, E. M., "From Practice to Theory: Community Mental Health Services and the Nature of Psychoses," *The Lancet,* 1969, pp. 721-724.

Gunderson, E. K. E., and Rahe, R. H., *Life Stress and Illness,* Charles C. Thomas, Springfield, Ill., 1974.

Gurland, B. J., "A Briad Clinical Assessment of Psychopathology in the Aged," in C. Eisdorfer and M. P. Lawton (eds.), *The Psychopathology of Adult Development and Aging,* American Psychological Association, Washington, D.C., 1973.

Gurland, B. J., "The Comparative Frequency of Depression in Various Adult Age Groups," *Journal of Gerontology, 31,* 1976, 283-292.

Haggerty, J., "Suicidal Behavior in A 70-Year-Old Man: A Case Report," *Journal of Geriatric Psychiatry, 6*(1), 1973, 43-51.

Horn, J. L., and Donaldson, G., "On the Myth of Intellectual Decline in Adulthood," *American Psychologist, 31,* 1976, 701-719.

Howells, J. G., "Family Psychopathology," in J. G. Howells (ed.), *Modern Perspectives in the Psychiatry of Old Age,* Brunner/Mazel, New York, 1975, pp. 253-268.

Jarvik, L. F., "Aging and Depression: Some Unanswered Questions," *Journal of Gerontology, 21,* 1976, 324-326.

Eisdorfer, C. and Blum, J. E. (eds.), *Intellectual Functioning in Adults,* Springer, New York, 1973.

Kahana, E., and Kahana, B., "Therapeutic Potential of Age Integration: Effects of Age Integrated Hospital Environments on Elderly Psychiatric Patients," *Archives of General Psychiatry, 23,* 1970, 20-29.

Kahana, R. J., "On Widowhood: Introduction," *Journal of Geriatric Psychiatry, 8*(1), 1975, 5-8.

Kahn, E., and Fisher, C., "The Sleep Characteristics of the Normal Aged Male," *Journal of Nervous Mental Disorders, 148,* 1969, 477.

Kahn, R. L., "The Mental Health System and the Future Aged," *Gerontologist 15,* (1:II), 1975, 24-31.

Kahn, R. L., "Perspectives in the Evaluation of Psychological Mental Health Programs for the Aged," in C. D. Gentry (ed.), *Geropsychology: A Model of Training and Clinical Service,* Ballinger, Cambridge, Mass., 1977, pp. 9-19.

Kahn, R. L., "Psychological Aspects of Aging," in I. Rossman (ed.), *Clinical Geriatrics,* J. B. Lippincott, Philadelphia, 1971, pp. 107-113.

Kahn, R. L., and Zarit, S. H., "Evaluation of Mental Health Programs for The Aged," in P. O. Davidson, F. W. Clark, and L. A. Hammerlynck (eds.), *Evaluation of Behavioral Programs,* Research Press, Champaign, Ill., 1974, pp. 223-251.

Kahn, R. L., Zarit, S. H., Hilbert, N. M., and Niederehe, G., "Memory Complaint and Impairment in the Aged: The Effect of Depression and Altered Brain Function," *Archives of General Psychiatry, 32*(12), 1975, 1569-1573.

Kalinowsky, L. B., and Hoch, P. A., *Pharmacological Convulsive and Other Somatic Treatments in Psychiatry* (2nd ed.), Grune & Stratton, New York, 1969.

Kastenbaum, R., "Beer, Wine, and Mutual Gratification in the Gerontopolis," in D. P. Kent, R. Kastenbaum, and S. Sherwood (eds.), *Research Planning and Action for the Elderly: The Power and Potential of Social Science,* Behavioral Publications, New York, 1976, pp. 365–394.

Kohen, W., and Paul, G. L., Current Trends and Recommended Changes in Extended-Care Placement of Mental Patients: The Illinois System as a Case in Point," *Schizophrenia Bulletin, 4,* 1976, 575–594.

Kramer, M., Taube, C., and Redick, R., "Patterns of Use of Psychiatric Facilities by the Aged: Past, Present, and Future," in C. Eisdorfer and M. P. Lawton (eds.), *The Psychology of Adult Development and Aging,* American Psychological Association, Washington, D.C., 1973.

Kuypers, J. A., and Bengtson, V. L., "Competence and Social Breakdown: A Social-Psychological View of Aging," *Human Development, 16*(2), 1973, 37–49.

Lawton, M. P., "Gerophysychological Knowledge as a Background for Psychotherapy with Older People," *Journal of Geriatric Psychiatry, IX*(2), 1976, 221–233.

Lazarus, R. S., Averill, J. R., and Opton, E. M., Jr., "The Psychology of Coping: Issues of Research and Assessment," in G. V. Coelho, D. A. Hamburg, and J. E. Adams (eds.), *Coping and Adaptation,* Basic Books, New York, 1974, pp. 249–315.

Lazarus, R. S., Averill, J. R., and Opton, E. M., Jr., "Towards a Cognitive Theory of Emotion," in L. Levi (ed.), *Society, Stress and Disease,* Vol. 1, *The Psychosocial Environment and Psychosomatic Diseases,* Oxford University Press, New York, 1971, pp. 190–205.

Levin, S., "On Widowhood: Discussion," *Journal of Geriatric Psychiatry, 8*(1), 1975, 57–59.

Levitt, E. E., and Lubin, B., *Depression: Concepts, Controversies, and Some New Facts,* Springer, New York, 1975.

Liberman, P. R., and Raskin, D. E., "Depression: A Behavioral Formulation," *Archives of General Psychiatry, 24,* 1971, 515–523.

Liederman, P. C., Green, R., and Liederman, V. R., "Outpatient Group Therapy with Geriatric Patients," *Geriatrics, 22,* 1967, 148.

Lipton, M. A., "Age Differentiation in Depression: Biochemical Aspects," *Journal of Gerontology, 31,* 1976, 267–71.

Lopata, H. Z., "Grief Work and Identity Reconstruction," *Journal of Geriatric Psychiatry, 8*(1), 1975, 41–55.

Lowenthal, M. F., and Berkman, P. L., *Aging and Mental Disorder in San Francisco,* Jossey-Bass, San Francisco, 1967.

Lowenthal, M. F., and Chiriboga, D., "Social Stress and Adaptation: Toward a Life-Course Perspective," in C. Eisdorfer and M. P. Lawton (eds.), *The Psychology of Adult Development and Aging,* American Psychological Association, 1973, pp. 281–310.

Lowenthal, M. F., and Haven, C., "Interaction and Adaptation: Intimacy as A Critical Variable," *American Sociological Review, 33*(1), 1968, 20–30.

Lowenthal, M. F., Thurnher, M., Chiriboga, D. et al. (eds.), *Four Stages of Life: A Comparative Study of Women and Men Facing Transitions,* Jossey-Bass, San Francisco, 1975, pp. 99–121, 163–175.

MacDonald, M. L., "The Forgotten Americans: A Sociopsychological Analysis of Aging and Nursing Homes," *American Journal of Community Psychology, 1,* 1973, 272-292.

Marshall, J. R., "Family Practice and Problems of Aging: The Geriatric Patient's Fears About Death," *Postgraduate Medicine, 57*(4), 1975, 144-149.

Mischal, W., "Toward A Cognitive Social-Learning Reconceptualization of Personality," *Psychological Review, 80,* 1973, 252-283.

Patterson, R. D., Abrahams, R., and Baker, F., "Preventing Self-Destructive Behavior," *Geriatrics, 29*(11), 1974, 115-118.

Paykel, E. S., Myers, J. K., Diemelt, M. N., et al., "Life Events and Depression," *Archives of General Psychiatry, 21,* 1969, 753-760.

Perlin, S., and Kahn, R. L., "A Mental Health Center in a General Hospital," in Z. J. Duhl and R. L. Leopold (eds.), *Mental Health and Urban Social Policy: A Casebook of Community Actions,* Jossey-Bass, San Francisco, 1968, pp. 185-212.

Pfeiffer, E., "Psychopathology and Social Pathology," in J. E. Birren and K. W. Schale (eds.), *Handbook of the Psychology of Aging,* Van Nostrand, New York, 1977, pp. 650-671.

Post, F., *The Clinical Psychiatry of Late Life,* Pergamon Press, 1965, pp. 52-76.

Post, R., "The Diagnostic Process," in K. W. K. Kay and A. Walk (eds.), "Recent Developments in Psychogeriatrics," *British Journal of Psychiatry Special Bulletin No. 6,* 1971, 63-73.

Power, C. A., and McCarron, L. T., "Treatment of Depression in Persons Residing in Homes for the Aged," *Gerontologist, 15*(2), 1975, 132-135.

Rahe, R. H., McKean, J. D. and Arthur, R. J., "A Longitudinal Study of Life Change and Illness Patterns," *Journal of Psychosomatic Research, 10,* 1967, 355-366.

Renshaw, D. C., "Sexuality and Depression in Adults and the Elderly," *Medical Aspects of Human Sexuality, 1*(1), 1975, 40-62.

Rodstein, M., "Challenging Residents to Assure Maximal Responsibilities in Homes for the Aged," *Journal of the American Geriatrics Society, 23*(7), 1975, 317-321.

Roth, M., "Classification and Actiology of Mental Disorders of Old Age: Some Recent Developments," in D. W. K. Kay and A. Walk (eds.), *Recent Developments in Psychogeriatrics,* Headley Brothers, Ltd., Asford, England, 1971.

Sadowski, A., and Weinsaft, P., "Behavioral Disorders in the Elderly," *Journal of the American Geriatrics Society, 23*(2), 1975, 86-93.

Scott, J. P., and Senay, E. C., *Separation and Depression: Clinical and Research Aspects,* American Association for the Advancement of Science, Washington, D.C., 1973.

Seligman, M. E., *Helplessness: On Depression Development and Death,* W. H. Freeman, San Francisco, 1975.

Silverman, C., *The Epidemiology of Depression,* Johns Hopkins Press, Baltimore, 1968.

Silverman, P. R., and Cooperband, A., "Mutual Help and the Elderly Widow," *Journal of Geriatric Psychiatry, 8*(1), 1975, 9-27.

Skelske, B. E., "An Exploratory Study of Grief in Old Age," *Smith College Studies in Social Work, 45*(2), 1975, 159-182.

Spence, D. L., Cohen, S., and Kowalski, C., "Mental Health, Age, and Community Living," *Gerontologist, 15*(1 part 1), 1975, 77-82.

Tobin, S. S., and Lieberman, M. A., *Last Home for the Aged,* Jossey-Bass, San Francisco, 1976, pp. 1-54.

Townsend, P., "The Effects of Family Structure on the Likelihood to an Admission to an Institution in Old Age: The Application of General Theory," in E. Shanas and G. Streib (eds.), *Social Structure and the Family: Generational Relations,* Prentice-Hall, Englewood Cliffs, N.J., 1965.

Tulving, E., "Episodic and Sematic Memory," in E. Tulving and W. Donaldson (eds.), *Organization of Memory,* Academic Press, New York, 1972.

Weinberg, J., "Psychopathology," in J. G. Howells (ed.), *Modern Perspectives in the Psychiatry of Old Age,* Brunner/Mazel, New York, 1975, pp. 235-252.

Weisman, A. D., and Kastenbaum, R., "The Psychological Autopsy," *Community Mental Health Journal, 4,* 1968, 1-59.

Whanger, A. D., and Busse, E. W., "Care in Hospital," in J. G. Howells (ed.), *Modern Perspectives in the Psychiatry of Old Age,* Brunner/Mazel, New York, 1975.

Zarit, S. H., and Kahn, R. L., "Impairment and Adaptation in Chronic Disabilities: Spatial Inattention," *Journal of Nervous and Mental Disease, 159,* 1974, 63-72.

Zerbin-Rudin, E., "Genetics," in J. G. Howells (ed.), *Modern Perspectives in the Psychiatry of Old Age,* 1975, pp. 1-23.

Chapter 8

Barrett, J., *Gerontological Psychology,* Charles C Thomas, Springfield, Ill., 1972.

Bender, J. J., "Marriage in the Middle Years," *Journal of Louisiana State Medical Society, 126*(9), 1974, 317-322.

Binstock, R., and Shanas, E. (eds.), *The Handbook of Aging and the Social Sciences,* Van Nostrand, New York, 1976.

Blau, T. S., *Old Age in a Changing Society, New Viewpoints,* Franklin Watts, New York, 1973.

Bouvier, L., Atlee, E., and McVeigh, F., "The Elderly in America, *Population Bulletin, 30,* 1975, 1-36, Population Reference Bureau, Washington, D.C.

Burnside, I., *Sexuality and Aging,* University of California Press, Berkeley, Calif., 1975.

Butler, R. M., "Family Life Style Characteristics and Child Health Care," in M. M. Lewis (ed.), *Social Work Services in Pediatric Hospitals,* USPHS, Department of Housing, Education and Welfare, Rockville, Md., 1972.

Butler, R. M., and Lewis, M. I., *Sex After Sixty,* Harper & Row, New York, 1976.

De Beauvoir, S., *Coming of Age,* Warner Paperback Library, New York, 1973.

Dressel, P. L., and Avant, W. R., "Neogamy and Older Persons: An Examination of Alternatives for Intimacy in the Later Years," *Alternative Life Styles: Changing Patterns in Marriage, Family, and Intimacy, 1,* 1978, 13-36.

Felstein, I., *Sex in Later Life,* Penguin Books, New York, 1974.

Fischer, D. N., *Growing Old in America,* Oxford University Press, 1977.

Freidson, E., *Profession of Medicine: A Study of the Sociology of Applied Knowledge,* Dodd, Mead, New York, 1972.

Glick, P. C., "The Future Marital Status and Living Arrangements of the Elderly," *Gerontologist, 19*(3), June 1979, 301-309.

Glick, P. C. (ed.), "Population and the United States, Trends and Prospects, 1950-1990," *U.S. Bureau of the Census,* U.S. Government Printing Office, Washington, D.C., 1974.

Glick, P. C., "Social Change and the American Family," *Social Welfare Forum,* 1977, 1978, pp. 43-62.

Glick, P. C., "Updating the Life Cycle of the Family," *Journal of Marriage and the Family, 39,* 1977, 5-13.

Glick, P. C., and Norton, A. J., "Marrying, Divorcing and Living Together in the U.S. Today," *32,* 1977, 1-39, *Population Bulletin,* Population Reference Bureau, Washington, D.C.

Gould, R., "The Phases of Adult Life: A Study of Developmental Psychology," *American Journal of Psychiatry, 129*(5), November 1972, 521-532.

Hauser, P. M., *"Aging and World-Wide Population Change,"* Chapter 3 in J. S. Binstock and E. Shanas (eds.), *Handbook on Aging,* Vol. 1, Van Nostrand, New York, 1976.

Hill, R., *"Decision Making and the Family Life Cycle,"* in B. Neugarten (ed.), *Middle Age and Aging,* University of Chicago Press, Chicago, 1975.

Hochschild, A., *The Unexpected Community,* Prentice-Hall, Englewood Cliffs, N.J., 1973.

Kahana, E., and Kahana, B. "Theoretical and Research on, Grandparenthood," *Aging and Human Development 2,* November 1971, 261-269.

Kart, O. S., and Manard, B. S., *Aging in America: Readings in Social Gerontology,* Alfred Publishing, New York, 1976.

Katz, S., Downs, T. D., Cash, H. R., and Gratz, R. C., "Progress in Development of the Index of ADL," *Gerontologist, 10,* 1970, 20-30.

Kobrin, F., "The Fall of Household Size and the Rise of the Primary Individual in the United States," *Demography, 12,* 1976, 127-138.

Krimm, I., *Sex Power and Health for the Middle Aged and Senior,* Happy Health Publications, Seal Beach, Calif., 1974.

Lawton, M. P., "The Relative Impact on Congregate and Traditional Housing on Elderly Tenants," *Gerontologist, 16,* 1976, 237-249.

Lopata, H. Z., *Widowhood in an American City,* Schenkman, Cambridge, Mass., 1973.

Mead, G. H., *Mind, Self and Society,* University of Chicago Press, Chicago, 1934.

National Council on Aging, *the Myth and Reality of Aging in America Today,* Washington, D.C., 1977.

Neugarten, B. L., and Havighurst, R. J., (eds.), *Social Policy, Social Ethics and the Aging Society,* Superintendent of Documents, U.S. Government Printing Office, Washington, D.C., 038-000-00299-6, Reprinted January 1980.

Neugarten, B., and Weinstein, K., "The Changing American Grandparent," in B. Neugarten (ed.), *Middle Age and Aging,* Chicago, University of Chicago Press, 1975.

Nydegger, C. (ed.), Measuring Morale: A Guide to Effective Assessment, *Gerontological Society,* 1977.

Peck, R. C., "Psychological Developments in the Second Half of Life," in B. L. Neugarten (ed.), *Middle Life and Aging,* Chicago, University of Chicago Press, 1968, pp. 88-92.

Pineo, P. C., "Disenchantment in the Later Years of Marriage," in B. Neugarten (ed.), *Middle Age and Aging,* Chicago, University of Chicago Press, 1975.

Riley, M., and Faner, A. (eds.), *Aging and Society,* Vol. 1, *An Inventory of Research Findings,* Russell Sage, New York, 1968.

Riley, M., Johnston, H. H., and Foner, A., *Aging and Society,* Vol. 3, *A Sociology of Age Stratification,* Russell Sage, New York, 1971.

Rosow, I., "The Social Contest of the Aging Self," *Gerontologist, 13,* 1973, 82-87.

Rosow, I., *Social Integration of the Aged,* Free Press, New York, 1967.

Segall, A., "The Sick Role Concept; Understanding Illness Behavior," *Journal of Health and Social Behavior, 17,* 1976, 162–169.

Shanas, E., "Family Help Patterns and Social Class in Three Countries," in B. Neugarten (ed.), *Middle Age and Aging,* Chicago, University of Chicago Press, 1975.

Shanas, E., and Hauser, P. M., "Zero Population Growth and Family Life of Old People," *Journal of Social Issues, 30,* 1974, 79–92.

Shanas, E., Townsend, et al., *Old People in Three Industrial Societies,* Atherton, New York, 1968 (out of print).

Siegel, J. S., *Demographic Aspects of Aging and the Older Population in the United States,* U.S. Bureau of the Census, U.S. Government Printing Office, Washington, D.C., 1976.

Sommers, T., "The Compounding Impact of Age and Sex: Another Dimension of Double Standard," *Civil Rights Digest* 7(1), 1975, 2–9.

Streib, G. S., and Schneider, C. J., *Retirement in American Society,* Cornell University Press, New York, 1971.

Sussman, M., and Burchinal, L., "Kin Family Network: Unheralded Structure in Current Conceptualizations of Family Functioning," in B. Neugarten (ed.), *Middle Age and Aging,* Chicago, University of Chicago Press, 1975.

Townsend, P., "The Emergence of the Four-Generational Family in Industrial Society," in B. Neugarten (ed.), *Middle Age and Aging,* Chicago, University of Chicago Press, 1975.

Treas, J., and Van Hilst, A., "Marriage and Remarriage Rates Among Older Americans," *Gerontologist, 16,* 1976, 132–136.

Uhlenberg, P., "Changing Structure of the Older Population of the USA During the Twentieth Century," *Gerontologist, 17,* 1977, 197–202.

U.S. Bureau of the Census, *Number, Timing, and Duration of Marriages and Divorces in the United States: June 1975,* Current Population Reports, Series P-20, No. 297, 1976.

U.S. National Center for Health Statistics, *Vital Statistics of the United States, 1974,* Vol. III, *Marriage and Divorce,* 1977(a).

U.S. National Center for Health Statistics, *Advance Report: Final Marriage Statistics, 1975,* Monthly Vital Statistics Report 26, No. 2, Supplement, 1977(b).

U.S. National Center for Health Statistics, *Advance Data,* 29, *A Comparison of Nursing Home Residents and Discharges from the 1977 Nursing Home Survey:* United States, 1978.

Westoff, C. F., and Rindfuss, R. R., "Sex Preselection in the United States and Some Implications," *Science, 184,* 1974, 633–636.

Chapter 9

Adler, J., *The Retirement Book,* William Morrow, New York, 1975.

Bartlett, D. M., "Retirement Counseling: Making Sure Employees Aren't Dropouts," *Personnel, 51*(6), 1974, 26–35.

Beverly, E. V., "Retirement: The Third Age—Turning the Realities of Retirement into Fulfillment," *Geriatrics, 30*(1), 1975, 126, 131, 132, 134, 139.

Blau, Z. S., *Old Age in a Changing Society,* New Viewpoints, Franklin Watts, New York, 1973.

Blayney, J. A. B., "Recreation—That Important but Often Forgotten Treatment in the Total Care of the Long-Term Care Resident," *Alabama Journal of Medical Sciences, 12*(2), 1975, 210-212.

Blonsky, L. E., "Factors Affecting the Prospect for Survival of a Jointly Sponsored Program for the Elderly," *Journal of Jewish Communal Services, 52*(1), 1975, 82-90.

Buckley, J. C., *Retirement Handbook,* Barnes & Noble, Scranton, Pa., 1974.

Busse, E. W., and Pfieffer, E., *Mental Illness in Late Life,* Washington, D.C., American Psychiatric Association, 1973.

Clark, F. L. G., *Work, Age, and Leisure,* Michael Joseph, London, 1966, p. 137.

Corlett, S., *Retirement Is What You Make It,* Warner Press Publications, Anderson, Ind., 1973.

Corrigan, B., *Retire with Pride, Purpose and Pleasure,* Exposition Press, Hicksville, New York, 1975.

Decarlo, T. J., "Recreation Participation Patterns and Successful Aging," *Journal of Gerontology, 29*(4), 1974, 416-422.

Evans, A., *Flexibility in Working Life,* Organization for Economic Cooperation and Development, Paris, 1973.

Fisher, P., "Labor Force Participation of the Aged and the Social Security Systems in Nine Countries," *Gerontologist, 2*(1), 1975, 1.

Gallaway, L. E., "The Aged and the Extent of Poverty in the United States," *South Econ. J., 33,* 1966, 212.

Harn, P., "Smoothing the Road to Retirement; Retirement Counseling," *Psychology Today, 9,* October 1975, 28ff.

Hayes, G. A., "Recreation and Leisure: Implications for the Aged," *Therapeutic Recreation Journal, 8*(3), 1974, 138-144.

Helping the Elderly: what fight is all About, *U. S. News and World Report, 80,* February 23, 1976, 71.

Hepner, H. W., *Retirement: A Time to Live Anew,* Robert E. Krieger, Huntington, N.Y., 1976.

Jacobs, J., "An Ethnographic Study of Retirement Setting," *Gerontologist, 14*(6), 1974, 483-487.

Jacobs, J., *Older Persons and Retirement Communities: Case Studies in Social Gerontology,* Charles C Thomas, Springfield, Ill., 1975.

Kimmel, D. C., *Adulthood and Aging: An Interdisciplinary Developmental View,* Wiley, New York, 1974.

Kinzel, R., "Resolving Executives' Early Retirement Problems," *Personnel, 51*(3), 1974, 55-63.

Klemme, H., "The Later Years—Are You Ready?" *Menninger Perspective, 5*(3), 1974, 4-11.

Kreps, J. M., "Where Is the Money?" *Trial, 10*(2), 1974, 14-15.

Matteson, S., "Spirit of 76—Independence in Old Age," *Trial, 10*(2), 1974, 20-22.

McCamman, D., et al., *Economics of Aging: Toward a Full Share in Abundance.* Prepared by Task Force for the Special Committee on Aging, U.S. Senate, 91st Congress, March 1969, p. 1.

Nystrom, E. P., "Activity Patterns and Leisure Concepts Among the Elderly," *American Journal of Occupational Therapy, 28*(6), 1974, 337-345.

Rogers, J. M., "Retired Couple's Budgets Updated to Autumn 1974," *Monthly Labor Review, R.98,* October 1975, 42–46.

Schwab, K., "Early Labor Force Withdrawal of Men: Participants and Nonparticipants Aged 58–63," *Social Security Bulletin, 37,* 1974, 24.

Sherman, S. R., "Leisure Activities in Retirement Housing," *Journal of Gerontology, 29*(3), 1974, 325–335.

Stevens, M. K., *Geriatric Nursing for Practical Nurses,* W. B. Saunders, Philadelphia, 1975.

Thurnher, M., "Goals, Values, and Life Evaluations at the Pre-Retirement Stage," *Journal of Gerontology, 29*(1), 1974, 85–96.

Chapter 10

Blonsky, L. E., "The Desire of Elderly Nonresidents to Live in a Senior Citizen Apartment Building," *Gerontologist, 15*(1), 1975, 88–91.

Brody, E. M., Kleban, M. H., and Liebowitz, B., "Intermediate Housing for the Elderly: Satisfaction of Those Who Moved in and Those Who Did Not," *Gerontologist, 15*(4), 1975, 350–356.

Carp, F. M., "Life-Style and Location Within the City," *Gerontologist, 15*(1 part 1), 1975, 27–34.

Carp, F. M., "Long-Range Satisfaction with Housing," *Gerontologist, 15*(1), 1975, 68–72.

Davis, B. H. A., *A Descriptive Exploratory Study of the Dimensions of Institutional Totality and Its Correlates in Proprietary Nursing Homes of New York City,* Doctoral Thesis, Teachers College, Columbia University, New York, 1974.

Flemming, A. S., "Commissioner Flemming Stresses Support for Home Winterization Program," excerpt from memorandum, A. S. Flemming, *Aging, 256*(4), February 1976.

Goldman, E. B., and Woog, P., "Mental Health in Nursing Homes Training Project 1972–1973," *Gerontologist, 15*(2), 1975, 119–124.

Guttman, D., "Roles and Functions of the Socially Oriented Manager in Congregate Housing Facilities for the Elderly," *Catholic Charities Review, 58*(6), 1974, 9–13, 22–23.

Hess, J. L., "How Referrals to Nursing Homes Are Made," *New York Times,* May 12, 1975, p. 18.

Kellogg, M. A., and Jaffe, A., "Old Folks' Commune; Share-a-Home Network in Orlando, Florida," *Newsweek, 87,* April 19, 1976, 97–8.

Kosberg, J. I., "Differences in Proprietary Institutions Caring for Affluent and Non-Affluent Elderly," *Gerontologist, 13,* 1973, 299.

Kramer, M., Taube, A., and Redick, R. W., "Patterns of Use of Psychiatric Facilities by the Aged: Past, Present and Future," in C. Eisdorfer and M. P. Lawton (eds.), *Psychology of Adult Development and Aging,* American Psychological Association, Washington, D.C., 1973.

Larson, C. J., "Alienation and Public Housing for the Elderly," *Aging and Human Development, 5*(3), 1974, 217–230.

Lawton, M. P., Nathemow, L., and Teaff, J., "Housing Characteristics and the Well-Being of Elderly Tenants in Federally Assisted Housing," *Journal of Gerontology, 30*(5), 1975, 601–607.

Lowy, L., "The White House Conference on Aging: Two Years Later," *International Journal of Aging and Human Development, 5*(2), 1974, 205–211.

McFarland, M. C., "Emergence of a New Concept Congregate Housing for the Elderly," *Aging,* February 1976, 256–257, 259.

Mehta, N. H., and Mack, C. M., "Day Care Services: An Alternative to Institutional Care," *Journal of the American Geriatrics Society, 23*(6), 1975, 280–283.

Nassau, J. B., *Choosing A Nursing Home,* Funk & Wagnalls, New York, 1975.

Nelson, L. M., and Winter, M., "Life Disruption, Independence, Satisfaction, and the Consideration of Moving," *Gerontologist, 15*(2), 1975, 160–164.

Reich, R., "Care of the Chronically Mentally Ill—A National Disgrace," *American Journal of Psychiatry, 130,* 1973, 8.

Ross, H. K., "Low Income Elderly in Inner City Trailer Parks," *Psychiatric Annals, 5*(8), 1975, 86, 89–90.

Sears, D. W., "Elderly Housing: A Need Determination Technique," *Gerontologist, 14*(2), 1974, 182–187.

Shanas, E., "Living Arrangements and Housing of Old People," in E. Busse and E. Pfeiffer (eds.), *Behavior and Adaptation in Late Life,* Little Brown, Boston, 1977.

Sherman, S. R., "Mutual Assistance and Support in Retirement Housing," *Journal of Gerontology, 30*(4), 1975, 479–483.

Sherman, S. R., "Provision of On-Site Services in Retirement Housing," *International Journal of Aging and Human Development, 6*(3), 1975, 229–247.

Sherwood, S., Morris, J. N., and Barnhart, E., "Developing a System for Assisting Individuals into an Appropriate Residential Setting," *Journal of Gerontology, 30*(3), 1975, 331–342.

Spence, D. L., Cohen, S., and Kowalski, C., "Mental Health, Age, and Community Living," *Gerontologist, 15*(1 part 1), 1975, 77–82.

Storandt, M., Wittels, I., and Botwinick, J., "Predictors of a Dimension of Well-Being in the Relocated Healthy Aged," *Journal of Gerontology, 30*(1), 1975, 97–102.

Tucker, S. M., Combs, M. E., and Woolrich, A. M., "Independent Housing for The Elderly: The Human Element in Design," *Gerontologist, 15*(1), 1975, 73–77.

U.S. Senate, Special Committee on Aging, *Nursing Home Care in the United States: Failure in Public Policy,* Report of the Sub-Committee on Long-Term Care of the Senate Special Committee on Aging, 1975.

Winn, S., and Kessler, S., "Community Mental Health Centers and the Nursing Home Patient," *Gerontologist, 14*(4), 1974, 345–348.

Woodard, H., Gingles, R., and Woodard, J. C., "Loneliness and the Elderly as Related to Housing," *Gerontologist, 14*(4), 1974, 349–351.

Chapter 11

Busse, E. W., and Pfeiffer, E., *Behavior and Adaptation in Late Life,* Little Brown, Boston, 1977.

Butler, R. N., *"The Life Review in Behavior and Adaptation in Late Life,"* in E. W. Busse and E. Pfeiffer, (eds.), *Behavior and Adaptation in Later Life,* Little Brown, Boston,

Butler, R. N., "The Life Review," in E. W. Busse and E. Pfeiffer, (eds.), *Behavior and Adaptation in Late Life,* Little Brown, Boston, 1977.

Butler, R. N., and Lewis, M., *Aging and Mental Health: Positive Psychosocial Approaches,* C. V. Mosby, St. Louis, 1977.

Cameron, et al., "Consciousness of Death Across the Life Span," *Journal of Gerontology, 28*(1), January 1973, 92–95.

Eliot, D., "Adjusting to the Death of a Loved One," in R. S. Cavan (ed.), *Marriage and Family in the Modern World: A Book of Readings,* Crowell, New York, 1974.

Fischer, G., "Death, Identity and Creativity," *Omega, 2,* 1971, 303–306.

Freud, S., *Our Attitude Toward Death, Collected Papers,* Hogarth Press, London, 1925.

Fullerton, G. P., *Survival in Marriage: Introduction to Family Interaction, Conflicts and Alternatives,* Holt, Rinehart, and Winston, New York, 1972.

Gunderson, E. K. E., and Rahe, R. H., *Life Stress and Illness,* Charles C Thomas, Springfield, Ill., 1974.

Hinton, J., *Dying,* Penguin Books, Baltimore, 1976.

Insel, P. M., and Roth, W. T., *Health in a Changing Society,* Mayfield Publishing, Palo Alto, Calif., Chapter 5, 1976.

Kavanaugh, R. E., *Facing Death,* Penguin Books, Baltimore, 1974.

Kübler-Ross, E., *On Death and Dying,* Macmillan, New York, 1973.

Palmore, E., and Maddox, G. L., "Sociological Aspects of Aging," in E. W. Busse and E. Pfeiffer (eds.), *Behavior and Adaptation in Late Life,* Little Brown, Boston, 1977.

Saunders, C., "Care of the Dying, St. Christophers Hospital of London," in R. N. Butler (ed.), *Why Survive? Being Old in America,* Harper & Row, New York, 1975.

Sullivan, H. S., *Clinical Studies in Psychiatry,* W. W. Norton, New York, 1956.

Trelease, M. L., "Dying Among Alaskan Indians: A Matter of Choice," in E. Kübler-Ross, (ed.), *Death: The Final Stage of Growth,* Prentice-Hall, Englewood Cliffs, N.J., 1975.

U. N., Department of Economics and Social Affairs Statistical Yearbook, 1980.

Chapter 12

Anderson, H. C., *Newton's Geriatric Nursing* (5th ed.), C. V. Mosby, St. Louis, 1971.

Beregi, E., et al. (eds.), *Pulmonary Pathology and Aging,* Vol. 1 of Gerontology Series, MSS Information Corp. 1974.

Birchenall, J., and Straight, M. E., *Care of the Older Adult,* J. B. Lippincott, Philadelphia, 1973.

Birren, J., and J. Renner. "Developments in Research on the Biological and Behavioral Aspects of Aging and Their Implications," in J. Birren and K. W. Schaie (eds.), *Handbook of the Psychology of Aging,* Van Nostrand, New York, 1977.

Bracklehurst, J. C., "*Textbook of Geriatric Medicine and Gerontology,*" Churchill Livingston, 1973.

Caird, F. I., and T. G. Judge, *Assessment of the Elderly Patient* (1st ed.), J. B. Lippincott, Philadelphia, 1974.

Cleverley, W. I., (ed.), *Financial Management of Health Care Facilities* (1st ed.), Aspen Systems Corp., April 1976.

French, R. M., *Guide to Diagnostic Procedures* (4th ed.), McGraw-Hill, New York, 1975.

Carlson, R. *The End of Medicine,* Wiley, New York, 1975.

Corso, J. "Auditory Perception and Communication," in J. Birren and K. W. Schaie (eds.), *Handbook of the Psychology of Aging,* Van Nostrand, New York, 1977.

Cosin, L. Z., "The Philosophy, Strategy, and Practice of Care of the Elderly," mimeographed paper, Tavistock House (South), Tavistock Square, London, W.C.I., 1975.

De Vries, H. "Exercise Intensity Threshold for Improvement of Cardiovascular-Respiratory Function in Older Men." *Geriatrics, 26,* 1971, 94–101.

De Vries, H. "The Physiology of Exercise and Aging," in D. Woodruff and J. Birren (eds.), *Aging: Scientific Perspectives and Social Issues,* Van Nostrand, New York, 1975.

Insel, P., and R. Moos (eds.), *Health and the Social Environment,* D. C. Heath, Lexington, Mass., 1974.

Kaplan, J., "The Hospital Model: Curse or Blessing for Homes Serving the Aged," *Gerontologist, 14,* 1974, 4.

Long, J. M., *Caring for and Caring About Elderly People: A guide to the Rehabilitative Approach,* J. B. Lippincott, Philadelphia, 1974.

Neelon, F. A., and Ellis, G., *Syllabus of Problem-Oriented Patient Care,* Little Brown, Boston, 1975.

Rahe, R., "Life Change and Subsequent Illness," in E. K. Gunderson and R. Rahe (eds.), *Life Stress and Illness,* Charles C Thomas, Springfield, Ill., 1974.

Rossman, I., "Anatomic and Body Composition Changes with Aging," in C. Finch and L. Hayflick (eds.), *Handbook of the Biology of Aging,* Van Nostrand, New York, 1977.

Schwartz, A., "A Transactional View of the Aging Process," in A. Schwartz and I. Mensh (eds.), *Professional Obligations and Approaches to the Aged,* Charles C Thomas, Springfield, Ill., 1974.

Schwartz, A., "Mental Health of the Aged and Long-Term Care," *Concern, 111,* 1977, 4.

Sherwood, S. (ed.), *Long Term Care: A Handbook for Researchers, Planners and Providers from Health Systems Management Series,* Halsted Press/Wiley, New York, 1975.

Snyder, L., Pyrek, J., and Smith, K., "Vision and Mental Function of the Elderly." *Gerontologist, 16,* 1976, 6.

Spencer, M. G., and Darr, C. (eds.), *Understanding Aging,* Appleton-Century-Crofts, New York, 1975.

Spiegel, A. D., and Podair, S. (eds.), *Medicaid* (1st ed.), Aspen Systems Corp., 1975.

Steinberg, F. U. (ed.), *Cowdry's The Care of the Geriatric Patient* (5th ed.), C. V. Mosby, St. Louis, June 1976.

Stevens, C. B., *Special Needs of Long-Term Patients,* J. B. Lippincott, Philadelphia, 1974.

Tiberi, D., Schwartz, A., Hirschfield, I., and Kerschner, P., "Correlates of the Medical and Psychosocial Models of Long Term Care." Paper delivered at 11th International Congress of Gerontology, Tokyo, 1978.

U.S. Department of Health, Education and Welfare, Public Health Service, National Institutes of Health, National Advisory Council on Aging, A Research Plan Toward Understanding Aging, No. 80-1446, 1980.

U.S. Department of Health, Education and Welfare, Public Health Service, A Guide to Medical Self-Care and Self-Help Groups for the Elderly, Washington, D.C., 1979.

Chapter 13

Abad, V., Ramos, J., and Boyce, E., "A Model for Delivery of Mental Health Services to Spanish-Speaking Minorities," *American Journal of Orthopsychiatry, 44,* July 1974, 584–594.

Alwin, D. F., and Hauser, R. M., "The Decomposition of Effects in Path Analysis," *American Sociological Review, 40,* February 1975, 37–47.

The American Alliance for Health, Physical Education, Recreation, Dance, "Newskit Update," March and November 1978, March and November 1979, March 1980.

de Vries, H. A., "Physiology of Exercise and Aging," in D. Woodruff and J. Birren (eds.), *Aging: Scientific Perspectives and Social Issues,* D. Van Nostrand, New York, 1975.

Edwards, J. N., and Klemmack, D. L., "Correlates of Life Satisfaction: A Re-Examination," *Journal of Gerontology, 28,* October 1973, 497–502.

Elrick, H., *Living Longer and Better,* World Publications, Mountain View, Calif., 1978.

Johnson, J. L., "Modern Maturity," American Association of Retired Persons, Long Beach, Calif., February–March 1979, p. 4.

Jones, H. B., "The Relation of Human Health to Age, Place and Time," in S. C. McKenzie, (ed.), *Aging and Old Age,* Scott, Foresman, Glenview, Ill., 1980.

Leslie, D., and McLure, J., *Exercise for the Elderly,* Iowa Commission on Aging, University of Iowa, Des Moines, 1980.

National Association for Human Development, *Basic Exercises For People Over Fifty,* Washington, D.C., 1976.

Palmore, E., and Luikart, C., "Health and Social Factors Related to Life Satisfaction," *Journal of Health and Social Behavior, 13,* 1972, 68–80.

President's Council on Physical Fitness and Sports, *Physical Fitness Research Digest,* Series 8, No. 2, Washington, D.C. April 1977.

Wilker, L., and Cantor, M., "A Causal Model of Psychological Well-Being Applied to White, Black and Spanish Elderly Men and Women in the Inner City," U.S. Department of Health, Education, and Welfare, *Administration on Aging,* Grant #AA 4-70-089-02, July 1980.

Index

DATE DUE